THE SOCIAL PHILOSOPHY OF GIOVANNI GENTILE

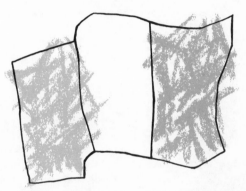

H. S. HARRIS

The Social Philosophy of
GIOVANNI GENTILE

UNIVERSITY OF ILLINOIS PRESS, URBANA AND LONDON, 1966

Dedicated to an unborn child

pensoso più d'altrui che di sè stesso

Petrarch.

ἀεὶ δ'ἀριδάκρυες ἄνερες ἐσθλοί
Proverb from the Homeric scholia.

That mankind is a community, that we all stand in a relation to each other, that there is a public end and interest of society which each particular is obliged to promote, is the sum of morals

P ler.

Es ist nicht davon die Frage: was *sie* nach meinen Begriffen tun sollen, sondern davon, was *ich* tun darf, um sie zu bewegen, dass sie es tun.

Fichte.

PREFACE

This book is a study of the practical aspects of the philosophy of Giovanni Gentile. Gentile was born at Castelvetrano in Sicily on 30 May 1875, and died by assassination at Florence on 15 April 1944. He was nine years younger than the other great figure in the revival of idealism in Italy, Benedetto Croce, whose international reputation almost completely overshadowed his own. Much less of his work has been translated into English, and knowledge of it in the Anglo-Saxon countries has always remained comparatively rare even among professional philosophers.

Even so there exist already in English several studies of different aspects of his thought. But no one has previously attempted, either in English or to my knowledge in any other language, a full-length critical study of his doctrine of the unity of thought and action. There are two reasons for this. In the first place, although the doctrine forms the core of his philosophy and appears in all of his works, Gentile himself did not expound it in detail or develop its consequences in a systematic way prior to the publication of his last book, *Genesis and Structure of Society* (1946).[1] Secondly, his association with Fascism, of which he was an ardent supporter from 1923 until his own death during the last throes of the Fascist

---

[1] As the readers of my fourth chapter will see, his earlier writings form a systematic whole; but some unresolved difficulties are apparent and the systematic relation is largely implicit.

Social Republic, prejudiced the issue. Critical evaluation of his political and social thought has been almost impossible for the Italians themselves because of the general climate of political opinion both before and after his death; and almost everyone outside Italy followed the lead given by Croce and dismissed Gentile's practical philosophy as unworthy of serious critical examination.

The aim of the present study is to set aside the polemical prejudices arising from Gentile's commitment to a particular political regime, and to consider his theory on its merits as a theory. For this reason I have tried first to trace his ideas back to their earliest germs in his pre-Fascist writings and to show how they were systematically developed *before* the March on Rome. In this way we are provided with a standard by which to judge whether Gentile's activities as a Fascist government official and publicist were a consistent application of his theory. In one sense our main problem is to see how far his 'actual idealism' can be disentangled from its Fascist connections. What is attempted here is in no small degree a rescue operation, or an essay in salvage. For if a theory which unifies thought and action necessarily leads in practice to the sort of policies and methods that the Fascists adopted, I do not suppose that many intelligent men will be convinced by it no matter how persuasively the case is argued. Indeed, if this were the case, we should have to hope that men would always allow such arguments to pass unheeded over their heads even if they were not skillful enough to expose them as sophistries; for in the long run nothing will protect us against the institutional abuse of human reason and human liberty if the practical common sense of ordinary citizens fails.

In fact, however, a much less gloomy conclusion is here arrived at. It can be shown that a great gulf always existed between the theory of 'Fascist idealism' and the actual practice of Fascism; and the very existence of this gulf is evidence for the further contention that 'Fascist idealism' is itself a radical deformation of Gentile's theory.

I have sought to buttress my conclusions by making my survey of the evidence as nearly complete as is humanly possible. The first version of this book was presented as a thesis in partial fulfillment of the requirements for the Ph.D. at the University of Illinois in January 1954; and the years of subsequent revision have accentuated rather than mitigated the tendency toward overabundant and overscrupulous documentation which reviewers are wont to complain of as a fault in academic productions of this sort. I hope at least that they will not find in this case that documentation has been substituted for critical intelligence. Gentile was a highly rhetorical writer, and because his philosophy was in any case dialectical he scarcely ever saw any reason to hold back the over-statement that came naturally to his Sicilian pen and tongue. For this reason his writings are full of superficial verbal contradictions and he is a very easy prey for the unfriendly critic; the only way to defend either his work or my own from the critic who is either honest but naive, or intelligent but malicious, is to show how far *all* of his utterances on a given topic can be reconciled with one an-other. Except for a tiny handful of minor items which have eluded me, I believe I have done this for all of his writings on social topics. I cannot claim to have made clear all the values and weaknesses of the writings to which I have referred, but I think that I have put them into correct perspective.

My thanks must go first to Professor Bellezza, without whose masterly bibliography [2] such an undertaking would have been in-conceivable; then to the many libraries in the United States and Italy that have aided me in locating materials—especially to the *Fondazione Gentile* and the *Scuola di filosofia* of the University of Rome, and to the *Istituto storico* in Croce's former home at Naples. Professor Max H. Fisch gave me much valuable advice and en-couragement in the writing of the earlier version; Professors Spirito of the University of Rome and Galimberti of the University of Genoa read that version in part and contributed useful criticism. The radi-cal revision and rewriting of the original Ph.D. dissertation were made possible by the grant of a research fellowship for 1957–58 from the American Philosophical Association.

Above all I must thank my wife, who has borne far more than a fair share of the duller tasks involved in preparing a manuscript for the eyes of others, and has never ceased to help and encourage me.

---

[2] Vito A. Bellezza, *Bibliografia degli scritti di Giovanni Gentile* (*Giovanni Gentile: La vita e il pensiero*, Vol. III), Florence, Sansoni, 1950. The numera-tion of Bellezza's *Elenco cronologico* has been used in references to Gentile's writings throughout. Thus confusions of the various editions, etc., are avoided: B.1279, for instance, refers the reader to the sixth edition (1944) of the *Teoria generale dello spirito*. (In order to avoid confusion I have accepted Wildon Carr's English title for this work—*The Theory of Mind as Pure Act*—but in making my own translations, as I have chosen to do throughout, I have always rendered *spirito* as "spirit" or "consciousness," never as "mind.")

CONTENTS

I

THE THEORETICAL PERSPECTIVE
OF ACTUAL IDEALISM

Idealism and Common-Sense Realism

Gentile called his philosophy 'actual' idealism because he refused to allow any divorce between theory and practice, between the level of eternal truth and the level of concrete actual experience. But in expounding his views he could not escape the necessity, imposed on us all by the structure of language, of talking either theoretically or practically, either logically or psychologically. Thus two distinct approaches to philosophy can be discerned in his work. On the one hand he tries to present it as the natural outcome of the whole Western tradition in philosophy; and though it reminds one a little of Hegel's ,*Phenomenology,* this must, for a variety of reasons which will appear later, be styled Gentile's 'logical' or theoretical approach. On the other hand, he offers it as an adequate analysis of the process of the individual reader's conscious experience of himself and the world. This can be fairly aptly described as his practical or 'phenomenological' approach.

Both of these approaches must be examined carefully, for the success of his whole enterprise depends on the possibility of demonstrating that they are in fact approaches to the same philosophy, that eternal truth and actual concrete experience are really wedded. We shall therefore begin by devoting a chapter to each of them. But before we can properly begin at all we must take into account a peculiarity that is common to them both. A Swiss scholar has remarked with some acuteness that Gentile demands of us an 'introversion' analogous to that which is required for the comprehension

1

of Bergson.[1] Actual idealism is not closely related to the philosophy of the *élan vital;* but they are alike in their resolute rejection of the habits of thought which are customary in the ordinary world of everyday life, the habits which go by the name of common sense. If we can once understand why Gentile feels that ordinary ways of thinking are inadequate to express the eternal character of truth or the full concreteness of experience, we shall be better able to guard ourselves against falling back into a common-sense attitude when we have to deal with his speculative theory—which is quite unintelligible from any point of view except his own.

Fortunately for us, Gentile did once try to explain his fundamental philosophical position to an audience of ordinary people—elementary-school teachers, to be precise—and the lectures were published and translated under the title *The Reform of Education.*[2] Here he expounded his basic philosophical position in fairly ordinary language, without assuming that his readers knew enough about the tradition of post-Kantian idealism to be able to understand his preferred vocabulary and the way in which he uses it. The result is necessarily a rather crude dichotomy but it is one that is vital to his thought, and it certainly provides the simplest introduction to his philosophy as a whole.

Gentile rejected the naive realism of common sense because of his intense conviction—probably the most fundamental motive of his philosophy—that any view of reality which reduces consciousness to the role of a mere spectator must be false:

Our whole life, when we consider it as it presents itself in experience, develops on the basis of a natural world, a world which does not depend on human life but is the condition of it. In order to live, to act, to produce or exert any sort of influence on the world around us, we must first of all be born. . . . Men derive life from a nature, organic and inorganic, which had to exist already before they could come into being; and when the conditions of human life fail within this nature, humanity will be extinguished, and nature will remain, though transformed into something cold, dark, and dead. . . .

. . . reality appears to us as already constituted prior to our existence and therefore conditioning it; it exists independently of us and perfectly indifferent to our being or non-being. But if reality is really what it appears to be and we are truly extraneous to it, the conclusion can also be drawn that we presume to know reality from the outside, and to move

---

[1] Fernand-Lucien Mueller, *La pensée contemporaine en Italie,* Geneva, Albert Kundig, 1941, p. 221.

[2] B.1128 (now Vol. VII of the *Complete Works*); English translation B.659.

round it although we are not ourselves this reality and have no part in it. In fact, the total complex of reality is conceived, however vaguely, by us; and reality as a whole is regarded as an object known to us, though independent of our knowledge of it. The whole of reality is exhaustively contained in this nature, which conditions our spiritual life; and our spiritual life can be the mirror of reality but can never itself be part of it. . . .

And we, then . . . considered as thinking beings and not as natural objects, considered as what we are when we affirm our personality and say "We," are less than the earthworms that creep about unnoticed by the foot that crushes them. We are nothing, because we do not belong to reality; and when we delude ourselves with the belief that we are acting, and doing something on our own account, we are actually doing no more than renounce all empty desires to create something or do something original and personal; we are simply letting go of ourselves and becoming confused with the eternal reality, letting ourselves be submerged in the flow of the irresistible current of its laws.[3]

The only way of escape from this ultimate nullity of thought lies in resolutely rejecting the instinctive realistic prejudice of mankind, and in seeing thought as the very soul of reality. Gentile thinks that it would be easy enough to do this on the theoretical side, if we could only muster up enough courage "to face the tremendous responsibility imposed on us by the truth that follows from it." [4] For when we reflect that all the evidence for this independent world is drawn from the consciousness that is said to be an empty shadow beside it, the contradictory character of all naturalism becomes apparent. How can the unreal guarantee the real? This is the *reductio ad absurdum* of what Gentile calls 'realism' as opposed to 'idealism' —though it would be more exact to say 'naturalism' as opposed to 'spiritualism,' since the majority of earlier idealists are 'realists' in Gentile's sense of the word:

We give the name *realism* to the method of thought that makes the whole of reality an independent object, abstracted from thought, to which thought as an activity should conform. By *idealism,* on the other hand, we mean the higher point of view, from which we discover the impossibility of conceiving a reality that is not the reality of thought itself. For it reality is not an idea which, as a simple object of the mind, may also exist outside of the mind, indeed must exist independently if the mind is to have the right or the power to think of it. Reality is this very thought itself by which we think of everything, for this thought must surely be something if by means of it we want, somehow, to affirm any reality whatsoever. It must be a real activity, if, in actual thinking, it does not become entangled in the magic circle of a dream but enables us to live

---

[3] B.1128, pp. 49–51, 53; cf. English translation (B.659), pp. 64–70.
[4] B.1128, p. 55; cf. English translation (B.659), pp. 72–73.

in its own real world. And if it is inconceivable that it should ever issue forth from itself, to penetrate the assumed material world, then that means that it has no need to issue from itself in order to come into contact with reality; it means that the reality which is called material and external to thought is in some way illusory, and that the true reality is just that which comes to be through the efforts of actual thinking. For, indeed, there is no way of thinking any reality, except by establishing thought as the basis of it.

This is the conception, or if you like, the faith, not merely of modern philosophy, but even of consciousness in general, the consciousness that has gradually been formed and molded through the profound moral sense of life fostered by Christianity. For it was Christianity that first set against nature and the flesh a truer reality—a world to which man is not simply born but must raise himself, a world in which he must live not because it is already there, but because it is his task to create it of his own will—the kingdom of the spirit.

According to this concept there is, properly speaking, no reality; there is only the spirit which creates reality, which is therefore self-made and not a natural product. The realist speaks of something already existent, a world into which man comes and must adapt himself. The idealist knows only the world that the spirit creates; a world in which nature itself is always internal to the progress of the spirit and throbs within the soul of man, who continually remakes it with his intellect and his will in a restless activity that knows no pause; a world that is never complete, because the whole of the past issues in the actuality of the present (the form that belongs to it and in which it really exists). . . .[5]

These two opposed conceptions of reality, the one in which it is simply an object contemplated by the intellect, and the other in which it is an activity generated by the will, are always present in Gentile's mind. He gives them technical names—the 'abstract logos' and the 'concrete logos'—and he finds them opposed, under various disguises, everywhere in the history of philosophy. But the reader who holds firmly to the distinction between 'realism' and 'idealism' here established should be in no danger of getting lost in the intricacies of the more academic works.

The 'Problem of Christianity'

As can be seen from the above quotation, Gentile holds that this new spiritual view of reality is rooted in the Christian tradition. The promulgation of the Gospel brought into the world something new; against the static contemplative attitude of the ancient world

---

[5] B.1128, pp. 55–57 (Gentile's italics); cf. English translation (B.659), pp. 73–75.

it asserted the primacy of the will. True reality, in the new dispensation, is the Will of God; and the fulfillment of God's Will requires human concurrence. This new voluntarist attitude is perfectly summed up in Paul's declaration that "though I have the gift of prophecy, and understand all mysteries, and all knowledge . . . and have not Charity, I am nothing." [6]

According to Gentile the central task of postclassical philosophy has been to find an adequate conceptual formulation for the Christian vision of man's spiritual destiny; and all attempts have so far failed because some elements of classical naturalism survived unconquered in every later formulation of the problem. Christ proclaimed the truth in religious terms; but the mystical transcendence that is native to religion proved an insurmountable obstacle to exact conceptual expression. The problem for a 'philosophy of Christianity' —if we may so speak without offense—was beautifully stated by St. Augustine in a sentence which Gentile frequently quotes or echoes: *Noli foras ire: in te ipsum redi; in interiore homine habitat veritas* ("Go not abroad; return into thyself; in the inner man abides truth").[7] But it was St. Augustine himself who worked out the doctrine of Divine Grace which restored man to a pre-Christian condition of impotence.

All attempts to express this truth of the inner man were in fact foredoomed to failure as long as the reality that they sought to explicate was accepted as a presupposition of the process of philosophical explication. Nothing that is accepted as absolutely given can be more than a reality of the intellect, something that is conceived statically on the model of the Being that forms the central conception of pre-Christian philosophy. To put the point more explicitly: if God—the supreme fount of all reality—is presupposed, how can the free spontaneity and creativity of man be real? St. Augustine's doctrine of Grace was the only logical answer to the question once it was framed in these terms. It was inevitable that Christianity, having conquered the world and set the seal on its conquest by closing the schools of Athens, should itself fall captive to the intellectualism of the past. The spirit of Greece could no more be overwhelmed by mere religious enthusiasm than by force of arms.

Only after many centuries of speculative struggling did the new wine begin to burst from the old bottles. The humanists of the Ren-

---

[6] I Cor. 13:2; cf. B.1224 (Vol. V of *Complete Works*), p. 34.
[7] *De vera religione*, 39:72 (Migne, *P.L.*, XXXIV, 154).

aissance, with their plethora of treatises *De dignitate hominis,* at last found the right starting point. Bacon translated this *dignitas* into *potestas* in his vision of a human conquest of nature through the advance of the natural sciences. Then Descartes recognized that the self-consciousness of the thinking subject is fundamental in all knowledge; but his thinking subject was still a substance immediately known, a presupposition like Bacon's sense experience.

The same weakness reappeared in their successors. Spinoza, the greatest of them, insisted strongly that the method of philosophy must be immanent—i.e., that the thinking subject must not be separated from the object of his thought—but he remained entangled in transcendence and therefore ended by resolving the subject into the object, man into God, rather than vice versa. Thus he worked out the intellectual theory of reality to its logical conclusion.[8]

The English empiricists, on the other hand, through their concentration on immediate experience, resolved the object into the subject, leaving only a flux of subjective impressions. Thus, in Gentile's words, philosophy was "constrained to oscillate between a world which is intelligible but not real (the rational world of the metaphysicians from Descartes to Wolff) and a world which is real indeed, and substantial, but not intelligible, though obscurely felt and able to shine through sense impressions, unconnected and manifold (the 'nature' of the empiricists from Bacon and Hobbes to Hume)."[9]

In Gentile's view, the skepticism of Hume provides a sufficient critique of both rationalism and empiricism; and by revealing the contradictions involved in any claim to possess knowledge of an object which transcends consciousness, Hume brought the 'modern problem' clearly into focus. The solving of this problem and hence

---

[8] Il metodo dell immanenza," in B.701, pp. 230 ff. (now in *Complete Works,* XXVII, 210–21). Spinoza's doctrine that truth is not to be fixed by reference to some reality that transcends it passes into actual idealism without substantial amendment, and Gentile acknowledges this by frequent reference to the Spinozan dictum *Verum norma sui et falsi.* The whole of actual idealism is, as it were, a translation into the first person of what Spinoza says in the third. Thus Gentile approaches the Spinozan synthesis more closely than any other Hegelian, precisely because he opposes it more directly: he does not criticize or correct, he simply converts. That is why, although he hardly ever mentions Spinoza without seeking to confute him, the spirit of the *Ethics* broods over and pervades much of Gentile's own work.

[9] B.1279 (now Vol. III of *Complete Works*), p. 72; cf. English translation (B.660), p. 73.

also the genesis of actual idealism begins in earnest with Kant's awakening from the slumber of dogmatism.[10]

Kant and the Synthesis a priori

Gentile claims that the germs of his philosophy were already discernible in his doctoral thesis, written in 1897 at the age of twenty-two, on Rosmini and Gioberti: ". . . in explaining the value of Rosmini's philosophy and hence of Kant's, my thesis brings out the profound difference between the category (which is the act of thought [*l'atto del pensiero*]), and the concept (which is the fact thought about [*il pensato*])." [11]

The synthesis a priori, by which Kant overcame Hume's skepticism, is a constructive activity on the part of the subject. It is a synthesis, not of concepts but of a concept and a sensation; and it is a priori because neither term can actually be conceived apart from it. The conceptual element involved is a pure form and is not a product of sense experience but rather a condition of it. Kant enumerates a finite set of twelve of these pure forms, which he calls functions of the understanding—or categories. On the other hand, the sensation which is united with the category in the synthesis is *not* a pure sensation: it is perceived through an intuition which has two fundamental forms, space and time. The source of the synthesis, the common root both of the sensuous intuition and the activity of the understanding, lies in the transcendental unity of apperception —the Ego.[12]

This conciliation of the dualism between mind and matter fails,

---

[10] Cf. B.1013 in B.1075, p. 20 (2nd ed., 1952, p. 18); B.296 in B.898, p. 24. But several important steps toward a solution had already been taken by Vico. The idealist interpretation of Vico, taken as a whole, is certainly debatable. But when Gentile writes "superare ogni immediatezza, *hoc opus, hic labor*" (B.1075, p. 97; 2nd ed., p. 87) he can legitimately point to Vico's criticism of Descartes as the first emergence of this ideal. At the beginning of the *Theory of Mind as Pure Act* he takes the famous aphorism *Verum et factum convertuntur* and revises it to make a motto for his own theory. One may object that when Vico wrote the *De antiquissima Italorum sapientia* his mind was still dominated by the neo-Platonism of the late Renaissance; but, for all that, Gentile's implied tribute remains a just one, since the *Scienza nuova* is only comprehensible if the 'making' of truth is a real creative activity, not an ideal re-creative contemplation. In this respect Vico does anticipate the great movement of German philosophy from Kant to Hegel (cf. B.656, pp. 57–62).

[11] B.296 in B.898, p. 14.

[12] This summary is framed in terms of Gentile's discussion in B.1251 (Vol. I of *Complete Works*), pp. 74–76.

however, because the content of the sensible manifold remains obstinately foreign to the elaborative activity of the mind. The Kantian category ought to be the actuality of the synthesis (*l'atto del pensiero*) but it remains a mere abstract term of the synthesis, a concept (*il pensato*). Kant could not hold firm to the identification of synthesis and category because he accepted the sensible manifold as a datum and did not clearly recognize that its constitution as a manifold involved the elaborative activity of the understanding. Having accepted the manifold as manifold, he needed a systematic multiplicity of judgments through which it could be ordered. Thus the category lost its truly transcendental character, its essential unity (which he was the first to perceive), and was degraded into a concept. This led to a series of mistaken attempts by Kant and others to restore unity by means of a 'transcendental deduction of the categories.'

This was by no means the sum of Kant's difficulties, however. For having accepted the sensible manifold as given, he was obliged to postulate the noumenal world as a transcendental ground for phenomenal experience; and under this guise the old realism, driven out at the door, crept back by the window. In relation to the noumenon the synthesis a priori of the understanding is conditioned and not free; and therefore human freedom, the autonomous nature of which Kant clearly understood, had to be relegated to the noumenal world and has no place in the *Critique of Pure Reason*.

When it is stated thus baldly, Gentile's interpretation of the Kantian problem may sound merely hostile and negative.[13] Never-

---

[13] It has sometimes been made a complaint against Gentile that he misrepresents the historical Kant (see, for example, Emilio Chiocchetti, *La filosofia di Giovanni Gentile*, Milan, Vita e pensiero, 1925, p. 69). When one considers his writings as a whole, I doubt whether the accusation can be made good; but, be that as it may, the complaint rests on a false premise. Gentile assumes an adequate knowledge of the whole history of German idealism on the part of his readers. The brief essays on the history of philosophy which serve as a sort of introduction to several of his systematic works, along with the chance remarks which are to be found on almost every page of his writings, are not meant to instruct his readers, but to illumine and interpret what they are assumed to know already. This assumption, as Collingwood remarked, is a serious obstacle to the understanding of his philosophy on the part of the ordinary layman (see the symposium: "Can the New Idealism Dispense with Mysticism?" in *Aristotelian Society Supplementary Volume* III, 1923, 169–70). It seems to be required, however, since his whole outlook is essentially historical; and there is little that anyone can do to remove the resulting barrier. This is the only excuse that I can offer for the unavoidably esoteric character of the present discussion.

theless it seems to me impossible to overestimate its importance as a catalyst in his own philosophical development. The identification of the category with the 'act of thought' was a crucial step for him. The distinctive motivation of his 'reform of the Hegelian dialectic' was therefore Kantian, and we might almost say that the moving spirit of his philosophy is Kantian rather than Hegelian. His aim is to confine philosophy within the bounds of actual experience, which is what Kant tried to do in the *Critique of Pure Reason*. But Kant was hampered by his dogmatic inheritance, which imparted a somewhat skeptical tone to his final achievement. Gentile seeks to rid the Critical Philosophy of this tendency toward skepticism by conquering the remnants of dogmatism. In this his attitude toward Kant differs from that of the German idealists, nearly all of whom overstepped in one way or another the limitations laid by the master upon the exercise of speculative reason. Schelling, Hegel, and Schopenhauer all came to rest in an Absolute which transcends concrete experience; and for all of them the Critical Philosophy was only a prolegomena or propaedeutic to a speculative or 'transcendent' philosophy of the kind which Gentile and Kant are united in opposing.[14]

To many critics it has seemed that Gentile is closer to Fichte than to Kant or to any of the other post-Kantian thinkers; and they have remarked with regret on the absence of a critical evaluation of Fichte in his writings.[15] At first sight the lack does seem perplexing, for Gentile recognizes in several places [16] that Fichte's ideal of

---

[14] Even the agreement of Kant and Gentile in this matter is somewhat deceptive. From Gentile's point of view, it cannot really be said that Kant was definitely opposed to metaphysics. His own theory of the noumenon constituted a metaphysics of the old-fashioned dogmatic variety. Sometimes, as Gentile puts it, Kant faces Hume's problem of how the mind passes to a knowledge of external reality—which is properly soluble only as Hume solved it—and resolves it by positing a *Ding an sich* which remains completely unknowable; and sometimes he faces his own true problem—of the process of consciousness from sensation to self-conscious reason. The former line of development leads to the replacement of metaphysics by science; the latter to the new immanent "metaphysics of the mind" (cf. "Il metodo dell'immanenza," in B.701, pp. 237–39; now in *Complete Works*, XXVII, 223–25).

[15] Cf. Roger W. Holmes, *The Idealism of Giovanni Gentile*, New York, Macmillan, 1937, p. 4; Patrick Romanell (Pasquale Romanelli), *The Philosophy of Giovanni Gentile*, New York, S. F. Vanni, 1938, p. 59; Mueller, *op. cit.*, p. 244n4.

[16] Notably in B.297 in B.1279, p. 244; cf. English translation (B.660), p. 254. Notice also that the full title of his *Logic* is *Sistema di logica come teoria del conoscere*.

philosophy as *Wissenschaftslehre* is, from his point of view, the right one. Fichte sought to do what Gentile claims to have done: to establish a 'philosophy without presuppositions'—a philosophy of freedom—by eliminating the dogmatic remainders in the Kantian synthesis. Furthermore, as Gentile also, though more hesitantly, recognizes,[17] it was Fichte who originated the dialectic method, which alone makes it possible to regard experience as self-constitutive and moral freedom as the ground of reality. But in spite of all this he deals with Fichte only briefly and in passing, as a stage on the road from Kant to Hegel; and though I agree with Mueller that it is a pity, I think we can see why he does not treat him at length.

Fichte, like all of the other post-Kantians, erred from the point of view of actual idealism in that he attacked the various dualities left in the Critical Philosophy in the wrong order. The fundamental problem that Kant bequeathed was the problem of integrating theoretical and practical reason. But this can never be done while the traditional dualism of thought and action is preserved. It is not enough to banish the *Ding an sich* and fill the gap by reversing the order of the first two critiques. This still leaves the heart of reality outside of actual thinking: one noumenon has been replaced by another but the result is not very different. True, the Fichtean Ego is no longer a substantial entity,[18] but it is still a reality presupposed by the thought which gradually recognizes it: the necessity of truth arises from the ontological priority of this transcendent act of self-positing.[19] As long as thought *follows* reality—in any sense of the word—truth is not and cannot be *norma sui:* it will always be the

---

[17] B.1013 in B.1075, p. 28 (2nd ed., p. 25). He always gives an unfairly large share of the credit to Hegel (cf. B.1224, p. 45).

[18] I cannot agree with Holmes when he argues that the Fichtean Ego is distinguished from the Gentilian by virtue of a certain substantial existence (*op. cit.,* p. 5). Fichte's Ego is as much a self-constitutive dialectic as Gentile's and he himself protests strongly against a 'substantial' interpretation. The *Ich* is an act, a *Thäthandlung* whose being coincides with its activity of self-positing. The difference lies rather in the relation of this original dialectical activity to the thought which is aware of it.

[19] If, as Fichte postulates, the dialectic that constitutes the Ego transcends the thought which thinks it, why prejudge the issue by calling it Ego? This seems to have been the substance of Schelling's complaint against Fichte and the motive of his search for a "point of union" between subject and object. Not merely the growth of the Ego in self-consciousness, but growth or life of any kind, can be shown to be constituted by a dialectical activity. Thus Schelling bequeathed the objective moment to the Hegelian synthesis, and Gentile passes over him, as he does over Fichte, because the problems implicit in the work of both of them become fully explicit in Hegel.

offspring of a contemplation whose content remains alien and indifferent. 'Alien' and 'indifferent' may seem overstrong expressions to apply to a reality as intimate as the self-positing of Fichte's Ego. But *any* transcendent reality is alien to a philosophy of freedom—the late-comer to the feast will always be without a wedding garment. Hence the resemblance that has been detected between actual idealism and the activism of Fichte is largely specious. Both philosophers assert, if you will, the priority of the will over the intellect—but whereas for Fichte the implied dualism is never successfully resolved, Gentile makes the assertion only after resolving it. For him the theoretical moment, grasped in its concreteness, *is* practical—indeed, it is the very soul of all practical activity. So that for him the 'priority' of the will means simply the universal priority of the act of thought (*pensiero pensante*).

The Hegelian Synthesis

According to Gentile, Hegel was the first to see clearly that the problem of the relation between being and knowing was essentially 'logical.' [20] He recognized that the dialectic was, properly speaking, a new logic of activity opposed to the traditional static logic of Aristotle; and therefore he drew a careful distinction between the 'understanding' which conceives things and the 'reason' which conceives spirit. But in his attempt to solve the problem which he had thus clearly formulated, he succeeded only in making explicit the intellectualism which had remained concealed in the theories of his predecessors.

Briefly, his method is at variance with his results. If we take his philosophy as a complete system of reality, the progress implied in the dialectic development of the Idea is illusory: his new logic is as static as the old because his 'solution' of the pseudo problem of the deduction of the categories is to conceive them as forming a great circle whose end is its beginning. And when we have completed this circle a further paradox comes clearly into view. Having followed the abstract universal to its point of fullest development we are unable to understand the leap by which we must now pass from the ideal universality of logic to the existent particularity of

---

[20] B.1224, p. 45; cf. n17 above. Hegel may have been the first to call the new method 'logic,' but it is debatable whether that was an advance.

nature.[21] Precisely where the dialectic becomes fully concrete it defeats our comprehension; and on re-examination we discover—what we might well have begun to suspect when we found that the dialectic of the Idea constituted a closed system—that the abstract dialectic of the *Logic* lacks the element of living contradiction which alone would make it cogent. Its apparent cogency is a mere seeming. For example, Being insofar as it is pure Being is distinct from non-Being; while, on the other hand, insofar as, by reason of its absolute indeterminacy, it is not distinguishable from non-Being, it is identical with non-Being. Inasmuch as it is self-identical it is distinct from non-Being; inasmuch as this identity is undetermined it is identical with non-Being. There is either a static distinction between the two terms (self-identity) or a static identity (equivalence). But there is no way in which from the two abstract concepts a third can be generated, for there is no unity of opposites but only the unity of identity.[22]

In fact, there can be no dialectic of ideas or objects of thought that is not ultimately reducible to the naturalism of the Platonic dialectic. No philosophy of freedom is possible upon such foundations. Hegel's method contradicts his result because it simply is not applicable to his premises; we have to choose between the method and the system. 'Actual' idealism is the logical result of a strict adherence to the method: it rests on a 'reform of the Hegelian dialectic.'

Bertrando Spaventa

This reform was not the achievement of Gentile alone. The problem of how, if reality is dialectical, Hegel's or any other systematic theory of it could be final or complete, emerged fairly early. The man who formulated the problem in the way in which Gentile received it was Bertrando Spaventa, a Neapolitan professor of the Risorgimento period.[23]

---

[21] B.1279, p. 66; cf. English translation (B.660), pp. 65–66.

[22] B.1279, pp. 55–56; cf. English translation (B.660), pp. 54–55.

[23] We should perhaps say, rather, that Gentile found intimations and anticipations of his own formulation of the problem in the often fragmentary essays of Spaventa which he edited and published for the first time. Spaventa was undoubtedly moving toward a philosophy of pure immanence, but it is not clear how far he actually saw, or would have been prepared to go, along the path that Gentile followed.

Spaventa was perturbed about the duality that survives in Hegel's work between philosophy and phenomenology. The *Phenomenology,* which describes the mind's progress toward a recognition of its own absolute character, is for Hegel only a sort of introduction to the systematic philosophy of the Spirit expounded in the *Encyclopaedia.* This means that an explanation of knowledge is not at the same time an explanation of the object known. Being still transcends the conscious mind. But to prove the identity of mind and being is the essential task of a philosophy of absolute immanence. Somehow the process of Absolute Mind must be seen as the process of the individual mind so that the propaedeutic character of the *Phenomenology* is canceled; for after all it is precisely the individual mind which recognizes its own absoluteness in the *Phenomenology.* If this were not so we could not understand the *Logic* at all.

Spaventa did not succeed in finding a way of reconciliation because he did not adopt a sufficiently radical attitude toward the Hegelian philosophy as a whole.[24] But in one of his essays he chanced upon the key to the problem. The way to unite the two 'proofs' (as he called them) of the ideal character of reality is to recognize the individual mind of the *Phenomenology* as the essential motive force of the *Logic.* Through the introduction of this active power the problem of the generation of the new concept Becoming from the opposition of Being and non-Being in Hegel's *Logic* can be solved. Spaventa realized that the Being that passes over into its own opposite is the *thinking activity.* An empty, dead concept is not enough; a living reality is needed. We have to turn from the content of thought to the act of thinking in order to find a basis for the dialectic:

In defining 'Being,' I do not distinguish myself as thought from Being; I *extinguish* myself as thought in Being; I *am Being.*

Now, this *self-extinction* [*estinguersi*] of thought in Being, is the *contradiction* of Being. And this contradiction is the first spark of the dialectic.

Being contradicts itself because this self-extinction of Thought in Being—and only thus is Being possible—is a negation of extinction [*un non estinguersi*]: it is a self-distinction [*distinguersi*], it is life. To think of not thinking, to make an abstraction from thinking, that is to say, to define Being, is to think. . . .

This immanent contradiction, that is, the unity in difference of Being and Non-Being, is what has been called the *unrest* of Being. . . .

Becoming is the *unrest* of Being: the Being which, inasmuch as it is,

---

is not. Becoming is the Being which is Non-Being, the Being which is Thinking, the Object of thought [*il Pensato*] which is itself Thinking [*Pensare*] (the Abstraction which is Abstracting). I think Being; and inasmuch as I think Being, I am Thinking, I am Non-Being; inasmuch as I abstract from myself as abstracting, I am abstracting. But Thinking itself, I do not think, at least I do not think it as Thinking, but only as an object of thought in a new act of thinking [*lo penso solo di nuovo come pensato*]. I cannot grasp myself as Thinking, as Non-Being; I grasp myself as Being: as Thinking I am the Being which is Non-Being. This sentence: *I am Thinking*, and I cannot grasp myself as Thinking—this unrest, this Being which is unrest itself—this is Becoming. (I cannot grasp the act as act—as energy, or I would like to say, *agens;* the act when grasped is no longer act: it is *Actum*).

Being and Non-Being when they are validated [*inverati*] in Becoming, are no longer what they were before being validated; they are each of them that same *unity in difference* which is Becoming, and in virtue of being this unity, they are truly, in other words *actually, distinct*. Precisely in virtue of their being truly one and distinct we say they are validated; that is they are *moments* of Becoming.

Being as a moment, is the *Being that becomes:* beginning, being born (self-distinction); Non-Being, as a moment, is the *Non-Being that becomes:* ceasing, dying (self-extinction).

Thus Becoming itself is a beginning that ceases, and a ceasing that begins; a birth that dies, and a death that is born (self-distinction that extinguishes itself, and self-extinction that distinguishes itself). *Eternal death, eternal birth.*

This eternal death that is eternal birth, this eternal birth that is eternal death, is Thinking.—I think, that is I *am born* as thinking; but I cannot grasp myself as *thinking*, but only as *an object of thought,* and hence I die as thinking. Yet *in dying* as thinking, I think; and hence I *am born* as thinking. And so on forever.[25]

This passage is quite a startling anticipation of the fundamental thesis of actual idealism. It follows from Spaventa's discovery that the whole problem of the categories, about which post-Kantian philosophy was so exercised, is an illusion. For at every stage in the concomitant progress of Thought and Being the logical situation is the same: the unique category, the source of the dialectic movement, is the concrete thinking activity of the subject. Actual thought is the only 'level of reality.' This conclusion, however, undermines the whole structure of Hegel's system; and Spaventa certainly did not envisage such a revolutionary denouement.

---

[25] "Le prime categorie della Logica di Hegel," in B.49, pp. 197–200. I have preserved the italics, capitals, and punctuation of the original.

The 'Method of Absolute Immanence'

It was left to Gentile to develop the consequences of this new interpretation of the dialectic some twenty-five years after Spaventa's death. Actual idealism is the result of a logical development of this single fundamental principle: that the activity of thinking is the only thing that is truly dialectical. The free spontaneity of thought must be both the foundation and the keystone of the modern spiritual view of the world. Only in this way can the Fichtean ideal of a *Wissenschaftslehre* be realized: a philosophy of freedom that makes no assumptions, and develops the Cartesian *cogito* to the full without appealing to any transcendent reality. Fichte and even Hegel fell short of this ideal because they continued to treat reality as a necessary presupposition of the activity which comprehends it. Even a reality *created by* the spirit is not a spiritual reality if the creation is already finished and complete—for there is then no room for free activity. Only if *thinking* is seen as the eternal creative act is the problem of freedom solved. In a truly spiritual account of reality there can be nothing external to this activity—everything must fall within it.

In this account of reality, therefore, method and result, logic and metaphysics, phenomenology and philosophy, must coincide. The method of philosophy cannot be an 'instrument' that produces an independent result. It is not a ladder to philosophy as Hegel's *Phenomenology* is a ladder to the Absolute; it *is* philosophy.[26] If the method of philosophy were only a means to the resulting 'system' then the system would be something transcendent relative to a thought that was still in search of it; and if truth were thus foreign to thought, then the actual process of discovering it would have no value. Hence thinking as *metodo strumento* is compelled to deny itself. But since even this denial would be an affirmation if the seeker after a transcendent truth were logical enough to arrive at it, it is obvious that even the theories of a transcendent reality are dependent on the living synthesis of actual thinking.

Kant remarked somewhere that there is no philosophy, there is only philosophizing. This is the essence of Gentile's 'method of immanence.' In it the Kantian category, the synthesis a priori, and

---

[26] The shadow of Spaventa's two 'proofs' survives in actual idealism in the shape of the two approaches described in our first two chapters. But if Gentile is right it is no more than a shadow.

the transcendental unity of apperception have coalesced, and the noumenon is finally banished. There have been philosophies of immanence before, from the time of Aristotle onward. But actual idealism is far more radical than any previous attempt in this direction. From Gentile's point of view, all previous philosophies are philosophies of transcendence—the Aristotelian individual, for example, in which the universal is immanent, is still a transcendent reality. It is posited as independent of *pensiero pensante,* and as such it is a mere abstraction, which must be brought back to the living thought that actually contains it and gives it meaning. It is this thought that is truly *individual,* a synthesis a priori of which we cannot say unequivocally either that it is particular (since it is a universal and infinite reality), or that it is universal (since its universality is a self-limiting actuality). We cannot define it at all, because we cannot objectify it. It is always precisely the consciousness that *contains* the object, i.e., it is the act of *defining.*[27]

The most important consequence of this assertion that thought is an act which eternally determines itself, and is not determined by anything external to itself, is that the familiar distinction between thinking and doing is thereby abolished. Thinking has become an activity; indeed, it is now the unique activity of which all others are simply facets. Traditionally it has been held that, while action is free, thought (or at least true thought) is determined by the truth that it knows, the reality that is its object—a reality which exists independently, whether it is known or not. It may seem that Gentile's denial of this distinction, and, in particular, his doctrine that thought is not directed toward an independent reality, simply opens the gate to relativism and absolute skepticism. That is far from his intention. If one wished to express the significance of his 'philosophy of freedom' briefly it would be fairer to say that he denies the subjectivity which naive common sense ascribes to action, than that he denies the objectivity ascribed to serious thought.

Freedom, for Gentile, means freedom in the Kantian sense—the moral autonomy of the good will. Thought must indeed be *true;* but, in his view, this objectivity is something that belongs to its own inward nature, just as duty belongs to the inward nature of the will. Truth is the *duty* of thought: it is a moral value. When he says that thought and action are both free he does not mean that either is the

---

[27] B.1279, pp. 8–9; cf. English translation (B.660), pp. 6–7.

result of a spontaneous impulse. An impulsive action is the very antithesis of freedom as he understands it, for no action can be truly *ours* if it is not mediated by our own conscious thought. Hence the free will of man cannot be established by asserting, as Fichte and Croce do, the primacy of the practical moment, the will. An act of which we *know* nothing until it is complete is none of our doing. It is just as foreign to us as a completely determined natural order which presents itself as 'given' by an unknown agent or by no agent at all. The spirit can know only what it has made knowingly. Free action must be *intelligent*, it must be guided by thought. Yet how can thought guide the active creation of a new world, if the world in which it has its own purely contemplative being is absolutely determined prior to its advent? This is the rock upon which all previous attempts to express the new *Weltanschauung* of Christianity have been wrecked. We have to grasp the concept of thought as active and creative, not passive and contemplative, if we are to understand the possibility of any freedom whatever.

But then, if my thinking *constitutes* my reality, am not I imprisoned in a world of illusions? Or in other words, how is this doctrine distinguishable from solipsism? If an absolute subjectivism of this sort is the price of an understanding of freedom, would it not be better to renounce such an understanding, and return to the Kantian world, in which all actual thought is determined by conditions that transcend it, and freedom is a mystery, postulated as necessary for the explanation of moral experience? In order to understand clearly how Gentile's philosophy evades, or claims to evade, this difficulty, we must reconsider the 'objectivity' that belongs to the act of thought.

Actual thinking is not mere idle imagining. It is not, indeed, determined by a reality which is external and indifferent to it; but it determines itself, and this determination is not a game but a serious business. Whoever thinks, thinks the truth. That is to say he thinks as well as he can and affirms his thought as true. But the truth that he thinks is never final—further investigation is always necessary; and in affirming it as true he objectifies it, cuts it off from himself, and makes it the starting point for criticism and reformulation.

This objectification also means that whoever thinks does not simply think *for himself*: in accepting his own thought he assumes that, if he can only make himself properly understood, others will agree with him. It is this universality, or rather this striving for and claim to universality, that constitutes reality. This is Gentile's 'transcendental Ego' in whom God and man are one. "Seek and ye shall find," says the Gospel; according to actual idealism, this is a way of saying that the finding lies in the moral earnestness of the seeking. A man will always find precisely what he deserves, and out of his finding he will build the actual world that he deserves. Thought is *free* precisely in the Kantian sense—its freedom is the willing acceptance of a universal law which it gives to itself. "Seek and ye shall find" is thus a direct translation of the Stoic maxim that "Virtue is its own reward" (*Praemium virtutis ipsamet virtus*).

In actual idealism, therefore, 'truth' and 'reality' are synonyms for 'value.' But what about 'truth of fact'? We should normally say that the statement "My pen is black" is *true* if and only if my pen *is in fact* black. If there is no place for truths of this sort in the new theory of truth, then Gentile's idealism is a very limited doctrine and one of doubtful utility.

We shall have to consider presently the general question of the 'poverty' of this theory of 'pure actuality'; but at least it is not limited in this sense. What we call 'facts' belong, in Gentile's view, to the *past* of the act of thought. Or rather, to be more precise, they form the *content* of the eternal present. For properly speaking the act has no past, since it is not in time, but generates time as a mode of order for this content. All thought requires a factual content into which it breathes life and value. The *logo astratto*, which is subject to the traditional abstract logic of identity and contradiction, is an essential moment in the *logo concreto* which is the dialectical logic of actual thought. It is true that, although Gentile can demonstrate the necessity of *some* factual element in all actual thinking, he cannot demonstrate the necessity of *any particular fact*. This has sometimes been urged in criticism of his theory.[28] But he never meant to do this. His theory certainly does not require him to "deduce his critic's pen," and I strongly suspect that it involves a denial that any such deduction is possible. Experience for him is an a priori synthesis of subject and object. That is to say that however far back we go in an attempt to trace an experience to some unique source we shall always find the duality. There is no Fichtean 'absolute seeing' which is not a seeing of anything, any more than there is an absolute Nature against which the truth of experience could

---

[28] Cf. Holmes, *op. cit.*, pp. 194–95; Romanell, *op. cit.*, p. 174.

be measured. The *fact*ual character of an experience is the *limit* of our actual comprehension. This limit is always there, but it is never final: we can never get to the bottom of Nature. It is in this sense that actual idealism affirms transcendence. The transcendent is perceived in and through the process of its immanent becoming; it has value, i.e. reality, in and for experience:

"resolving the whole worlds of nature and history in the act of thinking" does not imply that there is, properly speaking, a single massive absorption of the whole of reality; it means that the eternal resolution of reality is displayed in and through all the forms which experience indicates in the world. Experience is, from the metaphysical point of view, the infinite begetter of an infinite offspring, in which it is realized. There is neither nature nor history, but always and *only* this nature, *this* history, in *this* spiritual act.[29]

The expression "experience begets reality" is perhaps more fortunate than the more frequent variant, "thought creates reality." But we must not let ourselves think of experience as a *power*: it is just this begetting. The form is *all;* there is nothing behind or beyond. Even as the unresolved opaque element in thought, matter coincides with form. It is a negative form, a problem; it is ignorance, the present limit of our knowledge, a limit which is only real to us when it is somehow determined as ignorance about *something.* "So that ignorance is a fact to which experience can appeal only because it is known." [30]

Gentile and Croce

To anyone who has studied the early works of Croce the suggestion that the author of this 'absolute formalism' was ever a disciple of his is almost ludicrous. The whole of Croce's great system rests on the dichotomy between theory and practice. Certainly he felt the need to unify these two aspects of the spirit; but it is the dichotomy, not the unity, which is his key to almost all of the problems of philosophy, while for Gentile it is precisely the dichotomy which is the source of the problems. For a long period the two philosophers collaborated in a common struggle against the empiricism and positivism which were dominant at the time when they began to write. They were both interested in the tradition of

---

[29] B.297 in B.1279, p. 263; cf. English translation (B.660), p. 275.
[30] B.1279, p. 32; cf. English translation (B.660), p. 29.

German idealism and in the general history of Italian culture. Croce was the elder partner and his systematic philosophy was already before the public when Gentile's thought was approaching maturity. Thus there arose the natural but mistaken impression that actual idealism was more directly related to the 'philosophy of the Spirit' than was really the case.[31]

Nor can any serious student accept the view which has sometimes been put forward, that Gentile developed his doctrine largely out of a desire to separate himself from Croce, and that the personal breach which occurred after the March on Rome was always inevitable. I cannot pretend to solve the psychological question of whether Gentile aspired to be a new *maestro di color che sanno* or not.[32] It may be. But in any case his philosophy was an independent growth rooted in problems and preoccupations quite different from those of Croce—and these problems occupied his mind even before he came into contact with Croce. It was precisely this independence of their views that made the break between them, when it came, one of the saddest misfortunes in the history of modern philosophy.[33]

On the evidence of the early correspondence between the two philosophers, Ugo Spirito has argued that it was Gentile who was the dominant partner in the early years of their association. Taken literally this would be as misleading as the popular impression, and it is apparent that Spirito means it to be understood in a fairly limited sense. He is not concerned to deny the substantial independence of Croce, but rather to emphasize the originality of Gentile as emphatically as possible. At the least, he has clearly established that no reliable judgment about the early development of either thinker will be possible unless and until their early correspondence has been published in full.[34]

---

[31] Cf. B.1013 in B.1075, pp. 20–21 (2nd ed., pp. 18–19); B.296 in B.898, pp. 11–15.

[32] Cf. Mueller, *op. cit.*, p. 214.

[33] See further the note at the end of Chapter 6 herein.

[34] *Giornale critico*, XXIX, 1950, 1–11 (reprinted in *Vita e pensiero*, V, 255–67, and *Note sul pensiero di Gentile*, Florence, Sansoni, 1954, pp. 55–74). It seems to be fairly widely agreed now that in the early years of their association it was Gentile who influenced Croce rather than vice versa (cf. C. Sprigge, *Benedetto Croce*, Oxford, Blackwell, or New Haven, Yale, 1952, p. 18; E. Garin, *Cronache di filosofia italiana* [1900–1943], Bari, Laterza, 1955, pp. 245n, 259 ff.). But it has also been suggested (by Garin, *ibid.*) that the influence was largely an encumbrance to Croce ("a parenthesis"). Croce himself acknowledged his debt in his *Autobiography* (Oxford, Clarendon, 1927,

It seems, however, to be clear that the question of who was the dominant partner is of slight importance, since from the beginning each partner had his own personal outlook, no matter how much they learned from one another. Croce sums up his youthful attitude thus: "I soon settled down into a kind of unconscious immanentism, caring for no other world than that in which I actually lived, and not conscious in any direct or primary way of the problem of transcendence. Hence I found no difficulty in conceiving the relation between thought and being." [35]

From Gentile's point of view a confession of this sort is a kind of blasphemy that can only be excused on grounds of invincible ignorance. For it was this problem of "the relation between thought and being" that tormented him all his life.

Perhaps the best summary of the relationship that existed between the two of them was given by Croce in the Introduction which he wrote for the English translation of Gentile's book *The Reform of Education:*

. . . our general conception of philosophy as the philosophy of the Spirit—of the subject, and never of nature, or of the object—has developed a peculiar stress in Gentile, for whom philosophy is above all that point in which every abstraction is overcome and submerged in the concreteness of the act of Thought; whereas for me philosophy is essentially methodology of the one real and concrete Thinking—of historical Thinking. So that while he strongly emphasizes unity, I no less energetically insist on the distinction and dialectics of the forms of the spirit as a necessary formation of the methodology of historical judgment. [36]

This brief comment brings out the *complementary* nature of their philosophical speculation. The mutual independence in principle, upon which we have insisted, is counterbalanced by a remarkable degree of mutual dependence in detailed development. Each of them worked with one eye on what the other was doing, continually borrowing, criticizing, and reformulating. Sometimes the result was a logomachy, but in general the critical attitude adopted on both sides was fruitful for both; and a serious student of any theory advanced by either must always take account of the position adopted by the other on the same issue.

---

cf. pp. 61, 67, 93, 105) and in a note to the third edition of his *Logica* (7th ed., Bari, Laterza, 1950, pp. 210–11; cf. English translation, London, Macmillan, 1917, pp. 327–29). Spirito (*op. cit.*) has assembled other relevant references.

[35] *An Autobiography,* pp. 88–89.
[36] B.659, p. x.

It is doubly important to remember this mutual preoccupation in dealing with the writings of the later years, in which it is not always explicitly acknowledged.[37] After the advent of Fascism twenty-five years of *concordia discors* and active cooperation gave way to twenty years of bitter hostility and violent polemic (a polemic which Croce did not entirely abandon even after Gentile's death by assassination). The desire on both sides in this period was to accentuate differences, but the effective result was that the real differences were obscured in a sea of artificial verbal distinctions whenever they openly referred to one another; the constructive criticism went on, but it was covert. Unless we can keep this covert interaction before our eyes we may well be led into one or the other of two very serious errors. We may find ourselves taking the explicit polemic so seriously as to render a clear understanding of the views of either side impossible; [38] or we may be so disgusted by the shallow verbalism of the polemic as to push aside the real issues along with the illusory ones. Against both temptations we must be firm. The perspective of actual idealism is not the perspective of Croce; but Croce occupies an important and often vital position in the foreground—he is not simply a blot on the landscape.

---

[37] Thus, when in 1934 Gentile wrote an essay on "Economics and Ethics" (B.1107 in B.1139) he expressed himself entirely in terms of the concrete and the abstract logos, the fundamental categories of actual idealism; but he was thinking throughout of the dialectical theory of economics and ethics set forth in Croce's *Philosophy of Practice* and developed in *Politics and Morals* (cf. Chapter 7, pp. 230–36, herein).

[38] This is the pit into which Romanell has fallen in his *Croce versus Gentile*, New York, S. F. Vanni, 1946.

II

THE PRACTICAL PERSPECTIVE
OF ACTUAL IDEALISM

The Absolute Purity of the Act of Thinking

When Gentile first presented his 'method of immanence' as the logical outcome of the philosophical tradition of Western Christianity, Croce objected in a public discussion that the 'pure act' was a mystical reality about which nothing significant could be said; or that conversely, since everything was reduced to this pure act, the new idealism was a panlogism. In either case, having resolved all distinctions the actual idealist was quite unable to tell us just what makes any spiritual activity what it is.

Gentile defended himself indignantly against both charges, by pointing out that the unity of the pure act was not the mystical immediacy of a simple substance but an activity productive of distinctions. He was therefore not trying to destroy the distinctions but only to understand them. This, he said, was the aim of every philosophy worthy of the name, and his idealism was therefore no more and no less of a panlogism than any other.[1]

There is no need for us to become embroiled in this discussion at such a rarified level of abstract generalities. For apart from the metaphysical issue, there is a practical question involved about the adequacy of the 'pure act of thinking' as an account of ordinary conscious experience. It may be that *pensiero pensante* is always individualized and that the 'particular' moment of the dialectic is

---

[1] B.296 in B.898, pp. 11–35; Croce, *Conversazioni critiche* (*serie seconda*), Bari, Laterza, 1950, pp. 67–95; cf. the later violently hostile critical comments in *Conversazioni critiche* (*serie quarta*), Bari, Laterza, 1932, pp. 297–341.

not lost in the immediacy of a mystic universal; but if it has no necessary connection with any particular distinction considered in its particularity, how can it serve to illuminate our actual enjoyment of a life which is certainly far removed from 'pure thinking'? Thus even if Gentile were justified in theory we might still have to agree with Croce in practice; for although the philosophy of the pure act may be a system of necessary and universal knowledge, its very necessity and universality will render it valueless unless it helps us to deal with the personal problems of our lives as individuals.

This practical nemesis of 'panlogism' emerges clearly in Roger Holmes's contention, based on a careful and sympathetic study of Gentile's *Logic,* that

When the full expression of reality comes to be the "act of thinking," the Ego must necessarily fall with the Noumenon and the Absolute into disuse. The *Sistema di logica* possesses all of the ingredients necessary to this final step in the idealist's progress but it appears that the metaphysical vagueness of "Ego" is not noted by Gentile. The fault is undoubtedly explained by the nature of *pensiero pensante,* for it seems to connote a self-conscious thinking personality. But such a connotation would involve a presupposition, and it is precisely such presuppositions that *pensiero pensante* is brought forward to overcome. No thinker breaks completely from his past; his thinking develops out of his heritage. The "Ego" is Gentile's Darwin's Point.[2]

If the transcendental Ego is not really personal and Gentile's thought is not really egocentric but logocentric there is literally nothing left but the universal element and it is hard to see how actual idealism can be of any use to anybody. But then, why should we make the great mental effort necessary in order to understand actual idealism if, at the end of our "bold journey into the inner world of consciousness that draws us on into remote regions where the air may seem at times singularly rarified," [3] our only resource is finally to retrace our steps? In these circumstances the study of Gentile's philosophy might well be compared to the conquest of Mount Everest. A few intrepid spirits may have accomplished it, but their success can have but little relevance to the ordinary lives of the rest of us.

---

[2] Holmes, *The Idealism of Giovanni Gentile,* pp. 226–27.

[3] Mueller, *La pensée contemporaine en Italie,* p. 231.

Concezione umanistica del mondo

It is at this point that we must turn to consider what was called in the last chapter the 'phenomenological' approach to actual idealism. Gentile's philosophy is intended, far more literally than most speculative theories, as a philosophy of life. We have already seen that the pure act is never merely theoretical; it is not contemplation of the truth but rather the act of "cleaving unto it." It necessarily involves a sense of personal commitment and for this reason Gentile often refers to it as 'personality.' This is how he links the two aspects of human nature that used once upon a time to be called 'reason' and 'the passions'; and the maintenance of this bridge is vital to the success of his idealism as a working account not merely of human thought but of human action. He refers to the subject of the pure act as the 'Ego' because he recognizes, and wishes his theory to account for, the integral character of the individual human personality in all its aspects.

Holmes does not ignore Gentile's personalism, but in the light of his own analysis of the *Logic* he insists that "what Gentile should endeavor to stress is the *thinking* and not the *personality,* for it is the thinking that is central to his doctrine." [4] To this our initial reply must be that we cannot yet tell *what* is central to Gentile's doctrine. For even if it is true that the *thinking* appears to be central when he presents his doctrine as the logical result of the history of Western thought, it is certainly no less true that the *personality* appears to be central when he presents his doctrine as the only consistent theory of absolute humanism, the 'humanistic conception of the world.' If in the 'logical idealism' the personality of the thinking subject becomes diaphanous to the point of invisibility, in the 'actual humanism' the concept of thinking is stretched to the limits of paradox. Gentile did not take the "final step in the idealist's progress" because he was not simply an idealist, he was also a humanist. He was not simply a professor of the history of philosophy, he was also a would-be teacher of men.

This is, of course, not an adequate answer to Holmes's argument. He claims that Gentile ought to take the final step and abandon the Ego, because the Ego, the "thinking personality," would have to be just another presupposition of actual thinking. What we are say-

---

[4] Holmes, *op. cit.,* p. 171.

ing is that Gentile *cannot* surrender the Ego because it is the foundation of his absolute humanism. To this Holmes might reply that he was writing about the *idealism* of Gentile, not about his *humanism,* and that if the humanism really requires the Ego it is a different philosophy, and one which violates the 'method of absolute immanence.' Of course Gentile would not want to concede this, so that our task as defenders of actual idealism in its integrity must be to show that the Ego of which he speaks is *not* a presupposition of actual thinking. Only in this way can we avoid having to choose between the 'thinking' and the 'personality' as the 'center' of his doctrine. We shall not be in a position to fulfill this obligation properly until we reach the end of our investigation, but at least we can begin by showing that the Ego is something more for Gentile than a relic from the past which has lost its function.

In Gentile's practical conception of the world the transcendental Ego appears as the 'profound humanity' within us that makes *human* existence possible. He claims that in this respect his philosophy is rooted in the primitive intuitions of mankind. The anthropomorphic tendencies of primitive religion prefigure this truth in mythical form, for in his fables of the gods man makes a society between himself and his environment, and expresses the actual absorption of the environment into his own personality which comes about through his labors. Subsequently, as his powers of critical reflection develop and Nature becomes an impersonal concept, this primitive intuition of the truth is obscured.[5]

Rather than waste any idle regrets on this lost sense of the humanity of our natural environment, however, we must turn our attention to the far more important fact that this 'profound humanity' is the basis of human society in the ordinary sense, the ground of community between man and man. For it is only in virtue of his membership in a human community that the individual man thinks and speaks and wills; he becomes conscious of himself only within the society of others who form a social world. Here we can begin to see the answer to the complaint that the Ego is a presupposition. For this common humanity is not something that we simply discover in ourselves as we perceive it in others; it is something that we build together. It is culture, civilization, the fabric of which

---

[5] B.1013 in B.1075, pp. 5–6 (2nd ed., pp. 4–5). Thus, in a sense, the disenchantment involved in the development of scientific consciousness is a regression.

our individual lives are constructed and the metaphysical ground of our particular personalities. Yet it is not something prior to or independent of our responsibility: civilization is civilized living. In its simplest, most primitive form the transcendental Ego is not thinking, *pensiero pensante*, but feeling, *sentimento*—the feeling of universality which so grips us that "we cannot keep silent for our soul breaks out and speaks and sings." [6] This is the very heart of the act of thought in which everything is contained, "and apart from actual thinking the Ego itself is an abstraction to be relegated to the great storehouse of metaphysical inventions—pure creations of thought that have no real substance. The Ego is not soul substance; it is not a thing, even the noblest among things. It is everything because it is nothing. Whenever it is anything, it is a determinate spirit: a personality that exists in a world of its own—a poem, an action, a word, a system of thought." [7]

The self-determination of actual thought, the self-creation of personality, is the whole being of the Ego. Properly speaking it is the actualization of Royce's 'Great Person,' but it never loses its absolute historic individuality. It is *my* feeling, *my* striving after understanding and sympathy, however universal its scope or end. Gentile's doctrine that a *person is* precisely in *not being* is an attempt to express the concept of human perfectibility. The way to perfection is through the recognition of community—for "We are members one of another"; but the end is not a suprapersonal social order but rather the perfection of one's own personality—"Now I live, yet not I, but Christ liveth in me." The same Christ *in whom* we are members one of another is yet *in us* as a personal ideal. The transcendental Ego is thus the person that we aspire to be; but it is also the Great Person in whom all are united, since it would be impossible for us to feel that our duty was fulfilled in a world where there was still strife between ourselves and our fellow men.

Once we realize that Gentile's pure act is not merely thinking but also feeling, it becomes apparent that the thinking of the Ego is *not* more vital than its personality: the two are an indivisible a priori synthesis. The personality is always dual: there is the ego (particular or empirical) from which the dialectic begins and the Ego (transcendental) toward which it moves. The process of *pensiero pensante*, which is the life of both terms, is at the same time the

[6] B.1013 in B.1075, p. 26 (2nd ed., p. 22).
[7] B.1013 in B.1075, p. 27 (2nd ed., p. 23).

personality whose being consists in its not-being. In concrete terms this means that the individual maintains his individuality through his continual effort to create a real community.

Society is the dialectical product of this effort, and its progressive movement is what we call 'education.' We must never forget that throughout his life Gentile was actively engaged in teaching. He saw the world as primarily "a place of soul-making." His speculation did not merely arise in the schoolroom; it was to a large extent speculation *about* the schoolroom. Most of his typical ideas can be traced back to his preoccupation with the actual process of education, and it is almost impossible to study any aspect of his thought without taking account of these pedagogical roots. And it is notable that whereas in his other systematic works Gentile normally adopts the 'logical' approach, the *Summary of Educational Theory*, which was the earliest detailed exposition of his mature thought, begins with his most adequate account of the 'phenomenology' of the pure act.

The Analysis of Consciousness in the "Summary of Educational Theory"

The historical genesis of Gentile's idealism began, as we saw with the thesis of St. Augustine, *in interiore homine habitat veritas.* In his analysis of consciousness this thesis becomes the basic postulate for the interpretation of experience. He takes it to mean that experience is translucent but never completely transparent. "Cognition develops through infinite grades of perfection, without ever being absolutely perfect." [8] Conscious life is a continual advance toward the heart of things, a progressive evolution of new *meanings*, in virtue of which the world we experience becomes part of us. This evolutionary process is all that there is to experience. For if truth is within us we can only know that which becomes a part of ourselves. Knowledge is only possible if its object is somehow a part of us already; so that if there is to be knowledge at all, experience cannot be referred to 'something beyond.' But knowledge must be possible, for a radical skepticism would be self-contradictory.[9]

---

[8] B.1251, p. 5.
[9] Gentile is quite prepared to use the method of paradoxical refutation that is outlawed by Russell's theory of types. Indeed, even if we allow that the method has a certain validity it may well seem that he uses it far too much. It is worth

Therefore experience—i.e. actual consciousness, for a merely potential experience would be equivalent to the 'something beyond' of the realists—must be self-sufficient.

The way in which Gentile deals with the common-sense view that the physical world exists prior to our knowledge of it is interesting. He simply insists that inasmuch as we *presuppose* physical objects we do *not* know them. But time is a characteristic of things as *known*. Hence to say that the physical objects exist *before* we know them is simply to talk incomprehensibly.[10] The priority of the object known is a function of the knowing, and a reflection of the eternity and universality that belongs to all truth as possessing a definite value. The distinction of 'before' and 'after' results from analysis of a synthesis generated in the act of knowing, which constitutes the actuality of the knowledge, and which is, properly speaking, not temporal at all, but eternal.

Quite distinct from this knowledge, however internal, there is the knowing subject, "the *principle* of the world which is our world." [11] The knowledge we have of ourselves as *knowing* is *self*-consciousness, as distinct from our consciousness of the world known. But since all our knowledge is gained through a laborious process of absorbing the object into ourselves, *all* knowledge is really self-consciousness; and on the other hand, the knowing subject is the subject of precisely *this* knowledge. Simple self-consciousness and simple consciousness—'pure ego' and 'empirical ego' as Gentile calls them—are abstractions. The reality from which they are derived is a unity of self-consciousness with consciousness—the *act* of consciousness. The empirical ego whose biography can be recorded is always integrated into the actual biographer.

This synthetic, integrative activity which is the real subject of

---

quoting his comment an skepticism, however, since it shows clearly that in his own mind it is not the paradox so much as the definition of truth itself that is crucial: "to maintain the thesis that nothing can be known, one would have to maintain at the same time that the truth of this thesis is known. And one thing alone being known, that thing, that is that truth, would draw the rest after it" (*ibid.*, p. 11).

[10] I do not think we should be doing any violence either to Gentile or to Peirce if we borrowed the latter's terminology, and said that the fallacy which Gentile finds in common-sense realism lies in confusing the 'material qualities' with the 'meaning' or 'representative function' of the object cognized (the sign). See C. S. Peirce, *Collected Papers*, Cambridge, Harvard, 1931 ff., Vol. V, sec. 287 ff.

[11] B.1251, p. 15 (Gentile's italics).

experience is unique: there cannot be another like it. Hence it must certainly not be identified with any particular individual: "The conception of man as a particular individual is logically inconsistent with the conception of man as subject; and it should be noted that this inconsistency exists whether the particular individual involved is some other person or whether I consider myself objectively as a limited and particular being." [12] To identify the ultimate subject of all reality with a particular self would be solipsism; and solipsism is logically absurd because, deprived of any genuine *other* to which it can oppose itself, the ego remains self-identical. Alone in a world of mere things it is itself degraded into a thing, incapable of the act of self-denial which is the root of all development.[13]

In view of this analysis, one is tempted to ask how *any* unique subject, since it cannot oppose itself to other subjects, can avoid falling back to the status of a mere thing. Gentile's answer seems to be that the ultimate subject of experience never *is* at all; its life consists in a continual opposition within actual consciousness between the *thing* that I *am* "considered objectively as a limited and particular being," and the *person* that I *aspire to be*. For the ideal subject there can be no distinction of particular individuals—that is the meaning of the commandment to love our neighbors as ourselves. As subject, I cannot distinguish myself ideally from other subjects, once I have granted their subjectivity. But if I did not recognize others as subjects, the ideal unity between myself and my neighbor would be replaced by a material unity between myself and the world of objects. The difference between the ideal unity and the material unity is the gulf that lies between actual idealism and solipsism.[14]

But is the whole essence of humanity contained in this pure subjectivity? Man has a body, an object among others, spatio-temporally located, and objectively determined in a myriad of other

[12] *Ibid.*, p. 19.

[13] Cf. B.1013 in B.1075, pp. 35–36 (2nd ed., pp. 31–32). The vital need to avoid this degradation of the Ego is the source of Gentile's concern with the problem of human society. (I have consistently employed 'ego' for any subject that Gentile regards, or ought to regard, as degraded, and reserved 'Ego' for the genuine transcendental Ego.)

[14] Since no one is actually a solipsist, Gentile has to argue that the ideal unity is always realized in some measure, and that it is only from an external point of view that we can say that a certain person has betrayed it; whereas if we understood his act strictly as an act we should perceive its immanent universality. So that in a way his theory is a kind of moral solipsism—the solipsism implicit in the Gospel precept, "Judge not that ye be not judged."

ways. Furthermore his consciousness of this body involves distinguishable mental functions. On the basis of these functions it would seem to be possible to erect theories of human nature as something independent of historical development ('faculty' theories, or a system of 'grades of consciousness' such as Croce's). Gentile condemns all such attempts out of hand, on the ground that an analytical theory is bound, of necessity, to treat consciousness as a fact, rather than as an act; and he proceeds to a demonstration that the various functions of consciousness are in actuality forms or elements of *pensiero pensante.*

The most primitive level of actual consciousness is what is called 'sensation.' It is true that we do not normally accept our sensations as they stand, but try to classify them as 'internal' or 'external.' But when we do this we are simply trying to fix the spatial position of the supposed stimulus with respect to our own bodies; and both the 'internal' and the 'external' space is within consciousness—if it were not it would be possible to locate consciousness (the soul) within it. If we attend strictly to the sensation itself such spatial reference becomes impossible. Certainly we can distinguish our body from other things—but not in terms of simple sensation, for every sensation is complete in itself and unrelated to other things. All sensations have an identical form, and all are absolutely diverse in content. Even the distinction of form and content is not really legitimate since the sensing and the thing sensed cannot be separated: sensation is the most primitive form of the a priori synthesis of self-consciousness with consciousness, pure ego with empirical ego.

We might perhaps endeavor to establish a distinction between internal and external worlds by regarding immediate or external sensation as passive and opposing it to the psychic reaction of varying intensity which could in principle be assigned its place on a scale of pleasure and pain. But what should we mean then, by the 'inward state' that sustains this feeling? Is pleasure the mere absence or removal of pain (the fulfilling of a need)? Or, contrariwise, is pain simply an impediment in the normal flow of pleasure? These are insoluble questions as long as we cling to the fiction of a pre-existent soul that suffers and reacts to sensation. This presupposed substratum is only a shadow projected back into the past after sensation begins. The soul *is* actual sensation, and pleasure and pain are aspects of sensation, not reactions to it. Pleasure is simply the self-

consistency of sense experience and pain is the presence of an unresolved inconsistency. So that the former is the reality, and the
latter is a privation. Pain, like death, is not a positive part of life, but
only the sense of a limit. We cannot grasp it, for like Eurydice it
vanishes when we look it in the face. Feeling is always positive because it is the presence of self-consciousness to consciousness:

> . . . I cannot suffer without being aware of it. And when I become
> aware of it, it is not I who suffer, because I am rather the one who is aware
> of the suffering; and between suffering and being aware of suffering
> there is this not inconsiderable difference: that in suffering, the suffer-
> ing would have to be the act, the very life itself of the Ego (an absurd
> expression, since to suffer is to be passive, and a "passive action" would
> be like a "dark light"); while in awareness of suffering, the suffering is
> no longer the act of the Ego, the actual Ego: at the most it is what the
> Ego *was* previously, i.e. what it now *seems to have been*, in virtue of its
> present awareness of suffering.[15]

The pain may be said to grow with our knowledge of it. But this
knowledge is also a gradual alienation from it, which is why time
has the power to heal. Pain is gradually purified into pleasure; and
the positivity of pleasure consists in this catharsis. There is no
pleasure without its pain: in Arcadia the soul would vegetate and
become a thing.

We must pause for a moment to consider this doctrine, which
possesses a crucial importance because Gentile follows the same
pattern of argument elsewhere in dealing with such problems as
evil and error. The first thing to notice is that he seems to have
emotional suffering or grief in mind as his model or paradigm case
of *dolore*. Now, since disappointment or loss of this kind can only
be felt where the subject has freely surrendered its freedom, we
may say that all grief is voluntary. We can only grieve for a love
freely given. Hence the consciousness of grief, disappointment, or
toil is truly in 'overcoming' (*superamento*) of its negativity in that
our acceptance of it is a positive act of our own will. For pain in
this sense, Gentile's argument has a certain validity.

But he appears to imagine that it can be extended to cover all
the various meanings of the word. This would involve a disastrous
equivocation between the 'transcendental' Ego and the 'pure' ego.
Because I know that I 'have' a pain is it any the less I who am 'in'
pain? The only self that ceases to suffer in and through this aware-

---

[15] B.1251, p. 37 (my italics).

ness is not the actual Ego but only the empty Kantian 'form' of self-consciousness, the 'I think,' which Gentile himself has declared to be an abstraction. This is no place for final criticism but we may note that Gentile is here doing what Holmes says he should do and we say that he should not: he is emphasizing the 'thinking' at the expense of the 'personality.' But if his argument proves the formal legitimacy of Holmes's interpretation, it also exhibits its practical futility. For to suppose that a purely formal 'overcoming' of this sort is sufficient to solve the problem of pain and evil is childish. Gentile does in fact recognize that the real conquest of pain is a laborious process of self-formation. But his oft-repeated assertion that the being of a *person* lies in his non-being does not prevent him from slurring over the negative moment of the dialectic, and laying all the emphasis on the *positive* character of *pensiero pensante* when it suits him to do so. This point will be of some importance when we come to consider his theory of the inward nature of force and compulsion.[16]

Returning now to the course of the argument from which we digressed, we have seen that sensation and emotional reaction form an indivisible whole, a synthesis which is constituted only in and for our consciousness of it. What we call 'perception' is simply sensation in its full concreteness. Only in a very relative sense can we legitimately speak of perceiving some reality of which we were not previously conscious, and an 'unconscious sensation' would be a contradiction in terms.[17] In any ordinary sense of the terms, living does 'precede' philosophizing; but it is precisely the reflexivity of life that constitutes philosophy. Life is consciousness, sensation, and philosophy is the self-conciousness of that consciousness, perception. Sensation pure and simple is the past, the *logo astratto;* it only actually exists within the concreteness of perception. Hence all attempts to discover the cause of experience within the content of

---

[16] Cf. Chapter 4, pp. 111–17, and Chapter 9, pp. 302–4, herein.

[17] It is regrettable but perhaps not surprising that Gentile could see no value in depth psychology: "The science of the subconscious belongs among the natural sciences, not the sciences of the spirit; but it is only a spurious science, that applies improper methods to nature, just as magic and astrology did formerly" (B.1251, p. 42). I do not think he ever budged from this position of 1912. That such a negative attitude is not required in a philosophy which confides itself strictly to actual consciousness becomes apparent if one reads, for example, Collingwood's *Principles of Art* or Part I of *The New Leviathan,* with due care.

experience involve a hysteron proteron; and the same can be said of the attempt to explain the process of thinking and remembering in associational psychology, through the correlation of sensations regarded as abstract forms. No multitude of Humean impressions (abstract representations of past sensations) ever actually exists. Actual sensation is the unique process of a subject whose existence lies in preserving its own past and relating it to the present. Hence the problem of experience is not to explain memory but to explain forgetfulness.[18] How does the past lose its concrete determinacy, so that vast areas of our experience are reduced to abstract forms or types? Gentile's answer is that strictly speaking we neither forget nor remember. 'Memory' is simply the organization of present reality, and forgetfulness is the recognition of a limit in this process. "When we recognize that we have forgotten something we do not then recover our grasp of what had slipped from us, but we grasp for the first time what had never really been grasped." [19]

The great instrument in this organization of our experience is language. Of course in speaking of it as an 'instrument' we are treating it in the abstract; actually using language means actually organizing reality. No two utterances are genuinely identical, for one is *my* word—concrete, unique, intelli*gent;* the other is *a* word— an abstract, empty universal, the intelli*gible.* But how then do men come to agree on what they mean? Gentile's answer would seem to be that it is not certain that they really do agree, it is only certain that they morally ought to. What he says is simply that they would not be *men* if they did not: "the ears are different, but the spirit is the same." We understand by wanting to understand, and by working to attain community. A word is not a simple physical fact that we can abstract from the total context of language and culture, which is a universe of meaning. If we did not recognize its meaning, however imperfectly, the mere sound would not be a word. Language is the concrete consciousness that we have of our own sensations: it is the *body,* not the clothing or the vehicle, of thought, and it is always novel because thinking is self-creative. Where words refer to objects it may seem that the 'word' does not in fact coincide with the 'meaning.' But this is only in appearance. The word would not

---

[18] B.1251, p. 54. Gentile seems here to be indebted to Bergson's *Matter and Memory.*

[19] B.1251, p. 55.

have a meaning at all, if it did not coincide at least with an abstract representation of the 'thing' meant.[20]

Experience then is a developing process of sensation. There is no *absolute* immediacy anywhere, though looking back we can fix a single moment of the process and treat it as immediate. Only the total process might perhaps be called immediate—but it is really a process of self-mediation. In this process there are no absolute distinctions; more particularly, the distinction between theory and practice, thought and will is dissolved. This distinction arises from a comparison of certain psychic acts with certain others. Thought seems to presuppose the reality that is its object, whereas action creates its own object. But as soon as we see that the concept of reality which is here invoked rests on a mistake, it is not hard to show that this distinction is purely abstract. Once it is granted that the only reality that can be known is a reality which is self-generated, the opposition between knowing and doing becomes purely ideal. On the one hand thought does not presuppose its object, for a reality complete in itself and separate from thought is unthinkable; there is only the gradual increase of knowledge in experience. And on the other hand action does not produce an independent result: the will to do something is not a thing distinct from the doing of it. Premeditation, where it occurs, is part of the action—otherwise there would be no sense in calling it premeditated. Real thinking and real willing coincide in the experience of self-mastery; and mastery of self means mastery of the world of which that self is conscious. This coincidence of thought and will is what Gentile calls *autoctisi*, which may perhaps be best translated 'self-constitution.'[21]

Within the unified process of 'self-constitution,' the presupposed world of thought reappears as the *logo astratto*, the sensation contained in perception. Gentile says that this abstract content which appears as a presupposition is sheer unconscious will seen from the

---

[20] *Ibid.*, pp. 64–65. Gentile seems here to be leaving the *Ding an sich* unchallenged, because he thought it pedagogically advisable to let sleeping dogs lie. But perhaps he did not realize that his general position will not allow him to regard words as 'names' of substantial things at all. He ought to adopt a completely operational or phenomenological account of linguistic experience.

[21] The term was coined from the Greek by Spaventa. Κτίσις was the word used by the Greek Fathers to denote the creation of the world *ex nihilo*. (See further Chapter 9, p. 300, herein.)

point of view of conscious thought; it is a blind and opaque nature that gradually becomes self-conscious and intelligent. This is a strange and perplexing doctrine. It certainly seems rather strained to say that "Sensation is will and perception is knowledge," [22] for the world that appears to us in sensation is far from being willed by us. Yet that is what Gentile appears to claim. What he really means is only that the natural world is certainly there: it acts, it resists, it is stubborn.[23] What we call 'our' will as opposed to the brute persistence of natural facts is really *thought striving* to objectify itself, *to make itself will*, that is to make itself count in the world. Since Gentile has annulled the distinction between external sensation and internal impulse he cannot distinguish nature in general from the nature of the subject. The whole of reality has to be absorbed in the gradual conquest of self. The synthesis of self and world must be a priori, the distinction of external sensation and internal impulse cannot be granted, because only in this way can we escape from the paradox of self-conquest. The paradox is that on the one hand we cannot conquer ourselves until we are selves; and on the other, we cannot become selves except by self-conquest. We *must* say therefore that all consciousness is self-consciousness, that there is no sensation, however primitive or involuntary, that is not already instinct with thought. Or in short, that "the spiritual act is never a self-creation that must be contemplated and watched over afterward; it is always simultaneously a self-creation that is self-perception, and vice versa." [24]

Matter is thus resolved into spirit. 'Resolutions' of this sort are often dismissed as merely analytic or verbal; and when they are presented as the inevitable conclusion of a logical argument (as, for instance, in McTaggart) that is all that they can be. Gentile's argument certainly has a 'logical' appearance. One cannot, he says,

---

[22] B.1251, p. 84. This sort of remark lends color to the view that Gentile has merely brought Fichte to life again. But what distinguishes his view from Fichte's even here is the insistence that sensation, this preconscious will, is always and only an abstraction. (In his early work the priority of blind natural will is genuine; cf. Chapter 3, pp. 55–56, herein.)

[23] Gentile does not explain this doctrine himself. The proposed explanation should therefore be treated with caution. But some view of this sort seems to be implicit in what he says about Rousseau's theory of educational discipline (B.1252, pp. 38–39). Cf. also his later theory of 'economic' or 'corporeal' will described in Chapters 7 and 8, pp. 230–36 and 268–69, herein.

[24] B.1251, p. 84.

reduce spirit to matter because consciousness is a condition of any investigation of reality; and a coherent dualism is unthinkable because it is impossible to correlate spirit and matter without materializing the former. Matter is an essentially indifferent multiplicity —it is infinitely divisible. While the spirit has no parts but is an organic whole. Anything considered as having an essential unity is spiritualized; but as soon as we place it in relation to other things it becomes once again a material object. Even a plurality of spiritual reals would be material, at least to the extent of having certain relations to one another which were accidental to the reals themselves, like the relations which exist between atoms or parts of matter. For if these relations were essential then reality would be an a priori unity, not a plurality.

The real value of linguistic quibbles of this sort becomes apparent when we retort that the explication of experience requires the 'material' category of 'multiplicity' just as much as the 'spiritual' one of 'unity.' For must we not confess with Spinoza that we do experience bodies having spatial position in a world of external relations? Gentile's reply has two aspects. First, it is true that any reality can be regarded *in abstracto* as simply material: "As the cynical proverb reminds us, even the *Divine Comedy* will do to wrap the sardines in." [25] Secondly, the assertion that spirit is the sole reality is not meant to imply the nonexistence of the human or any other body, but only to deny the materialist interpretation of these indubitable realities. Reality is the actual process of experience; and this can only be understood as an organic unity, i.e. from within. The processive character of this unity involves a continual generation of multiplicity *within* the original synthesis. Life produces nature, which then remains as an obstacle to be penetrated and brought to life again. "We have only to think something, and it becomes unknowable; we have only to look within ourselves and we become alien to ourselves." [26] The point is that objectivity can be conquered. If it could not, consciousness would be altogether impossible. Thought is eternally negative; but equally it is positive. It separates itself from its object only to return to it, for the object constitutes its own history. The human body shares in this historical process—it *grows;* and as it grows to maturity man comes to control

---

[25] *Ibid.*, p. 94.
[26] *Ibid.*, p. 97.

it more and more. Only through it does his thinking become actual as an intelligent will.[27] The paralytic does not properly *will* to move, for 'will' implies 'can' just as much as 'ought' does. "In fact power is the essential constituent of the subject and is only distinct from it in the abstract." [28] The body is the product of the spirit so far as it is controlled by the will, and the effort to understand the body is an act of self-constitution. For the body is known only as a content of consciousness, and consciousness informs every physical movement with its own personality.

The arm of the paralytic is no longer truly his own and hence it is not felt as his own; but on the other hand, the sculptor's chisel is an essential part of his personality. In the normal course of events man exercises control far beyond the limits of his own body, and the control of matter is what Gentile seems to mean when he speaks of its 'spiritualization.' We have to follow nature, entering into the life of things, making them part of our spiritual community, in order to master them. The Ego, being one, has only one true body— the whole material universe. At this point Gentile's actual humanism links up finally with his logical idealism. For he could legitimately cite here the sentence of Pascal that stands as the motto for his *Theory of Mind as Pure Act:* "Par l'espace, l'univers me comprend et m'engloutit comme un point; par la pensée je le comprends." In his speculative theory he seeks to show that the first 'comprehension' is itself comprehended in the second, and gets its whole meaning therefrom. "And therefore," as he says at the conclusion of his analysis of consciousness, "man must return to himself, the absolute Subject, the subject that is wholly subject leaving nothing outside of itself, not merely to understand himself but to understand the world." [29]

---

[27] Thoughts as such have a moral value certainly—but of course there is no thinking without effort and bodily fatigue.

[28] *Ibid.*, p. 103.

[29] *Ibid.*, p. 106.

III

THE GROWTH OF GENTILE'S HUMANISM

Forward with Hegel

In the preceding chapters we have distinguished two aspects in Gentile's thought, calling them his 'logical idealism' and his 'actual humanism,' and treating them as, at least possibly, quite distinct in fact. Examination of his early writings will show, however, that the two trends did not actually develop separately, that they were inextricably intertwined in Gentile's own thoughts. Because our principal concern is with his theory of society, we shall here be concerned more with the genesis of his practical humanism, but in the course of our investigation we shall see that the development of Gentile's educational and social theory is dialectically related at every stage to the concomitant clarification of his metaphysical methodology.

Actual idealism came to birth in about 1912 after fifteen years of struggling toward a genuinely 'immanent' interpretation of human experience. The springboard for the continuing process of reformulation and reconstruction was provided in the main by Hegel; and this explains the curious ambivalence in Gentile's attitude toward him. It was natural enough, in view of the general cultural situation at the turn of the century, that the new idealism, in its reaction against the prevailing positivism, should turn back again to the great nineteenth-century tradition in Germany. The reinstatement of Hegel was its first task; his message must be understood and restated plainly enough to refute the ignorant criticisms and disdain of the positivists and others. But since the aims of this idealism were genuinely somewhat novel, there was a tendency in this 'reinterpretation' to confuse what Hegel said with what he ought to have said. 'What Hegel really meant' was often at odds with the system that the professor at Berlin actually constructed.

This Janus character in Gentile's early thought was a legacy from Spaventa, who remained all his life a loyal Hegelian, although in his continual efforts to rethink the whole course of the idealist tradition he was more or less unconsciously offering quite a novel interpretation of the Hegelian dialectic. Gentile held that a return to the teaching of Spaventa was the key to future progress. His teacher at Pisa, Donato Jaja, had been one of Spaventa's pupils and from him Gentile learned to revere the Neapolitan thinker as "the master of philosophic knowledge, not only at Naples but for the whole of Italy."[1] In 1900 he edited and published a volume of *Philosophical Writings*[2] by Spaventa which provoked some hostile criticism. But Gentile was not deterred;[3] and in the course of the next decade he edited and published several further volumes of Spaventa's work.

The first of these was the *Principles of Ethics* (1904)[4] for which he wrote an Introduction which provides a valuable index of his attitude to Hegel's political theory at that time. Political existence, it may be remembered, is for Hegel the 'objective' moment in the development of 'Spirit' which is the last great stage in the development of the Idea. The whole realms of Logic and Nature lie behind it and only the final great triad of the Absolute Idea—Art, Religion, and Philosophy—lies beyond. Gentile accepts and defends this overarching structure:

Everybody, I take it, admits . . . that logic should be considered as the introduction or the propaedeutic to all the sciences, and that its object . . . is therefore logically prior to the object of all the sciences of the spirit. And I do not suppose that there is any need to hold forth about the place that Nature and the Spirit, respectively, occupy in the triad;

---

[1] B.76 in B.618, p. 1.

[2] B.49; cf. Chapter 1, pp. 13–14, herein.

[3] In reply to the most prominent of his critics, Bernardino Varisco, he wrote: "In all honesty, his arguments cannot dissuade me from continually repeating to the people of Italy:—There is a tradition that we must take up again and develop if we wish to regain the right road; and that tradition is in the works of Spaventa" (B.68 in B.618, p. 52).

[4] Spaventa's own title, *Studies in Hegel's Ethics*, is a more modest and a more accurate description of the work, which is a lucid though brief commentary on the ethico-political theory expounded in the *Encyclopaedia*.

for nowadays there is even a tendency to overemphasize the dependence of the latter on the former, and everyone talks of *mens sana in corpore sano*.[5]

The only sign here of the revolution to come lies in the passing reference to the "tendency to overemphasize" the dependence of the Spirit on Nature.

Within the realm of Objective Spirit, which is the world of social relations, there are again three distinct moments: Abstract Right, Morality, the Ethical World. Gentile does not specifically associate himself with this triad but he does defend Hegel against certain misunderstandings, and he is implicitly committed to acceptance of his own interpretation of Hegel's meaning. The State, he explains, is the synthesis, the realization of the moral idea; but this does not mean that the sanctions of positive law are the source of the sense of duty. Morality is an earlier moment of the dialectic: certainly it is abstract and empty, and only receives content in history, i.e. in the ethical world of the State; nevertheless, "Custom is legitimated by morality; not vice versa." [6] The moral law of conscience is the transcendental ground of positive jurisprudence; similarly 'abstract right' is the transcendental original of all concrete civil rights. These transcendental presuppositions are ideal moments of the State: they are not realities. Consequently the genesis of 'morality' from 'abstract right' can only be an ideal one: abstract right is the *outward* fulfillment of liberty while morality is its inward recognition. The former is logically prior because what is moral must be right, while what is abstractly right need not be moral; so that morality involves right but not vice versa. The concepts of crime and punishment form the bridge between them because if the inner right were not violated in the outer world this nonequivalence of the two concepts would not become explicit and we should never progress beyond the first. But at this ideal level punishment is internal to the conscience of the criminal: it is the process through which he comes to recognize the law that he has broken.

At this point the reinterpretation and defense of Hegel has passed over into revision and correction. It can hardly be doubted that the account of 'abstract right' and 'morality' as transcendental presuppositions of political life is a correct explication of what Hegel

---

[5] B.98 in B.618, pp. 146–47.
[6] *Ibid.*, p. 148.

meant.[7] For that matter there is no question that punishment is a transcendental notion also; the reassertion of the law need not, as Hegel himself says, involve any attempt at the restoration of the empirical status quo. But where Spaventa (and Gentile) hold that the *criminal himself* must be brought to recognize that the law is the true substance even of his subjective criminal volition, Hegel seems to have thought that it is enough if this inner significance of punitive justice is appreciated by the judge as a rational observer. We are morally bound, in his view, to treat the criminal as a rational being in any event; if he has so abused his reason as not to appreciate rational treatment so much the worse for him. The difference between this view and the view of Spaventa and Gentile becomes most clearly apparent in the limiting case of the death penalty. Hegel, of course, supported the death penalty, arguing that it was the 'right' of the criminal as a rational being to sacrifice himself in order that the law which constituted his own moral personality might be vindicated. But if, as Gentile puts it in summing up Spaventa's doctrine, "the punishment of the delinquent . . . criticizes the individual subjectivity of his will, *in order to bring him to recognize the right in his own secret heart* [*sua stessa intimità*], and so to attain true liberty," [8] then the death penalty is automatically invalidated because it does not operate *within* consciousness. Spaventa explicitly says that "the death penalty and perpetuity of punishment are in evident contradiction with this conception." [9] Gentile clearly associates himself with Spaventa's view; [10] and his own mature theory of punishment is so closely related to Spaventa's that he ought always to have maintained the same attitude, though in fact he did not do so.[11]

For both of them this 'intimate self-criticism' was the transcendental ground and justification of all the external physical sanctions of the law, the executive and the judiciary. They held that since man is a social animal it is vitally necessary that the subjective inwardness of the moral conscience be objectively deter-

---

[7] Cf. T. M. Knox, *Hegel's Philosophy of Right,* translated with notes, Oxford, Clarendon, 1942, pp. 345–46, 347.

[8] B.98 in B.618, p. 151 (my italics).

[9] B.98, p. 114.

[10] Not merely in his Introduction to the *Principles of Ethics,* but in his biographical study of Spaventa; cf. B.49, pp. cxi–cxii, or B.775, pp. 131–33.

[11] Cf. B.1107 in B.1139, pp. 283–84 (cited and discussed in Chapter 7, pp. 232–33, herein).

mined by the machinery of justice. The sinner cannot be expected to rise above his sin simply by his own efforts. He "has need of the universal spirit," and therefore coercion is an instrument of the first importance in social education.[12] But it can be effective only insofar as he recognizes its rationality. Hence morality and coercion are not diametrically opposed; the former is not purely subjective, nor is the latter purely objective, since only through moral assent can coercion ever be successful.

The same tendency toward a 'subjective' interpretation of Hegel is observable in what Gentile goes on to say about his concept of the State. There is of course a certain ideal subjectivity in Hegel's account: 'the State' is a rational ideal excogitated by the philosophical historian. Any Hegelian would therefore support Gentile's contention that the will of the State must be moral and is not to be confused with any egoistic or arbitrary action.[13] But not all of them would go so far as to assert, in answer to the popular complaint that Hegel reduces the individual to a mere tool of the State, that "'Man' and 'State' are one and the same. Man is the State; and the State is man; and the State is the end of man, because man is his own end, inasmuch as in the State the political nature of man is realized." [14]

In his treatment of the transition from Objective to Absolute Spirit Gentile is again outwardly orthodox. The State, he says, is fully moral because it represents the moral ideal of man. But morality is not properly a characteristic of the Absolute Spirit. Within the world the spirit is necessarily moral, but in its *absolute* realization the qualification would be without meaning: "A single spirit, a solitary God, may create a thing of beauty, but he cannot do a good action." [15] Thus it would seem that in 1904 Gentile accepted

---

[12] B.98 in B.618, p. 155.

[13] Cf. Knox, *op. cit.*, pp. 362–63.

[14] B.98 in B.618, pp. 153–54. After all, Hegel did say "Es ist der Gang Gottes in der Welt dass der Staat ist," and one may well doubt whether he would have accepted the equation 'Gott = Mensch.' But Gentile rejected from the beginning any theological or transcendent interpretation of Hegel. In 1904 he found fault with Baillie for attaching too much importance to the theological element in Hegel's thought (cf. B.105 in B.701, p. 96; 3rd ed., p. 89). This tendency toward a completely *immanent* interpretation of Hegel is the distinguishing mark of the whole Italian school. But this particular example of it—the immanent union of individual and State—is more than an example of the general tendency: it is the germ of actual idealism.

[15] B.98 in B.618, p. 154.

not only the distinction of Subjective, Objective, and Absolute Spirit, but also the distinction of theory and practice.[16]

But, although this was probably the case, he was definitely moving already toward the resolution of both distinctions. For we find him insisting very strongly on the 'immanent' character of the Hegelian superworld of Art, Religion, and Philosophy. The 'eternity' of the three moments of Absolute Spirit he interprets as being simply a very qualified independence of historical conditions. Thus, although a great work of art, the emergence of a religion, or the promulgation of a philosophic truth is an important historical event, it must be conceded that the beauty of art, the God of religion, the truth of philosophy, are not essentially connected with the particular circumstances of their origin, as the events of history are with geographical and temporal conditions and particular agents. In this sense they are 'absolute.' But the superworld is still part of *our* world—the perfect liberation of the spirit takes place within experience. The Absolute is "neither above nor below the world, but within the world, and therefore within history, just as its critics would have it." [17]

The progressive deepening of this conception of the eternal within time eventually led Gentile to develop a philosophy of absolute immanence. But in 1904 he was still a long way from this goal. Everything which seems in Hegel's theory to fall outside of the real world of experience (the realm of Objective Spirit) is reduced in this essay to the status of an ideal moment or aspect of experience. But these ideal moments form an inviolable logical system to which the world of experience must conform. It is necessary that the universal—this a priori system—be immanent in the particular— the world of history; but this necessity itself is something transcendent, tyrannical. This contradiction betrays the weakness, the essentially transitional character of Gentile's thought in this early period.

---

[16] In 1921, when he reprinted this essay in the first volume of his *Critical Essays* (B.618), he added a footnote explaining that he was here concerned only with clarifying the interpretation of Hegel given by Spaventa. He refers the reader to the *Theory of Mind as Pure Act* for his own "more profound" theory. But, as we proceed, we shall see reason to believe that at the time of writing he shared Spaventa's view.

[17] B.98 in B.618, pp. 155–56.

Gentile and Marx

The same tendency toward absolute immanence combined with a belief in an a priori system of universal principles is apparent in Gentile's early writings on the theory of historiography.[18] Already in 1897 he was expressing some doubts about the distinction between the facts (*res gestae*) and the history of the facts (*historia rerum gestarum*) and thus moving toward a more extreme form of immanence than Croce ever held; yet at the same time he was ready to defend the idea of a 'philosophy of history' against Croce's attacks. Although he had qualms about the historian taking the facts as given, he allowed the possibility of the philosopher taking the history as given, and seeking to find an a priori pattern immanent within it.

His acceptance of the a priori method in philosophy led him to disagree with Croce about Marxism. He was never a Marxist; he was not even a pupil of Labriola as Croce was; [19] and he had little sympathy with the Socialist movement. But for all that, it is fair to say that he took Marx more seriously as a philosopher than Croce did.

In the first of his two essays on Marxism [20] he was concerned with its historical rather than with its materialist character. He agreed with Croce that to talk of 'historical *materialism*' was actually misleading since the materialism was only a later development grafted onto an already existing theory of history; but as against Croce he held that this original theory of history was a full-fledged philosophy, and not simply a practical method of inquiring into historical problems.[21] Gentile would never have concerned himself with

---

[18] Cf. B.14 and B.31 in B.615, pp. 137–52 and 1–60.

[19] We should note, however, that the two short monographs which he wrote on Marx before the beginning of his twenty-fifth year were strongly influenced by, and largely based upon, the writings of Labriola.

[20] "A Critique of Historical Materialism," originally published in 1897 (B.11 in B.1157, pp. 149–96; or in *Complete Works*, XXVIII, 11–58).

[21] In his Preface to the first publication of these studies in book form (*La filosofia di Marx*, Pisa, Spoerri, 1899) Gentile remarked that Marx's materialist metaphysics was an artificial construction produced long after the development of his revolutionary doctrine. Ugo Spirito (in *Note sul pensiero di Gentile*, pp. 18–21; cf. *Vita e pensiero*, I, 317) has drawn attention to the contradiction between this conclusion and an important passage in the second study (cf. B.1157, pp. 236–37; or *Complete Works*, XXVIII, 98–99) in which Gentile uses one of Marx's early letters to his father to prove that "the thought of Marx is essentially philosophical." But once we realize that one of the main

Marxism, if it had not seemed to him to be more than a historical method combined with a revolutionary program. He was interested in the theoretical relationship between Marx and Hegel, not in Marxian Communism and the social problems that it claimed to solve.

Hence he draws a careful distinction, at the beginning of this essay, between "existent social conditions," the content with which science begins, and the "formal elaboration of the spirit"—i.e. the discovery of an a priori pattern immanent in these conditions— which constitutes the essence of all truly scientific activity.[22] He considers that the originality of Marx as a philosopher lay in the fact that by applying the Hegelian dialectic he produced a new view of this immanent pattern. Marx boasted that he had put history back on its feet by substituting economic realities in the place of Hegel's Idea.[23] But his theory, like Hegel's, was an attempt to determine the course of human history a priori.

Of course, history is not mechanical but conscious; yet the stages of its development are necessary in the sense that they are immanent in the nature of things and can therefore be foreseen.[24] Marxism is scientific, antiutopian, precisely because it is founded on this a priori logic of reality. Croce protested that the political

ideas of the first study is to maintain, against Croce, that Marx's revolutionary doctrine is a *philosophy of history*, the contradiction vanishes. When Gentile says that Marx proposed "to take up a position in philosophy after conceiving his revolutionary doctrine" he is thinking of the metaphysics of dialectical *materialism*. Hence this contention is quite consistent with the view that the revolutionary doctrine is itself a genuine philosophy of history. In the very sentence to which Spirito refers Gentile expresses his conclusion thus: "the philosophy of history [*la filosofia storica*] did not develop out of the philosophy [*la filosofia*], but the latter was arbitrarily dragged out of the former" (B.1157, p. 144; *Complete Works*, XXVIII, 6).

[22] B.11 in B.1157, p. 152 (or *Complete Works*, XXVIII, 14).

[23] B.11 in B.1157, pp. 166, 174 (*Complete Works*, XXVIII, 28, 36). Gentile points out that Marx's naturalism was very different from evolutionary positivism because of its Hegelian roots. A theory of *socialism* cannot be founded on the biological struggle to survive since natural selection operates on a world of discrete individuals, whereas society and conscious social cooperation are a necessary presupposition of the class struggle. For Marx, as for Hegel, human existence is essentially ethical (B.11 in B.1157, pp. 166–69; or *Complete Works*, XXVIII, 28–31).

[24] Gentile insists that, since what the philosopher observes are the essential or universal qualities immanent in the *present*, no prevision is really involved in the philosophical analysis of history (B.11 in B.1157, p. 180n; *Complete Works*, XXVIII, 42n). This is just the sort of argument he later used to prove the essentially 'past' character of nature; so that from his mature point of view the philosophy of history, which he is here defending, stands condemned because it treats the spirit as if it were a natural phenomenon.

activity of Marx and Engels was eloquent testimony to their belief in the ability of the individual to reshape reality according to an ideal. Gentile replied that Marx and Engels would have argued that their moral fervor in the cause of Socialism was a direct result of the operation of this immanent law; it followed naturally from their understanding of the economic realities. A rational necessity becomes a moral imperative for those who understand it.[25]

In short, Marx did not make any formal innovation in the fundamental Hegelian conception of a dialectical philosophy of history; he simply substituted one content for another. And Gentile concluded that even this substitution was really only an apparent change, since the 'Hegel' and the 'Idea' which the Marxists rejected had never in fact existed anywhere outside of their own heads. The progress of Hegel's Idea is really identical with what Labriola called the "self-critical life of things" (*autocritica che è nelle cose stesse*).[26] But this self-criticism of *things* is only a metaphor, since all criticism has to take place in the consciousness of mankind. Thus the Matter of Marx is included in the Hegelian Idea, and if the meaning of his theory were adequately expressed the two conceptions would be seen to coincide.[27]

This conclusion demonstrates the strictly theoretical nature of Gentile's interest in Marx, for of course he did not mean that the theory of the class struggle was identical with Hegel's theory of history, but only that both were attempts to formulate the dialectic of the Idea immanent in history, so that Marxism did not involve a new metaphysical principle. He was at one with Marx in refusing to accept any theological interpretation of the Absolute, and he agreed that the task of reason was fundamentally practical, that "our business is not to understand the world but to change it." But his loyalty to the humanist tradition in education made it impossible for him to grant that Art, Religion, and Philosophy were

---

[25] B.11 in B.1157, pp. 187–90 (*Complete Works*, XXVIII, 49–52). This point is further elaborated in Gentile's second study (B.30 in B.1157, pp. 253–56; *Complete Works*, XXVIII, 115–18).

[26] B.11 in B.1157, pp. 175–76. Gentile rightly dismisses the interpretation of Hegel's theory of consciousness advanced by Engels in *Utopian and Scientific Socialism*—"instead of considering his own ideas as intellectual reflections of the objects and movements of the real world, he obstinately refused to consider the objects of the real world and the changes that they undergo, except as so many reflections of his own ideas"—as simply childish (B.11 in B.1157, pp. 176–77, or *Complete Works*, XXVIII, 38–39; cf. B.30 in B.1157, pp. 265–66 and n, or *Complete Works*, XXVIII, 127–28 and n).

[27] B.11 in B.1157, p. 193 (*Complete Works*, XXVIII, 55).

merely epiphenomenal. In his view, the claim that Hegel merely substituted a new philosophical heaven for the old one of the theologians only showed that Marx was blind to the highest values of human life, that he did not understand the absolute, as opposed to the relative, aspect of the Idea. A sort of uneasy consciousness that Marx, as a political revolutionary, represented a threat to the cultural tradition that enshrined his own deepest values probably accounts for the contrast between the general tone of Gentile's discussion and the violence of his closing verdict that Marxism is "one of the most calamitous deviations of Hegelian thought." [28]

In his second study [29] Gentile considered the metaphysical foundations of Marx's materialism,[30] and strove to exhibit the truth of his claim that the dialectical conception of matter coincides with the Hegelian Idea. In place of the dead object (*Gegenstand*) of earlier materialists, Marx substituted human sensitive activity (*sinnliche Thätigkeit*); and in so doing, according to Gentile, he returned from Feuerbach to Hegel, by positing a self-critical activity in things. It is true that for Hegel this activity was rational, whereas in Marx it becomes merely sensitive; but this is a comparatively unimportant if not completely illusory distinction. For once we admit that Marx's 'sensitive activity' is self-critical it becomes the root of everything that Hegel meant by 'thought.' [31] 'Sense' and 'reason' are simply opposite faces of the same coin; the identity between them is expressed in the principle that man can only understand a world that he has first created for himself; and this principle is the foundation stone not of materialism but of all immanent idealism.[32]

---

[28] B.11 in B.1157, p. 196 (*Complete Works*, XXVIII, 58).

[29] "The Philosophy of Praxis" (B.30, 1899), in B.1157, pp. 197–303 (or in *Complete Works*, XXVIII, 59–165).

[30] He had first to reconstruct this materialism for himself on the basis of the eleven theses of Marx against Feuerbach which Engels had published in his own book on Feuerbach (cf. "La filosofia della prassi," Chapter 2, *op. cit.*, pp. 206–9; *Complete Works*, XXVIII, 68–71). Spirito remarks that his reconstruction proved to be essentially accurate when Marx's original manuscript was published (*Vita e pensiero*, I, 321, or *Note sul pensiero di Gentile*, p. 27).

[31] We have seen already how in his mature thought Gentile strove to validate this claim by developing the experience of actual sensation into the fullness of rational will (Chapter 2, pp. 28–38, herein). He was bound to agree with Marx's implicit criticism of any abstract intellectualism: not for him the Olympian disinterestedness of Croce. The philosopher, if he takes his task seriously, cannot remain indifferent to practical programs, for his thought is a practical program—it is the practical self-criticism of the real world.

[32] Gentile finds examples of this same tendency toward concreteness in such various thinkers as Socrates, Vico, Fichte, and Froebel. It would be a mistake,

By substituting activity for passivity Marx freed humanity from the chains of mechanism. Man is not the product but the producer of his environment, and his world is an unending cycle of educational activity. "There is the society that educates, and the society that is educated: the same society when educated returns again to educating." [33] This perpetual interaction of subject and object is in itself a revolutionary social process (*umwälzende Praxis*) from which no one can escape—the individual and his environment are not entities having merely external relations, but terms of an a priori dialectic.

Viewed in this way Marxism is the absolute antithesis of traditional atomic materialism. The Marxian atom is determined by its relations to the whole, so that society is a fundamental necessity, not an accidental imposition as it was for previous materialists such as Epicurus or Hobbes. 'Man' can only mean 'man-in-society'; and being-in-society involves action and reaction, historical development. Society educates the individual and vice versa. On the one side, then, we have the *laudatores temporis acti,* on the other, the revolutionaries. In general, individuals play both parts: the revolutionaries get their way, only to find themselves defending their revolution against a new one. In striving to understand history, therefore, we must seize on the *essential* qualities of a situation and not be misled by survivals or aberrations, utopias or pockets of reaction. This was precisely what Hegel tried to do in his theory of the *Weltgeist*—"now an object of satire, but only for those who do not understand it." [34]

Certainly Gentile's initial attitude to Marx was unfriendly; but in the end he found himself defending the thesis that Marx was a philosopher before he was a revolutionary, and that his philosophy was basically sound. His original aim was undoubtedly to justify Hegel against the Marxists, but he fulfilled this intention by exhibiting Marx as a thorough Hegelian and a true pupil of the whole tradition of German idealism. This makes his uncompromising condemnation of Marxism in the first study look somewhat odd, for it is quite out of harmony with the sympathetic criticism of the second

---

therefore, to think that he is merely concerned with justifying Hegel against Marx, or idealism against materialism (B.30 in B.1157, pp. 210–19; or in *Complete Works,* XXVIII, 72–81).

[33] B.30 in B.1157, p. 222 (*Complete Works,* XXVIII, 84).

[34] B.30 in B.1157, p. 253 (or *Complete Works,* XXVIII, 115).

study. Here Gentile concludes more reasonably by insisting that Marx's metaphysical materialism was never properly absorbed into the dialectic of his philosophy of history, which was concerned entirely with living activity—"The whole history of previous philosophy should have warned him that his two principles—form (= praxis) and content (= matter)—were irreconcilable." [35]

It is not germane to our purpose, and indeed it scarcely lies within the competence of the present writer, to decide whether this completely Hegelian interpretation of Marx does justice to the great socialist or not.[36] For us the interest of the work lies rather in the extent to which Gentile agrees with the Marx he has pictured. He makes a strict distinction himself between form and content, the 'elaboration of concepts' and the 'actual conditions of society'; but he is at pains to make clear that the a priori method does not involve any attempt to dispense with experience,[37] and the ultimate outcome of his labors is almost a denial of the duality of theory and practice from which he begins.[38] For obviously the 'elaboration of concepts' is the explicit realization of that immanent self-criticism of things which constitutes the revolutionary activity. The owl of Minerva flies forth only at dusk—but the death of the old

---

[35] B.30 in B.1157, p. 301 (or *Complete Works*, XXVIII, 163). Even in the second essay, however, he ends on a polemical note by claiming that Marxism is only an eclectic mixture of contradictory elements, valuable only as a means of spreading Hegelian ideas (B.30 in B.1157, p. 303; *Complete Works*, XXVIII, 165).

[36] It should be mentioned, however, that Lenin himself declared Gentile's studies to be among the most noteworthy of those produced by non-Marxists: "The book of an Hegelian idealist, Giovanni Gentile, *La filosofia di Marx*, Pisa, 1899, deserves attention. The author points out some important aspects of Marx's materialistic dialectics which ordinarily escape the attention of the Kantians, positivists, etc." (V. I. Lenin, *The Teachings of Karl Marx*, New York, International Publishers, 1930, p. 45).

[37] Cf. B.30 in B.1157, pp. 281–86 (or *Complete Works*, XXVIII, 143–48), especially the quotation from Schelling.

[38] In his continual criticisms of the Crocean distinction between theory and practice—which can be found throughout both studies—it is apparent that he has already gone *beyond* the view of Kant and Fichte that the practical moment is somehow more fundamental than the theoretical toward the position that the theoretical moment is itself essentially practical. "Morality is a presupposition and not a product of a historical theory," and therefore Croce's complaint that historical materialism does not in itself provide a sufficient basis for socialism "presupposes a false point of departure and a false point of arrival (in other words a road that does not exist)" (B.11 in B.1157, p. 190 and n; or in *Complete Works*, XXVIII, 52 and n). This denial of the Crocean problem of how to pass from theory to practice is one of the most important seeds of Gentile's fully developed view.

day is also the birth of the new, and it is well to remember that the evening and the morning star are not two but one. So that eventually Gentile was logically bound to leave the study in which, at the beginning of these essays, he shuts himself away from the proletarian mob, and go down to struggle with them in the piazza. His *Studies in the Philosophy of Marx* seem to foreshadow the conception of a 'humanism of labor' which he set up against the Renaissance 'humanism of culture' in his last work. But we do not need to look so far ahead as that, for the echo of these studies in the view of life as a "continual revolution," which became one of the key ideas of his Fascism, is even more obvious.[39] And finally, although it would probably be a mistake to see in Marx the source of his conception of the universe as a great schoolroom, we must bear in mind that this fundamental motif of his mature philosophy was first expounded at length as part of his attempts to interpret Marx.[40]

Education and Culture

The fact that Gentile's vision of social history as a sort of cosmic educational process had no discernible effect on his attitudes toward educational problems in the strict or technical sense makes it plausible to suppose that in the first instance it was his educational preoccupations which molded his interpretation of Marx, and not vice versa. This would explain why the seeds of his later 'humanism of labor' present in the *Studies in the Philosophy of Marx* took so long to germinate. There is no sign in his essay of 1900 on "The Scientific Concept of Pedagogy," [41] for instance, that the broader conception of society as an educational dialectic influenced Gentile's pedagogical theory. The traditional 'humanism of culture' remains the dominant ideal of his early writings—as it does, indeed, even in his mature philosophy of education.

As early as 1900 he was already moving toward the identification

---

[39] Cf. Spirito, *Note sul pensiero di Gentile*, pp. 46–50 (or in *Vita e pensiero*, I, 332–33). See also Chapter 6, pp. 170–74, 179–82, 190–92, 201–4, and Chapter 8, pp. 273–78, herein.

[40] If it seems necessary to seek an external source for this idea, which is the very heart of his personal vision of the world, it would be best to connect it with the tradition of the Risorgimento and particularly with Mazzini's conception of humanity as "the man that is always learning" (*Duties of Man*, etc., Everyman, p. 37; cf. n76 in Chapter 4 herein).

[41] B.59 in B.1056, pp. 1–47.

of pedagogy with philosophy.[42] He insisted that the concept of pedagogy was an autonomous one, and could not be made dependent on ethics or any other science, as Herbart thought. But the autonomy that he accords to it is theoretical. He makes the same distinction between form and content, theory and practice, as in his social theory and philosophy of history, taking the empirical practice of education as the object of an a priori normative science of pedagogy. The theorems of this science provide imperatives for the guidance of educational practice, just as on this view the laws of the physical scientist have to be thought of as imperatives immanent in the material world, and would not be 'laws' if they did not express the inner, autonomous nature of that world.[43]

Gentile takes it that everyone would agree that the purpose of education is the *formation of man*.[44] It follows that the concept of Man—or more precisely, of the essentially human, autonomous element in man—is the fundamental concern of the autonomous science of pedagogy. Thus the idea of physical education is an error and a contradiction in terms: for although in common-sense terms a man is both soul and body, it is the soul that makes the body human. Nature is only a stage on the road to spirit, in which it finds its truth—so that in the final analysis "Man is not soul and body; but since he is soul, he is soul alone." [45]

The spirit (i.e. the autonomous element in Man) cannot be formed from without: it forms itself. Master and pupil must therefore be at one. Indeed, the empirical duality is quite accidental to the essential nature of education. It is spiritual unity that matters—for all attempts to teach would fail in the face of a pupil who lacked either the will or the ability to interpret the sounds and signs presented to him.[46] The abstract possibility of spiritual unity is furnished by the language system; and this accounts for the vital

---

[42] This identification is indeed specifically asserted (*ibid.*, p. 34); but the assertion does not here have the significance that it later acquired.

[43] *Ibid.*, pp. 15–17. Here more than anywhere else the Aristotelian notion of individuality, which Gentile later regarded as a prime error of his early speculation (cf. B.296 in B.898, p. 25), is apparent.

[44] B.59 in B.1056, p. 23.

[45] *Ibid.*, p. 30. What is called *physical* education is really part of the science of medicine (B.74). This conclusion is completely overturned in the *Summary of Educational Theory;* and the arguments provide as fair an example as could be desired of the practical difference between an idealism that presupposes nature and one that does not. In the later work the conclusion that man is "soul alone" remains, but the interpretation given to it is quite different.

[46] B.158 (1907) in B.1056, pp. 53–54.

importance of elementary literacy. A man who cannot read and
write is not more than half human. In virtue of his power of speech
he is a member of society, but his society is particular, and empirical,
because limited to the here and now. Thus the alphabet, as the key
to the universal society of humanity and historical civilization, assumes for Gentile a sort of sacramental significance: it is a second
baptism, the "baptism of reason," fulfilling the promise of the earlier
baptism of faith. Only through it does humanity enter into its own
past and thus come to understand its present: "Nothing in our environment is intelligible, and that means that nothing is truly seen
by us, apart from the knowledge of what has preceded it or what
corresponds to it elsewhere, apart from that knowledge which can
only be gained from books, which enables us to talk with men
long dead or living far away from us." [47]

With the acquiring of the basic skills of reading and writing the
development of the implicit nature of the spirit can begin. In an
essay of 1902 on "The Unity of the Secondary School," [48] Gentile
offered the following diagrammatic analysis of what is here involved:

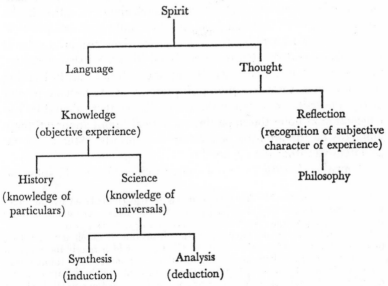

---

[47] B.154 (1907) in B.1056, p. 189. Cf. the whole passage, pp. 185–93; also
B.570 (1920).
[48] B.70 in B.813, pp. 9–51.

The detailed argument behind this schema is unimportant since with the full development of his idealism it was completely abandoned.[49] We must note, however, that Gentile already regarded the distinction of language and thought as purely ideal: language is the concrete form and thought the abstract content.[50] Hence it is language that must form the foundation of schoolroom education. Gentile proposed Italian, Latin (for the understanding of the Italian tradition), and (as a necessary complement to Latin) Greek. Turning then to the organization of objective experience he suggested history and geography (particular knowledge); mathematics and natural science (analysis and synthesis of universal concepts). Finally as the crown of secondary education there is philosophy.

Regarded as a theorem of his normative science the analysis of the implicit nature or logic of the spirit provided not only a guide for the construction of the curriculum, but a ground for the compulsory implementation of this unitary curriculum in the classical *liceo*. Gentile admitted that the *liceo* curriculum was overloaded, and at the same time that there was a case for further additions (especially modern languages). But he held that the main difficulties were not in the content of the curriculum but rather in the attitude toward it. Too many pupils whose only idea was practical profit were passing through the *liceo*. For them technical schools should be provided.[51] On the other hand the school should not try to do the work of a university. It was not its task to instill learning but to produce the *uomo puro e disposto*, ready to become scholar at the university or citizen in the world. Hence there should be less concentration upon the imparting of factual information and more emphasis on the arousing of interest and curiosity. Studies should be intensive rather than general.

About the *classical* nature of the curriculum he would suffer no

---

[49] See *ibid.*, pp. 28–34. The argument has here been replaced by the notes in parentheses on the diagram which were added by the present writer in order to indicate the principles upon which Gentile's analysis was based.

[50] We have here an anticipation of the distinction between *act* and *fact*, *pensiero pensante* and *pensiero pensato*. Cf. B.192, which rejects the proposal that the teacher of Italian should help in the correction of essays submitted in other disciplines. Even correct grammatical form is ultimately a matter of that discipline of thought of which the teacher competent in the special discipline must be the judge. Mastery of one's own language must be learned through the study of great literature. Ideally the teacher of Italian should be the classics master.

[51] B.143 (1906) in B.813, pp. 103–7.

compromise. Indeed, even if, as the present writer does, one agrees with Gentile about the vital importance of the classical tradition in European civilization, one cannot help feeling that he was unduly dogmatic about it. We must surely beware of using a priori arguments to justify the maintenance of the status quo, if *development* is the most fundamental a priori characteristic of reality. To deny all possibility of a 'modern classicism,' as Gentile did,[52] on the grounds that the roots of the Italian tradition were in Greece and Rome, is to betray this fundamental principle. For, after all, the roots of a tree spread more widely as it grows. Furthermore, some of his arguments were decidedly weak even from his own strictly theoretical point of view. It is true, for instance, that a knowledge of Greek literature is essential for a full appreciation of Latin literature, but it is not essential (as Latin literature is) for the sympathetic comprehension of the Renaissance or of Dante. Hence when Gentile claimed that those who are willing to sacrifice Greek were trying to compromise between two irreconcilable principles, and could find no theoretical justification for their position,[53] he was merely exhibiting cultural bigotry.

Some critics argued that the school should be a preparation for life, and that Gentile's program did not make sufficient allowance for the practical and moral aspects of education. He retorted that the *uomo puro e disposto* of his ideal—the man who is aware of his capacities and of the nature of the problems on which these capacities can be exercised—is prepared for life in the only way possible. The one alternative would be to try to include in the school curriculum everything that a good citizen should know. But any such "little encyclopedia" program is impossible because we cannot exactly define "the culture that is characteristic of the best citizens."[54]

The universal human spirit, on the other hand, *can* be defined, as we have already seen. For although men are irreducibly individual "it is undeniable that there is a *human nature,* that is, to be precise, a determinate organic system of spiritual attributes or activities."[55] But the definition can only be a theoretical one, since

---

[52] B.217 (1909) in B.813, pp. 139–40.

[53] *Ibid.,* p. 137.

[54] B.143 (1906) in B.813, p. 80.

[55] *Ibid.,* p. 83 (my italics). Here again the Aristotelian theory of the individual is very much in evidence.

the practical reality, with which we have to deal in moral education, is just blind impulse—the nature that is the presupposition of
the spirit.[56] Moral discipline must be achieved indirectly by developing the spiritual capacity of intelligence. The rational will is
simply a facet of the intellect.

This necessity for an indirect approach to the problem of building
character meant that moral education could not consist in the in-
culcation of precepts. Carrying the war into the enemy's camp,
Gentile argued that education by precept would indeed be too
theoretical—for "our actions follow from what we *are*, not from
what we *think*." [57] We must seek rather to arouse interest and to
guide it by setting an example. The most that we can do is to
point to the things that are of value; but this is still an important
office, for one cannot desire what he does not know. The pursuit
of truth is thus itself a moral discipline, for it produces intellectual
clarity which is the spiritual aspect of what we call strength of
character. If it is true in one sense that 'instruction' is only part of
'education,' it is equally true in another that 'education' (i.e. moral
education) is only part of 'instruction.' [58]

This doctrine is a long way removed from the view advanced in
the *Philosophy of Marx* that all theories rest on a practical moral
attitude; but at least in theory a reconciliation between them is
possible. For in both cases Gentile's fundamental thesis is that all
spiritual activity is essentially moral; and his emphasis here on the
morality immanent in pure thought considered as the search for
truth is as vital to his fully developed theory as his emphasis on the
practical genesis of thought in his study of Marxism. For it is this
emphasis that distinguishes his theory from the social pragmatism
or sheer historical relativism into which it might otherwise have
degenerated. At the same time, we are bound to recognize that the
detailed program for formal education contained in Gentile's earliest
writings reflects an extremely conservative intellectualism, which is
scarcely in harmony with the view that the whole world process is

---

[56] B.70 in B.813, pp. 30–32.

[57] B.121 (1905) in B.1056, p. 231 (Gentile's italics).

[58] B.70 in B.813, pp. 30–32. The opposition of 'education' and 'instruction'
comes from Mazzini (cf. *Duties of Man,* p. 84). It should not be forgotten that
Gentile advocated the teaching of dogmatic religion in the elementary school,
and insisted further that the secondary school should be inspired by a definite
philosophy (see pp. 66–76, herein).

an educational dialectic. These two almost opposite applications of a single principle provide an example of the conflicts that must be resolved if the 'immanent unity' of theory and practice is to be more than a collection of verbal ambiguities.

Liberty and Authority in School and State

From the fundamental principle that the curriculum of the secondary schools should be determined in accordance with the a priori logic of human nature, it follows that a single curriculum with very little variation or freedom of choice must be compulsory for all pupils. But at the same time Gentile held that the most essential character of the spirit was freedom, and from this fundamental principle it followed that the spontaneity of true spiritual life should be reflected in the schoolroom. This conflict of principles put him in somewhat of a quandary when he had to deal with the advocates of 'freedom in the school.' He admitted without hesitation that where the choice between uniformity and liberty is really forced on us, we must choose liberty.[59] But he felt that, in general, the option is a false one. We cannot mean by 'liberty' the arbitrary will of the individual; for, logically speaking, the individual qua individual is incapable of liberty—nature as 'given' has no liberty.[60] In order to educate at all we are bound to infringe upon the so-called 'liberty of the individual.' [61]

It is the spiritual liberty which the pupil *ought* to have that is the object of education. A naturally given tendency or capacity must be judged worthy of this ideal before it can be allowed. Certainly the vocation to thieving, for example, is not sacred. Furthermore, we cannot be content with simply disciplining the tendencies that naturally exist. We must also create those that should be

---

[59] B.70 in B.813, p. 25.

[60] B.115 (1904) in B.813, p. 59.

[61] B.216 (1909) in B.1056, p. 346: "Tom exists. But what does it mean to say that 'Tom exists'? What is 'Tom'? You may go to infinite pains to guarantee the sacrosanct individuality of this 'Tom' of yours; but yet Tom must *be something* even for you. If he were the 'shadow of a dream,' the problem of his education would never arise. He has to be something real, and, what is more, spiritually real. And this, whatever you may say, is the presupposition of your solicitude and concern for his ineffable individuality."

there.[62] Hence the liberty of the pupil effectively belongs to the teacher, who stands for knowledge against error (which cannot of itself recognize itself); and the teacher must not shirk his responsibility.

This granting of absolute moral authority to the teacher raises a fundamental problem. For how can such a grant be reconciled with the cardinal principle of post-Kantian idealism—the autonomy of the moral reason? Gentile argues that the freedom of the pupil should be thought of as preserved rather than canceled, since he can only come to understand his own moral nature through the subjection of his will to the law. But this paradox would seem to lead to some rather alarming conclusions. For if, wherever the spirit is present, liberty and autonomy cannot be absent, it would seem that we need never trouble ourselves about them. The fact that whatever the pupil learns, he will *ipso facto* learn voluntarily, is a sufficient guarantee of his freedom. As an individual he has no rights —all rights belong to the truth—which is personified by the teacher.

This is far from being what most of us normally mean when we speak of 'freedom'; all the same, it deserves to be considered carefully and not simply rejected out of hand. For Gentile is offering a solution to a problem which is all too often ignored. No one would hold that the schoolboy has a right to do what he likes, or that the thief has a right to steal. Somehow liberty must exist within the law. Hence arises the problem of the relation of liberty to the law. How is this limiting force to be determined? It is easy to answer, as skeptical utilitarians do, that everyone has a right to do whatever does not interfere with the equal right of everyone else to do likewise. But it is hard to see how this formal ideal can be given concrete application in any particular situation; it is even doubtful whether, by this criterion, anyone has a right to do anything— except perhaps breathe and think.

Moreover, even if this negative freedom could be determined, it would be a very poor sort of thing. To be absolute tyrant of a little world cut off and isolated is no fate for an essentially social being who is capable of a moral existence. Under such circumstances the real life of the individual, the one that matters not merely to others but to himself, would not be the private life that he enjoys in his subjective kingdom, but rather the life of sacrifice and suffering

---

[62] B.115 in B.813, pp. 59–60; cf. B.163 in B.1056, pp. 126–27.

beyond the limit, in the greater realm where absolute rights give way to responsibility and respect for law. He would be impelled voluntarily to surrender his private freedom, in order to devote himself to some cause which involves cooperation with others.

In point of fact, when we talk of 'freedom' we really mean the right to live according to our own conscience, and to make that conscience count for something in the world; and everyone will agree that a conscience which is to count for something in the world cannot be completely unrelated to the historical situation that actually exists there—people who have such 'irrelevant' consciences are regarded as mentally ill. In the normal course of events the conscience of the human individual acquires historical relevance to the world because it is formed in it. Surely, therefore, we cannot deny that the community has the right—and even the duty— to present itself to the conscience that is in process of formation, in whatever way seems to it to be best. This is the real significance of Gentile's insistence that in the relation of teacher and pupil the teacher must have ultimate moral authority. Even if we admit that the community might so abuse this right as to produce a situation of rigid social conformity approximating the state of things envisaged in George Orwell's *Nineteen Eighty-four,* we cannot deny its existence without abandoning education and communal existence altogether. As members of the community that authorizes the teacher, we must all admit, therefore, that the autonomy of the pupil is not *necessarily* inconsistent with the teacher's claim to exercise his freedom for him. The danger is that it *may* be; and the moral problem of education is to prevent this.

The solution of this problem clearly requires that there should be some sort of practical *conciliation* between the pupil's liberty and the teacher's authority; for when the pupil *feels* that his 'rights' are being absolutely ignored the educational process breaks down, and he simply educates himself in absolute opposition to the moral law in virtue of which the teacher claims to exercise his freedom for him. Hence it is vitally necessary, both from a theoretical and from a practical point of view, to consider *within what limits* and *by what methods* the teacher may *legitimately* exercise the pupil's freedom—*for he always needs the assent of the pupil.*

In his *theory* at least, Gentile never forgot this; that is why we can fairly claim that his is a philosophy of freedom. He often emphasized that the business of the school was to produce consciences which were alive and critical. Pupils—and indeed their parents also—should be aroused out of a state of social somnambulism, and brought to recognize their responsibilities as *makers*, not simply products, of society.[63] This was especially true, he felt, in the case of those who were being educated to join the ranks of the professions, for they would eventually provide the leadership and government of the country.

But in practice the truth as he saw it imposed itself on his will so completely that he was not unwilling to keep everyone else in leading strings until they could see it too.[64] This 'schoolroom fallacy' led him later to defend some very illiberal positions in his political polemics, and brought him at last to his death at the hands of an assassin.

In the early period that we are now considering the tendency even had a certain theoretical basis; for if human nature is bound to exhibit in history a certain definite form, then the ultimate authority on all questions is the philosopher who understands the a priori logic of the spirit. Hence the desires of the parents deserved no more

---

[63] Cf. B.143 (1906) in B.813, pp. 91–94. In the wider society beyond the schoolroom, the State and the government take the place of truth and the teacher. Hence the problem of pupil-teacher relations has important political repercussions. In his lecture "For the State Elementary School" (1907) Gentile made clear that the ethical character of the State does *not* set it above the criticism of individuals. But it is above mere grousing; criticism of the government must be constructive; then, as the political activity of responsible citizens, it coincides with the living process of the State: "Certainly, to be dissatisfied with the Government is right and good: it is a sign that we desire a better Government, more just, more intelligent, more active; in other words, that *we* aspire to greater justice and more intelligence. But a free people feels this aspiration not as a need that can only be satisfied by others when it may chance to please them; but rather as a duty that they, the people, have to fulfill. Do we desire greater honesty and justice? Well then let us form an alliance with the honest, let us gather round the banner of justice, let *us* do *our* duty in our role as citizens" (B.154 in B.1056, pp. 195–96).

[64] Gentile had, indeed, such a horror of anything resembling skepticism that even the self-doubt of people whom he believed to be mistaken about matters of practical policy filled him with disgust. To him the 'modesty' of one supporter of individual freedom in the school, who put forward his own proposals as mere suggestions, appeared to be either skepticism or hypocrisy. "For my part," he wrote, "I confess that I am convinced of just one thing: and that is that, though perhaps modesty is a great virtue of the character, it is by no means a great virtue of the intellect" (B.115 in B.813, p. 58). But a man who is not 'modest' in this sense will inevitably find it hard to accept anything less than absolute authority. Small wonder then that Gentile was tempted to assume the role of a philosopher-king—the schoolmaster of a whole society and guardian of its 'true' freedom.

attention, so far as Gentile was concerned, than those of their children. The State—the ideal State, Reason—must decide what is to be taught, not any individual interest.[65]

The same basic conflict between the 'freedom' and the 'logic' of the spirit is the key to his extremely ambivalent attitude toward the whole theory of democratic government.[66] Of course, his attitude was largely conditioned by his background. The cautious bourgeois intellectuals who made the Risorgimento after 1848 had little sympathy with those who interpreted the principle of popular sovereignty to mean popular democracy with universal suffrage. Even Mazzini felt that the people were too easily swayed to be trusted very far alone, and envisaged the gradual extension of democratic practice within the limits of a National Contract "made with the unanimous and free consent of *our greatest in wisdom and virtue*." [67] Gentile thought and wrote in this tradition. Thus he says in one place: "it is obvious that a free State in the modern age cannot but be a State governed by representatives of the people; and that these representatives can be representatives only if they are worthy of the people and the people of them. They are in truth the most genuine and authentic instruments of the political will of the people: we may even say that they *are* the people, organized politically and possessed of whatever value it has been able to attain." [68] But this affirmation does not make him a supporter of universal suffrage:

The demagogue who harangues a mob may exalt universal suffrage in the name of liberty. Yet the philosopher may fairly suspect that it is the negation of liberty, a failure to understand the dignity of the spirit and its pre-eminence over nature.

> . . . *Vogliam che ogni figlio d'Adamo*
> *Conti per uomo.*
> [". . . We mean that every son of Adam
> Shall count as a man."]

Well and good; but every son of Adam must count as a man, if he is a *man*: for many of Adam's sons are not *true men*, since they show no sign

---

[65] B.70 in B.813, pp. 27–28, 44.

[66] When a would-be reformer of the secondary school proposed that *different* curricula should be compulsory according to the career which the pupil desired to enter, and that the content of the various curricula should be settled by the professional bodies most nearly concerned, Gentile expressed scornful surprise that a philosopher should suggest the solution of a rational problem by majority vote (B.161 in B.813, p. 124).

[67] "To the Italians," in *Duties of Man*, p. 235 (my italics).

[68] B.154 in B.1056, p. 195.

of the breath of God, and have not attained to the actual exercise of that "reason" (concrete, historical reason) that is recognized as the specific difference of humanity. They have the appearance of men, but not the substance, the spirit, the true humanity; and hence they cannot count as men. And they cannot, for example, make laws; for the laws are a product of the human spirit.[69]

To exercise "concrete, historical reason" apparently means to have a social conscience and to be able to consider the interests of society as a whole. Thus it is identical in Gentile's usage with 'the State.' The doctrine that the State is immanent in the consciousness of the individual citizen can be found in his earliest writings, and is the foundation stone of his whole social theory. It is therefore of utmost importance to understand it aright. The most explicit comment on the relation between this philosophical concept of the State and the State as an empirical fact that I have found in any of Gentile's works occurs in the dedicatory letter to the volume *School and Philosophy* (1908).[70] Writing there to his friend Lombardo-Radice he remarks:

We want liberty—of this we have given proof in our writings, proof that even seems excessive at times—but liberty that raises itself to the State, and is not simply our own individual liberty, but the liberty of the law, that is in and for all men. Certainly the State is not quite what philosophy would like it to be, and we are always proclaiming the fact in no uncertain voice; but we remember the teaching of Kant, that the true politics is not that which looks only at the State as it is, but also at the State as it ought to be; and, to the best of our ability, we fight for this ideal State that is our heart's desire, the Lawgiver for all the practical activity in which the ideals of human culture are poured forth under the watchful eye of philosophy.

We have seen already that in Gentile's interpretation the Hegelian State is not alien to but rather immanent in the will of the individual. Since this immanent State is clearly identified above with the Kantian moral will, it is fair to say that when he talks about 'the State' Gentile usually means, or ought to mean, what we call 'conscience.'[71] As soon as this point is grasped many of the popular

[69] B.70 in B.813, pp. 25–26 (Gentile's italics).

[70] B.183; the letter is reprinted in B.813 (1925), pp. 5–8.

[71] "*We* are the State, all of us who feel ourselves organized and unified by a fundamental law, as a people possessed of independence; and all the defects of the State cannot but be our own defects. The individual who feels that this social organization is alien to him, and looks on all evil as alien likewise, and all good as accumulated in his own person, one who rebels against the State, is plainly an egoist who does not recognize that *the* good is the good of all men. . . . The State has a *raison d'être* insofar as there is something to be

accusations against his political theory can be recognized as mis-understandings; [72] and his indignant denial of the charge of 'Statol-atry' becomes intelligible.

The identification of State and conscience implies, of course, a completely social and historical view of morality. It is a denial of abstract rationalism in ethics. In Gentile's view, the ethical theory of Kant, in which the universal, rational nature of the moral consciousness was for the first time revealed, provided a final and perfect proof that it is impossible to give to this consciousness any determinate form by abstractly rational methods. Determination, i.e. concrete content, it receives only in experience.[73] There is no absolutely right and final code of morals; strictly speaking, in Gentile's terms, morality is not to be found in a code at all. The moral act is always unique; it springs out of a completely determinate historical situation that cannot recur. Hence there is very little that can be said about it in the abstract, and it should surprise no one to hear that the "Ethics" which Gentile promised the world in 1913 never materialized.[74] On the other hand, his whole view of life is ethical; there is for him no activity that does not possess moral significance. No one can hope to understand his work who does not appreciate the essentially ethical character not merely of his political and educational writings but even of more theoretical treatises such as the *Logic* [75] or the *Theory of Mind as Pure Act*. All his life he fought against the general tendency to abstract moral ideals from the actual situations of life, and to speak of 'what is' and 'what ought to be' as quite separate and distinct. He regarded the 'is' and the 'ought' as merely two aspects of a single dialectical

---

guaranteed; and in reality it guarantees all the economic activities of a people, by law against the enemies within, and by defense against enemies abroad; and thus it guarantees also all the moral personalities (chief among them, the family) to which human economic activity gives rise . . ." (B.154 in B.1056, pp. 196, 198).

[72] The empirical meaning of the word 'State' betrays him into dangerous ambiguities, however, about which even a careful and sympathetic reader cannot hope to become completely clear, since all too often the apparent cogency of the argument rests on the ambiguity of the term.

[73] Cf., for instance, his interesting remarks concerning Kantian ethics in his short review of Josiah Royce's *Philosophy of Loyalty* (B.270), which he rather unjustly regarded as no more than a restatement of Kant in a new vocabulary.

[74] B.296 in B.898, p. 32.

[75] Commenting on the promise of 1913 in his footnote to B.898, p. 32 (published in 1927), Gentile refers the reader to his *Logic* as the nearest approach to a fulfillment of it. But the *Philosophy of Law* should also be remembered (cf. n58 in Chapter 4 herein).

process—the self-criticism of reality, as Labriola and the Marxists called it. The separation of the real from the ideal was a 'sophism' and the cynics who boast of their 'realism' were merely confusing the issue.[76] Certainly action, if it is to be successful, must be realistic —but the real to which attention must be directed is the dialectic process as a whole. The 'facts' to which sophistic realism appeals are only facts within the framework of a theory.

The identification of the concrete moral conscience with the *State* is Gentile's way of recognizing the legitimate claims of 'what is.' For this identification implies that we must seek for the definition of our present moral duty in our social environment as it actually exists now; unless we are prepared to build on and within the social framework that exists, our volition will remain a merely subjective aspiration, lacking universality because it has not the power to objectify itself, to make itself real in the world. Objectivity, sheer power or effectiveness, is vitally important in Gentile's theory because it is a sort of guarantee of the universal value of the will; when we succeed in producing some definite change in a given state of affairs, our action ceases to be something merely personal, and assumes a value or significance in the eyes of *all* the other persons involved in that situation. His desire to obtain this guarantee sometimes leads him to confuse the transcendental State (the ideal of a morally responsible person) with the empirical State, because this latter is the greatest focus of social power. For instance, if we are good citizens in Gentile's sense we do not need to be told that the State is the only real source of authority. But this knowledge will not, as he appears to think, enable us to solve automatically the empirical problem of whether the national or the local authority should be responsible for the organization of public education.[77] The question is indeed one that must be settled by reference to the good of society as a whole, but there is no a priori way of showing that the paramount authority of society will serve the public interest better by direct action than by delegation of responsibility. It was perhaps logical for Gentile to hold that education is the most vital function of the State—he even says it would be the primary function of a supranational organization if one were established.[78] And it was therefore arguable that the national authority in a young nation

[76] Cf. especially B.216 (1909) in B.1056, pp. 341–48.
[77] B.154 in B.1056, especially pp. 176, 194 ff.
[78] *Ibid.*, p. 198.

such as Italy ought to supervise with considerable care the whole structure of elementary education, as the best means for the creation of a truly national consciousness. No one could deny that local control of education helped to strengthen the *campanilismo* of the average Italian, which was the primary enemy of this national consciousness. But such considerations as these are historical, not a priori. They are of the same sort as the counterargument, which Gentile dismisses in a very highhanded fashion, that the existing national authority had already shown itself corrupt and inefficient in dealing with the railways, and should not be trusted with the schools. As he says, the choice is always between two theories, and never between 'theory' and 'practice'; but it is still a choice that must be made with one eye on practical advantages and difficulties. The confident assertion that "True ideas find for themselves the way to reality . . . since where a road does not already exist, they create one" [79] is no recommendation for a practical proposal; and no matter how carefully the philosopher explains that his a priori method does not involve a dictatorship of the mind over reality, the practical politician will rightly continue to regard him as a weaver of utopias as long as he adopts this tone.

The worst danger involved in this tendency to confuse the transcendental State with the actual structure of governmental authority is that it leads with inevitable logic to a kind of intellectual despotism. For only a fully rational animal, a man possessed of a social conscience, is fit to be a citizen, and only the citizen counts in society. Thus we are faced with the problem of how to decide which featherless bipeds possess the requisite social consciousness. In Gentile's theory it almost seems that the philosopher (i.e. Gentile himself) is the ultimate judge. It follows that every tendency which the philosopher recognizes as 'rational' should be realized in institutions and voluntarily accepted by all citizens as part of their moral and civil life. Of course, it would be ridiculous to suggest that Gentile consciously held any such extreme view as this. But the tendency to favor government by the expert seems an ineradicable element of the Hegelian political tradition; Gentile never freed himself from it; and it goes far toward explaining his later career in politics.[80]

---

[79] *Ibid.*, p. 183.
[80] The seeds of his later Fascist theory can be seen even in his early attitude toward theoretical controversy. He inherited the Hegelian habit of regarding

Religion in School and State

When the State is regarded as the highest concrete expression of the moral conscience of mankind the problem of the relation between State and Church becomes more than usually complex. For on the one hand the State must possess moral autonomy, and not seek its authority from religion or any other external source. But on the other hand, religion, properly understood, must be immanent in the State; for the sense of universality and objectivity that should pervade the life of the good citizen is inseparable from a thoroughly religious attitude. Clearly if the Church is a united community these opposed requirements can only be met where it operates in close harmony with the State. The principle of the Peace of Augsburg, *cuius regio eius religio*, was a recognition of this. But in Italy the State had come into existence very much against the will of a long-established and closely united Church. The neutrality enshrined in Cavour's famous dictum, "A free Church in a free State," was the best that could be hoped for. Gentile, who was a passionately enthusiastic patriot, could not quarrel with this conclusion. But as a philosopher he could not regard it as final. A State which simply abandoned religion to its confessed enemies would in his view be committing suicide.

It seemed that the Italian government was not alive to this danger. The 'lay State' was responsible for the moral formation of the vast mass of its subjects through the national educational system; but it was tending more and more to shuffle out of this responsibility and leave the task entirely to the Church, which it did not officially recognize. The *Lex Casati* of 1859, which remained the legal foundation of the Italian educational system right down to

---

his own theories as 'Philosophy' with a capital letter; and because of the fundamentally ethical character of his whole view of reality, the inconsistencies of other philosophers appeared to him not as errors merely, but as sins. As he proudly proclaimed in 1907: "My friend Croce and I, traveling by different paths, arrive at this unshakable joint conviction: that theoretical errors have a moral root; and that it is not legitimate to regard as a man of good will one who does nothing to introduce a little order and intelligibility into his own thought" (B.176 in B.618, p. 238).

It is true that this was a polemical response to the accusation of De Sarlo, that he and Croce exercised "a kind of terrorism in the field of philosophy"; and that he goes on to characterize his own attitude as one of "free, insistent, and sincere criticism." But a strictly 'moral' approach even to speculative problems can hardly help becoming a semireligious fanaticism.

1923, made religion a compulsory subject of instruction in the schools. But during the first forty years of Italy's existence as a State this provision was gradually weakened, until at last it was on the verge of disappearing altogether. As early as 1870 religious instruction was made optional by an administrative decision—though this change was not definitely legalized until 1888. In 1904 the *Lex Orlando* finally omitted religion altogether from the list of subjects to be taught in the elementary schools. This provoked protests and a commission was set up to consider the matter.[81] While it was still at work, the federation of secondary-school teachers arranged to discuss the whole problem of the 'lay school' at their national congress in September 1907, and invited Gentile to prepare a statement on the subject. His report provides a valuable account of his views on the function of religion in society. Because it was primarily concerned with the problem of religious instruction in State schools the broader questions were only briefly dealt with, but the principles enunciated in it continued to dominate his thought on the subject to the end of his career.

The 'lay school,' he declared at the outset, must not simply be defined negatively. To say that it is *nonconfessional* or neutral in religious matters is not enough—there would be no progress involved in the simple creation of a *tabula rasa*. But when we seek to define it positively we find "at the root of the concept of the 'lay spirit' a certain element that essentially belongs to the religious spirit." [82]

The State can only distinguish itself from the Church on condition that it recognizes its own religious character; it can deny all external religious authority, but it cannot then deny the religious character of its own authority. "Only the State that is first of all religious can be a lay State. . . ." [83] Whatever its representatives may *say*, the State remains an ethical reality in its active existence; and only this absolute quality, this element of divinity within it, gives it the right and the power to reject all other authority. Because this ethical character is essential to the State, absolute autonomy has always belonged to every real State, even the so-called 'confessional' State, which in reality authorized its own subjection.

---

[81] Howard R. Marraro, *The New Education in Italy*, New York, S. F. Vanni, 1936, pp. 58–59.

[82] B.163 in B.1056, p. 97.

[83] *Ibid.*, p. 98.

The natural course of events, therefore, is for this autonomy to express itself ever more completely in the form of conscious liberty; the religious authority which appears at first as external gradually becomes internal. It is only through this internalization that the true character of religion as an ideal moment in the dialectic of the spirit becomes apparent. So that we can fairly say that the religious duty, which the 'confessional' State recognizes, is only properly fulfilled when the State becomes aware of its own ethical autonomy and responsibility. Religion gives way then to the full concreteness of philosophy, yet it is not thereby destroyed but rather fulfilled. It is no longer regarded as a reality but as an ideal, an eternal striving for the unattainable peace of absolute Truth.

From this speculative analysis of the nature of moral authority Gentile goes on to deduce the character of a really 'lay' school. It must be not less but more religious than the confessional schools, in virtue of a careful distinction between the arbitrary form and the essential content of religion. The main faults of the confessional schools arise from the arbitrary character of their conception of the Absolute. This arbitrariness must at all costs be avoided in any school that aspires to be 'lay'; but without *some* conception of the Absolute there can be no school at all.

In the confessional schools a definite religion is taught; and this gives them an exclusive character. The world is divided sharply into the two kingdoms of light and darkness—a division which is inconsistent with the ideal aim of education:

The school . . . is the teaching of truth and justice, which is or ought to be one for all men. Of its nature, the school makes men brothers, unites them in the spirit. . . . The confessional school on the other hand . . . takes away the faith native to the spirit, that truth and goodness are one, and splits the human race into two parts before the eyes of the pupil, the elect on one side and the wicked on the other. The first party are the privileged spirits, possessed of truth and justice; the second are those condemned to darkness, and divided in a thousand diverse sects erring in different ways in their vain search after a ray of light. Instead of brotherhood, division; instead of collaboration in the progressive determination of what we ought to know, and what we ought to do, intolerance! [84]

---

[84] *Ibid.*, p. 106. In later years this passage was often quoted by Catholics to prove Gentile's hostility to the Church and by Liberals to prove that his educational policy as a Fascist was a betrayal of his own principles. There is much justice in the Catholic claim, and little if any in that of the Liberals; but the attentive reader will see as we proceed that neither can legitimately be supported by appeal to this passage, because it contains only the negative aspect of Gentile's view.

Intolerance, however, is not the worst fault of the confessional schools; on that score one might *almost* say that dogmatic philosophy was as bad as dogmatic religion.[85] Their bigotry is a much less serious evil than their antipathy toward scientific advance—in the broadest sense of the term. And, worst of all, they destroy individual self-reliance and responsibility, by substituting a transcendent unchallengeable authority for the authority of reason in the individual conscience. This is the defect of confessionalism which a lay education must fight hardest to conquer, for it is the antithesis of real education.

But the fact that the confessional school does have a determinate conception of life is not merely the source of its weaknesses; it is also its one great merit. It may not be a very good school, but it really is a school, for it is founded on a definite faith, a concept of the supreme end. This basic conception is lacking in the existing lay schools; for intellectual instruction offers only a formal ideal. Certainly the spirit of scholarship is a serious one; but pure erudition ends in pedantic specialization and skepticism about the great moral issues of life outside the schoolroom. The true end of education is to understand life; and this requires a general conception of the purpose of existence.

A faith is therefore necessary, and it is bound to be a *philosophical* faith, for science cannot answer the ultimate questions that arise in experience, and a scientific neutrality or suspension of judgment is here impossible—we *must* face the problems of life and death. But we can avoid the dogmatism of a *credo;* we can avoid intolerance and partisan bigotry; and we can encourage the critical thinking that makes scientific progress possible. The lay school should be a *temple,* but a temple of the free advance of reason: reason must always be respected.

Here a problem becomes apparent. For how is complete respect for the free advance of reason consistent with the character of *faith* at all? Any faith worthy of the name must be determinate—it must have limits. Gentile gets round this difficulty by defining a philosophical faith as one that contains the seeds of growth beyond these limits. But his view still involves the rather unpalatable con-

---

[85] The point of the "almost" is that there is a vital difference between religious and philosophical dogmatism, in that a philosopher will always admit the appeal to reason, and hence the possibility of growth and change even in his most cherished dogmatic beliefs (*ibid.*, pp. 108–9).

sequence that individual teachers cannot have complete freedom in the interpretation of their material. Their freedom must be as great as possible, but some authority must set limits to its arbitrary exercise: "There are cases in which the knowledge and teaching ability of the teachers needs to be supplemented by advice, suggestion, and correction on the part of the director or overseer possessing the necessary authority and competence (which is something that needs very careful consideration) in order to prevent the occurrence of errors that can certainly be recognized as such."[86]

The way in which this thesis seems to look forward to the later excesses of Fascist educational policy makes it important to emphasize that the 1907 report, while surrendering the autonomy of the individual teacher, insists strongly on the autonomy of the profession. Gentile looks to the free discussions of the whole body of teachers to preserve academic freedom against any misuse of power by administrators. He stigmatizes the school where the teacher is not molested by the police so long as he minds his own business as a worse form of slavery than confessionalism.[87] We know already how vital the authority of the teacher is in his view. "The school is made by the master"[88] who forms the minds of his pupils; and their liberty is properly in his keeping, for education is a work of love and requires a "complete surrender" (*dedizione completa*). When parents send their children to public schools, they entrust their moral welfare to the schoolmaster appointed by the State. He has to create the conscience of the pupil, a conscience *worthy* of respect, before he can respect it. His school is a moral and intellectual preparation for life, governed by an ideal of what life can be.

Hence the details of the practical program to be adopted must be hammered out by continuous discussion at all levels of the organization of teachers. But the basic ideal to be inculcated is an immanent humanism quite distinct from and even opposed to any dogmatic creed: ". . . the reason for life is within life itself, not

---

[86] *Ibid.*, p. 124. The problems of a world divided into ideological camps have made us much better able to sympathize with Gentile than his audience was in 1907.

[87] *Ibid.*, p. 125. The explicit reference in 1907 was to the old Bourbon government of Naples. One wonders whether Gentile had any qualms about the existing state of things when he reissued the report in his *Collected Works* in 1931. He did make one significant gesture by reaffirming in a footnote his belief that reason and the right to think must always be respected (B.163 in B.1056, p. 123).

[88] *Ibid.*, p. 127.

outside of it; the reason for everything that we think lies at the heart of this reality that we perceive. Nothing transcends our world, rationally conceived; and therefore nothing transcends our spirit. Mysteries, incomprehensible fountains of human values are the negation of man's autonomy and hence of every human value." [89]

Having thus completed his analysis, Gentile concluded that religious instruction should not be banished from the schools. The moral consciousness can only be sound and objective if it is based on a vision of the whole of life. The requisite orientation of the individual in the world is something provided only by a religious doctrine or by a philosophy. But young children cannot be expected to achieve a critical intellectual understanding of their place in the world as a whole. Sound philosophy must grow out of religious myths and dogmas, and therefore religion is a necessary stage in the development of a philosophical attitude. [90] It followed that elementary education in Italy must be founded on the teaching of the Catholic doctrine, since virtually all Italians were Catholics. Open and critical rationalism, building on this foundation, would then provide a better education than the strict confessional school offered. And from the personnel of this new school no one could legitimately be excluded who was honestly interested in the total progress of culture. A modernist priest would even be preferable to a narrow-minded anticlerical.

Moreover, even in the secondary school, which should be philosophical and critical, there must be an over-all unity of outlook. The young mind must not be faced with violent contrasts of belief too soon, or skepticism, both moral and intellectual, would almost certainly result. "The ideal of the school is that it should have a single master." [91] School principals must therefore set the tone for the whole school. Only at the university level, when the student has acquired a definite consciousness of his autonomy and can make up his own mind, should the free play of opposed points of view be suffered. [92]

It is not to be wondered at that Gentile was accused of bad logic by some speakers at the congress. They found a contradiction between his critique of the confessional school and his whole argu-

[89] *Ibid.*, pp. 131–32.
[90] Cf. Gentile's reply to critics, B.165 in B.1056, p. 150.
[91] *Ibid.*, pp. 152–53.
[92] *Ibid.*, p. 153; cf. B.159 in B.813, p. 201 and *passim.* (Cf. Plato's warning of the dangers attending too rapid an approach to dialectic.)

ment in favor of an elementary education founded on dogmatic religion. Their bewilderment was reasonable enough, since according to Gentile's report the Italian school could not be a *lay* school in any real sense—but only in the transcendental sense in which all schools that are schools at all are *ipso facto* lay schools. Only the university in Gentile's proposal will meet the requirements of a lay school as it was defined, say, by Salvemini—one of his more moderate opponents. In all honesty, we must count Gentile as an opponent of the lay school, though he was by no means a supporter of confessionalism.

It is more surprising to find that Miss Lion, in her book on *The Idealistic Conception of Religion,* agrees that Gentile's views on religion and life in this paper were hopelessly confused [93]—for no one could describe her as a hostile critic. What troubles her, however, is the contradiction that she finds in Gentile's attitude to the *confessional* school. She claims that the impracticable nature of his proposals reflects a confusion in his ideas about religion at this time:

. . . Gentile tried in vain to reconcile what he had said of the excellence of the lay school with his emphatic proclamation of the superiority of the confessional school. His attempt made the contrast worse. For to be consistent he voted against the motion that the whole elementary school system should pass into the hands of lay men or women; and repeatedly demanded the introduction of definite religious teaching into these elementary schools. On the other hand, secondary schools were to have philosophical religious teaching; the teachers imparting philosophical faith. He could not have done much worse in the way of conciliation. . . .
. . . He foresaw all the difficulties and did his best to meet them. In spite

---

[93] She regards this report as belonging to the "early period" of Gentile's speculation about religion, and describes section 4 ("Religion, Religious Confessions and Philosophy") as "an unfortunate medley in which Vico's and Hegel's views are uncritically mixed" (Aline Lion, *The Idealistic Conception of Religion,* Oxford, Clarendon, 1932, p. 174). But it seems to me that she is the one who has created the confusion. We need to distinguish at least three senses of 'religion' in this essay. There is 'my religion' for the believer, 'such-and-such a religion' for the historian, and 'Religion' as a moment in the dialectic for the philosopher. All historical institutions have artistic, religious, and philosophical aspects; but since philosophy is the full self-consciousness of history, the philosophical aspect of an institution is normally what matters to a historian. Gentile makes it clear in section 4 that he is approaching religion from this point of view. He is seeking to determine, sufficiently clearly for his immediate purpose, what religion is in its concrete *historical* form. The immanent philosophy, which makes a determinate religion historically effective or significant, is bound to be immature and mythical in character or it would not be religious. Miss Lion treats this historical criticism of the Christian Church as if it were Gentile's own philosophy of religion.

of his efforts he could only make things worse by suggesting that each secondary school should try to select its teachers in a way that would ensure to single schools, at least approximately, unity in philosophical faith, so as to prevent the diversity of beliefs amongst the staff from breeding scepticism among students. To anyone used to the Gentile of later years and familiar with his speculative works, his attitude here seems almost comic. . . .[94]

It is not necessary for our present purpose to defend the conception of religion contained in "Scuola laica." But we must point out that Miss Lion's contention that Gentile's practical program reflects the confusion in his ideas about religion "at the time" is seriously misleading, because it is not true, as she continually asserts or implies, that Gentile's views, both speculative and practical, underwent serious modification in later years.[95] If Gentile was confused about religion in 1907 he always remained confused. In 1922 and 1923, whenever he discussed the reform of Italian education that went by his name, he referred back to his stand at this congress. In his reform he made religious instruction the center of elementary education, and a reformed philosophy curriculum the center of secondary education; he increased the authority of secondary-school principals and did everything he could to impress on them their over-all responsibility for what was taught under their direction. He justified all this by speculative reasoning which does not differ in any important respect from his argument in this report. Furthermore, in 1929, at the time of the Concordat, he still regarded the introduction of dogmatic religion into the secondary school as a mistake.[96] All this can hardly have been unknown to Miss Lion—whose book was published in 1932. Yet she talks as if

---

[94] *Ibid.*, pp. 179–80.

[95] It may seem both presumptuous and dangerous for one who knows Gentile only through his writings to challenge in this way one who was a personal pupil of his. But the consistency of every statement that Gentile ever published on the subject is so striking, and direct reference back to his stand in 1907 is so frequent, that I simply cannot comprehend how Miss Lion could ever have said that, to anyone who knew Gentile in later years, his attitude in 1907 "seems almost comic." As for her contention that "the philosophical faith which he propounded for the secondary schools could not have done the same service as the creed it was meant to supplant" (p. 180), I can only say that, true or false, it is a flat contradiction of the basic tenets of actual idealism.

[96] It would be difficult to supply chapter and verse for an explicit statement to this effect at that time, because Party discipline put a curb on Gentile's tongue; but his attitude emerges clearly in B.970 for example (see B.1104, pp. 95–96). Looking back in 1943 he did recall and reaffirm his opposition to the Concordat on just these grounds (B.1264, p. 8).

Gentile's view of the relation of religion and philosophy in his 1907 report were a mere aberration.

In his own Epilogue written after the congress Gentile himself showed how "Scuola laica" was integrally related to his over-all view of the relation between Church and State. With the political heritage of 1870 in mind, he remarked that his proposal was an ideal to aim at rather than a practical plan: "It means that *if the relations of State and Church in Italy permitted it* (*or whenever they do permit it*), the moral instruction in the elementary school would be (or must be) definitely religious." [97] Until then the spirit of elementary education should at least be concordant with the religious instruction given at home or in church. Only a proper relation of State and Church could bring the ideal of a fully religious elementary education to fruition.

Here if anywhere, there is a *genuine* contradiction in Gentile's views, and it is not a theoretical but a practical one. For it seemed to him that a proper relation or reconciliation between Church and State was in fact next to impossible. They were bound to remain suspicious of one another, because each claimed moral authority over the minds and hearts of their individual members. From the point of view of the State there were only two possible courses: either the claim of the Church to absolute authority was valid and should be admitted, or it was not and should be denied.[98] But if it were to be denied then the true source of authority would have to be pointed out; and this could only be the State itself, in its ethical character. Certainly religion as an ideal moment of the spirit transcends the State; and therefore religious freedom (as Cavour perceived) [99] is of the essence of the modern State. But the Church as a social institution is an organ of the State "which *in a practical sense* always creates it, inasmuch as it recognizes it." [100] The dis-

---

[97] B.1056, p. 162 (Gentile's italics). This Epilogue was first published in B.183 (1908).

[98] B.252 (1911) in B.898, p. 177.

[99] *Ibid.*, pp. 174–75.

[100] B.1056, p. 163 (Gentile's italics). This doctrine is probably unacceptable to any actual church. But it was the political principle accepted at the Peace of Augsburg, *cuius regio eius religio,* and it is reminiscent of Luther's claim that Christ delivered the keys to Peter as representative of the community. The conflict of moral authority between Church and State, which Gentile seems to endow with an almost transcendental significance, only exists where the church concerned transcends national boundaries. Thus Gentile wished the Italian State to come to terms with the *Italian* Church, but his philosophical

tinction here drawn is founded on Gentile's immanent interpretation of Hegel's Absolute Triad which we discussed at the beginning of this chapter. He elaborates on it as follows: "Philosophy is superior to the State, and contains it; but the professor of philosophy is an organ of the State; similarly religion contains the State, but the State contains the Church. The theory of the separation of State and Church willfully ignores this difference between religion as a moment of the spirit and hence a private matter, and the Church as a social institution and hence a matter of public concern of which the State must take cognizance." [101]

The State is the moral limit of the citizen's individuality; and the citizen is the whole man. Hence the State can exercise a negative control over his whole life: no more than Jove can it undo what is done, but it can deny public effect, i.e. universal significance, to a deed of which it disapproves. Thus it may censor works of art and remove professors from their official positions.

The Church on the other hand is not a form of the State itself but only of the 'people,' who are, as it were, the raw material of the State. Hence, if the State allows the Church an important role in education, no surrender of authority is involved. It is simply the case that religion has its own proper place in cultural development. The State itself can profess no religion. What religion should be taught is an empirical matter to be settled so as to satisfy as many people as possible; but that there should be religious instruction is an a priori necessity, and hence the State cannot heed the protests of private individuals who oppose religion altogether. "In

---

convictions compelled him to resist to the last any rapprochement with the *Vatican*. The difficulty of clearly distinguishing these two bodies, together with his confused intellectual/emotional conviction that Catholicism was the 'true' religion because of its explicit universalism, prevented him from seeing clearly that the problem is a contingent historical one. His Catholicism was confused because it *ought* to have been purely speculative—as his enemies always thought it was. Both religion and philosophy are universal values. Hence both the Church and the State will be universal in tendency. But a Church that is empirically more 'Catholic' than the State must inevitably create conflicts of loyalty for its members. The paradoxical position of the Established Church of England, which claims to be part of the 'Catholic' Church while remaining 'national,' seems most nearly in accord with the principles of actual idealism.

[101] *Ibid.*, p. 163. The difference between this immanent interpretation of Hegel which Gentile owes to Spaventa and his own mature view can be judged from the fact that whereas here he follows Hegel in saying that religion is a private matter insofar as it transcends the State, he argued in 1922 that religion is a private matter insofar as the State transcends *it* (cf. the following note).

this case also the cultural and moral purpose proper to the State should prevail as against the pseudo purposes of private persons, in order that the true purposes of these very private persons (although they may be ignorant of them or willfully ignore them) may at last prevail." [102]

Freedom must be built on faith. Hence religion is eternal because it corresponds to a "childhood of the spirit" that must be eternally renewed. Democracy is the reign of immanent reason in politics. But like Antaeus it can live only while it maintains contact with the earth from which it springs.

---

[102] B.1056, p. 166. I do not think that this typical example of Gentile's rational authoritarianism means that a particular creed should be taught to private individuals or their children against their will. For this would be inconsistent with the Hegelian point of view that he adopts here—according to which religious belief is a private affair. Yet it is hard to see how the purpose of the State can prevail in any other way. When he was in a position to put his ideas into practice in 1922, he no longer admitted that religious belief *was* a private affair—since, in his fully developed idealism, the distinction between public and private was completely abolished. But he still held that the State should permit freedom—since it would fall short of its strictly *philosophical* ideal if it insisted upon a *determinate* religion. His view in 1922 was that "every faith is sacred; but *a* faith there must be" (B.668 in B.1057, p. 17); and this seems to be what he really means here also. The Royal Decree of 1 October 1923, No. 2185, put this policy into effect by enacting that "Children whose parents wish to provide religious education personally are exempted from religious instruction in the schools" (Marraro, *Nationalism in Italian Education*, New York, Italian Digest and News Service, 1927, p. 109).

IV

THE MATURE SYSTEM

Prospect and Retrospect

By 1912 the 'method of absolute immanence' had crystallized definitely in Gentile's mind. From this time forward his thought is a continual effort to apply this new instrument more and more widely over the whole range of human experience. Hence there is a new unity of treatment about his work after this year. But the dominant concerns of his philosophy do not change; indeed, it would be surprising if they did, for it was the attempt to clarify his own humanism that guided him in his criticism of the past history of philosophy, and eventually produced the new logic of the pure act.

Gentile studied Hegel in the light of his Kantian inheritance and decided that the current interpretation of the philosophy of the Spirit was mistaken: Objective Spirit, the State, is not opposed to the human subject but immanent within him; and Absolute Spirit, the supramundane realms of Art, Religion, and Philosophy, is not opposed to, but rather immanent within, the real world of Objective Spirit. The State is the concrete historical will of the good citizen; and Art, Religion, and Philosophy are on the one hand transcendental—the ideal moments through which that will determines itself —and on the other hand actual—i.e. determinate objects or institutions which fall under the dominion of that will.

Having gone this far, within the Hegelian pattern, toward a philosophy of strict immanence, the ideal of strict adherence to actual experience presented itself clearly as the aim of philosophical investigation. But a strict application of this criterion inevitably undermines the whole fabric of the Hegelian system. The absolute freedom involved in the identification of the rational individual with the State as an *ethical* reality requires that there be no pre-existing absolute Nature behind, and no logically determined program of development ahead. If Logic is to be unified with the philosophy of the Spirit, as it must be in a completely immanent interpretation of reality, then the philosophy of nature must disappear—for it is only an illusion resulting from their separation. But also Logic itself must lose its absolute objectivity, its systematic completeness; not only the philosophy of nature but everything that has traditionally been called the philosophy of history must go by the board.

A philosophy of pure immanence must necessarily deny that the traditional distinction between particular and universal is speculatively valid; and, as a result, the 'philosophies' of nature and history become illegitimate, since it is no longer possible to distinguish the 'particular' facts from the immanent 'universal' meaning of the facts. The philosopher can no more 'presuppose' the work of the historian (as Gentile had proposed in 1897) than the historian can presuppose the facts. In short, the logic of the universe cannot be separated from the actual history of the world; and therefore the traditional a priori method of absolute idealism (which Gentile had defended in the *Philosophy of Marx* and applied in his own 'science of pedagogy') rests upon a mistake. All that remains of the imposing fabric of Hegel's Logic in actual idealism is the dialectic of Absolute Spirit —the three 'transcendentals,' Art, Religion, and Philosophy. A priori schemas of spiritual development (such as Gentile had employed in his defense of the classical *liceo*) are rejected as mere abstractions dangerously tainted with empiricism.[1]

It was necessary to treat the earlier writings separately, even at the expense of a certain amount of repetition; for it would be difficult to bring out the significance of this revolutionary simplification in any other way. The first important work in which the new method is consistently employed is the *Summary of Educational Theory;* and the analysis of the master-pupil relationship in that work is the root analogy upon which Gentile's whole approach to the problem of human society depends. We shall not begin with this analysis, however, since it seems best to present his mature 'phenomenology

---

[1] The main fault of the schema mentioned (given on p. 53, herein) is the misconception of the relation of history and science that is involved in it. The real difference between these two activities is not that the former deals with the particular and the latter with the universal, but that the former deals with the concrete, and the latter with the abstract universal.

of the social spirit' as an organized whole, which means that we must consider first of all his mature views about the most primitive and fundamental of human societies—the family.

The Child and the Family[2]

We saw at the end of the last chapter that as early as 1907 Gentile regarded the moments of the Hegelian Absolute as being truly absolute, in the sense that as ideal elements or tendencies they are present in every determinate form of human consciousness. Thus, although we call some experiences by the general name of 'Art,' others 'Religion,' and others again 'Philosophy,' there is really no experience that does not involve a subjective moment, an objective moment, and their immanent synthesis; the empirical classification is merely an indication that one or another of these aspects is, or at least appears to be, predominant. We saw also that in Gentile's view the predominance of one of these ideal moments in a total conception of life is characteristic of certain stages of human consciousness. Every individual must grow through the prior stages in order to rise finally to the synthetic (philosophical) viewpoint—a self-consciousness which though not complete (for no one is ever completely self-conscious) is at least disciplined, reflective, and critical.

In the light of this conviction, Gentile, like Vico, found metaphysical significance in the tendency of young children to weave private fantasies and perform symbolic imitations. In order to perceive this significance we must enter into the child's world. His activities cannot be measured and judged in relation to an abstract norm like the one established by empirical psychology; scientific attempts to construct a formal scheme of child development result merely in the creation of a mechanical toy—*il fanciullo fantoccio,*

---

[2] Two short essays (B.718 and B.722) referred to in this section were written as opening speeches for congresses which Gentile addressed as Fascist Minister of Public Instruction. There are traces in them of Gentile's own *stile fascista* and they therefore belong properly to a later chapter. But I have chosen to deal with them here in order to make the total picture complete.

I have also kept in mind two lectures of 1934 on the place of woman in society (B.1103). But in these lectures the Party line is very obvious, and I do not feel they provide reliable evidence: the view that the woman's place is in the home is not required by the logic of actual idealism. Indeed, Gentile is obviously a little uneasy in arguing for it (cf. *ibid.*, p. 12).

"the doll-child," as Gentile calls it.[3] The real child is an individual with a life of his own, a world of his own, and we must respect his individuality. He is not aware that his world is not the real world, that his experience is not mature. In the moment of actual experience, as Gentile points out, we are all children in this sense: our present experience would not be what it is if we were *already* conscious of it as incomplete and imperfect. It is only *for the adult* that the child is a *child*—an immature human. He appears to us as rapt in a dream, but *in* the dream there is no other reality than the dream world. It is only in the waking world that the dream becomes a part and not the whole of reality; there would be no sense in calling it a dream if we never awoke.

According to Gentile this dreamlike quality is the essential characteristic of art; and he draws quite a detailed parallel between the situation of the child and that of the artist. The characters of an artist's world are always new creations, and they follow the will of their creator. This is true even if, as in the *Divine Comedy*, they are historical persons; for Dante has removed his characters from the context of the real world, and placed them in a dream, in which they have a new life quite independent of anything that may be discovered by scholars about their historic originals.

Within his ideal kingdom the artist is absolute lord and the external world is quite irrelevant to him. But at some point he must issue from its magic confines, and enter the real world in which his will is not absolute, though like the rest of us he possesses at all times some measure of artistic spontaneity. We sometimes 'get our own way,' to use the common idiom, even in the harder world of real life.

Like the artist the child constructs a dream world; but he does not realize that it is a dream, and so it falls to us to awaken him. In his world he affirms his own personality, his own will, and he does not recognize the limiting power of the real world. But even he does have an end in view, which possesses for him an independent value. There is an objective religious moment in the most spontaneous artistic activity, and a real morality underlies even the self-assertive egoism of the child.

Certainly this aesthetic morality has little connection with the practical world of adult human society; but in the child's play

---

[3] B.1225, pp. 11 ff.

there is a seriousness which we miss if we view it only from the outside, and not from his point of view.[4] His imitative activity expresses his determination to assimilate the world, and set the seal of his own subjectivity upon it; and in his habit of destroying something that he has done with, he evinces his anxiety to progress. These are the primitive elements required for the development of a sober yet critical moral consciousness. Without them the child would grow into a sort of vegetable in human form. The subjectivity that he so strongly affirms is what makes him really human.

But, when all is said and done, the child's seriousness—his primitive sense of objectivity—does not properly involve any sacrifice of self. Certainly he sympathizes intensely with all the 'persons' in his orbit—they may include his pets, his toys, and all kinds of other things. But a real sacrifice of personal will implies a recognition of social responsibility—and the first society into which he really enters is the family. Among his toys and his pets he is a despot— no matter how benevolent; but in the family he is so no longer. That is how the family raises man above the beasts.[5]

There is an essential difference between the human family and any form of animal organization. The latter is always characterized by a fundamentally instinctive quality, whereas the former is from the first a result of conscious volition: "This character of conscious-

---

[4] Gentile held that most play-theorists of education did serious violence to the moral nature of the child by advocating play as a pedagogic method while adopting an adult view of 'play' as opposed to 'work' (*ibid.*, pp. 42–43).

[5] *Ibid.*, p. 70; cf. B.718 in B.1057, pp. 88–89. For Gentile, as for Hegel, the family is important as the first determinate form of human community, the first objectification of the spirit; but there is an interesting contrast in the ways in which they deal with it. Hegel recognizes that it has an important educational function, but he is primarily concerned with the institution of marriage: he sees in the child an objective fulfillment of the moral contract, an outward expression of the meaning of the institution, the deliberate perpetuation of the species. For Gentile on the other hand, the subjective attitudes of the persons concerned, and especially of the child, are of vital importance. It is the society of feeling into which the child enters that is important—far more important than the material sustenance he receives.

I do not, by any means, wish to imply that Hegel denied the importance of the subjective side of family life; it was he, I believe, who first called it the "society of feeling." What is important is the different attitude the two thinkers adopt toward 'feeling.' For Hegel it is something primitive and immediate, and there is not much that can be said about it; whereas for Gentile nothing is strictly immediate, and 'feeling' is the determinate concreteness of the act of consciousness, which is his most fundamental concern. Their conceptions of 'feeling' are not so very different, but in Gentile it is never destined to be finally transcended as it is in Hegel.

ness, this expression of will, is the keynote of every later relationship that man may establish between himself and creatures like himself, or between himself and the natural world." [6] The link that binds us to the family is one that may be broken. For at the root of the family, as of all other human communities, there is an act of will apart from which father, mother, and child would not exist. The biological link is in itself only a fact like other facts, and does not necessitate any kind of conscious relation.

The essential task of the family is to get the child to recognize and share in this family will, and thus to teach him something of the virtue of self-sacrifice and respect for others. This enlargement of consciousness is the whole purpose of education. Hence formal education should not be thought of as diverging from domestic education, or even as proceeding alongside it:

. . . all education moves along this same path on which man sets foot as an infant, from the moment when he learns to look into the face of his mother, and begins, as the old poet says, to recognize by her smile the one who assists him . . . welcomes him to her own heart, and thus makes him rise to a social existence, a higher spiritual life, which belongs no longer to one individual but to two; a social life: the life in which he discovers himself outside of himself, his own heart in the heart of another, his own soul and his own feeling in another's breast. [7]

Education begins within this first primitive society; but the social bond itself is more primitive than the educative activity. The parents are morally bound to the child from the moment when they realize that it will be born, for "from the time when we first receive a human being into our thoughts, we cannot but feel ourselves bound to him by moral ties." [8] And this primitive family society is not simply absorbed into a wider scheme of things when the child goes to school. It is transcended, but it is not left behind—it remains always as the foundation stone of all formal education.

Domestic education itself never ceases, and there is one way in which the family is superior to any other school: it possesses in a high degree the religious character which is essential to education, and indeed, as Gentile rather gratuitously adds, fundamental "in every truly human spiritual relationship." [9] The family is the eternal

[6] B.1225, p. 71.

[7] B.718 in B.1057, p. 90.

[8] *Ibid.*, p. 92.

[9] *Ibid.*, p. 94. A special emphasis on the 'religious' character of society is the keynote of the *stile fascista* as it appears in Gentile's work during the early years of the Regime.

guardian of that *pietas* on which civilization depends; the *pietas* which expresses itself in respect for traditions and institutions, and in willingness to die in their defense. The child's relationship with his mother provides him with an example of, and an opportunity for, self-sacrifice; and his father's authority has a natural quality, a felt absoluteness, that no external authority can ever have. If the family does not send children to school with a natural readiness to give trust and accept authority, the teacher is in a very difficult position.[10]

For Gentile, who could never allow that education was only an incidental or particular function, this preparatory opening of the mind was the real essence of family relations: "The education of children is the very problem the family exists to solve." [11] The problem of education expresses the meaning of the family for the parents as well as for the children, since it is a task which they can only perform if they have already opened their own hearts and minds. It is a mistake to think that the parents sacrifice themselves for the children; all benefit alike from a general surrender of the lesser self to a greater: "What do we mean by going about talking of the duties of gratitude that our children owe us, as if our own children were separate from us, foreign to our own personality, passers-by who come to the door of our house to ask us for something which we might refuse them? Our children are our very selves, our own soul, our personality. In educating them we educate ourselves; in order to educate them we have to create the family for ourselves continuously, day by day, as the expression of our humanity." [12]

This is the ideal of the family, and it is an ideal to which reality must somehow or other approximate. It is a matter of concern to the State—in which the purpose of the family receives complete and concrete expression—that *some* institution should perform the task of the family, if for any reason the family itself fails. Hence the provision of orphanages and similar institutions is a public duty.[13] The old view that education and family life are no concern of the State becomes nonsensical as soon as we grasp the ethical character of human community. Education is the business of the family; but domestic education is only a foundation—though a necessary

[10] *Ibid.*, pp. 94–96; B.722 in B.1057, p. 124.
[11] B.718 in B.1057, p. 98; cf. *ibid.*, p. 88.
[12] *Ibid.*, p. 98.
[13] B.722 in B.1057, pp. 122–23.

one—for the formal education provided by the greater community: "the work of the family must be sensible of, and support at every moment, the work of the school, in which it should concur." [14] "Thus the family is absorbed and elevated, its work consolidated, by the higher activity of the State." [15]

The 'natural' character of the family, which might perhaps seem to give it a certain *independent* value, is really ambiguous. So far as it is strictly natural it can have no moral value; but, as we have seen, it is never really a bond of sheer instinct. To separate the element of natural impulse from that of moral volition in family relations is very difficult; but the same is true in all other realms of experience:

Where does the love that seconds and sustains the family finish, and that which maintains and strengthens the domestic bonds as *duties* begin? Human life is all woven out of this ambivalence in our nature: on the one hand, it seems to us that everything grows naturally. Love takes possession of our hearts unobserved, it grows up on a sudden, and seems to draw us on; but on the other hand, reflection always intervenes, weighing, valuing, distinguishing, in order to destroy, to extirpate the weeds, and guard the plants whose flowers are the ideal of life.[16]

The family is to the school as the body to the soul. It is the organic base and fountain of life on which the whole structure of self-conscious existence must be built. It is an essential element in human personality; but it is properly an instrument of the higher life of reflective consciousness rather than an end in itself. Above it stands the school, and above the school, the State. But just as the school must be restored to health before the State can be made healthy, so the family must first be sound before any reform of the school can take effect. For within the family *man* is born not merely in the literal but in the spiritual sense—man, the moral individual, who is the substance of family, school, and State alike.[17]

The School and the Pupil

The school completes the spiritual awakening of the child. In his eyes, therefore, it is bound to represent discipline, objectivity, even sheer force; yet it can only achieve its task through the creation of

---

[14] B.718 in B.1057, p. 88.
[15] B.722 in B.1057, p. 123.
[16] *Ibid.*, p. 125; cf. also the analysis of the sex relation in B.1103, pp. 6–8.
[17] Cf. B.718 in B.1057, pp. 93, 99.

a spirit of freedom and sympathy. This is the antinomy of all education. The object must be resolved in the subject: education means the conquest of the world by the spirit, not the domination of the spirit by the world. But it begins, and it must begin, with the actual recognition of the world as something that has to be conquered, and cannot simply be ignored. The school, therefore, is the repository of cultural tradition; the repository of a past with which the present—the consciousness of the pupil—must come to terms because it is the proper content of the present. "The school begins when man acquires consciousness of an existing social and cultural patrimony that should not be wasted." [18]

This cultural patrimony seems at first sight to be an independent and self-sustaining reality; but it is not. It is true that the mind quails at the prospect of the enormous mass of funded experience in books and libraries, and one important task of the school is to make an initial selection from this mass, to provide, as it were, a "sheltered cove" for the first encounter with the "ocean of knowledge." [19] But this selective activity in practical education is the very life of the mass. All the books in the libraries remain without significance until they come to life in the mind of the reader. Hence the whole life of the school is internal to the consciousness of the pupil, and his liberty must on no account be suppressed; he must not be frightened into pessimism. The school has a moral mission which is the second moment of the antinomy of education: it must develop in the pupil a sense of his independence of the objective world and foster in him that awareness of moral responsibility which is concrete liberty. "By liberty we mean the power, proper to man, of making himself what he is, and hence of initiating the series of events in which all of his activity manifests itself." [20] This moral liberty, though it is proper to man, is something more than the spontaneity of fancy and sentiment that he possesses quasi-naturally. Indeed man himself is not a natural entity—something that simply exists—in any sense of the word:

. . . from the moral point of view, man is man insofar as he is capable of resisting and withdrawing himself from the overpowering force of passion which impels him to return evil for evil and hatred for hatred. He *ought* to pardon, he *ought* to love the enemy who does him wrong. Only if he can understand the beauty of this pardon and this love, and is so

---

[18] B.1128, p. 58; cf. English translation (B.659), p. 76.
[19] B.1128, p. 60; cf. English translation (B.659), p. 79.
[20] B.1128, p. 33; cf. English translation (B.659), p. 41.

attracted by it that he no longer does what might be expected of him in the natural order of things, does he cease to count as a merely natural being and attain to that higher world of the moral law, in which he must gradually develop his specifically human character.[21]

This ideal moral freedom is at once the presupposition and the end of education, and indeed of all human activity. Any deterministic account of human behavior involves a contradiction, since it could only be posited as *true* by an intelligence that was free to think the truth.[22] If it were possible to conceive of liberty as emerging gradually out of compulsion, the antinomy of education would not be difficult to resolve. We could simply say, as Gentile did in his early writings,[23] that in the early stages the pupil's liberty is in the teacher's keeping. But now this will not do. It is not a solution, but merely one aspect of the problem. We have to recognize on the one hand that the teacher represents the universal values of truth, beauty, law or religion—not, of course, because they somehow belong to him personally, but because he speaks for humanity—as against the particularity of the pupil; and from this point of view the teacher's authority must be recognized and the pupil's liberty denied absolutely. But on the other hand we must not forget that education presupposes the moral freedom and responsibility of the pupil, and aims at its continual increase.[24]

The true solution is to be found not in the consciousness of the teacher but in that of the pupil. The school is not organized because someone wishes to teach, but because someone wishes to learn. In the *will to learn* the moments of authority and liberty are reconciled and the duality of teacher and pupil becomes merely apparent. The pupil, therefore, is the "living center of the school," [25] and the school "fulfills its whole being within the consciousness of the learner." [26]

What then are we to say of the many situations in which this condition is *not* fulfilled? When the pupil does not wish to learn, his will is opposed to that of the teacher and the duality becomes

---

[21] B.1128, pp. 34–35 (Gentile's italics); cf. English translation (B.659), pp. 43–44.

[22] Cf. B.1128, pp. 35–40; or English translation (B.659), pp. 45–51.

[23] Cf. Chapter 3, pp. 57–61, 70, herein.

[24] Cf. B.1128, pp. 29–32; English translation (B.659), pp. 36–40. Cf. also B.1252 (Vol. II of *Complete Works*), pp. 47–48.

[25] B.1251, p. 189.

[26] B.1128, p. 64; cf. English translation (B.659), p. 85.

real. To overcome this duality is the problem of discipline which we must now go on to discuss.

The speculative solution of the antinomy in terms of the 'will to learn' remains always problematic. It is never finally or completely achieved; for here again, as in the case of the family, the solving of the problem constitutes the actual existence of the institution. The school is precisely this problem of the reconciliation of the master's authority with the pupil's liberty, and it could not exist if the problem did not present itself continually in new forms. Our solution must therefore be taken as a regulative ideal, "a way along which every man of judgment and good will can gradually progress as he continually solves his own problems"; [27] and the "man of judgment and good will" on whom the burden of responsibility falls is the schoolmaster. For although the school is constituted entirely by the pupil, it cannot exist without a master: it is an aspiration on the part of the former toward the culture that the latter already possesses,[28] and it is up to the master to see that the aspiration is fulfilled.

Hence Gentile's theory of educational discipline is extremely ambivalent. Much of what he says is hard to reconcile with the view that the school "fulfills its whole being within the consciousness of the learner," for in spite of this assertion he generally looks at the problem from the point of view of the teacher. He still insists even in his mature writings that the teacher is morally responsible for the pupil. The teacher's authority in his view is simply the authority of the moral law which is immanent in his will, just as, according to the definition of Aristotle, it is immanent in the will of the judge: "For the judge wishes to be, as it were, justice ensouled." [29] Through the mediation of the teacher, the law acquires power and becomes an active force. It would be inaccurate to say either that the law confers authority on the will or vice versa. Authority is simply their coincidence; and the recognition of authority involves a similar coincidence of the law with the will of the individual subjected to it—in other words it involves willing obe-

---

[27] B.1128, p. 31. (The English translation, B.659, made from the first edition, B.557, which I have not seen, is barely recognizable at this point; cf. p. 39.)

[28] B.1128, p. 59; cf. English translation (B.659), p. 78.

[29] B.1252, p. 28; cf. B.1157, p. 101. ὁ γὰρ δικάστης βούλεται εἶναι οἷον δίκαιον ἔμψυχον (Aristotle, *Eth. Nic.*, V, 7, 1132a21).

dience. The abstract objectivity of the law, its 'otherness,' is in this way destroyed; only the sense of its concrete objectivity, its universal validity, remains—that is to say, its fulfillment becomes a moral duty.

Thus the meaning of the claim that the teacher is morally responsible for his pupils is that his will must express for them the content of the moral law. It is clear, therefore, that his decisions must be impartial; they cannot be simply the product of a personal whim. If he wishes to discipline his pupils he must first discipline himself: *"Discipline is not the duty of the pupil, but rather the fundamental duty of the master."* [30] While there is a plurality of wills there is still no real authority; but if many empirical individuals are to concur in one active will, the content of that will must be universally valid for each of them; that is to say, it must be truly objective and not bound up with the particular desires of any one of them. Discipline must be sternly enforced, for the law is immutable. But the spirit of enforcement must be rational. The necessity that is characteristic of true discipline is not a suppression of liberty but rather a necessary condition of it.

This is where the ambivalence of Gentile's attitude becomes apparent. In view of his analysis of 'education' and of 'authority' he ought surely to argue that all real discipline is voluntary, since the necessity of the law does *not* suppress the freedom of the subject so long as its rationality is recognized—i.e. so long as it is accepted as fair. But he does not say this—or at least not immediately. He chooses rather to maintain that even slavery involves some measure of this moral freedom. "Here again," he remarks, portentously, "we must repeat: the spirit is always free, and yet never free." [31] One might perhaps be tempted to reply that when liberty becomes so equivocal that it does not exclude slavery it is not worth having. At this extreme Gentile's moral freedom seems as worthless as Hobbes's natural right.

A careful analysis will show, however, that this is not the case. For the point is that slavery can only become established as an institution when it is regarded as a moral relationship. A man whose every thought still centers on escape from bondage is not yet a slave at all.[32] On the other hand, when his spirit is absolutely broken,

---

[30] B.1252, p. 37 (Gentile's italics).
[31] *Ibid.*, p. 41.
[32] And hence in Hobbes's view his captor retains the right to kill him;

and he is completely subservient to his master, the condition of slavery is 'natural' to him in Aristotle's sense—i.e., it is the best thing for him.[33] Between these two extremes there lies an infinite variety of possible relationships involving some degree of moral authority and some degree of moral rebellion; and in these cases it is not altogether trivial to say that the slave is really free insofar as he recognizes his master's will as just.

Even such a limited experience of justice may educate the slave to rebel intelligently, in defense of his moral rights. But we must *not* argue that the moral value of slavery lies simply in arousing him to rebel, for then it would no longer be slavery if the rebellion were finally crushed, no matter what means of 'pacification' was employed; and this conclusion makes complete nonsense of the context in which this discussion of slavery forms only an unfortunate digression.[34]

It is quite typical of Gentile that immediately after describing slavery as a stage in the development of liberty and respect for law, he goes on to identify discipline with *love*.[35] He explains that by 'love' he means here a real community of will, not an ideal com-

---

cf. his distinction between a subject and a prisoner in bonds (*Leviathan*, Chapter 21).

[33] It would be foolish to pretend that when we campaign against an institutional abuse we are always doing what is best for those who suffer under it. It may well be that the institution has molded the persons involved in it until they are unfit for any other condition; and in the case of an immoral institution such as slavery this is the very best reason for opposing it.

Moreover, even if we are solely concerned with the welfare of those who have been demoralized—a problem which is only incidental to the main issue, but one which certainly cannot be ignored—we must remember that there are two sides to the question: the welfare of the master must be considered as well as that of the slave. In this connection there is a passage in one of Gentile's later essays that deserves to be quoted: "As man gradually comes to understand his own free nature, he achieves freedom both for himself and for his fellows; and the slave is released from bondage when his master becomes definitely conscious of the chains by which he himself is bound as long as he does not free himself from the completely selfish and irrational [*passionale*] instinct that leads him to use the slave as a mere instrument . . ." (B.1103, p. 8). This analysis of the situation seems to me to be much more valuable than the conclusion quoted in the text.

[34] This interpretation is required by Gentile's theory of discipline as a whole, and more especially by the context in which this passage stands. But Gentile is not always so careful in interpreting his own doctrine as we have been (see pp. 92–93 herein).

[35] B.1252, pp. 42–44; cf. B.1128, p. 2. (This last passage is not to be found in the English translation, B.659, as Gentile rewrote the first chapter as an introduction for non-Italian readers.)

munity of sentiment. Disciplined love is not, like Cupid in the legend, blind; it is the mutual trust and understanding that grows up when a community is tried and tested. In this interpretation discipline is merely the ethical moment of the acquisition of knowledge—in other words it is an aspect, not a prerequisite, of the actual process of learning and teaching. The beginning of true discipline is the recognition by the pupils that the teacher can give them something that they need. Given this recognition obedience becomes voluntary and even spontaneous, so that from this point of view there is no 'problem of discipline.'

But in order to keep the problem from arising we must maintain the thesis that all discipline is self-discipline. One way in which this might be done would be by outlawing any kind of coercion; but Gentile will have none of that.[36] He objects to the use of prizes and rewards in the schoolroom [37] but he insists that punishments are necessary and inevitable. 'Perfect discipline' is synonymous with the 'will to learn,' which, as we have seen, is only a regulative ideal toward which we must continually advance in the classroom. Punishment is a stage in this advance and as such it is the 'right' of the pupil as a moral being, or to be more precise it is the right of the future repentant pupil.

This view contradicts the thesis that we have just enunciated, however, and hence the problem of discipline recurs. For on this interpretation punishment is not *self*-discipline. The pupil does *not* regard punishment as his 'future right' *when* he is punished—for him it is only an unpleasant natural fact existing in the present. It is the *teacher* who sees the punishment inflicted as a right of the future pupil; and only by an act of faith can we say that it is "the future man who demands of the educator the punishment that will redeem him by subjecting him to discipline" or "the future redeemed sinner who already from afar points out the punishment to which he has a present right." [38] This talk of the future having rights is

---

[36] "Alas for the school in which everyone understands from the very first day, and the most perfect concord reigns between master and pupils! In that school it is not the pupils who have risen to the level of the master, but the master has descended to their level and is betraying his human duty. If the school is a school, if someone has to learn something, there will be fatigue and effort: and hence failure and recovery, sin and expiation" (B.1252, pp. 51–52).

[37] *Ibid.*, pp. 56–57.

[38] *Ibid.*, p. 53.

only a pompous disguise for the uncomfortable fact that the teacher is obliged to take a step in the dark, and act as the conscience of another human being. Certainly he must do it, but under the circumstances it would be wiser to do it humbly and in doubt rather than in the full confidence of self-righteousness.

Because he is acting as the conscience of another person, the teacher *cannot* be sure that his punitive action will be successful. If discipline means the effective establishment of a community of purpose in the minds of teacher and pupil, then the penalty that the teacher inflicts can only have a disciplinary value when it is recognized as just by the pupil. From the teacher's point of view there is *no* solution of the disciplinary problem, precisely because all discipline is self-discipline.

A consistent account of punishment as a means of discipline can only be given from the point of view of the pupil; and when Gentile considers the meaning of punishment for the pupil he does finally offer an acceptable analysis: "Given the concept of discipline as the actual production of spiritual unity between master and pupil, the primary consequence [of punishment] will be the breach [*dissidio*] between them: this is the original and fundamental punishment to which all others can be reduced." [39] The sense of this *dissidio* arises only where the pupil respects the teacher who punishes him. But if the teacher fulfills his own fundamental duty of self-discipline, and succeeds in incarnating the moral law, as Gentile's theory of authority demands, there can be no difficulty here. The pupil must inevitably feel that he has fallen short of his own ideal; punishment both reveals and helps to resolve a conflict in his own personality.

When punishment fails it must be for one of two reasons: either the teacher lacks the will to teach or the pupil lacks the will to learn. In the former case the hurt inflicted is clearly not punishment at all, but a rank injustice. With that possibility therefore we need not be concerned. In the latter case the pupil's attitude will presumably be one of defiance; and the failure of the punishment will be evident because of a continuation and even an accentuation of this attitude. Since Gentile holds that the school is based on the will to learn, it would seem that in this situation he ought to lay upon the teacher the task of arousing the pupil's interest; and certainly

---

[39] *Ibid.*, p. 54.

he ought to declare the continued use of punishment unjustified.

He does clearly recognize that his theory of discipline imposes certain limitations on its use:

The appropriate limit for punishment is indicated by the end to be attained: a punishment that nullified not merely what is accidental and particular but even the essential and universal element in the mind of the transgressor would cease to be punishment and become a crime.

Punishment is justified by the good that it produces.[40]

But when he comes to discuss the absolute breakdown of communication that is here postulated, he uses just the kind of argument that we have outlawed above in discussing his view of slavery. He claims that all is still not lost so long as the teacher's authority is maintained as a limit to the pupil's freedom:

. . . even here if the master is not just slack, but exerts a real spiritual power, the persistence of the limit is of value in the spiritual development of the pupil. For he is not crushed—the liberty of his nature is incoercible —but rather provoked into affirming his own personality even more vigorously, by this improper educative activity. So that even in this case the school is the forge of liberty in spite of the contrary intentions of the teacher. The school without liberty is the school without life.[41]

We must all of us have encountered, in our years at school, pupils who did react to discipline in just this way. But that does not justify the adoption of the corresponding attitude on the part of the teacher. As we have had occasion to remark before, a freedom that is so intimate as to be beyond coercion is all too easily ignored.[42] Gentile's argument provides a perfect alibi for pedantic tyranny. Nowhere is the abstractness, the disastrous ambiguity, of his theory of pain and compulsion [43] more clearly revealed than here. He must surely have known that, for all their 'incoercible liberty,' many pupils *have* emerged from bad schools with their wills broken or their characters twisted.

This tendency to justify brute force as a moral power is the worst aspect of Gentile's Hegelian heritage. It might possibly be made

---

[40] *Ibid.*, p. 56. Gentile goes on to point out that this immanent limitation provides no grounds for outlawing corporal punishment. The body is a part of the concrete personality—and indeed there is no way of inflicting punishments of any kind except through the mediation of the body.

[41] B.1128, p. 47; cf. English translation (B.659), p. 62. Notice the contradiction between the claim that the teacher's power is "spiritual" and the admission that with respect to the pupil it is "improper."

[42] Cf. Chapter 3, p. 58, herein.

[43] For Gentile's theory of pain, see Chapter 2, pp. 31–33, herein; for his theory of compulsion see the present chapter, pp. 112–17.

to appear consistent with the authoritarian view that punishment is the 'right' of the future repentant sinner; but it is completely inconsistent with the view that punishment should create the sense of a spiritual 'breach' between teacher and pupil.

One reason for Gentile's failure to live up to his own principles in this instance may be that he never had any conception of how the difficult child feels. In his vision, the child comes to school with great eagerness:

"As man with rumored beauty falls in love" . . . so it happens that even before we have ever been to school, we may already desire to go. (Oh the sweetness of anticipated joys in childhood, when we first dreamt of all that the school promised, as the day drew near when we were to go, with our older brothers and our friends a little bigger than ourselves, forward into that life which so strongly attracted us as we glimpsed it in their tales and the tales of our parents.) [44]

One detects here a note of autobiography. Certainly not all, and perhaps not very many, children actually experience this eager anticipation, and if they do they are speedily disillusioned. But Gentile was one of the exceptions whose eagerness was too great to suffer disappointment.

The child is normally disappointed because when he comes to school he has still hardly begun to awaken from his daydream world of spontaneous impulse to the realities of life in a wider community. Through the discipline of the school he learns or should learn to appreciate objectivity. And Gentile does recognize the danger that he may come to terms only partially with the new world. He may limit his responsibility and adopt an egoistic attitude. The school will then have failed in its task of opening the mind. Education can never be morally neutral. But a purely intellectual conception of education may well be morally disastrous: "For man is always moral within his world. But his world ought to be continually growing. The scholar who is also a bad citizen is a sound and honest enough man in the world of his learning; and outside of it there is no world for him. The peasant who has learned to read and write, and sends out demands for ransom, has been most inadequately instructed in school—we might even say that he has not really been instructed at all. . . ." [45] This final defeat can only be averted

[44] B. 1128, p. 68; cf. English translation (B.659), pp. 90–91. The line "Com'uom per fama s'innamora" is a slight misquotation of Petrarch, *Canzone* 53 ("Spirto gentil che quelle membra reggi"), l. 103.

[45] B.1251, p. 238; cf. B.570, and B.154 in B.1056, p. 186.

through a clear recognition that the problem of discipline is the fundamental problem of all education.[46] The ultimate task of the school is to produce a full consciousness of what it means to be a human person; and only a really critical vision of life as a whole can provide a firm basis for the morality of the citizen—the human person who recognizes and fulfills his social duties.[47] The moral purpose of all education is thus at the same time a *philosophical* purpose; and for this reason formal philosophy is the proper crown of any adequate education.

A critical or philosophical vision of life will only lead to the requisite moral responsibility, however, if it rests on an initial acknowledgment that the objective world possesses spiritual value even in its primitive 'otherness'; and this acknowledgment is the essence of what Gentile calls 'religion.' "The fear of the Lord is the beginning of wisdom"—or in other words, responsibility must be accepted before moral freedom can be exercised. The religious view of the world—a quasi-immediate sense of the Whole—forms a natural foundation for the critical and creative attitude of philosophy, just as the family provides a natural foundation for the initial, religious phase of education.[48] Human development, however, is not progress in a straight line, but the gradual growth of an organic universe in which nothing can ever be completely new. Hence at every stage of the pupil's development the educator's attitude should be prophetic of its philosophical culmination [49]—even the dogmas of religious faith need not and should not be taught dogmatically.[50]

Gentile never gave sufficient attention to the question of how religious dogmas could be taught in an undogmatic fashion. This would certainly not be easy unless religion was taught 'comparatively'—which Gentile did not intend and which would have defeated his purpose. His hope in 1923 was that the religious instruction given in elementary schools would become more 'historical' in

---

[46] B.1128 or (English translation) B.659, Chapter 8 *passim.*

[47] B.1252, Part II, Chapter 4; cf. B.1251, pp. 251–52.

[48] For the corresponding moment in the life of the State—the institution of monarchy—see B.504 in B.561 (cf. pp. 122–25, herein).

[49] Cf., for example, B.1251, pp. 255–56; B.1252, p. 207; B.1128, pp. 176–80 (English translation, B.659, pp. 240 ff.).

[50] B.1252, pp. 193–94. Of course the teacher must not fall victim to the secular dogma of complete and perfect 'science' either (B.1128, pp. 105–7; cf. English translation, B.659, pp. 142–44).

the higher grades as a preparation for philosophy in the secondary schools. But if the 'historical' account were completely reverent it would almost have to be, as in Vico, a 'sacred' history quite distinct from 'gentile' history; and this was not what Gentile wanted. If on the other hand it were taught like ordinary history it would lose its 'absolute' character as a foundation for morality.

So far as I know the only time that Gentile tried to deal with this antinomy was in his Epilogue to "Scuola laica" (1908), where he met the objection that no modern 'lay' teacher could give religious instruction without being a hypocrite, by saying that it was not a matter of teaching what one did not believe, but of putting what one believed into a form in which it could be appreciated. "I have many things to say unto you: but ye cannot bear them now" was the text that he recommended to the elementary-school master.[51] This view of the place of religion in education is reminiscent of Plato's use of myth in the *Republic*. But Gentile's conception is Hegelian rather than Platonic. He regards the religious dogma as something destined to be transcended, whereas Plato seems to have regarded the mythical form itself as ultimate and inescapable, though any particular myth might be transcended.[52] The Christian Fathers were able to make use of the Platonic conception by substituting the fixed value of 'revealed truth' for the free variable 'myth.' The fact that the Church as an institution is founded on this *fixed* or dogmatic expression of the transcendent truth is what makes Gentile's program unworkable. His 'Guardians'—the educators—need to be above the myth altogether; but in fact they do not even have the power which, if I am right, Plato's Guardians had, of varying the form of the myths. Clearly they cannot adopt a 'philosophical' attitude toward their material without setting themselves from the beginning against the conception on which the Church is founded. The Church, however, is one of those animals that are so ill behaved as to defend themselves when attacked; so there would be a tug of war between Church and school for the allegiance of the pupil, which would destroy the certainty that Gentile hoped to obtain from his religious foundation.

---

[51] B.1056, pp. 158–61.
[52] This would account for Socrates' suggestion that the Guardians, and not merely the populace, should believe in the 'myth of the metals' (*Republic*, 414d).

Here we have touched upon the basic weakness of Gentile's educational theory. He ignores the institutional framework within which education is carried on. Not only does he seem to forget that the school itself is not a little world in isolation, that it exists in a complex of institutions, some of which may react upon it in such a way as to nullify or completely alter its intended effect; he seems to forget that the school itself is an institution. His whole conception of the educational process is much too strictly *personal*. He writes always of a direct relation between teacher and pupil, in which 'purpose' and 'law' are purely regulative ideals. But in actual fact every school has a code of rules in which these ideal notions achieve objective existence. The school rules were not made by the teacher, and the pupil knows that they were not; this is vitally important, for no one can be expected to accept another person as the mouthpiece of Reason—even when he appears to be a perfect example of the discipline he is trying to enforce—except, perhaps, after long acquaintance with him and experience of his character. Again, the practical conflict of authorities in a single school, which constitutes for Gentile a difficulty that can only be resolved empirically, is actually resolved in a speculative sense through the idea of the school as an institution above the teachers, an institution having a life of its own founded not merely on its rules but on the tradition that slowly grows up in the course of its history. Anyone who has passed through a school that possesses a corporate existence of this kind will agree that his own education for citizenship rested far more on his conception of 'our School' as a society to which he owed allegiance as a member than on regulative ideals such as Art, Science, Philosophy, Religion, Right, or Morality.[53] It may be that Italian schools in 1913, when Gentile wrote his *Summary of Educational Theory*, gave little sign of possessing a corporate existence and tradition of this kind. Even so it is strange that he did not pay more attention to the possibility of developing the school as a social organism, when we remember that in his view the primary duty of the school is to produce good citizens. He says often enough that a school must be a spiritual unity. But when he speaks of this unity he seems to be thinking only of the classroom relation in which the teacher is necessarily dominant; and the *spirit* of the school about which he talks so much is just the universal tendency—i.e.

---

[53] See B.1252, p. 48, for this list of universal values which the teacher should represent. Cf. also B.1128, p. 30 (English translation, B.659, p. 36).

the philosophical attitude—immanent in the process of teaching. He never thinks of the school as a place in which children are educated, largely by one another, in the difficult art of living together—for them the 'school spirit' means something quite different. Yet there can be no school which does not fulfill this function in some measure, and one would have expected him to perceive its importance.[54]

As a matter of fact education seems in his mind to be a transaction between *one* teacher and *one* pupil in which *"The consciousness of the master is the infinite moment of the self-consciousness of the pupil."* [55] Everything must begin from the finite moment of the pupil's consciousness, his past experience, what he already knows; but if there is to be any learning this moment must be transcended, and the teacher's knowledge is the means to this self-transcendence. For the pupil to have any other incentive than the simple desire to know is immoral and dangerous. The teacher may be a man of flesh and blood with economic incentives; but the pupil should not even compete for prizes[56]—he is like a novice in a monastery, alone with his god whose name is Knowledge. It may be doubted whether this austere intellectualism is the best attitude to adopt in opening the mind of the young. The truth is that as a professor Gentile could not help regarding the school simply as a breeding ground for university students, in spite of the fact that in his speculative theory it has a much broader significance.[57]

---

[54] Of course, we must never forget the material poverty of Italy and of Italian schools. Doubtless this accounts in part for Gentile's extreme emphasis on the personal and spiritual aspects of education. (Cf. the account of the way in which the *Riforma Gentile* was implemented in some village schools near Palermo given by Alfred Iacuzzi in *School and Society*, XXV, January 1927, 74–76.)

[55] B.1252, p. 73 (Gentile's italics).

[56] Contrast B.189 with B.1252, p. 56.

[57] At the university level, where the master-pupil relation gives way to a more equal kind of cooperation in the quest for knowledge, Gentile was well aware of the value of a community in which young scholars live together with their professors. In this respect the *Scuola Normale Superiore* at Pisa is, I think, unique in Italy; and Gentile's years as a student there had an unforgettable effect on him (cf. B.191 in B.813, pp. 232–96; B.976 bis, B.1019, B.1067 or B.1084; B.1132 in B.1139, pp. 183–203).

The Fascists showed that the school was a community that could 'educate' in a nonscholastic sense, and even usurp the authority which in his view belonged to the teacher. Gentile himself was led to protest against the pressure exerted by Fascist student groups in the universities (B.991 in B.1057, p. 467; cf. Chapter 6, p. 195, herein). Of course the Fascist groups did not educate

Good and Evil

Gentile's rather narrow conception of the practical process of education stands in sharp contrast with the speculative vision and boldness with which he generalized from his analysis in theory. The account of school discipline in his *Educational Theory* is of fundamental importance for the whole of his social philosophy; and in particular it provides the key to his *Foundations of the Philosophy of Law* (1916).[58] In its original form this book was a summary treatment of three main problems:

(1) the relation of the individual to society;
(2) the relation between force and law;
(3) the relation between law and morality.[59]

But before we proceed to consider his treatment of these problems, we must deal with Gentile's general view of the relation between good and evil, since he regarded an understanding of this problem as a necessary prerequisite for the comprehension of his philosophy of law.[60]

According to his analysis, reality in its moral aspect—or in other words, the spirit as creative activity—is a dialectical unity of good and evil. The human good is a process: it is the gradual realization of the good will which occurs in the conquest of evil. Hence it can never exist in a state of final perfection, for its perfection would

---

in the true sense, for no one would say that they 'opened the mind.' They were probably instrumental, however, in opening *Gentile's* mind to the wider implications of his own view (cf. Chapter 3, pp. 50–51, Chapter 6, pp. 178–82, 192, Chapter 8, pp. 273–78, herein).

[58] B.354. This small volume was based on a course of lectures delivered at the University of Pisa in that year. Gentile had not previously concerned himself with legal philosophy, and it might well appear that the book was the accidental product of an academic task. But it has been shown fairly conclusively that it was actually the result of several years of meditation and discussion which began in 1913, just at the time when he was finishing the second volume of his educational treatise (see the article by Arnaldo Volpicelli in *Vita e pensiero*, I, 364–79).

[59] To the first version of the book Gentile added at various times an introduction—see the following note—and two essays on political philosophy written in 1930 and 1931 (B.989 and B.1017) which are discussed in Chapter 7, pp. 236–43, herein.

[60] In 1914 Gentile wrote an essay on Rosmini's ethics for an edition of that author's *Il principio della morale* (B.308). This essay was reprinted as an appendix to the second edition of the *Philosophy of Law;* and appeared as an introduction to the third edition (B.1157) with the title: "Introduction to the Study of Practical Philosophy or of the Moral Life."

imply its annihilation—if the process were completed there would be an end to all value. The good is not so much the palm of victory over evil as the actual winning of the battle. Objective evil is the obstacle, the reality which the will seeks to remold; and evil in the will is simply absence of self-consciousness—failure to will the good.[61]

It would be easy to simplify this view into a kind of Socratic intellectualism; but it would also be a mistake. Gentile would certainly agree that "virtue is knowledge," and it is obvious that he must also hold that "no one willingly does wrong." But this does not mean that evil is simply an illusion, a will-o'-the-wisp of ignorance. It is as real as good; the two forms of value are inseparable.[62] The doing of a good action—which exhausts for Gentile the whole reality of goodness—is always the perception and removal of some evil. There is no perfect way of life: the moral man is never without a sense of sin. Even his good action, as soon as he regards it as completed, is no longer an act but a fact, which is good, if it is good at all, only in virtue of his critical reconsideration of it. Empirically speaking, such reconsideration is a *new* act,[63] so that it necessarily contains a negative moment, or involves the perception of some further evil—for there is always some further good to be done. What in the original act was the solution of a moral problem becomes a new problem as soon as it is thus objectified. *The* good is always in the future, eternally real and eternally unreal.

Even if we set aside the charge of intellectualism, however, the fact remains that Gentile takes a completely negative view of evil. His theory is not far removed from the orthodox Christian tradition in which evil is treated simply as a privation of good. Many thinkers have rejected this view on the ground that it fails to account for the concrete and substantial character of evil in human experience. Gentile considers the alternative view that evil is a positive reality, and condemns it as a complete error—though he admits that it is an opinion which is hard to eradicate from men's minds. To illustrate the nature of the fallacy that is involved in it he tells the story of the simpleton Mancini, who hired a train of asses to take his grain to market. On the way home he felt tired and mounted one of them; then, when he counted them he was alarmed to discover that

---

[61] Cf. B.308 in B.1157, pp. 7–11.
[62] B.354 in B.1157, p. 70.
[63] *Absolutely* speaking, it is *the* act, and is not part of a series of acts.

there was one missing. He left his wife in charge of the string when he arrived home, and rode back along the way seeking the missing animal. At last in despair he turned back again for home:

And only when he reached home, long after nightfall, and his wife persuaded him to dismount, did he discover the ass that he had been seeking so wearily.—One who perceives evil without perceiving the good in which that evil is conquered and annulled sees the asses that he has in front of him, but not the one on which he is riding: he sees the will opposed to his own, and which he calls evil, but not his own in virtue of which he calls the other evil, and apart from which the other would not exist as evil. It is not really possible to be aware of the evil that exists in this world without thereby achieving an attitude of mind that is morally superior to it. For evil cannot be treated as an indifferent fact of nature; it is judged; and the judgment is a condemnation, which is a rebellion of conscience—that is, an act of good will. So that evil is not, and cannot be, evil in itself. When evil is evil, it is already dead in the purifying conscience that judges it.[64]

We had occasion, in dealing with the very similar account that Gentile gives of pleasure and pain, to remark that he lays too much emphasis on the formal 'overcoming' of the negative moment that is involved in the simple consciousness of it. If we accept this metaphysical conquest of evil at face value, we must find Gentile guilty on the charge of Protagorean subjectivism.[65]

But a narrow-mindedly literal interpretation of this sort makes Gentile a supporter of skepticism and abstract individualism—the very attitudes that he most abhorred. This conclusion seems to prove the inadequacy of the critic rather than the inadequacy of the doctrine, for, as Vico says, it is only "men of limited ideas" who "take for law what the words expressly say." If we consider what Gentile says about the conquest of evil in the light of what we know of his general attitude we shall see that his claim that "when evil is evil it is already dead" does not mean that when we have decided that a thing is evil, we are entitled to ignore it. It means rather that the evil is 'dead' or 'overcome' if and only if we have decided that we must spare no effort to eradicate it. Then again, the *good* with which Gentile is concerned is not some utopian ideal, by which we measure the world and our own activity in moments of dispassionate re-

---

[64] B.308 in B.1157, p. 12.
[65] The ethics of actual idealism on such an interpretation would be very close to the skeptical solipsism of Pirandello as certain critics have claimed; cf., for instance, Angelo Crespi, *Contemporary Thought of Italy*, London, Williams and Norgate, 1926, p. vi.

flection. It is the ideal that we actually live by, and strive for—and, in the last analysis, this means the thing that we are prepared to die for. A philosopher like Aristotle, who founds his whole theory of ethics on the distinction between intellect and will, would retort that in many situations there is a great difference between what *is* good and what *seems* good to the individual agent involved. Gentile does not and indeed cannot make this distinction. But at least he can argue that what seems good *to* us is not the same as what seems good *for* us as individuals. The good in his view is precisely that element in our lives which seems to us to be *objective*—something that possesses an absolute and universal value, which others can and shall be made to recognize even if we die for it. The moral conquest of evil that is involved in its recognition as evil is nothing else but our ultimate readiness for such a sacrifice. "The act of condemning evil and that of willing good are one and the same act." [66] Gentile's theory of good and evil is therefore a tremendous challenge to sincerity: only a man who accepts absolutely the maxim that an intellectual conviction must be demonstrated in practice before it can be accepted as genuine can be an actual idealist.

In this view of the moral life the distinction between knowing and doing is abolished; but the distinction between will and intellect is not altogether lost, though it does assume a rather paradoxical form. For even in Gentile's theory there remain *two* ways of looking at the world. When we look at it from the outside any event is simply a natural fact, an expression of 'will.' It is something already done and finished, whether it be "by an empirically assignable subject (human volition) or by a subject assignable only metaphysically (nature)." [67] While on the other hand the world that we know from within is a conscious activity which opposes itself to this practical reality while at the same time positing it: "So that, when we look inward, thought is found to be not something opposed to volition, but rather a volitional activity in itself." [68]

---

[66] B.1157, p. 69. All further references to B.1157 in this chapter are to B.354 therein.

[67] *Ibid.*, p. 61; cf. Chapter 2, p. 36, herein. Notice also the contrast with Gentile's earlier view (Chapter 3, pp. 55–56, herein).

[68] "Sicchè a guardarsi dentro, il pensiero non si trova ad essere pensiero contrapposto a volontà, bensì pensiero come volontà" (B.1157, pp. 61–62). The reality that is thus 'posited' in moral consciousness is never really posited as independent of that consciousness: the end of all action is the self-realization of the subject—which is what the empirical psychologist calls 'pleasure' (cf. Chapter 2, pp. 31–32, herein).

Conflict and Society *in interiore homine*

Within thought understood in this active sense there is always an obstacle or an 'enemy.' It makes no difference here whether we should ordinarily describe this enemy as 'internal' or as 'external,' whether we are concerned about our own vices or about some abuse existing in the world around us. Morally speaking the enemy is always 'internal' because it is *our* enemy. Even if we found our morality on some theory of natural law, that law itself must become the voice of conscience before it can assume an ethical value. The realization of justice is a developing process, a continuing tragic struggle in which the individual strives to conquer his own selfish egoism, and advance the common good by action that is in accordance with the law.

The fact that man is self-conscious raises him almost automatically above the level of mere animal instinct, the mechanical and immediate response to a stimulus. Hence the strictly *atomic* individualism of Hobbes, for example, is not a tenable position, for even at the most primitive level in conscious development the human will has already a moral quality because its end is considered as absolute: the *bellum omnium contra omnes,* if it existed, would not be a war between individuals at all, but a war waged by *the* individual against forces which in his eyes were merely natural. In the world of the egoist, where the primitive instinct of self-preservation becomes a categorical imperative, all of life is like a shipwrecked sailor's struggle with the sea: "The egoist's mistake lies not in giving a wrong solution to the problem of his life, but in formulating the problem wrongly: once the problem is stated in his terms, it cannot be resolved by the moral consciousness (universal will) in any other way." [69]

Gentile finds in this "mistake" the source of war. He does not seem to feel that there is any inconsistency in arguing on the one hand that the *bellum omnium contra omnes* is the "figment of a materialistic imagination" (i.e. that Hobbes is mistaken), and on the other hand that egoism is the cause of conflict (i.e. that Hobbes is correct). For him both theses are reconciled in the conception of war as the process through which the error of egoism is brought to light (which, of course, was what Hobbes also maintained). In the

---

[69] B.1157, p. 72.

course of the struggle the abstract plurality of the opposed wills is mediated: the individuals are compelled to recognize their particularity, and the war finally ceases when a truly universal will emerges. Thus war, as the process of mediation, is the establishment of peace; and since mediation is always necessary, 'war' and 'peace' in this speculative sense are not empirical states but dialectical moments that are eternally necessary to each other: "Some conflicts may be more violent, and some less; but the will is always a *concordia discors:* and the discord in which particular interests are apparent is a moment of the concord in which the divergent interests are reconciled in the universality of the will of the whole [*volere unico*]." [70]

In considering this theory of conflict as a necessary moment in human relations, we should remember that Gentile's *Philosophy of Law* was written during the first World War. In October 1914 he delivered a lecture on "La filosofia della guerra," [71] and it is obvious that the ideas of that earlier essay were still very much in his mind two years later when he was sketching the outlines of his legal and social philosophy. In it he distinguished three different conceptions of war: first, the *metaphysical* conception of war as the mother of all things, expounded by Heraclitus; second, the ordinary *empirical* conception that Kant opposed in his pamphlet on *Perpetual Peace;* and finally, the *historical* or genuinely philosophical conception that Fichte invoked in his *Addresses to the German Nation.*

Of these three conceptions, Gentile dismissed the second as irrelevant to philosophy—though he could not resist the temptation to make sarcastic remarks about pacifism and "idyllic" conceptions of life in general.[72] He then went on to argue that Heraclitus' meta-

---

[70] *Ibid.*, p. 73.

[71] B.306 in B.497, pp. 1–24. This title is ambiguous: it can mean "The Philosophy of War" or "The Philosophy of *the* (present) War." Gentile deals with both topics—and, to make matters worse, he concludes that they are concretely identical.

[72] He seems to think that, because many of the theoretical defenses of pacifism belong to the period of the Enlightenment "which was *the* antihistorical century," and because we have discovered that "questions like that concerning perpetual peace are absolutely without philosophical significance," it follows that "the propaganda of the pacifists is one of the most naive and quixotic ways of wasting time" (B.306 in B.497, pp. 4–5). His premises here are questionable; but even if we accept them, the conclusion does not follow. A convinced actual idealist could still be a pacifist in practice, though the kind of argument he could offer for his position would probably not be 'absolute' enough to satisfy a tribunal in wartime. Gentile remarks that certain Hegelians

physical principle is merely a superficial and external conception of the real conflict within consciousness itself. The universal flux of nature is only an abstraction contemplated in imagination; the concrete universal must be sought for in the dialectic of the human will, where conflict is necessary and eternal precisely because the opposites form a unity. The 'other' to whom 'I' am opposed is within me; and hence 'I' cannot avoid the conflict. This war in which 'I' am unavoidably involved is the war with which Fichte was concerned. This, then, is the unique concept of war, the only one with which the philosopher can properly concern himself:

> The war that I fight with someone else, or that a people, once it has established a national personality, fights with another people, does not spring from the diversity of persons or peoples, but rather from the fundamental identity that is realized through this diversity. For it is evident that in the world as it reveals itself to us when we study it in the inwardness of our own spirit—which certainly is a world, and the world in which all past wars have arisen and all future ones will arise—identity without difference is impossible.[73]

This philosophical thesis provoked by the existing situation exerted great influence in Gentile's mind. It seemed to him self-evident that any situation that could arise within consciousness must presuppose the ideal unity of self-consciousness; in situations of conflict this formal unity becomes the ground of a moral imperative: it is the duty of the knowing subject to produce a unity of will within his world, corresponding to the abstract unity of his knowledge of it—only in this way can his knowledge be certified as genuine. Since Gentile's view of reality was essentially moral—his whole philosophy might be summed up by saying that consciousness of a thing implies moral responsibility for it—he was naturally led to emphasize the omnipresent element of conflict in human affairs, and he even seems to have inclined to the mistaken view that situations of extreme conflict involve a higher kind of morality than other more normal conditions.[74]

It is, of course, a commonplace that war brings out the best in people; but ultimately it involves a threat to the ideal unity that is

---

were guilty of a speculative abuse (*un vero abuso gnoseologico*), in that they confused the 'philosophical' with the 'empirical' concept of war, and were thus led to exalt physical warfare. We might fairly say that this is just what Gentile himself does in his criticism of pacifism; and thus it is out of his own mouth that he is judged. (See further Chapter 9, pp. 325–27, herein.)

[73] B.306 in B.497, p. 6.

[74] Hence his later support of Fascist militarism and 'war-mindedness.'

the ground of all moral value. If war brings out the best in man, it also brings out the worst. It may increase the intensity of moral resolve, but it also has a disastrously narrowing effect on moral sympathies and responsibilities.[75] Both strength of resolve and breadth of sympathy are essential to the ethics of actual idealism, since it is founded on the immanent unity of will and intellect. Gentile seems to have thought that the sympathy would inevitably grow as long as the resolve was genuine—but there is no sense in proclaiming a synthesis if you are then going to let one of the terms take care of itself. No doctrine can give way to sheer voluntarism like this, and remain viable as a social theory; for although there has to be a certain formal unity of consciousness for all parties to a conflict of wills, in the sense that they must inhabit a common world, this provides no guarantee that the conflict will eventually give rise to a genuinely *moral* unity. There is no a priori reason why the war of all against all should not go on eternally; and when Gentile attempts in the *Philosophy of Law* to derive social relations from purely economic conflict, the ambiguity of his argument is only concealed by the extreme brevity and abstractness of his exposition.

In economic conflicts of interest the unity out of which the conflict springs is provided by the *object* upon which the interests of the opposing parties converge. If someone else happens to want something that I wish to obtain for myself, his will appears as a negative moment of *the* will for whose affirmation I stand. This sort of conflict of desires may easily occur even within the consciousness of a solitary individual:

. . . Robinson Crusoe on his island, in the days before he met Man Friday, was bound to realize his own will by going through the same process that is proper to the will of every individual living in a social group: that is to say, by negating the element opposed to his will as a universal value, which constitutes the particular or finite moment of the will in society. Hence society, though empirically it may be the accord of individuals, is speculatively definable as the *reality of the will in process of development*. The universal value is established through the immanent suppression of the particular element. Society, therefore, is not *inter homines* but *in interiore homine;* and it exists *between* men only because all men, with

---

[75] The more critical the situation, the more evident this becomes. In 1914 Gentile himself, for example, found an ideal unity beyond the *patria* in the tradition of European culture. But in 1943 he had to appeal to cultural tradition to preserve the *patria* itself; and he seems to have lost sight of all the bonds uniting Italy to her enemies (cf. Chapter 8, pp. 286–88, herein).

respect to their spiritual being, are one single man with a single interest that continually grows and develops: the patrimony of humanity.[76]

If we ask why it is necessary to consider all conflict in this way, why all conflicts of interest must be considered as having their roots in the common interest of humanity, Gentile's answer seems to be that otherwise the conflict could not be 'spiritual'—it would be simply an expression of natural appetite, and moral action would be impossible. But this introduces a new premise altogether and is, in effect, an admission that objective convergence of interests is not enough. For it is implied that *unless* an overarching *spiritual* unity is recognized by both parties to a conflict there can be no society between them. The common objective is certainly the ground of the conflict; but it provides no basis for interpersonal relations. We should not say that the sailor forms a society with the gale, though a conflict of will certainly exists between them regarding the course of the ship. Gentile is right in saying that individuals involved in economic conflict "feel their egoistic and repellent particularity inasmuch as they come together and encounter one another, as two contradictory acts of judgment about an object of will that is identical for both." But if we agree with his further assertion that the contradiction about the object is really "in the will itself, the one judgment standing for the affirmation and the other for the negation," all genuinely social relations between the contestants become impossible. Conflict as such is not a social relation: we cannot pass from an objective coincidence of wills to a subjective identity of will.[77] Only when the conflict is already, at least ideally, overcome in an incipient cooperation (felt identification) of wills does society begin to exist.

Thus, Gentile's attempt to derive society from economic conflict by way of the moral conscience fails. And the reason is not far to seek: it lies in the fact that the dialectic of morality is a dialectic of particular and universal moments. If this pattern of universal against particular is imposed upon all interpersonal relations we

---

[76] B.1157, pp. 75–76 (Gentile's italics). Gentile claims in a footnote that his last sentence provides the true explanation of Rousseau's theory that the General Will is sovereign. But it is more directly related to the Mazzinian conception of humanity as a man who is always learning, which he traced back to Bruno (see B.275 in B.1223, pp. 331–55, especially pp. 349–52).

[77] B.1157, p. 75. The only logical conclusion if we regard economic conflict in this way is the Marxist theory of class war with its absolute conflict of values. Aristotle pointed out the ambiguity that is here involved (see his discussion of ὁμονοία in *Eth. Nic.*, IX, 6).

can never get beyond the *bellum omnium contra omnes*. It is true that the will of the other opposed to ours will appear to us as internal, but it will not thereby become *social*. On the contrary, society will become, if anything, even more impossible. If there is any situation that is less social than that of the sailor in a gale it is that of the saint vis-à-vis the lusts of his own flesh. St. Francis could even recognize a bond binding him to brother Fire and sister Water; but for his own body he had no such sympathy. If the relation between two persons were as simple as that between Robinson Crusoe's moral will and his particular desires, each party would identify himself with the moral will and his opponent with the particularity, and both parties would remain complete egoists, each seeing only the egoism of the other. This rudimentary relationship of absolute individuals would not then constitute a society at all, despite the coincidence of interest in a single object; for the concrete universal will—the history that actually evolves through their conflict—would remain transcendent for both sides.[78]

Society cannot be founded on any dialectic of particular and universal moments, because a truly social relationship, a relationship between persons, requires that each side should recognize that the other has a certain universal value which must not be negated. The moment of conflict is certainly present in social relations; but if society exists at all, the moment of perfect universality is an ideal above the conflict for both parties. Sheer opposition, war to the death, is the negation of society.

Gentile would undoubtedly protest at this point that no war is really war to the death; [79] as Hegel pointed out, the conquered enemy is not he who is killed but he who submits. We may allow this claim. But what follows is that war is the cradle of society as slavery is the cradle of liberty; and any recourse to force in human relations is a regression toward the impotence of an infant, not an advance toward a higher morality, since the universality, the common humanity of the opponent, is denied. In war it is denied absolutely, even to his annihilation in death.

----

[78] The tendency to view any serious conflict in which we may become involved in these terms is the reason for that disastrous narrowing of sympathy in war to which we have already referred; and since it is clear that any use of force must involve, or at least seem to involve, a claim to represent the universal moment of the moral will, there is, after all, some philosophical significance in the conception of "perpetual peace."

[79] Cf., for instance, B.1250, pp. 329–30.

Strictly speaking, it is the immanent sense of cooperation in human relations that constitutes society, not the undeniable moment of conflict. The conflict assumes a truly social character insofar as the conflicting parties both concentrate on reaching agreement (an ideal universality that neither side claims to possess already), and each recognizes the sincerity of the other in this effort, and respects his integrity as a person. To be valid as a foundation for human society, therefore, the internal dialectic must be conceived not as a dialectic of ideal moments but as a dialectic of persons. By the time that he published his *Prolegomena to the Study of the Child* (1921), Gentile had already realized this. He there restates his conception of internal society thus:

. . . we believe that the individual contains society in himself, and develops a social life within himself originally; and that this society immanent in his spirit is only afterward realized progressively in all the infinite forms of social reality, in that system of spheres whose radius has become ever greater throughout the history of humanity.

Each one of us, though from the outside he may seem absolutely isolated and possessed of a completely unconditioned liberty, still recognizes in his inner consciousness, within his own "self," an "other" to whom he is bound by rights and duties. When in the biblical phrase we say "Woe to him that is alone" we ought not to think of the man who cannot establish a society with other empirically determinate individuals, but of the one who does not know how to establish bonds of community and of unity with the "friend" and the "judge" who lodges within him.

. . . by way of this "other" within ourselves we become members of every other form of society. The words of comfort that come to us from without are received as such because they are the words that we have already addressed to ourselves; and in fact we hear in them the throb of a voice that seems to break forth from the inwardness of our own being. In the same way, when we turn to this "other" that is within us, and speak to him alone, our language is universal and is universally understood.[80]

All of Gentile's works from the earliest to the latest lay stress on the coincidence of particular existence and universal meaning in the phenomenon of language.[81] For him language is not simply the garment in which thought is clothed; it is the bodily substance through which it is expressed.[82] Thought must be individualized in

---

[80] B.1225, pp. 73, 75.

[81] Cf., for instance, B.70 in B.813, p. 39 and n; B.158 in B.1056, pp. 53–55; B.1251, pp. 56–65, 104, 130; B.1128, pp. 19–23 (English translation, B.659, pp. 21–26); B.1250, pp. 319–22; B.1012, pp. 225–30; B.1013 in B.1075, p. 26 (2nd ed., p. 23); B.1288, Chapter 4.

[82] Cf. Chapter 3, p. 54, herein; also the first reference in the preceding note.

order to be concrete; hence language is the most primitive form of human personality. Yet this language, which is the ground of our possession of everything that is most truly ours because through it we give determinate form to our own thoughts and feelings, is at the same time essentially *public* and communicable. Even the most private code must have a key.[83] The foundation of Gentile's theory of knowledge is provided by the fact that our very self-consciousness necessarily carries with it the possibility of understanding others, and of their understanding us. He interprets *all* knowledge as an extension of the inner dialectic of subject and object through which we obtain knowledge of ourselves. Everything known is *ipso facto* subjectified and even personified. Our own past becomes an 'other' within us; the moral law speaks in the still small voice of conscience.

But in the last analysis this subjectification of the object does not amount to a really personal relationship. The internal 'friend' is not really what its name implies: it is in fact *pensiero pensato*, the not-self, the object, the past, everything that imposes a moral limit on individual liberty.[84] The dialectic of *pensiero pensante* and *pensiero pensato* may be what constitutes personality, but it is not a dialectic of persons. We have said already that when we identify ourselves with the universal moment of the dialectic there is no social relation between us and our 'enemy.' What we have now to add is that the same is true if we reverse the roles and regard the

---

[83] B.1128, p. 22 (English translation, B.659, pp. 24–25); B.1288, p. 16 (English translation, p. 82).

[84] The way in which, in the *Prolegomena to the Study of the Child*, Gentile equates the internal 'other' of consciousness with the metaphysical object of thought throws light on the passage in the second volume of the *Logic* in which he speaks of Nature being personified and uttering "the great word 'I'" (B.1250, pp. 19–21; cf. Holmes, *The Idealism of Giovanni Gentile*, pp. 79, 169, for a translation of the relevant passages). Holmes objects to this passage as "sheer fancy" (*ibid.*, p. 170), and uses it as a key passage in his indictment of the Ego, which he wishes to see banished from actual idealism. But if he had carefully considered that the 'act of thinking' only becomes determinate through the object thought (its own past), he would have realized why Gentile insists that reality is *personal*. Gentile says that Nature answers thought by saying "I am Nature," in order to indicate that the only 'Nature' that can be known is that which becomes part of the personality of the knower. "It is a law . . . of the knowledge of spiritual reality that *the object be resolved in the subject*" (B.1279, p. 14; cf. English translation, B.660, p. 10). Through this resolution the *person* is constituted; thus the person is not—as Holmes seems to fear—a presupposed ghost, but it is just as essential to Gentile's doctrine as the act of thinking of which it forms the object (cf. the remarks in Chapter 8, p. 283, herein).

object as our 'judge,' as "the first recognition of the law" or "the first tribunal." [85] Self-consciousness, as Gentile expounds it in the *Prolegomena,* involves at best a partnership between 'the Self' and 'the Other' (Man and God) rather than one between 'a self' and 'its own other' (man and man).[86] His theory provides a speculative foundation for the inner acceptance of the State and its laws as a moral authority, but he does not demonstrate the existence of *society* in the inner man.[87]

The reason for his failure is that it is always possible, thus far, to identify the 'other' within the self with one or another of the moments of the dialectic. It is the *enemy,* the particular moment (as in "The Philosophy of the War" and the *Philosophy of Law*) or the judge, the object, God, the universal moment (as in the *Prolegomena to the Study of the Child*). Even the reference in this latter work to the 'other' as 'friend' seems to pass over very easily into the notion of a 'Divine Friend'—"the Holy Ghost, the Comforter." But there is one passage in the second volume of the *Logic* (1922) which does seem to verge on a really 'personal' conception of the internal society:

. . . man in solitude holds a dialogue with himself; he creates his own other within himself; and he labors in the secret colloquy with the interlocutor that he has made for himself in the abstract solitude of his own particular world, in a drama identical with the one in which everyone of us is enmeshed as a particular being engaged in the actual business of living together with the whole world that is ours. He has no less need to come to terms with this secret interlocutor, conquering him or yielding to him or subjecting himself to him; and in him he finds now a satanic tempter, now a mentor austere or gentle, now a criminal or a judge, and in general an associate.[88]

Even the roles and attitudes here suggested—'tempter,' 'mentor,' 'criminal,' 'judge,' 'subjection,' 'conquest'—are slightly suspicious. But the general conception of a dialogue and the concluding char-

---

[85] B.1225, p. 75.

[86] It is interesting to compare G. H. Mead's theory of the "generalized other" as a constitutive element of the self with Gentile's theory in the *Prolegomena.* (For some comparative remarks on Gentile and Mead, see Chapter 8, pp. 261–63, herein.)

[87] Gentile does not appear to have distinguished clearly between the problem of community and the problem of authority. In "The Idea of Monarchy" he sums up his whole theory of *societas in interiore homine* as a theory of the *State in interiore homine.* But it seems to me that there are two distinguishable problems involved (cf. B.504 in B.561, pp. 154–57).

[88] B.1250, p. 110.

acterization of the interlocutor as *un socio* are definitely prophetic
of the doctrine of the *socius* elaborated twenty years later in *Genesis
and Structure of Society*. In their context, however, these few sentences are only intended as a criticism of the classical ideal of the
rational soul at peace with itself in contemplation of the truth.
Gentile is simply seeking to show that the nature of reason precludes all possibility of rest; he is not concerned to make this argument a metaphysical ground for anything. And although both here
and later in the same work he does remark that empirical society
depends ultimately on man's ability to understand his own thoughts
when he "converses with himself and discourses mentally," [89] this is
an argument which we have already found in several of his other
works; the later theory of a transcendental dialogue between self
and *socius* is still only implicit within it. Taken as a whole, the second volume of the *Logic* is thoroughly pervaded with the religious
spirit, the sense of *the* Other, God, Truth, the Law, the Universal;
and it was not until he wrote *Genesis and Structure of Society* that
he systematically developed the implications of the "secret colloquy." Only then did he give an adequate account of *societas in
interiore homine*.[90]

Force and Law

We have already remarked, however, that even if the arguments
of Gentile's early works are not an adequate foundation for a social
theory, they do at least show us what he meant by saying that the
State was internal; and they do provide a firm metaphysical basis for
the moment of authority which he regarded as omnipresent in human society. In the family, authority normally rests with the father;
and in the school it rests with the teacher. But Gentile argues that
even in social relationships like friendship, where authority does
not rest with any of the parties involved, there is an overriding
will that is sovereign. The sovereign will need not *necessarily* be
personified precisely because it is *always* ultimately internal:

. . . the superior directing will . . . gains its title to superiority not
through a mechanical force that works upon the wills subjected to it
from outside, but through the respect (in the widest sense of the term)
of which it appears worthy, and through the intrinsic value that is at-

---

[89] *Ibid.*, p. 320.
[90] See Chapter 8, pp. 254–65, herein.

tributed to it. It is not the master who by his authority gets the truth accepted, but the truth that confers authority on the master. And the *ipse dixit* is not born *ex abrupto;* it presupposes a long-established and well-warranted experience of the master's great familiarity with the secrets of knowledge. In any case, whatever degree of rationality the considerations that induce us to recognize an authority may possess, the authority is only real in virtue of our recognition; and all the speculations, in which philosophers have attempted to base the power of the laws to which our will is subjected on an authority superior to our will, have always been vain logomachies. For it is quite clear that, however exalted this authority may be, it can never be exalted higher than we have ourselves exalted it. Speaking of "authority" is just the same as speaking of "*law*": but of course we are referring to the fundamental law, the law that is absolute.[91]

Our membership of any social organism depends ultimately on our acceptance of the sovereign will that gives it organic form. From this acceptance springs our obedience to particular determinations of the sovereign will in positive laws, and, at the same time, our recognition that these positive laws may be changed. For although the sovereign will is not a thing numerically distinct from its particular determinations, these determinations themselves are never absolute: the law-giving power is inseparable from the laws that it gives, but these laws are not given once and for all—they are always dependent on the sustaining will of the sovereign power, which is identical with the moral conscience of the subject who recognizes his duty in its dictates.

Having thus declared that the sovereign will of the State is identical with the inner conscience of the citizen, Gentile has to face the fact that there is an undeniable and seemingly irreducible element of compulsion in human society.[92] He poses the problem in its most extreme form, by admitting that, from the point of view of a strict naturalism, Spinoza was right in regarding *force* as the basis of legal right; while at the same time, from the spiritual point of view, Rousseau was right in defending the ideal character of law as something distinct from and opposed to brute physical compulsion. This antinomy of legal compulsion arises, says Gentile,

---

[91] B.1157, p. 77. The passage "Comunque, quale che sia il grado di razionalità delle considerazioni che c'inducono a riconoscere un'autorità, questa è reale in forza del nostro riconoscimento . . ." ("In any case, whatever degree of rationality etc.") points forward to the notorious remark about the blackjack as a means of persuasion in *Che cosa è il fascismo* (see Chapter 6, pp. 174–76, herein).

[92] B.1157, Chapter 5, pp. 80–86.

because force can be considered from two quite opposite points of view. Spinoza looks at it from *within*, i.e. from the point of view of the *agent* who employs it; while Rousseau looks at it from *without*, from the point of view of the *patient* against whom it is employed:

> The force of the agent is the affirmation of the spirit, its realization; while the force of the patient (the force that he consciously suffers) is the negation or suppression of spiritual reality. The first indeed generates the second, but only by positing two absolutely different spiritual situations, one of which is the actual creation of spiritual value, and the other of spiritual disvalue. Now, when Spinoza attributes to every individual (we should say, to the spirit) the *ius summum ad omnia quae potest* ["supreme right to everything within its power"], he is thinking of force in the first sense, the sense in which it is creative of value; Rousseau, on the other hand, in denying that force can generate any value, clearly has the second sense of the word in mind.[93]

Thus each side is justified in its own terms; what is needed is a synthesis that takes account of the elements of truth contained in both views. Gentile feels that this has in fact been provided by the idealists. The 'might' that constitutes 'right' in the naturalist theory is not simply a natural fact, completely determined and particular, but a spiritual striving toward universality: "Hegel and Ihering have shown clearly, as Vico had done earlier, how slavery—the institution that typifies the 'law of the stronger'—is the cradle of liberty." [94] Rousseau himself, the severest critic of this 'law of the stronger,' still held that we ought to use force in dealing with children and reason only with adults. Gentile therefore concludes that the problem of physical coercion admits of no precise answer. The important question is always whether the use of force in any actual situation serves a genuine educational purpose; and this means that like every other educational process the coercion must be internalized.[95] But this is almost a tautology for "strictly speaking, external forces simply as such have no value for the spirit, or in other words they do not act or exist as forces." [96] The coercive power of an external force is experienced as *pain*, the inner consciousness of spiritual non-being.

This use of his metaphysical theory of pain in order to put coercion on a par with other methods of education is one of Gentile's

---

[93] *Ibid.*, p. 82.

[94] *Ibid.*, pp. 82–83.

[95] *Ibid.*, pp. 83–84. Gentile himself refers the reader at this point to the first volume of his *Educational Theory*, especially Part II, Chapter 4 (B.1251, pp. 125–31).

[96] B.1157, p. 85.

worst mistakes. His argument is invalid because it rests on the fundamental assumption that his metaphysical theory applies equally to all forms of pain. As we have already pointed out, the theory cannot legitimately be applied to physical pain because, unlike grief, physical pain is not voluntarily accepted. The attitude of the will toward it is entirely negative; it remains simply a natural fact, to be removed if its removal proves to be feasible, or, if not, to be suffered as calmly as possible until an opportunity of escape occurs.[97] Never, except in the last resort, is it accepted with resignation—only what *can't* be cured *must* be endured.

As a transaction between two *persons* physical coercion can establish only a negative relation. In a sense Gentile recognized this, when he pointed out that the spiritual situation of a person suffering violence or coercion is quite different from that of the person who inflicts the violence. But this admission betrays the weakness of his speculative position. He does not seem to see a contradiction between the claim that the 'force of the agent' is an 'affirmation' or 'realization' of the spirit, and the admission that it *generates* the 'force of the patient' by positing two different spiritual situations. A 'realization' of the spirit means a 'universal' value; and it is 'concretely' universal when it is possessed by a community. Thus the very admission that the agent's force generates the patient's is *ipso facto* an admission that it is *not* a realization of the spirit,

---

[97] Cf. Chapter 2, pp. 32–33, herein. Francesco De Sarlo claims that, in his account of pleasure and pain, Gentile confuses the fact of pain as an event of conscious life, with the interpretation of the fact in an ethical and teleological conception of the universe (*Gentile e Croce*, Florence, Le Monnier, 1925, pp. 158–59). Like most of his criticisms, this complaint rests largely on a complete misunderstanding—even, one might say, a willful refusal to understand. For Gentile, the 'fact' of pain—like any other 'fact'—is an abstraction; hence one cannot treat a *determinazione della vita spirituale* as a mere *dato di fatto* as De Sarlo does. In any concrete "determination of the spiritual life" the "factual datum" is only an abstract element, whose objective immediacy or givenness is already resolved into the will of the subject. The *fact* of pain is concretely inseparable from its moral significance for the sufferer: the reality of which he is conscious is the fact in the total context of its interpretation. Thus any kind of pain which is voluntarily accepted is satisfactorily explained even as a 'fact' by Gentile's ethical and teleological interpretation.

Even in the case of physical pain, where, as our discussion seeks to show, there is some truth in De Sarlo's complaint, it is not strictly correct to oppose the 'fact' to the 'interpretation.' The distinction of the fact as 'simply a natural fact' takes place within the interpretation (which is still the total or concrete reality); within this interpretation the fact is opposed to—instead of being identified with—the will of the conscious interpreting subject.

but at best a blundering aspiration toward the spiritual reality that it can never possess until it ceases to be coercion. By using force rather than reason, the agent demonstrates his conviction that only *his* will is of any value: the patient's will is a mere natural obstacle to be subdued, not a living spirit deserving moral respect. Similarly, for the patient the coercive will is simply the non-being of his own spiritual activity, a problem, or an impediment to be removed. Yet each party is aware of the other as a person, and not simply as a natural obstacle to his own self-realization; and, as Gentile himself said in discussing the relation of parents to an unborn child, as soon as we recognize any being as human we are linked to it by moral ties.[98] Hence the two situations—which are indeed "absolutely different" when considered in the abstract, that is from a strictly egoistic point of view—are really elements of a single spiritual whole. The parties themselves bear witness to this, by each declaring that his opponent's will, far from being merely a natural fact, is a positive moral evil—'criminal' says the agent, 'tyrannical' or 'unjust' says the patient. Thus they each give the natural obstacle a moral status but precisely by so doing they destroy any possibility of a 'realization' of the spirit.

The very possibility of a positive relation between persons requires that this kind of moral attitude should be rejected as absolutely *im*moral. "Condemn not, that ye be not condemned," "Love your enemies," "Bless them that persecute you," says the Gospel; for until we can admit that our opponent's will is in some fundamental sense 'good,' we can achieve nothing because we lack the good will in ourselves. When he recognizes the 'patient' as a person, the 'agent' is logically bound to recognize at the same time a moral obligation to come to an agreement with him about the nature and value of any act in which they may both be involved. The moment of compulsion is the negative moment of the dialectic, the moment of multiplicity and opposition, and this opposition can find its meaning only in the synthesis. Every action involves, in some degree, the use of force; so that all 'agents' must look to their 'patients' for the only moral justification they can ever hope to receive.

In short, Gentile's distinction of the aspects of force possesses only a negative significance. To suppose that it gives us grounds for adopting the positive point of view of the agent would be to

---

[98] B.718 in B.1056, p. 92; cf. p. 82, herein.

reduce actual idealism to the crudest kind of moral solipsism. The separation of 'my' act from the action as it appears to those who 'suffer' it is, in reality, only a refined form of the old distinction between 'intention' and 'result,' which did so much to make 'casuistry' a word of opprobrium. In common parlance the tendency to separate these two aspects of a single indivisible whole is called 'hypocrisy'; and if I have rightly understood the ethical significance of Gentile's philosophy, hypocrisy, in his system, is the sin against the Holy Ghost.

Fortunately, however, this dangerous, indeed disastrous, tendency is not the only one that is apparent in his theory. Just as in his account of school discipline, so here in his analysis of legal coercion there are two distinguishable lines of thought, one of which is more truly in accord with the general spirit of actual idealism than the other.[99] Alongside his attempt to prove that all force is fundamentally spiritual in character (which corresponds to his justification of punishment as the 'right of the future' and his insistence that the authority of the master must be maintained, since even tyranny does not really suppress liberty), there is his insistence that force must evolve into reason and that the law immanent in compulsion should become the conscious will of the person subjected to it (which corresponds to his declaration that the real meaning of punishment lies in the pupil's sense of the *dissidio* between himself and the teacher). From this latter point of view 'might' is never 'right' until it ceases to be regarded as 'might'; and the employment of physical force for a moral purpose must therefore involve an act of faith. Unless the faith is justified the morality of the act will remain merely subjective and abstract. There is no way out of this dilemma. The action of the court which passes sentence on a criminal is *actually* moral precisely so far as the judge and criminal eventually come to agree that the sentence is or was deserved. The spiritual reality of all coercion lies not in pain simply, but in repentance, which is a *self-imposed* 'pain' arising from an active change of heart; and this in turn is not simply a change of outward behavior, though it can only receive concrete expression through such a change.[100] The coercive power of the law is intended to procure the real inward change; the way in which this

---

[99] Cf. pp. 84–94, herein.
[100] Cf. Spaventa, *Principi di etica* (B.98), pp. 106–14.

should be done, and the circumstances under which it *can* be done, are matters of vital moral principle, not merely empirical questions of what is practicable or politically expedient, as Gentile seems to have assumed.[101]

Law and Morality

Having dealt with the problem of legal coercion, we come finally to the question of how positive law is related to the moral law. As we might expect, Gentile bases his answer on the familiar distinction between act and fact, *pensiero pensante* and *pensiero pensato*. The actual moral will (*pensiero pensante*) is a synthetic union of self-consciousness with consciousness, of will as activity (*volere come volere*) and will as object (*volere come voluto*).[102] Positive law falls naturally enough into the category of *pensiero pensato;* it is the objective content of the moral will, its past. Thus it has two aspects, depending on whether it is considered as a term within the synthesis (i.e. as consciousness) or in abstraction (as potential consciousness, or a mere content of consciousness). As a concrete actuality (i.e. within the synthesis) it is internal to the will of the citizen. But it can be separated from the will, and considered abstractly in itself; indeed, if this analysis and abstraction did not take place in ordinary experience, development would be impossible, and we should not be able to talk of the will at all, for there would be nothing in the world except mechanical instinct. It is through the process of abstraction that we free ourselves from the burden of the past and continually reassert our freedom.

At this point a serious problem arises, for, as we saw, Gentile has already used this same distinction of *pensante* and *pensato* to elucidate the problem of good and evil.[103] He argued then that evil is the metaphysical past of the good act—the abstract content of the purifying consciousness which judges and so 'overcomes' it. In applying the same pattern of analysis to positive law he certainly cannot mean to imply that law, considered abstractly, is identical

---

[101] This point is developed somewhat in the following section (pp. 120–21). The consequences of Gentile's error will be seen in his apologia for Fascist violence (see Chapter 6, pp. 174–77, herein). For a full discussion the reader should refer to the conclusion of the present inquiry (Chapter 9, pp. 307–30).
[102] B.1157, p. 87.
[103] Cf. pp. 98–101 herein.

with 'evil.' In order to see how this conclusion is avoided, we must examine carefully what Gentile says about the process of abstraction:

> The separation of the object willed [*il voluto*] from the act of willing [*il volere*] manifestly transforms the object of present will [*l'attuale voluto*] into an object of past will [*il già voluto*] but without thereby withdrawing it from the dialectic of the will. If the object willed were thus withdrawn it is clear that it would become a nullity [*cadrebbe nel nulla*], since the spiritual dialectic of the spirit exhausts all being; and to go completely outside the circle of this dialectic must mean annihilation. But the object willed is not annihilated; and it is not annihilated because it is spirit, even if it is only a negative form. It is conserved in its negativity. I will *a;* and I am *a;* but if I did not will something else, I should not will any longer; hence I should not be *a,* for I am *a* only while I will to be *a.* Hence to have willed *a* [*voler già a*] involves willing a^1, a^2, a^3, etc.; and willing a^1 means no longer willing *a* (which would involve not willing a^1); and if I am to will a^2, I cannot any longer will a^1, and so on. In short, willing something involves unwilling it [*disvolerlo*], by willing an object that contains the first will-object [*voluto*] but in a higher form, in which it is to go on realizing itself ever more completely through the dialectic.[104]

Il già voluto would seem to be identified here with the absolute Object recognized in the religious moment of spiritual development, and with the 'Other' involved in the transcendental society.[105] It is past and complete but it is not dead (evil). It is a negative form of the spirit because its life, its spiritual reality, consists in being continually *negated* as an object in order to be preserved in the subject. Simple contemplation of it is not possible because consciousness is essentially activity. Hence when some definite goal has been achieved, and the process of actual willing is complete, the object in which the satisfied will comes to rest can only continue to possess spiritual value in virtue of a new volition for its active preservation and defense.

Thus, considered simply as *past,* whatever the spirit has already willed is simply a brute fact that compels our attention. We may grant it not merely attention but respect, in which case it is "conserved in its negativity," it becomes *law,* the force that is freedom;

---

[104] B.1157, p. 88; cf. Spaventa, *Principi di etica* (B.98), p. 114.

[105] I am referring, of course, to the transcendental society as expounded in the *Prolegomena* and other writings of this period. The 'other' who is *socius* in the *Genesis and Structure of Society* is a *person* who cannot and must not be identified with *il già voluto* or any other pure *category.*

or we may decide that it ought to be "annihilated" as evil.[106] For a time we may even be neutral. In action that is only outward obedience to the law, the law itself represents merely the limit of the freedom that belongs essentially to the act, and so long as it appears simply as a limit we are aware of it merely as force. But when we recognize it as a necessary condition of our present freedom it gains moral and spiritual value, and becomes a standard to which our action must now conform, on a par with anything that we approve of as right or good in our own personal past. The philosophy of law therefore is an aspect of moral philosophy and the two are concretely identical. Law is the past of morality, but it is the past *of the present,* the living content which gives to the present its determinate individuality. To use a traditional Hegelian phrase, the past is *aufgehoben;* as particular (evil) it is canceled, but as universal (law) it is preserved.

Gentile derives some interesting and important corollaries from this thesis about the relation of law to morality. To begin with, he thinks that in the light of it the traditional opposition between *lex* and *ius* can be seen to be merely an abstract antithesis, originating in that first moment of the dialectic when the law is not really law at all but sheer force. 'Rights' are in fact simply the correlatives of the 'duties' imposed by the law. The 'subjective' right of a creditor exists inasmuch as there is an 'objective' right (a law) which obliges the debtor to pay him what is owing. The universal force of this objective right is, according to Gentile, the only spiritual reality; [107] and in it debtor and creditor are one, their right is completely identical. That is why *consciousness* of a subjective right is unimpor-

---

[106] It is easy to see, therefore, that Father Chiocchetti's summing up of Gentile's theory of evil—"Evil is what I thought (or willed) last year, yesterday, a moment ago!" (*La filosofia di Giovanni Gentile,* p. 297)—is only a travesty of Gentile's meaning; and Croce's criticism, which Chiocchetti cites with approval, really expresses Gentile's own opinion: "The past! But when I (or anyone else) examine the propositions I have uttered in the past, I distinguish quite clearly those of them which were thoughts, poor thoughts, but now revived and enriched in new thought, from those that were not thoughts, but mere sounds without meaning, or at least without precise meaning, suggested or imposed on me by the practical situations in which I found myself. And I feel pleased with myself about the former, while for the latter I blush. . . . And so likewise, among my past actions, I distinguish those which pass calmly before the eye of conscience from those others that disturb me as evils that must be amended . . ." (*Conversazioni critiche,* II, 76).

[107] For a criticism of this view see n112 below.

tant. A man *has* rights quite regardless of whether he avails himself of them or not.

Another traditional problem that vanishes is that of the *princeps legibus solutus*. For legal coercion is not the activity of an independent sovereign power upon its subjects; it is the moral experience of the subjects operating in and upon their present wills. Ideally, the coercive power of the law has nothing to do with the existence of empirical sanctions or guarantees, though there is a natural tendency to buttress anything recognized as law in such a way that it will command respect and obedience. The real 'sanction' of the law is the respect that it commands when it appears to us simply as law, that is, as a voluntary decision (*un voluto*) which is not identical with our present activity of willing but forms its proper content.[108]

The most important and the most dubious of these corollaries, however, concerns 'freedom of conscience.' Gentile contends that once we have understood the ideal *inward* character of law we are bound to see that any attempt to distinguish the 'inner' life of the person from the public life of the citizen is foredoomed to failure. In defense of the distinction he quotes Spinoza:

. . . no one can transfer to another his natural right, or his faculty of reasoning freely and of judging about any matters, nor can he be compelled to do this. Hence it is that the exercise of authority over men's minds is regarded as violence, and that the highest majesty is seen to do wrong to its subjects and to usurp their right when it wishes to prescribe to each what is to be embraced as truth and what rejected as falsehood, and even by what opinions the mind of each individual is to be swayed in his devotion to God; for these questions belong to the right of every man, which no man can surrender even if he wishes to.[109]

But he considers that this argument must give way before the reply that he borrows from Augustine:

It is better indeed (who would doubt it?) that men should be led to God's service by teaching, than that they should be driven to it by the fear of or the actual pain of a penalty. But the fact that the better sort follow the better way is no reason for neglecting those who are incapable

---

[108] We might say, from another point of view, that Gentile has not abolished the antinomy but exacerbated it, by substituting an internal relation for the traditional external empirical one. For man as a moral philosopher (which means every man faced with a moral problem) is literally *legibus solutus*. His decision creates the law that he obeys, so that he is at once bound and not bound by the law.

[109] *Tractatus theologico-politicus, cap.* 20; cf. B.1157, pp. 95–96n.

of it. For it has profited many (as we have found and are finding in practice) to be driven first by fear or actual pain, in order that they may later be taught, or may translate into deeds what they have already learned in words.[110]

Here again, Gentile leans too heavily on his metaphysical explanation of pain. Only when an individual feels that his existence as a person is being respected is there any hope that he will really learn his lesson, no matter what compulsion is employed. If he feels that his personality is being violated, the coercion will appear to him simply as *evil* (the 'past' that is a natural obstacle to be annulled) and not as *law* (the 'past' that is deserving of moral respect). He may submit outwardly until he gains courage to assert his moral character in political rebellion or social revolution; his will may even be completely broken—but then he will never be able to learn anything properly. In view of the fundamental importance of conscious mediation in Gentile's writings and his claim that thought is always free and self-critical, Spinoza's position seems far more consonant with the spirit of actual idealism than the strict dogmatic attitude of St. Augustine on this point.[111]

Finally, whether or not we agree that the resolution of law into morality helps to solve or avoid traditional difficulties, there is no doubt that it raises one ancient problem in its most extreme form. If all law is moral law, how can any law be unjust? Here Gentile reaps the benefit of the paradoxical proximity of law to evil in his dialectic. He defines both terms as 'the past of the will,' and then, as we saw, he has to distinguish the *non-being* of the spirit which is

---

[110] *De correctione Donatistarum* (Epistle 185), *cap.* 6 (Migne, *P.L.*, XXXIII, 802); cf. B.1157, p. 96n.

[111] We know, of course, that what justifies Augustine's appeal to force in Gentile's mind is the educational aim (*ut postea possent doceri*). But if to be *taught* something means not just to be convinced, but to understand, Spinoza's position is unassailable. The *imperium quod in animos est* can only be used to establish a faith which is either above or beneath the level of human intelligence. Gentile unwittingly anticipates here the educational policies of the Fascist regime. I say "unwittingly" because when he was actually faced with the *imperium in animos* he seems to have perceived his error. He declared in the senate in 1926 that an intellectual dictatorship was a *controsenso*, and that in the field of thought there is no life without liberty and autonomy (B.877 in B.937, pp. 130–31). This is just a moralized version of Spinoza's more neutral statement. In the later years of the Regime he often protested that an undue emphasis on discipline and the religious attitude typified by St. Augustine's argument would lead to merely formal obedience and internal rottenness (see Chapter 6, pp. 206–7, etc., herein; and for a discussion of the whole problem of toleration and freedom of thought, see Chapter 9, pp. 323–30, herein).

abstracted as past in order to be annihilated, from its *being* which is abstracted (negated) in order to be preserved. In the limiting case of the unjust law, the moral being of the spirit passes over into its non-being (evil). The law must therefore be abrogated. But until it is abrogated by due process of law, it must be obeyed:

. . . for since the unjust law, as long as it is not yet abrogated, is the will of that State which is immanent in the citizen, its injustice is not wholly injustice. Rather we may call it a justice *in fieri*, which will mature little by little to the point when the law itself is abrogated. And the citizen who obeys it, despite his recognition of its injustice, does not really obey *that* law, but a higher law that *is* just, of which the unjust law is a particular detail that can only be corrected if the higher law is observed, as Plato demonstrates in the *Crito*.[112]

The Theory of Monarchy

In an essay written shortly after the first World War Gentile considered the question of how this higher law can *best* be determined in a system of government.[113] In classical theory this appears as the problem of the 'ideal constitution'; but Gentile grants at the outset that this is only a pseudo problem, since the way that a State is organized is a function of the special historical tradition and evolution of a community. We must therefore, presumably, take his argument in favor of monarchy as a demonstration of the philosophical coherence of the Risorgimento, rather than as a criticism of constitutions having a different tradition behind them. But the arguments that he employs are a priori ones derived from his general speculative theory; so that they do represent criteria applicable to *any* situation, and we can say that even if there is no perfect constitution, there are at least certain canons by which all sound constitutional development must be guided.

The State is the authority which appears to us as the universality

---

[112] B.1157, p. 102. Antonio was therefore morally obliged to honor his immoral bond—but was Shylock morally justified in insisting on his legal right, let alone morally obliged to insist on it? Or again: it has been observed that where trial by jury exists, a jury will tend to acquit rather than condemn an accused person, even when his guilt is clear, if the penalty appointed by law appears to them to be unduly severe. Is such evasion necessarily immoral? I think that Gentile goes too far in his insistence that 'objective' right is all that counts. 'Subjective' right plays an important part in the dialectic of legal history. It has a real, though negative, spiritual influence—which is exerted through a deliberate *refusal* by the individual to exercise his right, or by the community to impose penalties that infringe it.

[113] B.504 in B.561, pp. 147–61.

of our own moral will. Its constitution or fundamental law is the moment of passage, the point at which the moral law passes over into positive law; and since we are none of us moral without a struggle this passage exhibits for us a double aspect. On the one hand it is something required of us (the law, authority, our duty); and on the other hand it is something we have actually achieved (autonomy, freedom, our right). No State, however autocratic, could long endure without the consent of the governed; and the good State is the one which genuinely expresses the will of its citizens, whether it is formally classified as a 'democracy' or as a 'tyranny.' But if it did not first appear to us as a transcendent power we could not be free moral beings, for we could not exert our freedom in order to become moral. It represents, so to speak, the religious moment in the cosmic process of education, the fear of the Lord that is the beginning of wisdom. So that the thesis that all government rests on the consent of the governed must be complemented by its antithesis: no government, however democratic or libertarian, can exist without authority backed by force. Since the moment of authority is eternally necessary to the dialectic of social existence, the distinction between government and governed, sovereign and people will always exist in any political situation. The ideal of a classless society or a perfect democracy is an illusion: "The notion of a State involves law and authority. This authority cannot but present itself initially as a limit to liberty, precisely in order that liberty may be able to express itself in its full concrete infinity. And all authorities based on election presuppose an authority that legitimates the election." [114]

A constitution will only be stable if it gives determinate existence of some kind to the eternal moments of the dialectic. But, on the other hand, the embodiment of the moment of authority cannot be complete and perfect, for its existence, even as a limit, must already contain the possibility of its being overcome. All authority is properly internal; it is an activity of self-limitation, and its final destiny is to be recognized as such and become identified with the liberty of the subject. It is not the free activity of the will that presupposes the limit, but rather the limit that presupposes the free activity:

Thus there is the activity that posits the limit, the limiting activity [*l'attività limite*]; and there is the activity that is faced with the limit, and recognizes it as its own limit: the limited activity [*l'attività limitata*].

[114] *Ibid.*, p. 157. For Gentile's views on democracy cf. B.518.

There is the free popular will that creates, maintains, and guards the State, and there is the will that fulfills and resolves its own liberty in the recognition of the State that it has itself created. Without this circle of the will, at once the beginning and the end of political reality, politics becomes quite inconceivable to us moderns; for we recognize the completely spiritual nature of the State, and the consequent necessity of its immanence in the spirit.[115]

Now the only kind of existence that is determinate yet at the same time spiritual is *personal* existence; it follows therefore that the representative of the general will should rightly be a specific limited human person rather than a fundamental law or charter which is fixed, final, and inviolable.[116] The monarch represents tradition, but not in a dogmatically determinate form. By reason of his own personal limitations he is a living proof of the possibility of further progress. His will is the 'natural' root of the State—a firm and abiding point of reference throughout all the changes and vicissitudes of the popular will in its history:

Constitutionality, as Kant observed, makes a monarchy resemble a republic; but its hereditary character withdraws the monarchic regime from the vast, infinite field over which it is right that the liberty of the popular will should range and come to fulfillment, making the State in its original nucleus an antecedent of liberty, and a secure guarantee of its every possible experiment. The hereditary character of the supreme power in the State introduces a quasi-natural element into the realm of politics [*il circolo della volontà politica*]. . . .[117]

The phrase "a quasi-natural element" should prepare us for what follows by recalling to our minds the 'quasi-natural' character of the bond that binds the family together. The authority of the monarchy, Gentile concludes, can only have a 'natural' value if the nature is *our own*, and is recognized—or, in other words, felt [118]— as such:

---

[115] *Ibid.*, p. 158.

[116] It is very important to understand the argument leading to this conclusion, if we wish to comprehend why Gentile acted as he did when faced with the Armistice in 1943. It is because the limit is not something complete and absolute but a *product* of free activity that it should properly be represented by a human person. But equally because it is not absolute it may be renounced. Thus the ground of Gentile's monarchism is also the ground of his right to reject the king's government as he did.

[117] *Ibid.*, p. 159.

[118] As in the case of the family bond it is the feeling that creates the bond itself, and only the relatively immediate quality of the feeling that gives it the apparent immutability of a natural instinct (cf. pp. 81–84, herein).

A people . . . has in its monarchy the basis of its political life, but only insofar as it has an immediate sense of the monarchy as its own, as something which is completely at one with its tradition, with its past, with that personality which is the heritage of its historical experience, and on which it must lean in facing the history that is to come. The person of the King is that sacred, inviolable person which the citizen must find, if he can, at the heart of his consciousness of the nation; it is his own true personality. And where this profound inward unity has not been formed, or has disappeared, the legitimacy, which gives spiritual value to the institution and authority of the monarchy, is lacking or has died out. For in such a case the duality exists, but it is not a duality that can be conciliated in the peaceable process of actual political life, since the fundamental unity is lacking out of which the two terms ought to have arisen.[119]

Culture as a National and Universal Ideal

We have now reached the point at which we can survey Gentile's theory as a whole. The moral community which Socrates exalts in the *Crito* under the name of 'the City' is replaced in Gentile's view by the Nation-State as symbolized in the person of its monarch. But the underlying pattern remains Socratic. The essential task of education is to produce good citizens, and the good citizen is one who hears the voice of 'the State' within him. Like Socrates' City, Gentile's State is an ideal entity, not to be confused with the government that exists at any given moment. But in an idealism that strives to be strictly historical, the distinction between State and government, though always asserted when the point is raised by critics, is hard to maintain in practice. The strong emphasis on individual personality that is fundamental to actual idealism makes it tempting to pass over the ordinary citizen and exalt the heroic leaders who personify the ideals that lesser men ought simply to accept.

This temptation is very apparent in Gentile's lectures to the elementary-school teachers of Trieste in 1919. The existence of a

---

[119] B.504 in B.561, pp. 160-61. This passage presents us with yet another version of the theory of society *in interiore homine*—and a much sounder one than that which is based on the metaphysical principle of conflict. But, although it is also more definitely personal than other expressions of the doctrine, it reveals quite clearly the basic difficulty in Gentile's early view. Can we really establish social relations with a king *as king*—sacred, inviolable, 'the Lord's Anointed One'?

Nation, he declares at the beginning, is not necessarily dependent on community of territory or language, or even on cultural tradition, though any or all of these elements may assume special significance in national life when the Nation is once established. Despite all appearances it is the 'State' which constitutes the 'Nation,' not vice versa; where by 'State' we mean the fundamental community of will that expresses or at least strives to express itself in all the institutions of social life.

Because it is this community of will that is important and not any quasi-natural community or heritage, there can be no 'natural right' to nationhood. The Nation, as Mazzini saw, is a *mission*. Its right to exist is not a natural property but a spiritual conquest; it is not established in law courts but on the battlefield.[120] Nor is it ever established finally and completely—the national mission is something essentially incomplete. It is not strictly correct to say that any community is already a Nation-State, for the State is always something that we have to establish, here and now, by our own action.

But after clearly affirming this Socratic conception of the State as an ideal, Gentile proceeds directly in his second lecture to assert that any act of will that is successful is *ipso facto* the will of the State. This would mean that, by and large, the State is equivalent to the government, as long as the government—however tyrannical—can maintain its power. Gentile himself admits this: ". . . the tyrant destroys the liberty of the *patria* by substituting a new State for the old; likewise the rebel, by killing the tyrant, makes the revolution if he succeeds, and establishes liberty. And if he does not succeed, he is conquered, and his will returns to subjection and conformity with that of the State he could not overthrow."[121]

The ideal mission of the State has scarcely any place in a historicism as strict as this, for it can scarcely be called moral at all.[122] Yet Gentile would certainly not admit that his historicism is amoral. He would argue that such a criticism can only be advanced from an

---

[120] B.1128, pp. 9–12; cf. English translation (B.659), pp. 8–12. For the political undertones of this statement see Chapter 5, pp. 140–41, herein.

[121] B.1128, p. 26; cf. English translation (B.659), p. 31.

[122] The actual idealists claimed that Croce's view that the individual is never, properly speaking, responsible for any action destroyed the basis of morality. But this same conclusion seems to be an inescapable corollary of their own theory, if what the individual really wills is always precisely what the sovereign power wills that he should will (cf. B.1128, p. 25; or English translation, B.659, p. 29).

intellectual or external point of view, and that the ostensible equivocation between the assertion that the State is always an *ideal* and the apparently contrary assertion that it is the only *reality* arises from a refusal to adopt a strictly spiritual, internal point of view in both cases. The State is always an ideal for those who belong to it, though in a tyranny such spiritual citizenship may well be almost totally confined to the ranks of the tyrants themselves.

This, however, does not solve the problem: the State is *either* an ideal *or* it is the reality. It cannot without equivocation be both at once even in a dialectical theory of history. For if the State is the moral ideal, and at the same time it is the one effective will as opposed to the many vain strivings after the impossible, there can be no moral duty except that of being on the winning side. Gentile must tell us whether it is our duty to be successful or to abide by the dictates of our conscience.

His response to this challenge can be clearly seen in his own career: the ideal was more 'real' for him than any existent entity. "One must walk as conscience wills. This I have preached all my life," he wrote at a moment of crisis shortly before his death.[123] When he says that the only real will is that of the State, he means that everything that is real is real precisely insofar as it realizes the ideal. "The State, in short, is not moral inasmuch as it is a State; but it is a State inasmuch as it is moral." [124]

It follows that actual existence cannot be the criterion of goodness, and that Gentile's historicism does not preclude the possibility of moral judgment. The pity is that he often talks as if existence were the criterion of goodness and not vice versa. It is nonsense, for instance, to say that a would-be tyrannicide who fails is *ipso facto* vanquished. He may die the death of a martyr, and symbolize the aspirations of his people for centuries. History offers many instances of individuals who opposed the will of existing authorities and were crushed, but who achieved more universal significance in death than they ever had while they were alive. Consider Socrates, for example, or Giordano Bruno, who, like Socrates, told his judges that they who sentenced him stood in greater fear than he who was condemned: did *their* wills return to conformity with that of the State which they could not overcome? The focusing of attention upon successful action because it represents the final concreteness of actual existence

---

[123] *Vita e pensiero*, IV, 40 (letter to his daughter Teresa).
[124] B.474 in B.497, p. 216; cf. B.382 in B.497, p. 52.

destroys the ethical significance of historical idealism.[125] It involves a shortsighted and narrow-minded interpretation which coincides at the extreme limit with the crudest positivism or naturalism. Morally speaking it is the apotheosis of hypocrisy.

The regulative ideal toward which the Nation-State conceived as a moral mission aspires is what Gentile calls 'culture.' As the supreme form of internal community culture forms the copestone of his conception of personality. The man of culture is one who, while submitting to the discipline of objectivity, remains conscious that his acceptance of the world is fundamentally a subjective act of will. He acts responsibly, but with a due awareness that the responsibility is his own. He does not simply look after his own personal interests but strives to do justice to the universal interests of his community; and he does not merely accept those interests as they are presented to him in existent institutions or traditions; he criticizes the world. He is no longer simply being educated—he has become an educator.

As we saw earlier in the present chapter, Gentile opposes this dynamic conception of cultural tradition to the ordinary 'realistic' view of it as something preserved in books and libraries. Knowledge, in his view, must be an active force, guiding the personal life of a cultured individual and gradually reshaping the whole of the community. The ideal of 'pure scholarship' or contemplative knowledge is itself just like a dream; [126] and the proper task of the school is to awaken man from the dream of childhood, not to deceive him with a new kind of mirage.

The 1914–18 war provided Gentile with a magnificent opportunity to show how the ideal of culture, even in the most strictly academic sense of the word, could be an active force. He extolled it in his lecture on "The Philosophy of the War" as the basic unity which alone could give meaning to the conflict. For no one could be

---

[125] As does the insistence upon the metaphysical *superamento* of pain and evil—and for the same reason. In the present case the source of Gentile's error seems to be an excess of patriotic fervor rather than the desire for an easy speculative victory. We should remember that these early lectures in *The Reform of Education* were addressed to an Italian audience in a city which had just been liberated after a very hard war which ended with Italy's one great victory. One cannot but regret, however, that this blemish should occur in what is, on the whole, the most attractive of Gentile's works, and far the best introduction to his thought that has been written by anybody. (For Gentile's feelings during his visit to Trieste, see B.539.)

[126] B.416 in B.937, pp. 8–11.

our enemy if he did not "share with us in a community that is the root both of our spiritual being and of his"; and from this it follows that

. . . our being is not confined within our "Country" egoistically understood; and that for very love of our Country, in order that it may have its proper value, and our devotion to it may be sanctified in the absolute act that is our duty, we must all of us look beyond our Country to a higher end.

Our Country is a sacred thing, but only if it lives in hearts sanctified by agreement with the absolute will of God: governed, that is, by the universal laws of the spirit. A people firm in its loyalty to Country above all else is certainly a strong people, a people that has in itself the stuff of greatness; but the greatness is barbaric, and therefore bound to fall. . . .

Our Country is not an end in itself, any more than the individual is an end in himself. The only end in itself is the spirit, which becomes real in the one and through the other. The same humanity lives and moves both within and beyond the frontier: the humanity that constitutes our whole value, everything that we are and that we wish to defend.[127]

This fundamental common humanity is embodied in the cultural tradition of the civilized world. It was therefore the duty of philosophers and men of letters, according to Gentile, to emphasize this common human heritage and keep the universality of cultural values unsullied by partisan emotions. As we shall see in the next chapter, his own practical activity was, in fact, largely guided by this ideal throughout the conflict.

It must be noted, however, that Gentile's own conception of the supreme ideal has still something of the flavor of 'pure scholarship' about it. Most of his writings and speeches were, of course, addressed to an audience which like himself was professionally interested in culture in the academic, intellectual sense of the word; and it was therefore natural for him to think primarily in academic terms. But even when he spoke or wrote for a nonacademic public—which was comparatively rarely—he never gave to 'culture' the broad sense that it must have if it is to serve as an ideal for ordinary men, and not simply for scholars;[128] and one cannot escape an uneasy suspicion that his theory of society rests on an aristocracy of the intellect very similar to that of Plato. In his ideal world the philosopher should be king, and those who

---

[127] B.306 in B.497, pp. 18–19.
[128] Cf. B.416 and B.658 in B.937, pp. 1–37. The comments of this paragraph should be read in the light of the discussions in Chapter 3, pp. 45–62, and Chapter 8, pp. 273–78, herein.

understand should have the authority to teach those who do not. His unwillingness to allow doubt and argument to enter education below the university level means inevitably that only the so-called 'upper' classes can be cultured in the creative sense that he gives to the word. For the ordinary citizen, the will of the real State—the 'governing class'—must suffice. The guardians of the ideal, who spur the governors to self-criticism, are the university professors.

It is important to recognize that the notion of a governing elite is not a necessary corollary of Gentile's philosophy. Obviously any attempt to divide the world neatly into educators and educated could only succeed through drastic oversimplification; in reality we all have something to teach and a great deal to learn. By emphasizing the fact that each has a contribution to make, a proper balance can be restored to his theory. But this means that we must resist all temptation to personify the moments of the dialectic. The State is an ideal; it cannot and must not be identified with a human personality or group. So that a really scrupulous regard for the spirit of Gentile's philosophy is all that is needed to destroy the foundations of his Fascism.

V

THE FIRST WORLD WAR
AND AFTER (1914-22)

War and Nationalism

The period during which Gentile was developing the systematic
views summarized in the last chapter was also that which saw the
beginning of his career in politics. Before the first war his practical
activity was mainly confined within the charmed circle of the
academic world. By environmental tradition and personal inclination he was a 'Liberal of the Right,' that is to say, a conservative in
the tradition of Cavour, and a strong supporter of the national State
against the proletarian internationalism of the 'Reds' and the clerical
universalism of the 'Blacks.' But his main interest was centered in
the field of educational reform, and it was only his strong feelings
about Italy's part in the war that led him to take an active part in
general politics.

When the war broke out in 1914, Italy was not immediately involved, and it was by no means certain that she ever would be.
Gentile was, as he confessed publicly after Caporetto, an interventionist from the beginning. But he took the view that private
citizens, and even politicians, should keep their opinions to themselves and leave the king's ministers free to take whatever action
seemed best.[1] Party conflict and the free play of opinion were essential to the normal political life of the nation. But a moment of

---

[1] This was the policy that he advocated in his lecture of October 1914 on
"The Philosophy of the War" (B.306 in B.497, pp. 1–24), which was his
first public utterance on the subject. But see more particularly B.333 in B.497,
pp. 25–31, where by tacit use of the principle *salus populi suprema lex* Gentile

national peril was a time for resolution, not for bickering: the motto for the moment should be *provideant consules ne quid respublica detrimenti capiat.*

In this same year Donato Jaja died and Gentile succeeded to his former teacher's chair, moving from Palermo to Pisa. There he became a member of the city's Committee for Civil Preparation and Mobilization; but although Italy entered the war on the side of the Allies in May 1915, he was not directly concerned with the war during its first two years. Like Croce he devoted himself rather to the defense of the world of academic studies against the twin heresies of war hysteria and extreme nationalism.[2] He condemned heartily the general tendency to decry all things German, greeting the popular thesis that everything of value in German philosophy derived from French sources with the comment that if it was true that Kant would not have been what he was but for the influence of Rousseau, it was also true that he found truths in Rousseau which other readers had not recognized: "So that even as a condition of Kant, Rousseau is important not because he *was* a condition, but because Kant made him one." [3]

It was, of course, undeniable that much nineteenth-century German scholarship and speculation was marred by nationalistic excesses of the same kind; and Gentile did not try to blink the fact. But he emphasized that in this respect two blacks did not make a white: "If Fichte was wrong in considering his own as the chosen people, there is no need to commit a like error, when one seeks to confute him." [4] One ought to seek out the kernel of truth even in one's opponent's errors. Gentile himself absolutely rejected the gos-

---

subsumes this case under his general philosophy of law: ". . . just as a single man has no real individuality or will of his own, when every conflict of motives remains unresolved in his mind, so there is no real Nation or State where the parties do not submit loyally to the law, even though it may not conform to their aspirations: to that law which has in fact emerged as the resolution and composition of the mutually conflicting social forces that contribute to the life of the State" (p. 27).

[2] Here again he was following the policy laid down in "The Philosophy of the War"; cf. Chapter 4, pp. 128–29, herein.

[3] B.361 in B.497, p. 168.

[4] *Ibid.*, p. 173. Shortly after Italy entered the war, Gentile himself reviewed an Italian translation of the *Addresses to the German Nation*. Instead of the mordant criticism that would have been so easy and must have seemed so tempting, he gave it very sympathetic treatment, quietly pointing out that Fichte's belief in the essential superiority of the German people was merely a personal prejudice which ought not to blind us to the value and importance of his speculative theory of nationality (B.341 in B.497, pp. 156–61).

pel of German imperialism with its tacit assumption that might was right; he regarded Treitschke's doctrine that the State is a mere concentration of power as a sophism. But he always insisted that it was only a perversion of what was originally a sound tradition; and even while the tide was finally turning against Germany we find him insisting that the Latin nations could learn an important lesson from this tradition.[5] The Germans had long understood that liberty was impossible without law, and that power—even moral power—was inseparable from discipline. The great tradition of German idealism had not lost its value simply because certain elements of it had been taken out of context and shockingly misused by propagandists.[6]

This critical defense of the cultural tradition of the enemy was accompanied by a severe critique of the nationalist extremists at home. Gentile's relations with the Italian Nationalist party were always ambivalent. He shared in their reverence for the Nation but he felt that they did not really understand the logic of their own position. It seemed to him that many nationalists tended to regard the Nation as an existent entity which it was the citizen's duty to guard like a loyal watchdog; and even those who knew better still treated it as a presupposition, an outward reality rather than an inward ideal.[7]

Their contempt for the liberal tradition and liberal values he could not understand. In 1918 the Nationalist leader Corradini published a book called *The Regime of the Productive Bourgeoisie*, the central thesis of which was that the liberal parliamentary system was a fraud: political power ought to belong to the productive members of the community, and especially to the active bourgeoisie who controlled the processes of production. His argument foreshadowed the Fascist Corporate State; and for this reason Gentile's reaction is especially interesting. He agreed that the party conflict typical of democratic government was only possible where the basic structure of the State was strong and stable. But he felt that the essential liberal tradition had always presupposed a strong State, and that by confusing liberalism with individualism the Nationalists

---

[5] B.468 and B.432 in B.497, pp. 195–206, especially pp. 202–3; cf. B.433 in B.497, pp. 207–12. Even when analyzing the spiritual weakness of *Realpolitik* in order to explain the significance of the Allied victory, he still drew attention to its positive value (B.408 in B.561, pp. 11–14).

[6] B.474 in B.497, pp. 213–18; cf. B.480 in B.497, pp. 219–23.

[7] B.382 (March 1917) in B.497, pp. 48–52.

were helping to destroy the things in which they most believed: ". . . I cannot grasp the reason for the author's pitiless aversion to liberalism, which—though it may be convenient enough for the Socialists to confuse it with individualism—was never individualist except in its origins in natural law theory, and then only for completely transitory reasons of history."[8]

Gentile continued to carry out in this way the policy which he had advocated at the outset of the war, until the great Italian defeat at Caporetto in October 1917. He had become a contributor to the Bologna newspaper *Resto del Carlino* early in the year, writing at first only occasionally and on cultural topics. But he was apparently a member of the editorial board, and when the crisis came he produced a steady stream of articles and editorials, signed and unsigned, dealing with the general political situation. In January 1918 he even began to write regularly for a second newspaper, the *Nuovo giornale* of Florence.[9] He did not cease calling for national solidarity and discipline; but now, instead of passing over the existence of party strife in silence, he began to castigate the various sections of the 'Liberal' party for their lack of any abiding faith, and did not hesitate to accentuate the dilemma of the Socialist and Catholic parties, whose members were faced with the choice between their loyalty to the nation and the supranational ideals which their respective parties existed to serve. He even acknowledged the existence of a large group of neutralists, people whom he especially despised because they were still living in the "dead" past of the days before the intervention, and refusing to face the "historical necessity" of the actual situation.[10]

---

[8] B.481 (August 1918) in B.497, pp. 55–56. A few years later he was extolling the 'totalitarian' spirit of Fascism and generally condemning the egoistic individualism of the Liberals. For the transition, see Chapter 6, pp. 167–78, herein.

[9] I have not been able to discover when his association with *Resto del Carlino* began or how close it was. Bellezza in his *Bibliografia di Gentile* says that Gentile "collaborated" in it "during the war 1915–18." But the earliest article he has identified was printed in February 1917 (B.381); and Gentile continued to contribute articles sporadically until January 1922. His active career as a journalist really lasted from December 1917 until September 1919, during which period he wrote one hundred articles for the two newspapers mentioned in the text.

His association with the *Nuovo giornale* appears to have lasted from the beginning of January 1918 until the end of February 1919.

[10] Gentile had really no right to speak of "historical necessity" at all—as he did in "24 maggio 1915" (B.437, May 1918, in B.497, pp. 115–19). Such talk was misleading in his mouth since he did not believe in the sort of

A few weeks after the disaster, on 6 November 1917, Gentile drafted a proclamation for the Pisan war committee previously referred to, calling on the people to remain calm and steadfast under the threat of invasion. In December he made his own profession of faith in an article entitled "Examination of Conscience." Where others, who in 1915 had clamored for intervention while he was counseling and observing the discipline of silence, were now silent in dismay, Gentile chose to proclaim himself an interventionist: "I also—and I am glad to turn back and declare it at this moment—was firmly of the opinion that a great people . . . could not stand aside as a mere spectator of the struggle in which the future of all humanity was at stake. . . ."[11]

The role of passive spectator of events was one which he consistently rejected. For him a historical situation was always either a problem or an opportunity. He regarded the war as an opportunity for Italians to show that the myth of decadence and *dolce far niente* was without foundation; and Caporetto was a test of the genuineness of the Risorgimento. If the Italian nation was simply the diplomatic achievement of a few individuals aided by good fortune, if it had no roots in the lives and hearts of the people, then its disappearance would not matter to anyone except a few hundred lawyers who could no longer assemble in Rome and gossip about the interests of their clients in Parliament: "An Italy destined to perish as the result of a military defeat would no longer have been worthy to live—if it ever had been."[12]

In the next few months Gentile conducted a kind of post-mortem over the disaster. His conclusion was that it had come about because Italy had never really seized her opportunity: her intervention had been a pretense and not a reality. Following the lead already given by General Cadorna in announcing the catastrophe, he found the root of the trouble in a failure of national morale; but he gave this view a personal twist by adding that if the schools had created a genuine sense of patriotism before the war, the military disaster would never have happened.[13]

---

transcendent compelling power or inevitable fate that the words suggest to the ordinary reader. His real view was that the war was a test that Italy had to undergo in order to wipe out the disgraces of the past (cf. B.424 in B.497, pp. 191–92) and set the seal on her existence as a great nation.

[11] B.384 in B.497, p. 61.

[12] *Ibid.*, p. 62.

[13] B.422 in B.497, pp. 79–83. It is of course questionable whether Caporetto should be blamed on a failure of nerve at all. But the hysterical reaction of

We might be tempted to say that Gentile was merely claiming for himself the role of Cassandra, since we are bound to be reminded here of his plea at the 1907 congress for something like a religious faith at the foundation of elementary education.[14] But this is not the only moral to be drawn—nor is it perhaps the true one. Gentile insisted continually that all must share the responsibility for the national disaster. Conservative interventionist opinion blamed Giolitti for the disaster; and Gentile himself was disposed to agree that *giolittismo* had much to do with it.[15] But he made a clear distinction between the man and the system, arguing that a people gets the government it deserves, and that Giolitti's power had been delegated to him by the people as a whole including those who were now so ready to condemn him.[16] In laying the responsibility on the schools, Gentile was reacting *against* the search for a scapegoat and almost saying *mea culpa*. In his view it would do no good to shift the blame onto others since "every punishment that is not a violent and destructive vendetta must come from within, not from without"; [17] and to maintain a vendetta under the existing circumstances would be ruinous, for in the defeat of the nation all parties alike would be "morally suppressed." All should therefore stand together and resist the enemy.[18]

The ultimate enemy, in Gentile's eyes, was the defeatism of the Italians themselves. He felt that the need to restore morale and build a sense of national solidarity was urgent and vital enough to justify even the suppression of profiteering scandals by the official censorship. The pessimism and self-distrust that masqueraded as tough-minded realism seemed to him far more dangerous than the Germanophiles, pacifists, smugglers and spies of the popular imagina-

---

which Cadorna's communiqué was the first evidence shows how torn by inner guilts and fears the nation was. The Italians themselves did most to create the Caporetto myth which other nations accepted; the military defeat was such a magnificent opportunity for self-exculpation and recrimination. In this sense there is justice in Gentile's analysis, whether or not it applies to the battle itself.

[14] See Chapter 3, pp. 66–76, herein.

[15] Between 1900 and 1915 Giovanni Giolitti was the most important leader of the group of factions that went by the name of the Liberal party. Through his appreciation of the parliamentary balance of power and his skill in the manipulation of patronage he created something like a parliamentary dictatorship in this period.

[16] B.421 in B.497, p. 76.

[17] B.420 in B.497, p. 70.

[18] B.428 in B.497, pp. 95–99.

tion.[19] He himself, perhaps pardonably under the circumstances, blamed "Germanic thought" for creating the myth of the indolent and cynical Italians out of what was merely a legacy of the centuries of decadence.[20]

By the time Gentile had completed this analysis of the situation it was March 1918; and despite his plea for no recrimination he had himself attacked first the Vatican and then the Catholic party as early as January; at the end of February he turned on the Socialists; and finally in June he bitterly criticized the members of the Italian Parliament as a whole.

This apparent inconsistency is not hard to explain. While he was considering why national morale had not been built up before the war, Gentile was moved to comment on the divisions in Italian life before 1914. Liberalism, he said, had then been faced by two forces —the Socialists and the clericals—whose attitude toward the national State was purely negative; and failing to find a positive ideal to set against them, it had itself been reduced to sterile negations. The war, however, provided in his eyes a national ideal with positive content, and thus marked the beginning of a new period in Italian history. In the light of this new situation the liberalism of Giolitti was only a relic of the dead past, and the supranational ideals of the Catholics and Socialists were revealed as ambiguous and negative. So that, although it was fruitless to repine about the past, all of these partisan factions deserved to be condemned for their attitude in the present.

The Vatican, of course, was an external force in any case. And since Gentile held that it had no legal right to the independence which it claimed, his attitude toward it as an independent power *de facto* was naturally hostile.[21] As early as February 1918 we find him protesting that the Holy See must not have a seat at the peace conference, and that no proposal for the internationalization of the Law of Guarantees should be admitted.[22] Benedict XV's peace

---

[19] B.430 and B.431 in B.497, pp. 100–104, 105–9.

[20] B.434 in B.497, pp. 110–14. The Germans were not the only begetters of the myth of *dolce far niente*. The English certainly contributed. But the Italians themselves were more to blame than anyone else for its persistence.

[21] In an article of January 1918 he reiterated his view that the 'separation of Church and State,' essential to the Risorgimento tradition, involved a claim by the State to be an autonomous source of spiritual value, and added that the majority of Italian Catholics accorded it this autonomy (B.462 in B.497, pp. 138–41; cf. also B.443, August 1918, in B.497, pp. 146–49).

[22] B.426 in B.497, pp. 142–45.

message at Christmas 1917 drew from him the acid comment that His Holiness' conception of war was "Arcadian and even materialist" and most certainly not that of the Christian who seeks peace with God by doing His Will; he even added the cynical suggestion that the Pope was really afraid of the war because it made men conscious of the ethical and religious character of the State.[23]

His main complaint against the Catholic party concerned the ambiguous allegiance which it owed on the one side to the State and on the other to this power that claimed to be independent of the State. He distrusted it because its policy emanated from higher authority and did not grow up spontaneously; so that the undeniable fact that the majority of ordinary party members were unconscious of any conflict of loyalties was no real guarantee against subversion, since the directive impulse did not come from the majority.[24]

The Italian Socialist party, dominated at this time by its revolutionary wing, was officially neutral in this 'bourgeois' war. They bickered among themselves; but not even the moderates, though they protested that they were loyal Italians, were ready to abandon the ideals of the International. To Gentile their attitude seemed completely illogical. The class war was not, he argued, a sort of division of labor; Marx himself had recognized that absolute neutrality was impossible in history. The Nation had a place in the dialectic that was to bring about the triumph of the proletariat, and therefore it behooved all good socialists to make up their minds what that place was. They should decide whether the governing classes were fighting for the revolution or against it, and either help or hinder them accordingly. Prophetically anticipating the Red bogy from which the Fascists were later to 'save' Italy, Gentile warned the moderate socialists that if they persisted in fighting only for class interests, they would create in Italy a situation comparable to the chaos of the revolution in Russia. It was no use their simply affirming their loyalty: they should recognize, as the German Social Democrats had done, that the national capital must be preserved, even if its preservation involved preserving the capitalist class also. Otherwise the revolution, when it came, would be a Pyrrhic victory for the proletariat.[25]

As for the Italian Parliament, it had not been of one mind since the very beginning of the war; and its members had never ceased

---

[23] B.418 in B.497, pp. 124–28.
[24] B.419 in B.497, pp. 129–33; cf. B.423 in B.497, pp. 134–37.
[25] B.427, B.429, B.472 in B.497, pp. 237–52.

to advertise the fact to the world at large. Many of them had been opposed to Italy's intervention, and all alike were ready to make party capital out of any turn of events. In June 1918 Gentile declared in disgust that men of good will had begun to distrust everything that was said on Montecitorio, because of the eternal petty squabbling; and he prophesied that the continual refusal to accept communal responsibility for anything would bring dishonor on the whole institution of Parliament:

A chamber that persists in ignoring the need ["to unite together soberly and sincerely, with a communal sense of dignity and determination, in support of an agreed program"] is no use to the country; and certainly it cannot arouse respect and trust. The deputies themselves confess it once they are away from Montecitorio. But a people that despises its own institutions cannot stand erect. All the parties should reflect thoroughly about this, for when they have made this Parliament, which they are allowing to fall so low, completely impotent, what will they put in its place that can satisfy and safeguard the very interests which each party represents? [26]

As we have seen, Gentile himself felt that the war had opened a new epoch for Italy. The crisis of October 1917 was the greatest challenge the nation had faced since 1870; and the recovery, with the eventual halting of the Austrian invasion on the Piave, proved to him that the spirit of the Risorgimento was not dead.[27] But this spirit must somehow be kept alive in Italian political life after the war; [28] and it certainly was not to be found on Montecitorio. Nevertheless Gentile did not yet despair of parliamentary government as such. He was later to become a leading apologist for the Corporate State. But in 1918 he showed himself very unsympathetic to all brands of syndicalism. He defended the liberal ideal of respect for the free development of the individual person against the "regime of the productive bourgeoisie" proposed by the Nationalist leader Corradini; [29] and he dealt equally faithfully with analogous proposals from trade unionists at the opposite political pole.[30]

---

[26] B.475 in B.497, p. 123.

[27] B.439 in B.497, pp. 315–18; cf. B.467 in B.497, p. 268.

[28] Gentile gave cordial support to movements formed by young servicemen with this aim in mind; and he also suggested that the problems of demobilization, etc., should be studied carefully in advance (cf. B.476, June 1918, in B.497, pp. 258–62).

[29] Cf. pp. 133–34, herein. By this time, however, he was much more friendly to the Nationalists than in 1917—witness a very friendly article on Alfredo Oriani's *La rivolta ideale* published not only in *Resto del Carlino* but in the Nationalist organ *L'Idea nazionale* (B.441 in B.497, pp. 309–14).

[30] B.461 in B.561, pp. 95–100; see Chapter 6, p. 180, herein.

The League of Nations and the Peace Conference

As it became obvious that victory was only a matter of time, Gentile, like everyone else, turned his attention toward the problems of the Peace. His general attitude can best be described as one of moral intransigence. He was not disposed to be conciliatory to the Germans—still less to the Austrians. Indeed he was not even prepared to trust them; he advocated caution in dealing with their early overtures, and insisted that they must accept and fulfill Allied terms to the letter.[31] One suspects that he was not very anxious for the war to end because he felt that national solidarity still needed the external stimulus of an enemy in arms.[32]

Gentile was not much inclined, therefore, to join in the chorus of popular acclaim in which President Wilson was hailed as the architect of the future peace of the world, when he made his tour of triumph before the peace conference began at Versailles. He was ready enough to admit the greatness of Wilson as a warleader who had led the United States out of isolation, and thereby turned the scale in the European conflict. In this capacity he really had done something to achieve the triumph of peace and justice in a 'Society of Nations'; and, as an 'armed apostle,' moreover, he stood in marked contrast to Benedict XV, with whom his Catholic admirers were coupling him.[33] But Gentile was very skeptical about the general idea of settling historical problems by the application of abstract canons of rightness or morality. He felt that to talk of such things only made matters worse by rousing vain hopes and futile aspirations; and that it was, at the same time, merely a veil behind which the real interests which statesmen stood for continued to operate. Even while joining as far as he could in the popular enthusiasm, he pointed out that America had entered the war for reasons of her own. And a few weeks later, when Italy's troubles at Paris had begun, he drew the moral that Wilson had triumphed

---

[31] B.448, B.449, B.451, B.454 in B.497, pp. 342–45, 346–50, 351–55, 361–65, respectively.

[32] His earliest comment on "The Society of Nations" (B.411, February 1918) bears this out. He ends by saying that the idea is founded on a false conception of the State, which "has war within when it does not have war without, and the former is all the more violent . . . when the common dangers and the responsibilities of the latter are less felt." This passage echoes his caustic remarks about the Pope's Christmas peace message a few weeks earlier (B.418; cf. pp. 137–38, herein). See also n42 below.

[33] B.516.

as the representative not of the Fourteen Points but of the Monroe Doctrine extended to the whole world.[34]

We can see why Gentile took this attitude by applying his own canons to himself. His dislike of the Fourteen Points and of Wilson's attitude in general is explained by the fact that he was an interventionist and a nationalist. He saw from the beginning that Wilson's peace program was incompatible with the Treaty of London and the hopes with which Italy had voluntarily entered the war. He had no sympathy with the minority groups in the old Austro-Hungarian Empire who were clamoring for their 'national rights'; and it infuriated him to see Mazzini's gospel of the Nation as a moral mission to be accomplished through strife, sacrifice, and endurance, degraded into a mere matter of counting heads.[35] Here we have one of the roots of his Fascism. When he had to make a choice between parliamentary democracy and his interpretation of Mazzini there was never any doubt about which he would choose. He insisted that Mazzini himself had put the interest of the Nation above all else—and that where necessary he had appealed to strategic and other nonethnic considerations in deciding how a national boundary should be drawn.[36] And even Wilson had recognized that the principle of self-determination could not be applied to the six hundred thousand Italians in New York! [37]

---

[34] B.525. This article was published just a week before Wilson's manifesto on the Adriatic question set Italian public opinion unanimously against him. The history of the U.N. suggests that if Congress had not refused to ratify Wilson's work, and if the League had ever come to exercise any effective authority, this prophecy might not have been too wide of the mark. Gentile, with Hegelian malice, added that the Monroe Doctrine is "the radical negation of every principle of the 'Society of Nations.'"

[35] B.505 and B.506 in B.1280, especially Chapter 2.

[36] B.450 in B.497, pp. 330–35. It is obvious that Gentile's lack of sympathy with the principle of self-determination is largely conditioned by his patriotic concern over Italy's interests in the Adriatic and the North. He lays special emphasis on the fact that Mazzini's pronouncements about the Adriatic question were inconsistent, and that no conclusion could legitimately be drawn from them (cf. also B.444).

It is easy to see why he was disturbed about the application of the plebiscite method to the Italian frontier problem. But I confess that I find some of his diatribes against the 'rights' of small nations very puzzling. After all, the Austrian Empire had to be dealt with on some principle; and Gentile certainly held no brief for its preservation. The only small nation apart from the new Austria whose 'rights' might threaten Italian interests was Serbia; and against her his argument was not valid. For Serbia had demonstrated the genuineness of her mission through sacrifice and endurance more clearly than any other nation in Europe.

[37] B.517 in B.561, pp. 102–3. For Gentile's most considered criticism of Wilson's political philosophy see B.555.

Against the Wilsonian idyl of universal concord based on government by consent Gentile set his own view of history as an essentially tragic conflict of opposed ideals. In abstract terms this means that there is always more than one moral principle that is genuinely applicable in any situation; only through suffering and strife, therefore, can mankind advance toward a real Society of Nations.[38] As he explained to the reporters of the Nationalist newspaper *L'Idea nazionale* in January 1919, the 'Society of Nations'—which he appears to have identified with the 'brotherhood of man'—is an ideal that is as old as man; and it is gradually though imperfectly realized throughout the whole of history. The Wilsonian attempt to conceive this ideal as an existing organization he stigmatized as a utopian fantasy born of the unhistorical atomism of the Enlightenment.

Careful examination of the argument by which Gentile justifies this thesis reveals the equivocal character of the whole dispute. He takes the question at issue to be not whether an international organization can or should exist, but rather what status it can have in social theory. We must understand first what we *mean* by a 'society.' Tempering the winds of his idealist doctrine to the shorn intellects of ordinary newspaper readers, he solves this problem in traditional Aristotelian terms by saying that the State is a true society because the individual is inconceivable apart from it. It exists as an institution only in order to modify and regulate social relations that have always and must always exist.

But, of course, if social relations bind men into groups there must always be some specifiable relations between these groups. Hence the Society of Nations has the same transcendental or eternal status as the State itself, and Gentile is compelled to admit that a supranational organization is possible. There is no sound speculative reason why international relations should not be modified and controlled by objectively established institutions, just as interpersonal relations are. An international juridical order must inevitably be something that evolves gradually, and it can only be effective if it takes account of the actual interests of nations. Physical warfare can be abolished, but only if all parties honestly indicate the things that touch their interests most nearly. Italians cannot surrender the

---

[38] B.540 in B.561, pp. 114–19; cf. B.460. In B.530 Gentile draws the logical inference that the Allied powers cannot claim to "represent the civilized feelings of humanity as a whole" or hope to "restore perfect justice on earth."

interests of Italy, since Europe and the world exist for them only as functions of their own awareness of nationality.[39]

Thus Gentile's philosophical objection to the proposed League of Nations really amounts to no more than this: that it is impossible to organize the world once and for all, and to banish all conflict finally. Whenever he spoke of the Society of Nations he seems to have had this utopian dream in mind; but he did recognize that some of the supporters of Wilson's proposal—Lord Cecil for instance and perhaps even Wilson himself—had quite a concrete and historical conception of their task.[40] It would seem, however, that he did not really approve of the idea even when it was conceived properly; and that is probably why he concentrated his attention upon the utopian conception, of which he could legitimately disapprove as a philosopher. For he felt that from *any* point of view a Society of Nations implied a somewhat Arcadian ideal of life; faced with the proposal that international war should be abolished he was obviously uneasy.[41] In his essay on Mazzini he cited the message which the great Genoese sent to a pacifist conference: "Peace cannot become the law of human society except through strife. . . . A strife which is necessary, a war which is as sacred as peace, since the triumph of the Good is to result from it." [42] A very similar personal feeling colors everything that he wrote about Wilson and the League. He insists always on an absolutely precise and universal

---

[39] B.515 in B.497, pp. 371–77 (cf. B.411, B.460). It is instructive to compare this view with that of Kant in *Perpetual Peace*—which is clearly what Gentile is thinking of when he claims that Wilson's ideal has its origins in the Enlightenment. Kant also lays it down that there can be no lasting pacification without full statement of all grievances. But he seems to think that once stated the grievances can be finally dealt with. Whereas Gentile clearly feels that there will always be irreconcilable conflicts of interest. In the current phraseology, the best we can ever hope for is to replace 'hot' wars by 'cold' ones.

[40] B.515 in B.497, p. 376 (for Cecil); B.516 (for Wilson). It was already clear to everyone by 1920, he thought, that the utopian ideal was a fantasy generated by war weariness. "Who remembers any more," he asked in the Preface to *After the Victory*, ". . . the Society of Nations which made so many hearts beat faster?"

[41] See B.515 in B.497, p. 376; and cf. n32 above.

[42] B.1280, p. 22. In B.537 he even gives his assent to the curious view that the "true author of the disarmament imposed on Germany was not Foch but Lloyd George," and agrees that it will weaken the Latin nations more than the Germans because it will make the majority in those countries feel that military preparedness is an unnecessary luxury whereas the Germans will be eager to regain their former position of strength.

interpretation of what his opponents say, and often appears to think that the resulting inconsistencies are a sufficient refutation of the thesis which they advance. But his own pronouncements would not stand up to this sort of treatment, and he is always ready to find an acceptable interpretation of the expressions used by those with whom he is in moral agreement. His attitude is, therefore, to say the least of it, disingenuous.

But even if he refused to believe that the Allied victory had concluded the 'war to end war,' Gentile was far from cynical about it. For him, just as much as for the supporters of Wilson, the victory was a triumph of the ideal of international justice over national egoism. The Kaiser's Germany as a whole—including the German Socialists—needed to fight the war, to suffer defeat and all its consequences, in order to be purged of the "fever of dominion that invaded it after 1870." [43] The German people, therefore, should not be allowed to evade the penalty for their misdeeds by shifting responsibility onto their former autocratic leaders and pleading a change of heart.[44] Actions are performed and decisions frequently made by individuals, and the particular agent is always responsible for his action. But when he acts on behalf of a whole community and that community does not denounce the action, but rather demonstrates support for it in innumerable ways, no room remains for a distinction between 'public' and 'private' morality. In fact there is never room for the distinction, for all moral action is action on behalf of a community: the conscience of the citizen is "always individual but never private." [45]

This doctrine provides the key to Gentile's two articles on the proposal to punish the Kaiser, articles which on the surface are

[43] B.460. Cf. B.408 in B.561, pp. 3–25, where Gentile argues that the German *Machtpolitik* was a last echo of Renaissance individualism having its roots in Machiavelli's theory of *virtù*. Since it was individualism at the level of the State, it was Germany, and not just the Kaiser, that needed to be taught that all power must be governed by immanent moral law. For the mere *virtù* of the individual perishes with the individual and can achieve nothing lasting, because it has no roots in any universal value.

[44] B.455 in B.497, pp. 366–70; cf. B.460, etc. The explosive combination of Gentile's violent antipathy to socialist internationalism with his uneasy distrust of democracy produces in B.455 the harsh judgment that the German's new-found "democratic faith" is a greater blot on the national escutcheon than the mere fact of military defeat. In B.525 he suggests that the reality behind their internationalism is the old imperialism of the Kaiser. In B.530 he associates himself specifically with the punitive aims and views of Clemenceau.

[45] B.408 in B.561, p. 14.

more remarkable for emotional fervor than for logical rigor.[46] In
the first, provoked by Lloyd George's electoral slogan "Hang the
Kaiser," he protests that "to take arms against the Kaiser is to dis-
arm against the German people" and claims that if the punishment
of the Kaiser personally were justified the Allies would have a duty
to help the German people stricken by disaster in their innocence.
Here we might feel that although the argument is not logical, it did
nevertheless correctly interpret the 'let's not be beastly to the Germans' mentality. But when in the later article he has to deal not
with Lloyd George but with Clemenceau's reply to German protests at the harshness of the treaty, and we find him insisting that
precisely because it is just that the German people should suffer,
it is wrong that the Kaiser should be punished individually—that
in order to secure the 'greater' justice we *must* let the 'lesser' justice
go—he seems to be in flat contradiction with his own principle. For
if communal responsibility does not destroy or even essentially alter
individual responsibility, why should not *both* the community *and*
the individual source of community initiative be subject to justice?

The answer which is presupposed though not stated in Gentile's
articles is that the individual conscience becomes moral by identification with the will of the community. No individual can do
more than act for the good of his community as he sees it; and no
individual can receive justice except from his community, so that
if the Kaiser's actions did not express the will of Germany it belonged to his people and to them alone to punish him as an individual. When an individual joins in a criminal or seditious conspiracy and the plot is discovered, the wider community is able
nevertheless to punish him as an individual because it treats his
participation in an immoral community as being precisely what
constitutes *his* offense. That is to say it treats him as an individual
with a conscience of his own of which it, the State, is the proper
expression and therefore the legitimate guardian; the *individual*
responsibility is apportioned as accurately as the nature of the case
will allow, precisely because the conspiracy itself is not regarded
as a proper focus of responsibility. Where the conspiracy is too
widespread to allow of its being thus treated as an accidental con-
fluence of individual wills, the State may for reasons of expediency
and self-interest elect merely to punish the ringleaders so far as they

---

[46] B.460 and B.530.

can be distinguished. But even then the lesser accomplices escape punishment precisely because, as in the former case, the conspiracy is not admitted to exist as a moral community at all. Thus if the Kaiser was to be tried for the crime of plotting war, the whole German nation would have to be treated as a chance aggregation of individuals, and in principle every State would have to be so regarded. On this Gentile harps continually. But instead of explaining carefully why it is so, he surrounds it with so many rhetorical flourishes and dubious corollaries that the ordinary reader may be pardoned if he fails to get the point altogether.[47]

A State cannot be regarded as an accidental agglomeration or the individual moral conscience would have no objective foundation. Thus when an individual can say he has acted in the service of his State he is the "minister of a dominating historical law" and cannot be held responsible as an individual any further. But if the State is a genuine, i.e. a moral community, how can we grant that its will is evil, and what court could have authority to call it to account? This problem brings Gentile to the verge of ultimate moral despair, for it is a case of "If the salt has lost its savor . . . ?" But as we know, he regards the final conquest of evil as a contradictory ideal, so that for him it is a matter of a dialectical extreme, "a fever of dominion" in one nation, destined to be overcome by the community of nations. The court is provided, as in Hegel, by world history as an organic whole. We have reported above his conviction that the Allied victory was a victory for the moral will. But he did not hold that all responsibility for the war rested on the central

---

[47] As an example of a rhetorical flourish we may take the description of those whose decision initiated the war as "ministers of a dominating historical law." The argument that the Allies would have a duty to help the stricken Germans can be regarded either as rhetorical excess or as a dubious corollary. But much clearer examples of the latter are to be found in B.530, where Gentile claims that if responsibility for war rests on the German governing class then the Socialists were right to contract out of a 'bourgeois' war, and further that if justice is to be meted out to the Germans as individuals, the Allied powers cannot possibly defend a treaty which will impose hardship on innocent women and children and on generations yet unborn. What the former argument proves, if anything, is that the German Socialists were *certainly* wrong in giving their government full support, and the socialists in Allied countries at least *possibly* wrong so far as they remained aloof; while the latter argument merely points to an imperfection that is ineradicable in all forms of human justice. The innocent relations, and even the friends and acquaintances, of any criminal may suffer as a result of his punishment in ways which the legislator and the judge do not intend but which they can neither foresee nor prevent.

powers, and he would not concede that the Allies could speak with full authority for "the civilized feelings of humanity as a whole." Thus his answer was, in effect, that we can never allow that the salt has completely lost its savor.[48] World history is a "tragic poem" in which justice is never complete.

The Kaiser's Germany, then, deserved to perish—but only history would show whether it had really perished—inasmuch as it had ignored its moral responsibilities. In any case, the nation created by Bismarck remained; and Gentile foresaw that it would eventually absorb the new Austria, since it was the spirit of nationalism that had at last destroyed the Dual Monarchy.[49]

We have already spoken at some length about Gentile's conception of Italy's part in the war. In his view the victory at Vittorio Veneto had redeemed Caporetto and fulfilled the Risorgimento.[50] When the peace conference slighted the claims of the newborn Italian nation, therefore, he was roused to a fury of patriotic indignation.[51] Was it not Italy who had broken the deadlock of the war? [52] Yet now she was despised and threatened by her erstwhile allies and her extremely modest needs and aspirations were passed over, etc., etc.

What really galled Gentile about the rejection of Italy's claims

---

[48] The Germans should receive clement conditions of peace, Gentile says, not on any Wilsonian humanitarian grounds, but because the logic of history requires that the victor should not annihilate the vanquished but preserve him as witness of his victory (B.525). This "collaboration in the new society created by the victory" would be his answer to the problem "wherewith shall it be salted?" The worldly wisdom, at least, of his conception can be seen by examining what happened in and after the *second* World War. By their policy of unconditional surrender the Allies proclaimed that the salt *had* lost its savor. But this policy was only carried through to the bitter end—the destruction of Germany as a united nation—because the Allies themselves did not trust one another. They had no common moral will. Thus the salt had *indeed* lost its savor; and the division of Germany must continue until this hiatus in the moral conscience of the world is somehow ended, and a sense of community of purpose restored. What makes the hiatus so perilous is precisely the fact that the Germans of course cannot possibly accept the moral vacuum that it imposes on them. So far as they remain conscious of being Germans they must insist that they are a nation, and that their salt has *not* lost its savor.

[49] On the fate of Germany, cf. the definite verdict of B.408 in B.561, pp. 3–25, with the uncertainty of B.460 and the prejudiced foreboding of B.525; on Austria see B.408.

[50] B.456 in B.561, pp. 26–30; cf. B.527, B.534, etc.

[51] For what follows down to the end of this section, the major source is B.508 in B.561, pp. 69–91.

[52] Cf. also B.525 and B.532 for extravagant claims of this sort.

at the peace conference was the fact that it enabled those Italian politicians who had opposed Italy's intervention in the first place to say "We told you so." [53] His own support for the intervention had never rested on the material and diplomatic benefits promised by the Treaty of London. He emphasized continually that the real benefits of the intervention were spiritual.[54] But if the treaty was simply set aside, he feared it would lead to a return of the cynical spirit of *dolce far niente*. And his fears were not without foundation: there was talk of inquiries to establish where the responsibility for the intervention lay—as if the whole thing had been a mistake.[55] Reacting violently against this resurgence of the backbiting spirit which had already made a badge of shame out of Caporetto, Gentile hailed the seizure of Fiume by the poet D'Annunzio at the head of a rabble as a "generous gesture." [56]

In all this he sounds almost like a drawing-room version of Mussolini. But, unlike the tiny group of Fascisti, he was not so much interested in violent reactions against the peace treaty [57] as in preserving the spiritual gains of the war by persuading the Italians to see the intervention and the victory in the right light, and not judge it in terms of material profit and loss. He certainly preferred moral indignation over Italy's treatment at Versailles to cynical fatalism. But he was consistent in his rejection of abstract moralism. Italy received, in his view, a raw deal; but it was foolish, he said,

---

[53] Cf. B.527.

[54] The best way to see the continuity and consistency of Gentile's views about the real purpose and value of the intervention is to examine first his lecture on "The Philosophy of the War" (B.306 in B.497, pp. 1–24), then his first article after Caporetto (B.384 in B.497, pp. 60–64), and finally his articles for the anniversary of the intervention (B.437 in B.497, pp. 115–19, and B.527). But references could here be multiplied *ad nauseam*.

[55] Cf. B.533.

[56] B.508 in B.561, p. 76. Italy had no claim to Fiume under the Treaty of London; and Gentile admits that no one would have thought of demanding it before 1915. But he felt, or affected to feel, that possession of it was vital for the defense of the Dalmatian fringe. In any case, since the dispute over Fiume had been the occasion of Italy's withdrawal from the congress at Versailles, D'Annunzio's action symbolized dramatically the contrast between the true spirit of the intervention and the prudent bickering and calculating of the politicians.

[57] But revision did remain one of his long-term aims apparently: "the man who possesses self-respect . . . goes calmly to meet the inevitable, in the conviction that the force to which each of us should bravely entrust his ideals is not violence, which strives to break down obstacles at a stroke, but constancy of will, which perseveres in the patient resistance that brings us to our goal" (B.534).

to expect "gratitude" at a peace conference, which was bound to be a war of interests. Italian politicians ought never to have been deceived by the Wilsonian dream of an 'Age of Gold.' Nitti deserved all honor, he felt, for frankly explaining to the Italian people that they must give up their hopes of a favorable solution to the Adriatic question in order to obtain the American credits that were vital to economic recovery.[58]

La vigilia

As time passed it seemed more and more evident, however, that Gentile's hopes were not going to be fulfilled. The old faces reappeared at Montecitorio and there was no sign of his much talked of resurgence of the national spirit within the framework of liberal democracy. The Church—that old enemy of the liberal State—made a decisive entry into the political arena in the form of the Popular party (*Popolari*), founded and led by the Sicilian priest Don Luigi Sturzo. The Socialists continued to preach revolution in theory and accept parliamentary government in practice—salving their consciences by refusing to share any responsibility for the government.[59] It seemed that in spite of the war the Liberals had still to find a positive ideal; and Gentile was obliged to admit that even among those who were imbued with the spirit of Vittorio Veneto there was still too much shouting and talk. At first he counseled patience just as he had done in 1914. The new Italy could not be created by violent revolutionary action. It must have time to grow. Milk and honey would not suddenly begin to flow just because the war was over.[60]

The worst problem, of course, was economic. Italy was born with an unbalanced budget and virtually no resources. From any point of view, except that of the Socialists, the achievement of stability could only mean retrenchment. Gentile urged that the government should actually practice austerity and not just preach it—for instance they should meet the civil servants' demands for higher pay, but first they should reorganize the administration and abolish the great number of wartime temporary posts.[61] His usual comment on

---

[58] *Ibid.;* cf. the preceding note.
[59] B.508 in B.561, pp. 77 ff.; cf. B.569 in B.818, p. 247.
[60] B.458 in B.561, pp. 43–48.
[61] B.528.

strikes was that the common good must be preferred to the interests of particular pressure groups. But behind this rather empty platitude a recognizably 'bourgeois' conception of economic life can be discerned. Gentile habitually contrasts the "just claims of the working *classes*" not with the claims of 'capital' or 'the managerial classes' but with "the general necessities of national life"; in other words there is an implicit and quite illegitimate identification of the national interests with that of the bourgeoisie.[62]

He was indeed aware of a certain bias in his own attitude. He felt that the socialist ideal of the withering away of the State was absolutely opposed to the true spirit of liberalism; but he admitted that it was permissible for a genuine liberal to support the moderate wing of the Italian Socialist party in the belief that if they came to power the Socialists would be obliged to accommodate their theoretical ideals to the practical realities of politics. His own sympathies, however, were conservative; and he claimed that liberals who themselves favored more radical policies should for their part admit the value of a conservative counterbalance against revolutionary socialism. In other words, a liberal should not be too dogmatic in his party allegiance, since the sense of mutual solidarity between liberals of opposite persuasions was the best defense against revolution.[63]

His attitude toward the *Popolari* was equally ambivalent. All his life he remained suspicious of the Vatican, and held that any attempt to cover up or explain away the breach of 1870 was contrary to the interests of Church and State alike.[64] Hence he was bound to feel that the position of an officially Catholic party was hopelessly

[62] B.536 in B.561, pp. 63–68.

[63] B.521, B.522, B.524 in B.561, pp. 162–87. Although, as we saw previously (see p. 138, herein), one of his wartime articles anticipated the 'Red peril' from which Mussolini later claimed to have saved Italy, Gentile does not seem to have been very impressed with it in this period of its supposed existence; even later on, when it was an article of Fascist faith, he does not seem to have placed much emphasis on it. The only result of the revolution in Russia so far as he could see was anarchy; and in November 1918 he wrote that outside of Russia the specter of Bolshevism was merely "the last bogey of the defeatists who have survived the victory"—a specter against which the memory of victory was the best defense and "the strongest guarantee of social concord for all classes" (B.457 in B.561, pp. 42, 40). In July 1919, when the momentary threat of a general strike was averted, his confidence remained unshaken: "Italy is Italy and no misfortune or injustice can ever make it a Balkan country" (B.532).

[64] B.535 in B.561, pp. 134–40; cf. B.673.

equivocal; and the "nonconfessional Catholicism" of Don Sturzo appeared to him to be a contradiction in terms. But he admitted that there was a certain breadth and elasticity about Sturzo's views— there was a feeling of life in his very inconsistencies which was lacking in the orthodox clericalism of the right-wing *Popolari*. It is clear that Gentile regarded Sturzo as a possible recruit for the defense of parliamentary liberalism.[65]

Gentile was probably right in feeling that the war had made a difference in the attitude of the Socialists on one side and the Catholic party on the other toward the national State. But by 1920 he had begun to realize that the war had not produced the spiritual revolution in his own party, the fruits of which he was so patiently expecting. This realization was the beginning of his ultimate disillusionment about parliamentary government, and his conversion to Fascism. He always insisted that Fascism was the embodiment of genuine liberalism; and by this he meant that it was imbued with the spirit of Vittorio Veneto which the Liberals had allowed to perish.

When we examine what he meant by this 'spirit' it is easy to see that his disillusion was more or less inevitable. It is not really possible to arrive at any complete or satisfactory conception because Gentile himself did not know and emphasized that we *could* not know precisely what to expect. But apparently he believed himself to possess criteria by which he could recognize it wherever it appeared; and in spite of some appearance of inconsistency, I think we can reconstruct these criteria from what he says about it.

It was, in the first place, a spirit of free spontaneity, a spirit of youth and almost of recklessness, where 'recklessness' is meant literally as refusal to make careful prior calculation of results before embarking on a course of action; the reason being that the action is regarded as an end in itself and not a means to any results. This was how Gentile regarded Italy's part in the war and it is easy to see how in this light he could applaud the escapades of D'Annunzio.

But there is another aspect to it, which is rather darker and probably more important. The spirit of the war was the spirit of the trenches, of military discipline and obedience, sacrifice of self and

---

[65] B.541 and B.538 in B.561, pp. 128–33 and 141–46 respectively; by 1921 he seems to have become convinced that the old wolf was just as dangerous in the new sheep's clothing (cf. B.625 in B.813, pp. 392–95). His refusal to admit the possibility of "nonconfessional Catholicism" is odd considering that following Gioberti he always claimed to be a Catholic 'in his own way.'

death at one's post. Gentile wanted to see the attitude of the good soldier carried over into civil life, he wanted peacetime reconstruction regarded as a continuation of the war.[66] But this presupposes several conditions which are hardly ever satisfied in ordinary political life. First, everyone must agree on what the basic aim is; one does not, as Gentile himself said, die for a party but only for the *patria*.[67] But the Italians did not agree even in basic outline about the kind of society they wanted.[68] Secondly, the question of who is to give the orders must be clearly and unequivocally settled.[69] But how is this consistent with a democratic conception of government? Thirdly, the officers, however designated, must give orders without fear or favor; the good officer spares his men when he can, but equally he does not hesitate at a critical point of the battle to demand the last ounce and more from them, and in particular to demand more from some than from others if they chance to be in a crucial position. This is the absolute antithesis of the fairness and respect for the individual which we take to be proper to peacetime government, and which can only be abrogated by a special grant of emergency powers.

These two aspects are, of course, antithetical. On both counts Gentile was disappointed. But on the side of free spontaneity this was merely a contingent fact and did not arise from the essential inapplicability of his criterion to peacetime, as it did on the side of discipline. In a war, because the common aim is clear and needs no discussion, the antitheses become reconcilable. What we mean when we say that morale is high is that the exigencies of discipline

---

[66] Cf. B.519, B.520, B.531, B.532, B.537.

[67] B.531. Because of this Gentile did not approve of any attempt by ex-servicemen to form a political party. He agrees that they stand for something which can be regarded as a "program," but he insists and reiterates in B.519, B.520, B.531 that they must not regard themselves as a special group, that even during the war they were the spearhead of a whole nation which shared their hardships, and that now in peacetime they must infect the whole nation with their discipline.

[68] For Gentile's recognition of this see especially B.533. His insistence that the victory "*shall* bear fruit" is the first echo of the 'religious' spirit he later found in Fascism.

[69] In Gentile's view this should be done through the education system. Hence when the elementary-school teachers went on strike he was morally appalled, although he himself agreed that the improvement of their financial condition was the first essential for a sound educational system. It was as if the junior officers charged with training the raw recruits should engage in mutiny (cf. B.529; the military metaphor, however, is mine and not Gentile's).

are not corroding the sense of spontaneity. But in peace, where the fundamental task is to work out a common aim through free discussion and a tug of war of interest which by an unspoken and virtually unconscious agreement is kept within certain limits, a perfect reconciliation is impossible. Life, however, is full of fallacious appearances; extremes may meet and seem for a moment to be united. It is easy to see, therefore, how Gentile could have believed, at first, that Fascism met his criteria, that the new spirit had at last come to bloom. The astonishing thing is that he never lost his faith that the fruit, whose bitterness he could not deny, would one day ripen.

His disillusion with parliamentary liberalism was signalized by an article in the review *Politica* for April 1920 which marked the end of his active involvement in general political discussion until the March on Rome. Under the title "Realism and Political Fatalism" he offered a critique of the 'philosophy' of Francesco Nitti— the prime minister whose resolute frankness he had earlier praised —based on a distinction which he had drawn two years earlier between 'intellectualism' and 'spiritualism' as opposite attitudes toward the world.[70] For the intellectualist, reality is something already complete and perfect; it forms the necessary presupposition of consciousness, while remaining quite independent of any consciousness that may actually exist. Practical wisdom on this view lies in 'conformity to Nature'; morality is a matter of resigned obedience to a law for which the moral subject is not responsible. The ideal life, therefore, is a life of maximum passivity—a dispassionate contemplation of the natural order involving action only when personal adaptation to that order becomes necessary or advisable. For the spiritual idealist, on the other hand, consciousness is the very substance of reality and is inseparable from it. Morality means autonomy and it is Nature that must be molded into conformity with the moral law; being moral involves not resignation but self-assertion, not obedience but mastery.

This opposition is the keystone of Gentile's whole philosophy. His

---

[70] B.569 in Appendix to B.818, pp. 245–58. The distinction between 'intellectualism' and 'spiritualism' was drawn in "Politica e filosofia," an article for the first issue of *Politica* in December 1918 (B.409 in B.561, pp. 188–216). It corresponds to the distinction between 'realism' and 'idealism' in his Trieste lectures on *The Reform of Education* (B.1128, English translation B.659; cf. Chapter 1, pp. 2–4, and Chapter 4, pp. 125–28, herein).

main aim, as expounded to the schoolteachers of Trieste in 1919, was to produce a self-consistent theoretical account of the 'spiritual' conception of reality. The 'spirit of Vittorio Veneto' as he understood it was typified by this same quality of moral creativity and responsibility; whereas those who wished to liquidate the war by remaining passive were intellectual fatalists.[71] By 1920 Gentile was convinced that Nitti belonged to the latter party because he continually claimed that actions were forced on him by the necessity of events. As a result the government merely drifted, and economic egoism grew ever stronger among the citizens, since in the absence of a definite social initiative everyone was bound to begin looking out for himself. Nitti's alibi was invalid because within consciousness there is only *moral* necessity; only through the general acceptance of responsibility for whatever we take to be necessary in our common world can there be any escape from natural egoism.

We can all agree with Gentile in this condemnation of political drifting; and no one can study the history of Italy in these four years without feeling that the successive governments generally had no policy but simply resigned themselves to events. But, since Gentile declines to offer a policy himself,[72] it cannot fairly be said that he advances beyond the view that he criticizes. For in the absence of a positive policy, the negative criticism he offers would have been fully answered by the simple admission on the part of the "liquidators of the war" that what they called the necessities of the situation in no way diminished their responsibility, but rather constituted the very morality of their actions. This is all that Gentile's distinction of 'realism' from 'fatalism' absolutely requires. It was all very well for Gentile to counsel patience and discipline in order that the new spirit born of the war might grow to maturity. Life was going on all the time; and only those who were prepared to say what decisions were consonant with the new spirit had any right to criticize those who acted in accordance with the old. Such advice as Gentile was prepared to give sprang only from the negative disciplinary aspect of the new spirit; it was too authoritarian to be heeded by any parliamentary government. He did not exactly drift into Fascism as the country did; but he did not yet see where he was going.

---

[71] Cf. B.569 in B.818, p. 251.
[72] *Ibid.*, p. 255.

Toward the *Riforma Gentile*

In one respect, however, he *did* have a policy. For during the last year of the war he made proposals concerning the organization and finance of Italian education which were substantially identical with the regulations that he later enacted as Minister of Public Instruction in Mussolini's first cabinet. In 1918 the Minister of Public Instruction (Signor Berenini) published a plan for the reform of the normal schools, of which Gentile did not approve; [73] and in support of his criticisms he made a number of counter-proposals in a series of articles which were almost immediately collected and issued as a pamphlet entitled *The Problem of the Schools After the War*.[74]

The root of the problem, as he saw it, was economic. The financial condition of the teaching profession was such that only a hollow mockery of education could exist in Italian schools. In order to earn enough to live on, the teacher was obliged to take on a heavy schedule of extra classes (*classi aggiunte*), and even to give private lessons, in addition to his regular work. Because of this burden, no teacher could do his job properly and there was no incentive even to try. Hence men of ability were deserting the profession and it was being flooded with women even at the higher levels. Gentile was very alarmed about this since he did not think that women possessed or ever could possess "the spirited originality of thought or the iron strength of character which are the highest intellectual and moral endowments of humanity and should be the core of the school that molds the higher culture of the country." [75]

For Gentile, as we already know, the central aim and purpose of the school as an institution was personified in the teacher: "there can never be real pupils where masters are lacking." [76] Somehow or other, therefore, he had to find a way to reduce the economic pres-

---

[73] Cf. B.465 and B.470 in B.497, pp. 269–81.

[74] B.498 (1919); in the present discussion the second edition (B.562, 1920) and the Appendix to B.813 (1925) have been used for references.

[75] B.435 in B.562, p. 14 (B.813, p. 329). Elsewhere he is slightly more tactful on this point: ". . . women can never completely replace men and it would be a very bad thing if they were in a majority; in any case, their preparation is not equal to that of the men" (B.413 in B.562, p. 72, or in B.813, p. 359).

[76] B.413 in B.562, p. 71, or in B.813, *loc. cit.;* cf. Chapters 3 and 4, pp. 57–58, 70, and 87–88, herein.

sures: extra classes and private lessons had to go. The state must pay its teachers enough to live on.

But how could this be done? In the case of elementary education there was no possible alternative to an increase in the budget. Elementary education had to have absolute financial priority because there could be no question of the State's obligation to provide gratuitously the education which establishes the basic community of culture that is its own abstract essence, and which all citizens are therefore required by law to undergo.[77]

Secondary education, however, was quite another matter. The preservation of culture at the higher levels is certainly vital to the health of the State. But it would be impossible, and absolutely wrong, to apply the same democratic equalitarian principles in this case. Society needs engineers and doctors; but there is no reason why every citizen should be trained to perform these functions. Given the common basis provided in the elementary schools, every citizen should go on to develop his own personal culture in accordance with his position and task in society as a whole. The task of secondary education in the academic sense of the word is to develop an intellectual aristocracy. The principle of democratic equality justly requires that everyone should have an equal opportunity to become a member of this aristocracy. But this requirement is met by establishing competitive examinations as the only means of access to the State secondary schools.

Gentile maintained that there was *no* real secondary education in Italy because this aristocratic purpose had been lost sight of. Multitudes of students were passing through the *liceo*, and even going on to the university, simply in order to obtain diplomas that would enable them to enter some special trade or profession. The whole system was overloaded with this "ballast" [78] which must somehow or other be disposed of. Both the number of secondary schools and the number of students admitted to them must be drastically reduced; and some less costly and elaborate way of training people for particular trades and professions must be devised. The multitude of smaller universities could then be left to justify themselves in an economic struggle for existence which would result, at least, in the disappearance of a number of superfluous faculties.

---

[77] B.413 in B.562, pp. 75–76 (B.813, p. 362); cf. B.529 and n68 above.

[78] *Zavorra*—this was a word that Gentile had borrowed from Salvemini years before (cf. B.217 in B.813, p. 136).

Being a nineteenth-century liberal, Gentile recognized that this severely aristocratic conception of secondary education could not be justified if any one authority retained a virtual monopoly in the field. His idea was that the State should set an example which other institutions were free to follow, and a standard by which their achievements could be impartially judged. It was therefore essential to his plan that private schools should be given a fair chance in competition with State schools. But he was in somewhat of an embarrassment here—an embarrassment which was only increased by the enthusiastic welcome accorded to this aspect of his program in the Catholic press—for he had always maintained that the State was the only source of public activity, and he certainly did not wish to withdraw from this position. He got around the difficulty, as best he could, by pointing out that he was not advocating complete independence for private schools; the State must remain responsible for the quality of education in all schools and all schools must recognize its authority. The teachers in recognized secondary schools must be duly qualified and their pupils must pass State examinations.

There is a certain irony in his use of the proposed *esame di Stato* to meet the doctrinaire liberal claim that responsibility for all education must rest with the State. For he was here appealing to that part of his proposal which was best calculated to strengthen the private schools. Until his great reform in 1923, they were hampered not merely by their inability to compete economically with the State schools where fees were kept very low, but also by the fact that all official examinations were set and graded locally *in* the State schools *by* the State teachers. Pupils in private schools were therefore most unfairly handicapped even if the State teacher was absolutely conscientious; and only the establishment of independent boards of examiners for each district—which was what the supporters of the *esame di Stato* wanted—could give them a fair chance.

Considering Gentile's plan as a whole in its relation to the social and political situation at the time, it is not easy to see how a better one could have been devised. The economic situation of the teacher had to be improved, and more elementary teachers had to be trained and paid. But Italy has always been poor, and her existence as a nation was from the beginning overshadowed by a chronically unbalanced budget. In these circumstances economies had to be made somewhere. Gentile's was probably the best way in which to make them.[79] There is, however, one remark in the minister's reply to his open letter that should give us pause: ". . . we must look at the scholastic problem as a whole and ask ourselves whether the 'ballast' that he has made so much play with does not contain other and different properties, which, if they were differently developed, instructed, and educated, might bear fruit in ways which are socially more valuable than the scramble after jobs, even jobs obtained by way of examinations, for which the candidate prepares himself as well as he can [sc. on his own as Gentile proposed]." [80]

In justice to this objection we must admit that Gentile's solution of the problem, though perhaps it was the best possible, was given too 'absolutely.' He talks like Plato as if every man should be trained simply for his particular task. But it is by no means obvious that "secondary education is, of its very nature, aristocratic" unless we accept a very narrow and academic definition of what education is. The zavorra might well be capable of benefiting in a different kind of school. Under particular circumstances it may be impossible to do anything about this; but the fact that Gentile ignores the possibility, and talks as if his solution were speculative and not empirical, is evidence of sheer academic snobbery.

His plan did not pass altogether unheeded. In June 1920 Nitti's cabinet fell, and the old master Giolitti emerged from the shadows to form a government himself. He persuaded Croce to become Minister of Public Instruction; and Croce in his turn appointed Gentile chairman of a committee to draft proposals for secondary-school reform. This committee produced bills for the reduction of extra classes and the establishment of the esame di Stato (independent boards of examiners for the certificate of graduation whether from private schools or from State schools). But these proposals were rejected by the education committee of the Chamber of Deputies and did not even come to a vote in the Parliament itself. Shortly afterward Giolitti tried the experiment of a general elec-

[79] Some orthodox liberals proposed a large increase of fees. But Gentile regarded this as a more serious infringement of the principle of State responsibility than his own solution. If and insofar as the preservation of culture was a national concern, the cost should not be borne simply by the individuals who profited directly by its preservation. Fees should remain low, and selection should be by examination (cf. B.512 in B.562, pp. 101–6, or in B.813, pp. 380–84).

[80] B.562, p. 30 (not in B.813).

lini's *Fasci di Combattimento,* though later on many of them followed Gentile into the Fascist party. Their closest political ties were with the Nationalist party. But they were ready to accept any alliance which would help them put their plans into force; [3] and Mussolini, who had no educational program and no real interest in the subject, was quite willing, at first, to give them a free hand.

Seeing things as we do, in the perspective of later history, it is hard to realize that Gentile's acceptance of Mussolini's offer was not a fateful or irrevocable step. The Fascists had come to power in a very unorthodox way; but the situation was critical, and to many thoughtful observers on the right, the need to overcome the existing paralysis of government seemed urgent enough to justify overlooking this. The government was, after all, still a coalition of a fairly familiar type, and it seemed reasonable to hope that, once the crisis had passed, Fascism itself, being merely one of the symptoms, would disappear. The new Minister of Education—whose very appointment was for other intellectuals the most reassuring thing about the whole situation [4]—had no interest in the ultimate fate of Mussolini or his party; he saw only an opportunity to put the results of his long meditations to the test. He came to power with definite views about what he wanted to do, and by the force of his example he managed to inspire many of his collaborators with an energy and enthusiasm that almost equaled his own. In the space of a few short months he reorganized the Italian educational system more or less from top to bottom. In the process he annoyed a fairly large number of people and became the target of a great deal of parliamentary criticism.

---

[3] The *Popolari,* for reasons explained in the last chapter, supported one major part of their program, the *esame di Stato.* According to Prezzolini (*op. cit.,* p. 157) the Fascist group of professors had declared against this proposal at the conference in Naples a week before the March on Rome. This in itself is a sufficient commentary on the claim that the Gentile reform was "the most Fascist of the reforms."

[4] The general bewilderment of the academic world over the new turn of events is well described by M. Ascoli in "The Press and the Universities in Italy," *Annals of the American Academy of Political and Social Science,* CC, November 1938, 248 (or in F. Keene, ed., *Neither Liberty nor Bread,* New York, Harper, 1940, p. 116). All were reassured by Gentile's appointment but even among his friends the uncertainty is apparent. Thus *Levana,* the educational periodical edited by Codignola, greeted the new minister with an unsigned editorial which was already redolent with the 'Fascist idealism' of five years later (I, 1922, 369–72), while Lombardo-Radice in his journal *L'Educazione nazionale* signed his name to an equally enthusiastic salute, but did not try to hide his doubts about Fascism itself (November 1922, pp. 2–3).

His success and the criticism he aroused were perhaps partially responsible for his decision to join the Fascist party in May 1923. The Party certainly wanted to take the credit for his achievements; and Gentile needed firm political support in finishing his work. Mussolini referred to the reform of education as *la più fascista delle riforme*, "the most Fascist of the reforms"; but all that this meant was aptly summed up by Giuseppe Bottai when he set to work years later to produce a genuinely 'Fascist' educational system. He replied to those who cited this authoritative judgment with the simple observation that the *Riforma Gentile* was indeed "the most Fascist" reform at that time—because there were no others!

Gentile himself always claimed that his work was truly 'Fascist' in spirit; but this was simply a way of saying that for him Fascism was the embodiment of the 'spirit of Vittorio Veneto,' or the continuation and fulfillment of the liberal tradition as he understood it.[5] The reform was actually based on principles laid down in his report to the 1907 congress on "The Lay School" and was foreshadowed in outline in the proposals of 1919 which were described at the end of the last chapter. We shall here be concerned with it only as a realization of his pre-Fascist theories.[6]

At the elementary level the outstanding novelty of the reform was that the teaching of Christian religious doctrine according to the Roman Catholic tradition became the core of the curriculum; in the higher grades religious instruction was to be given 'historically' —so as to provide a kind of bridge to the secondary school in which no dogmatic religion was to be taught, its place being taken by

---

[5] See Chapter 5, pp. 151–53, herein, and the next section of the present chapter (pp. 167–78).

[6] Those who are interested in the Gentile reform as a working system of education should refer to the brilliant critical and historical study by Dr. Minio-Paluello, *Education in Fascist Italy*, and the earlier volume, *Making Fascists* (University of Chicago Press, 1929), by H. W. Schneider and S. B. Clough, which provides some interesting illustrative material such as quotations from approved textbooks. Since in this chapter and the last I am concerned with Gentile's political activity only insofar as it mirrored or reacted upon his social and political thought, I have been obliged for the most part to concentrate on his own view of events. The fact that his beliefs and expectations were often out of harmony with the realities of the situation is treated here only as a ground for criticizing the speculative assumptions on which those beliefs and expectations were founded. It is no part of my present purpose to offer an objective critique of Gentile's achievement as a member of Mussolini's cabinet or of his subsequent career as a Fascist publicist. A balanced judgment of the history of Fascism does not seem to me to be possible as yet. Certainly I am not in a position to offer one.

philosophy. Apart from this major innovation no other great change was introduced; but there was a slight increase of emphasis on such artistic activities as drawing and singing.[7]

In the secondary schools the 'organic' character of Gentile's approach is immediately apparent. The reforms introduced affected the structure of the school system perhaps more than anything else. The classical *ginnasio-liceo* continued to exist unchanged, offering a unified program of studies which extended over eight years and gave access to the university. This was the heart of the secondary-school system as Gentile conceived it. Classical and Italian literature and history formed the core of the curriculum; and philosophy was given an important place in the programs of the higher grades (the *liceo*). Other secondary schools were organized as nearly on this model as their particular purposes would allow. The normal school, for example, which had hitherto accepted pupils from a variety of sources, was provided with its own preparatory division entered directly from the primary schools; the complete curriculum was planned to extend over seven years; Latin occupied a central position in the syllabus for every year; and philosophy, especially the philosophy of education, was to be taught in the higher grades in place of the old dogmatic pedagogy.

Even the more strictly scientific institutions conformed largely to the same pattern. The technical institute was provided with a preparatory section strictly adapted to its own needs, in place of the old technical school, which had contained many pupils who merely wished to continue their education for a year or two. In the curriculum of this new lower course Latin was one of the most important subjects. The 'modern' section of the old classical *liceo* was combined with the physics and mathematics division of the technical institute to form a new school, the *liceo scientifico* or science lyceum, which gave access to the scientific faculties of the universities. In this case, however, an exception to the rule of organic autonomy was made. The science lyceum provided a course of only four years and could be entered after four years of satisfactory work at any other secondary school.[8] There was naturally

---

[7] Cf. Gentile's proposals of 1907 described herein in Chapter 3, pp. 66–76, and his theory of child development, Chapter 4, pp. 79–81, 93–95.

[8] This exception was made necessary by the over-all need for economy; Gentile revealed in 1937 that he would have founded a *ginnasio scientifico* if he had had the financial resources possessed by some of his successors (see n116 below).

a strong emphasis on scientific subjects, especially mathematics and physics, in the curriculum, and there was no Greek; but the pattern of the classical lyceum was maintained in that an important place was given to Latin, and philosophy was taught in the higher grades.

In the original plan there was one other school which was not an organic whole, complete in itself, the lyceum for girls (*liceo femminile*), which was a sort of three-year finishing school for girls who did not intend to take up a career; it could be entered after four years at any other secondary school. This school was a complete innovation; but it proved unsuccessful and was abolished after a few years.

This reorganization of the secondary schools was, as can be seen even in this brief sketch, a notable advance toward the ideal of organic unity which receives so much emphasis in Gentile's philosophy of education. For each different kind of pupil, a different school; and within each school a strictly regulated unitary curriculum.[9]

But far more important than the new organization, at least in the minds of the reformers, was the change that would be wrought by the new 'spirit' in education. "The letter killeth but the spirit giveth life." The mechanical grind of the school dominated by the 'realistic' prejudice which Gentile had studied and criticized so acutely in *The Reform of Education* was to be replaced by the freedom and spontaneity of the new idealism. To this end greater freedom and responsibility were given to the teachers; they were informed that the detailed syllabus provided for each grade by the ministry was intended only as an indication of what would be expected in the examination, not as a strict program for the teachers, whose proper task was to encourage the free development of their pupils rather than to provide them with factual information.

Unfortunately, the new spirit made very little headway against the weight of tradition and the normal human unwillingness to accept freedom and responsibility. Nor is this surprising, for a candid study of the reform reveals that spontaneity could never flourish within such a rigid scheme of things. To begin with, the pupil had no real liberty at all; his curriculum was fixed and he had to pass one examination after another in all of the subjects involved. The teacher, on the other hand, knew that his success in

---

[9] The higher technical institutes had different specialized programs; but even these appear to have been strictly regulated.

getting his pupils through these examinations, like circus animals through a series of hoops, was the criterion by which his capabilities would be judged; and whatever the minister's instructions to the examiners might be concerning the evaluation of the candidate's *personal culture* and *general intelligence*, all parties involved in an examination were bound to recognize that it is impossible to make a reliable estimate of such subjective elements on the basis of a single meeting. 'The facts' considered as the material presupposition of the school are objective; the question of whether a particular candidate is acquainted with them can be decided more or less impartially. Hence the teacher must tend to concentrate on them and on the examination, because the pupils will recognize thereby that his judgment and his purpose are truly objective, and not conditioned by his own arbitrary caprice. We have here a speculative ground for the 'realism' that is natural to the school; a speculative ground to which Gentile did not pay sufficient attention either in theory or in practice. Men will always cling to institutions as a relief from personal responsibility and active morality: liberty and spontaneity in education will always be an ideal approached only by a few. But except in a system of maximum flexibility, in which it is impossible either for the teacher or for the pupil to evade responsibility altogether, and possible for both parties to accept a great deal, even this minority cannot hope to exist. The rigidity of Gentile's curriculum was certain to stifle the new spirit wherever it raised its head; especially in view of his concern for strictness and objectivity in the enforcement of regulations and the raising of standards. He claimed, for instance, to be striking a notable blow for idealism against realism and spiritual sloth, by substituting a list of philosophical classics in the place of the old textbooks of 'philosophy.' But it is questionable whether this advance was not more than nullified if, as seems probable, the classics were then studied simply as examination material. To degrade the *Republic* into a textbook is perhaps worse than learning by heart a summary of Plato's 'philosophy' supplied by some academic hack.

In accordance with Gentile's view of their place in the development of the spirit, the universities were granted complete autonomy. They were left to organize themselves, subject only to the minister's approval—which proved a sufficient check, however, to make the return to strict State supervision in 1936 quite easy.

Along with the reorganization of the school system there went several important administrative reforms, designed in the main to secure financial economies. The staff of the ministry, which was renamed the Ministry of National Education in homage to the new spirit, was reduced in various ways, and greater power and responsibility were given to the principals and heads of schools.[10]

The universities were divided into three classes, A, B, and C: those in Class A were maintained by the State, those in Class B received State assistance, and a number of the smaller universities (Class C) were left to fend for themselves entirely. No university was completely abolished—indeed a new medical school with university status was actually established at Bari—but it was anticipated that financial necessity would cause the abolition of some faculties at universities which lacked State support. The number of secondary schools was reduced (especially the normal schools) and for teaching purposes various subjects (Latin and Italian, philosophy and history, physics and mathematics, etc.) were combined.[11] The size of classes was limited, and the *classi aggiunte* were abolished. The many teachers, inspectors, and others who lost their positions seem to have been either genuinely inefficient or else simply the unlucky ones; I have seen no suggestion anywhere that political criteria were employed [12]—though 'political unreliability' became common enough in later years as the official grounds for dismissal. In general this aspect of the reform seems to have been quite successful.

It is obvious that the whole reform was conceived in terms of Gentile's own philosophy; and critics were not slow to complain

---

[10] For this, however, Gentile could offer a philosophical justification (cf. Chapter 3, p. 71, herein).

[11] There was much criticism of the somewhat doctrinaire fashion in which this was done. The scientists complained that while it was reasonable to expect a physics teacher to teach mathematics the converse was not so natural; and both philosophers and historians were dissatisfied. But instead of simply recommending that combinations be made in accordance with the training and interests of available staff, Gentile persisted in imposing his uniform pattern. In the particular case of philosophy, the implication was clear—anyone whom *he* would be prepared to call a 'philosopher' should be able to teach history, and vice versa. Of course, this consideration could only be regarded as conclusive on the assumption that in future all teachers of philosophy or history would be more or less members of Gentile's school. So that his intransigence in this matter lent color to the frequent accusation that he was seeking to set up an "intellectual dictatorship."

[12] But military service was speedily recognized as deserving special consideration (cf. B.720 in B.1057, p. 112).

about this. The Catholics, especially, objected to his conception of religion, and to the restriction of religious instruction to the elementary schools. Gentile, influenced perhaps by political considerations—for the new government needed the support of the *Popolari* —replied that the reform must be judged independently of his philosophy; that his opinions had very little to do with the matter since the results would be not his work but that of the whole teaching profession; [13] and that most of the reforms he had instituted had been recommended by others who did not share his speculative views.[14] There is this much to be said in his defense: the majority of schoolchildren would receive a not too dogmatic grounding in the Christian faith according to the Roman confession, without ever so much as hearing of actual idealism unless they went to the *liceo* or into the teaching profession. Gentile was well aware of this; it forms a striking proof of the sincerity of his own religious convictions; and I do not think that the Catholics have ever given him due credit for it.

From Liberalism to Fascism

In the midst of his reforming labors the minister was visited by the Secretary of the National Fascist Party, who came to offer him a Party membership card. He replied in a letter to Mussolini [15] which deserves to be quoted in full because it strikes the keynote of his attitude in the succeeding years:

(Rome, 31 May 1923)

Dear Mr. President,[16]

As I am today making my formal act of adherence to the Fascist Party, I beg you to allow me a brief declaration, in order that I may tell you that in this adherence I believe I am fulfilling a moral obligation of sincerity and political honesty.

As a liberal whose convictions are deep-rooted and firm, during these months in which I have had the honor of collaborating in your great task of government and sharing closely in the development of the principles that inform your political action, I have become absolutely convinced that Liberalism, as I understand it and as the men of the glorious Right that guided Italy in the Risorgimento understood it, the Liberalism of

---

[13] Cf. B.789 in B.1057, pp. 257–62.
[14] Cf. B.826 in B.1057, p. 312.
[15] B.723 in B.1057, pp. 127–28.
[16] Mussolini was officially President of the Council of Ministers.

liberty within the law and therefore within a State that is strong, and a State that is conceived as an ethical reality, is not represented in Italy today by the liberals who are more or less openly opposed to you, but in actual fact by yourself.

And therefore I am likewise convinced that between the liberals of today and the Fascists who understand the thought behind your Fascism, a genuine liberal who disdains equivocations and desires to stand at his rightful post must range himself at your side.

Cordially Yours,
G. G.

Naturally enough many liberals were deeply offended at Gentile's suggestion that Fascism was the true liberalism; and they accused him of cloaking betrayal with hypocrisy. Gentile responded that they did not understand his liberalism, and that he had never been the sort of liberal whose creed was the antithesis of Fascism, as his critics claimed that it should be. And in fact his adhesion to Fascism was simply the culmination of the disillusion of which we saw the beginning in our last chapter. Even before the March on Rome he had joined with a group of friends in planning a review to be called *The New Liberal Politics;* and for the first issue which appeared in January 1923 he wrote an article on the contrast between the true 'philosophical' tradition of liberalism and the classical political theory that arose in seventeenth-century England.[17]

The change in attitude which the writing of this article implied can be seen when we remember how, during the war, he had met the Nationalists' attack on 'liberal individualism' with the retort that liberalism had *never* been a doctrine of individualism "except in its origins in natural law theory, and then only for completely transitory historical reasons."[18] The implication of his argument then was that individualism was only a passing phase which had soon vanished; and although he knew that this view scarcely corre-

---

[17] B.707 in B.818, pp. 119–22. Answering the later cry of betrayal he wrote: ". . . even when we were liberals and did not yet believe we could become fascists we felt, nonetheless, the need to speak of 'new liberal politics' so as to make it clear that we had no intention of becoming confused with the gray mass of the indefinite liberals" (B.845 in B.818, p. 172). But the *Nuova politica liberale* was not in fact the organ of a coherent group. Among those associated in the original project (cf. *Giornale critico,* III, 1922, 419) were Croce, who withdrew before the first issue and became the severest of the critics Gentile was trying to answer, and Lombardo-Radice, who remained hostile to Fascism though he did not personally quarrel with Gentile.

[18] B.481 in B.497, p. 56; cf. Chapter 5, pp. 133–34, herein.

sponded with the historical facts,[19] he was confident that the war had finally destroyed the false liberalism of abstract individualism. After the war he refused for some time to recognize that the old enemy was not dead. But the reappearance of Giolitti and the Liberals who had opposed Italy's entry into the war convinced him finally that his was not the only liberalism that counted.

The liberalism that he opposed was the cosmopolitan humanitarian creed of the French Revolution: the creed in which the individual man has 'natural rights' *against* the State or any other social organism. His own view was that the State is the actual embodiment of the citizen's ethical personality. He distinguished this thesis from the 'statolatry of socialism' by saying that the Ethical State is not a material entity but an ideal toward which the individual aspires. The key to the relation between State and citizen for Gentile lay in the readiness of the patriot to die for his country—and clearly a view of this kind has nothing in common with "the great lottery of mob democracy." [20] On the contrary, the religion of the *patria* is the foundation of the *Stato forte*, the strong State.

Gentile claimed that his was the liberalism of the Risorgimento and of those men of the 'Right' who carried on the Risorgimento tradition down to 1876. And it can scarcely be denied that the 'moderates' who put the House of Savoy on the throne of Italy were inclined to authoritarian habits of thought and action. None of them hesitated to infringe on the most sacred 'rights of man' when they felt that the interests of Italy required it. Ricasoli's record of authoritarian government in Tuscany is the prime example. Cavour, who was thoroughly imbued with the classical English liberalism, was, as Gentile himself admits, a partial exception; [21] but even he was quite prepared to impose a strict censorship of the press, and justified his action by declaring that States were brought to ruin by an undue respect for abstract principles.[22]

To have the 'moderates' on his side, however, was not enough. He claimed, above all, the support of Mazzini. The evaluation of this thesis is more difficult. We have already had occasion to mention

---

[19] A little further on in 'the same article he admits that the tradition of anarchic liberalism continued to exist alongside the deeper humanism of the German philosophers.

[20] B.707 in B.818, p. 121.

[21] B.824 in B.818, pp. 179–96, or B.1139, pp. 97–113; cf. B.785 in B.818, p. 130.

[22] Cf. *ibid.*, p. 127.

Mazzini's theory of a National Contract as "the inauguration, the baptism of the nation . . . the initiative that determines the normal life, the successive and peaceful development of the forces and faculties of the country." [23] This element in Mazzini's writings, along with his theory of the "privilege of genius" and of the Nation as a *mission* which is the highest moral duty of the citizens, is obviously consistent with Gentile's rather totalitarian liberalism as well as with his later Fascism. But there are other elements in the gospel of the great Genoese, which can scarcely be reconciled with Gentile's Hegelian view of history. Mazzini continually exalts 'association' as a principle of the new age, and this association is voluntary in the strongest sense of the term. Numerous positive liberties were to be guaranteed to the individual by the Nation—some of which were denied by the Fascists from the beginning; and even if Mazzini was not unconditionally in favor of universal suffrage, there can be no doubt that he held firmly to the principle of free election. Recognizing the difficulty, Gentile tries to argue that we must seize the essence of Mazzini, his religion of the Nation, and cast aside the "outdated formulas that Mazzini accepted from the various revolutionary currents with which he was obliged to ally himself." [24] But an interpretation of Mazzini's 'spirit' that makes it necessary to cast aside many of the beliefs and ideals for which he worked and suffered is not to be trusted. Mazzini would have admitted that the representative principle was not something absolute and inviolable; a vote can have no value if it is not cast with a sense of moral responsibility. But he held, nevertheless, that "a democratic inspiration is the soul of every rising faith," [25] and I do not think for a moment that he would have been satisfied with Gentile's argument for the 'democratic inspiration' of Fascism. It is well to bear this in mind when we approach Gentile's writings in defense of Fascism, which are full of the 'spirit of Mazzini' as he understood it.

The Liberal opponents of Fascism naturally found Gentile's defense even more offensive than the crime of which he stood accused. It was nonsense, they said, to suggest that the great heroes of the Risorgimento were all Fascists. But this, of course, was not what Gentile meant. He protested that he had "too much respect for history to want to give a party card to Spaventa or to anyone else

[23] *Duties of Man*, p. 236; cf. Chapter 3, p. 61, herein.
[24] B.505–6 in B.1280, p. 32 (pre-Fascist essays later dedicated to Mussolini).
[25] *Duties of Man*, p. 289.

among the political leaders of the prewar period." [26] Any such suggestion, he added, would be quite unjust to the Fascists, who had produced a great revolution in Italian political life—a revolution which involved a return to the political principles of the 'Right,' but certainly not a return to 1876. Gentile recognized that even the era of 'transformism,' which was so repugnant to him, had achieved something essential by bringing the mass of the people into politics, making them citizens and giving them a share in governmental responsibility. The "making of the Italians," which D'Azeglio had foreseen as the task of the newly made Italy, was begun by the Socialists and completed by the war, which corrected the abstract universalism of official Socialist doctrine, and taught the whole nation the lessons of discipline and self-sacrifice. Out of the war issued Fascism, *a mass movement* embodying this new spirit of national discipline. The healthy element of the socialist tradition— Sorel's syndicalism—had been absorbed by the new movement; and the revival of idealism in the years before the war had prepared the way for the new spirit.[27] Meanwhile the survivors of the old 'Right' continued to do reverence to the Nation with their lips; but many of them were so enamored of their ideal that they could not bear it to be contaminated by real application—especially when its reality involved some definite sacrifice and discipline on their part.[28]

The twin ideas of sacrifice and discipline were, according to Gentile, the keynotes of the new movement. In this way it was linked with Mazzini: the battle cry of Fascism was *Pensiero ed azione*, "Thought *and* action"; and since its attitude was fundamentally religious, it was bound to be absolutely intransigent toward its opponents. By its unbending earnestness it had bestowed something of dignity and seriousness even on the other parties, who had hitherto been content to squabble with one another in pursuit of their own

---

[26] B.834 in B.818, p. 138. The Spaventa referred to is *Silvio* Spaventa (brother of the Hegelian philosopher Bertrando), who was a major figure among the leaders of the 'Right' in the generation after the death of Cavour. He was also the uncle who became Croce's guardian after the earthquake that rendered him an orphan.

[27] Cf. B.785 (October 1924) in B.818, p. 129; B.778 (March 1924) in B.818, pp. 52, 56–60. Gentile claims in several places to have been a precursor of Fascism by virtue of his part in this revival; cf. B.729 in B.1057, pp. 167–68, and B.726 in B.1057, pp. 141–42. His view of the period, although expressed mainly in the form of Party propaganda, must always be kept in mind when reading Croce's *History of Italy*, 1871–1915.

[28] B.735 (October 1923) in B.818, p. 124; B.778 in B.818, pp. 51–52.

advantage, interpreting the public good as equivalent to the satisfaction of their own selfish egoism. Here was something that was more worthy of consideration than futile arguments about the liberties that it had 'destroyed.' Families were divided against each other and old friendships broken. But this was not something to be regretted but rather to be accepted without bitterness or malice. A real faith always sends "not peace but a sword" on the earth. History is a long battle of tragically opposed ideals, not a quest of peace and comfort.[29]

This 'religious' character of Fascism seemed to Gentile to be something that transcended the Party itself. It was the inward essence of the movement, the spirit immanent in it which conferred upon it a universal significance. Regarded simply as a political doctrine, Fascism was bound to remain partisan, for not everyone could be a party member. But this spiritual essence—the religious, totalitarian view of life—should and eventually would inform the consciousness of all citizens. Moreover, being totalitarian, it must penetrate every sphere of human activity: "It is impossible to be Fascists in politics, and non-Fascists . . . in school, non-Fascists in our families, non-Fascists in our daily occupations." [30]

It is difficult, however, to see how anything as nebulous as this 'spirit' of Fascism could exist and work anywhere outside of the imagination of an idealist philosopher. 'Taking life seriously'— which seems to be almost all that this 'spirit' amounts to—will not distinguish a Fascist from any other person who acts upon a strong religious or moral conviction. Indeed, since a conviction which is to lead to action must be determinate, it would be impossible for the Fascist to exist *as such* without some definite belief. It is impossible simply to be religious—one must be religious in a definite way.

Yet Gentile insisted that the new spirit should not be allowed to ossify into a *credo* or a system of dogma; [31] he emphasized that his

---

[29] B.833 in B.818, pp. 143–51. The echoes of Matt. 10:34–38 in this article were not mere rhetoric but expressed Gentile's real sense of loss through the breach with Croce which became final about this time (beginning of March 1925). He refers to the breach without mentioning names on pp. 147–48. For further details see the note at the end of the present chapter.

[30] B.837 in B.818, p. 38.

[31] B.818, p. 95. It is clear that Gentile wished to maintain the doctrinal flexibility of the Party in order to make eventual reconciliation with its liberal adversaries possible without sacrifice of conscience (cf. B.796 in B.818, pp. 139–41, written during the Matteotti crisis).

own Fascism was only a personal interpretation of this spirit.[32] On the surface it might seem that this line of argument leads to the Protestant theory of 'private judgment,' which Gentile cordially abhorred; but since in fact politics cannot be made out of a group of philosophical doctrines which the author admits to be only moral ideals, the 'religious spirit' of which Gentile talked so much was actually bound to produce just the opposite result. It meant that ultimately no sincere Fascist could attach any value to his personal interpretation of Fascism. So long as the new faith lacked a doctrine and a program—upon which a *really* 'personal' view might be founded, that is, a view which possessed a certain objective validity —it inevitably resolved itself into simple acceptance of orders received from above. And this conclusion is just as inconsistent with the whole tenor of actual idealism as the theory of 'private judgment.' [33]

Certainly, the acceptance of authority was typical of the 'religious' frame of mind as Gentile interpreted it; but equally certainly he did not mean this when he spoke of a return to the religious spirit, as he often did,[34] in the years before the March on Rome. To suppose that he could rest content with a politics of religious obedience would make nonsense of his work as a philosopher. His continual reiteration of the religious character of Fascism is perhaps, in part, a criticism of its speculative weakness, its lack of self-awareness and self-understanding.[35] But he meant in the main to exalt it for its objectivity and universality, which were the essential prerequisites of any truly responsible, self-conscious (philosophical) approach to politics. Given this sound basis, he put his faith in the power of time. Fascism was bound to grow up; Vichian barbarism was only its first transitional stage. The violence of the *squadristi* had been necessary, but it was only a passing phase through which

---

[32] B.837 in B.818, p. 10.

[33] Similarly in a school where there is no established doctrine the pupil must either absolutely accept or absolutely reject the authority of the teacher. But Gentile, wiser in the schoolroom than in politics, points out that the religious trust of the Pythagorean student's *ipse dixit* "is not born *ex abrupto*" (B.1157, p. 77).

[34] See especially B.568 (1920) in B.1100; and cf. Chapter 5 herein, *passim.*

[35] Even in the midst of his apologies, he is obviously uncomfortable in dealing with the problem of *squadrismo:* in his attempts to dismiss the whole problem as teething troubles there is an implicit admission that religious enthusiasm can sometimes lead to excesses (for references see the following note).

the nation had to pass in order to achieve a philosophical understanding of its own liberty.[36]

Gentile's account of the liberty that was to be born of this religious revolution is at first sight simply a repetition of the philosophical doctrines with which we are already familiar.[37] Liberty, we
should be prepared to agree, belongs not to the particular individual
as a natural entity, but to the self-conscious personality in its endeavor to obey the moral law: man demonstrates his liberty, so far
as he issues from his own private world and accepts responsibility
for happenings in the public world which belongs alike to all men.
This public world as an organism unified by law is the State, so
that through the individual's acceptance of public responsibility the
State ceases to be thought of as an external power imposing its will
on him. The real State *in interiore homine* is not a system of related
atoms but the concrete realization of the one individual, whereas the
conception of the individual as an atom possessed of liberty against
all comers makes it no more than an instrument in the service of
individual interests and factions. Gentile contended that this degradation of the State had happened in Italy after the fall of the
Right.[38] And, if indeed the Fascists really did deny the egoistic
liberty of classical liberal economics, we must agree that they were
right to do so.[39]

There seems to be nothing particularly dangerous or reprehen-
sible in all this; but Gentile in a university lecture hall (even the
lecture hall of the 'Fascist University' at Bologna) is almost another
person from Gentile as a supporter of the Fascist party. "Liberty,"
he told his fellow Sicilians in a speech before the elections of 1924,

is certainly the supreme end and rule of every human life, but only so
far as individual and social education make it a reality by embodying the
common will, which takes the form of law and hence of the State, in the
particular individual. . . . From this point of view State and individual
are identical, and the art of government is the art of so reconciling and
uniting the two terms that a maximum of liberty harmonizes with a maximum of public order not merely in the external sense, but also and above

[36] B.837 in B.818, pp. 29–33; B.735 in B.818, p. 124; B.830 in B.818, p. 157;
B.836 in B.937, p. 56 (cited p. 183, herein).

[37] As expounded in a lecture on "Liberty and Liberalism" at the 'Fascist
University' of Bologna on 9 March 1925 (B.828 in B.818, pp. 65–94).

[38] B.783 in B.818, p. 214; cf. B.778 in B.818, p. 45.

[39] B.828 in B.818, p. 86; cf., for example, B.778 in B.818, p. 49 (but contrast
B.785 in B.818, p. 126).

all in the sovereignty ascribed to the law and to its necessary organs. For always the maximum liberty coincides with the maximum force of the State.[40]

This passage contains the crux of the theory that the State is internal to the consciousness of the individual. For the State that makes its will to coincide with that of the individual, through the educational control it exercises, is certainly not—so far as it actually exercises control—a State that includes its own opponents. It is the government purely and simply; and though there may be some disagreement among the members of the government, there is no room for disagreement on the part of the ordinary citizen. His part is to obey; otherwise he is a criminal—one who has betrayed his status as a free and moral being.[41]

Certainly it is right and natural for the duly constituted representatives of a State or society of any kind to endeavor to generate in its members a spirit of common loyalty; and certainly a member who is imbued with this loyalty will readily agree that the laws and commands of the governing body must be obeyed even when one disagrees with the government. But no one can long continue to make this distinction between the government with which he disagrees and the State to which he owes allegiance, unless within the framework of the State there is a means by which he can make his own will felt, and reverse the educational relation subsisting between himself and the official authorities.[42] The error in Gentile's

---

[40] B.778 in B.818, p. 50. A longer extract including this passage is given in H. W. Schneider's *Making the Fascist State*, New York, Oxford, 1928, pp. 346–47.

[41] Cf. B.818, p. 104, where the State is acknowledged to be an ideal—but an ideal which, thanks to governmental activity, tends to be ever more completely embodied in the government.

[42] Mazzini recognized this very clearly, and he saw that it necessarily involves the right to organize an opposition party: ". . . National Education shall at the conclusion of its teaching dismiss the pupils with these words: 'To you, destined to live under a common compact with us, we have taught the fundamental bases of this compact, the principles in which your nation believes today. But remember that the first of these principles is Progress. Remember that your mission as a man and as a citizen is to improve the mind and the heart of your brothers wherever you can. Go, examine, compare, and if you discover a truth superior to what we believe we possess, publish it boldly and you will have the blessing of your Country.'

". . . The State represents a certain sum and set of principles in which the universal body of citizens are agreed at the time of its foundation. Suppose that a new and true principle, a new and reasonable development of the

defense of totalitarian government lies in treating the coincidence of liberty with State power almost as if it were an immediate identity rather than a process of give and take; and he proceeds to a justification of Fascist violence which became notorious even outside of Italy. His argument will not surprise attentive readers of our fourth chapter: it rests on his refusal to recognize any distinction between 'moral' and 'material' force. There are those, he admits, who "distinguish moral from material force: the force of the law freely voted and accepted, from the force of violence which is rigidly opposed to the will of the citizen. But such distinctions are simple-minded when they are sincere! All force is moral, for it is always directed at the will; and whatever method of argument is adopted—from sermon to blackjack—its efficacy cannot be anything but its power to convince men in their hearts and persuade them to agree." [43]

When the speech was printed Gentile added a footnote explaining that his remark about the blackjack (*manganello*) was not meant to justify sheer bullying directed to a selfish end, but only the material force of the State, normally represented by the police and the army, "which everyone has always admitted and respected as moral." The *squadristi* stood for this force at a time when the official representatives of the State had completely failed to face their responsibilities. As soon as their task was fulfilled they were disbanded and given a formal legal position as the Fascist Militia. [44]

---

truths which give life to the State, is revealed to some of the citizens; how can they spread the knowledge of it without association? . . ." (*Duties of Man*, pp. 88–89, 92).

Mazzini's political doctrine is one which, *as a whole*, is consonant with all that is best in actual idealism. It is a pity that Gentile did not accept it as a whole, but only in fragments which lent themselves to the support of a reality which would have horrified Mazzini.

[43] B.778 in B.818, pp. 50–51. It is interesting to notice that immediately after this Gentile insists that rulers must recognize that the State in whose name they claim to act is not something that they possess already, but an eternal ideal. But the government which is so confident that its view is correct that it employs the blackjack against those who disagree is claiming to *be* the State *already*.

[44] Schneider (*op. cit.*, p. 347) inserts the salient parts of Gentile's footnote into his translation of the passage. But it was the speech and not the footnote that was remembered and quoted, and it was right that this should be so, for the footnote was not published until after the election. Professors who are accustomed to the use of footnotes to correct polemical exaggerations and false impressions should not make fiery political speeches. In any case the footnote does not affect the essence of the problem. Gentile's

Considering the state of Italy at the time, we may allow that this view of *squadrismo* must have seemed plausible to people who had supported Salandra's government in 1915. But Gentile's argument, coming as it does immediately after his conclusion that "the maximum liberty always coincides with the maximum force of the State," involves a deliberate ambiguity.[45] Properly speaking, the earlier conclusion ought to mean that the more fully an individual is able to realize the moral ideal of his own personality within a community, the stronger will his loyalty to that community be. Taken in this sense, Gentile's paradoxical aphorism is the best epitaph for the Fascist State that could be devised. For it contains the reason why a State which turns itself into a schoolroom with the government in the role of the schoolmaster cannot long endure: no morally adult individual can agree to remain in a community in which everything important is decided for him. At the very least he will demand the right to change his teacher and to follow a curriculum of his own choosing.

The saddest thing about this whole unhappy episode is that, as we have already indicated, this attempt to make Fascist violence an expression of the new philosophical freedom does not represent Gentile's own considered opinion. He was himself too thoroughly imbued with the respect for law and order of the good conservative to feel happy about the unorthodox way in which the Fascists had come to power. His usual attitude toward Fascist violence was that

---

position appears to be that all force is moral force when it is the force of the State, and that only the force of the State is really *forza* because *forza* means actual effectiveness. But then it is clear that there is a real distinction between 'moral' and 'material' force, or rather between moral 'force' and material 'violence.' *All* coercive methods of persuasion are ambiguous because one does not know whether they really have 'force' or not. Gentile, having identified 'force' with 'effective power,' overlooked this ambiguity of common usage. This was disastrous, since coercive violence, even if it is spiritually null, is a very real and pressing problem. It may come to nothing but it is not simply nothing. It is one obvious form of the actuality of evil. Reflection on this actuality might have made Gentile's 'solution' of the problem of evil less abstract; in any case it would have changed his attitude toward the political use of coercive methods. One may have to do evil that good may come; but if one knows that that is what one is doing one cannot take comfort in the pious reflection that if the good does not come the evil will not amount to anything really—which is what Gentile's argument about the "efficacy" of the blackjack amounts to (cf. the discussion of his theory of educational discipline in Chapter 4, pp. 84–94, herein).

[45] Croce was one of the first to observe and analyze this ambiguity accurately (*La critica*, XXIII, 1925, 253–54; cf. Chapter 9, pp. 317–18, herein).

it was all past and done with, and should not be used in criticism of what they were doing with their power now that they had it. History alone could decide the rights and wrongs of the seizure of power; opponents of the new government should have patience and wait for its verdict.[46] To revive the memory of those scandalous times before October 1922 was "bad faith"—a worse violence against the spirit than the violence of the *squadristi*.[47]

Constitutional Reform and the Corporate State

His reputation as an old-fashioned Liberal with an intense re- spect for the constitutional way of doing things was doubtless the reason why, after his resignation from the cabinet at the end of June 1924,[48] Gentile was appointed to head the Committee on Con- stitutional Reform established in October of that year.[49] His public utterances as holder of this office are an eloquent testimony to his naturally conservative attitude and his respect for tradition. He was at pains to emphasize that the Fascists were come not to destroy the law but to fulfill it. Their aim was to return to the true spirit of the statute of 1848 paring away the accretions of demagogic liberal- ism and reinterpreting the original in terms of the new twentieth-

---

[46] B.837 in B.818, p. 30.

[47] B.834 in B.818, p. 138.

[48] Cf. B.794 in B.1057, p. 303. Gentile made many enemies by his personal intransigence; and the sweeping character of his education reforms aroused much opposition and bitterness (cf. Ascoli, *op. cit.*, p. 249, or in Keene, *op. cit.*, p. 117). He resigned after a mere twenty months in office. Schneider (*op. cit.*, p. 127) connects his resignation with Mussolini's attempts to restore the popu- larity of his government during the Matteotti crisis. This is chronologically plausible since the murder of Matteotti took place in June. Schneider may be right, moreover, in thinking that the setting up of the constitutional com- mission in August was part of this pacific policy. Actually it only exacerbated the opposition, but the prompt elimination from its terms of reference of the questions about relations between the State and the press, the banks, secret societies, and international parties is an argument for this view. In presenting the report of his commission to Mussolini, Gentile mentions the problem of secret societies, but as Schneider says, the commission actually dealt only with relations between the legislative and the executive, and between the State and the syndicates. Gentile's tone of moderation and conservatism fits very well into this interpretation (*ibid.*, p. 94). He was doubtless chosen for the task because that was the kind of man he was.

[49] Strictly speaking there were two successive committees—the first con- sisting of fifteen members (October–December 1924), the second of eighteen (January–July 1925).

century situation.[50] He insisted—and, so far as I have been able to discover, his insistence was justified by historic precedents—that the *Statuto* was not a sacrosanct document but a living institution that must grow and be adapted; that the Italian constitutional tradition, like the British, had always been one of gradual modifications and adaptations. The Liberals themselves had set up constitutional commissions on this assumption; only they lacked the energy to pursue the matter to a conclusion.[51]

We have already seen that, in Gentile's view, the task of the Left had been completed before 1915 and sealed by the war: the masses had been brought into politics. Through the efforts of the Socialists the working class had been transformed from a mere aggregate into a group of corporate personalities—the trade unions or 'syndicates.' The task of the constitutional reformers therefore, as Gentile conceived it, was to take account of this development; the syndicates must be organized within the total framework of the great national personality—the State. Otherwise the State would again be degraded into a mere instrument, or a battleground of selfish egoism on the corporate level.

This was the basic premise of the Corporate State, which was voted into existence in 1925. Some of the Liberals complained that the unity of the State was being sacrificed in this legal recognition of a multiplicity of corporate bodies; but this was a somewhat naive complaint to raise, at least against *Fascist* syndicalism, and Gentile had no difficulty in answering it. The syndicates of workers and employers were to be controlled by the State through the new 'corporations' to which both sides were subordinate. The corporations in turn were organized under a single minister, and in this way the anarchy and division which had formerly existed would be articulated into unity: "Recognition [of the syndicates] apart from

---

[50] B.844 in B.818, p. 238.

[51] B.783 in B.818, pp. 212–14. It is tempting to correlate Gentile's insistence that the constitution is not sacrosanct with his doctrine that the underlying unity of the State must center on an incomplete and finite personality (the king), not on a personality complete and perfect (for instance, the historical enactment of a fundamental law; cf. Chapter 4, pp. 122–25, herein). But I hesitate to do so because although the position that he actually took over the constitution is consistent with his theory in "The Idea of Monarchy" I cannot help suspecting that he would have taken a very different attitude if it had been the *Socialists* who were trying to adapt the *Statuto* to the requirements of a Corporate State (cf. B.461 in B.561, pp. 95–100; discussed pp. 180–81, herein).

the Corporative Organization seemed to the Commission to be dangerous to the sovereignty and power of the State about which the liberals also claim to be concerned." [52]

Actually the corporations did not come into existence until 1934, while the syndicates recognized in the law of 1925 were present realities. But since there was no decadent liberal democracy involved, there was never any threat to the unity of the State. Authority in the Fascist State proceeded downward: the officers of the syndicates had to be approved by higher authorities—and at least in the case of the workers' syndicates they were generally directly appointed.

Gentile himself had offered a more serious objection to the whole idea of syndicalism in criticizing a plan put forward by the Confederation of Labor in December 1918.[53] They proposed to transfer the powers of Parliament to syndical committees of experts. After remarking that this 'new' idea went back to Plato, Gentile commented that the fallacy of the idea lay in the fact that political questions were not simply technical: no problem could be solved simply by reference to the interest of particular classes. On this point he would have been provided with a ready if somewhat specious answer in 1925—the Corporate Organization. But he went on to claim that the liberty to be had in a Nation-State was better and richer than that which was offered by the medieval corporations; and this seems to me to be an unanswerable argument from the point of view of actual idealism. In the Corporate State the great majority of citizens are assumed to be incapable of consciously willing the State which *ought* to be the substantial concreteness of their own personality. They are doomed to remain always at the moment of self-dissociation, obeying the law of the State as a power stronger than themselves but quite foreign to their own will. This is a situation familiar and unexceptionable in traditional Hegelianism, in which the moments of the dialectic are spatio-temporally dissociated; but it is definitely not in accordance with Gentile's integral humanism. Instead of providing a challenge to the citizen to transcend his own private interests, the Corporate State encourages him to pursue them as single-mindedly as possible; its own interest, which is quite separate and forms the direct concern only of a gov-

---

[52] B.843 in B.818, p. 227.
[53] B.461 in B.561, pp. 95–100; cf. B.658 in B.937, especially p. 35.

erning elite, almost requires that the ordinary citizen should *not* concern himself with the common good (since he would thereby weaken his own volitional effectiveness and indirectly lessen the power of the State). For the ordinary citizen morality should consist simply in a loyal acceptance of the umpire's decision.

Taken as a whole, there is a remarkable consistency about Gentile's political career which might lead one to suppose that his political action followed from his own interpretation of his philosophy as applied to the existing political situation. But a careful study of his change of front on this question of corporate organization may persuade us that ideas and prejudices of a not very philosophical nature had much to do with his political attitude. When we consider his work in its organic unity it is apparent that his lifelong preoccupation was with the higher intellectual culture, and particularly with the intellectual and literary tradition of his own country. These were not interests that the majority of ordinary people could either share or appreciate. Hence his abiding distrust of democracy and, in particular, his strong aversion to the Socialist party with its strictly 'economic' interpretation of reality and its ignorant contempt for national tradition. It was therefore natural that he should perceive clearly all the discrepancies between his philosophical outlook and any program advanced by the party of materialists and philistines. But when a similar program was presented with a different end in view, it was equally natural that he saw in it only a means of discipline and control for those who could not rise to higher things. The hierarchic character of the Corporate State agreed very well with his general educational program; especially since in his view secondary education (the stage of philosophy and personal autonomy) was essentially aristocratic. But for all that it was essentially contrary to the spirit of his philosophy of society.

Gentile tried hard to overcome the difficulty, but he only succeeded in making it ever plainer. In his inaugural address to the Fascist Institute of Culture, for example, he argued that Fascism was no enemy to democracy, if by democracy we mean the education of a whole people called to participate in their own government "all alike, men and women, from the so-called governing classes to the must humble laborers." [54] But the vocation must be

---

[54] B.836 in B.937, p. 51.

genuine, and therefore the people must be organized according to the categories in which their own life and interests are articulated, *in order that* the individual may be ever more conscious of the indissoluble unity between his interests and those of society as a whole.

This argument involves two conflicting conceptions of the 'corporation' at one and the same time. It is legitimate to conceive it as an instrument of government in the authoritarian sense, that is to say as a way of educating and disciplining the citizens. Putting the best construction on their efforts, this was what the Fascists tried to do through the corporative system. As we have said, this fits in very well with Gentile's organic conception of education, and his experience of the Corporate State did much to broaden his conception of his own educational humanism.[55] But then it is idle to say that the Corporate State is a form of *self*-government or a more concrete form of democracy on the grounds that it articulates actual interests. It does, indeed, articulate them; but it does so precisely in order to *prevent* their expressing themselves freely. One can have a corporate system of civic education; or one can, perhaps, in spite of the objection raised above, have a syndicalist system of democratic government. But I do not see how one can have both at once.

'Fascist' Culture

After the murder of Matteotti in June 1924, Mussolini made great efforts for a few months to placate liberal parliamentary opinion. Finding this impossible, he began to construct an overt dictatorship in January 1925. The majority of the intelligentsia were now definitely alienated from the new Regime. Croce, who had supported the government even during the Matteotti crisis, now became and ever after remained the principal representative of this alienation; Gentile became the leader of the minority who made the opposite choice. The group of Fascist intellectuals met at Bologna at the end of March 1925 and sought to define their position; Gentile argued against Panunzio that Fascism was a totalitarian religious spirit rather than a religious or philosophical creed, and his view

---

[55] See Chapter 8, pp. 273–78, herein. The first germ of an authoritarian conception of the corporation in Gentile's mind seems to be B.625 in B.813, p. 399; cf. Chapter 5, p. 159, herein.

was triumphant. He was charged by the congress with the writing of a Manifesto stating their views; and what he in fact produced was an idealized account of the history of the Fascist movement and of its relation to the Risorgimento. The new ideal of the Corporate State was favorably compared with the old liberal parliamentary system but otherwise the Manifesto contained no explicit doctrine.[56]

In December of the same year the National Fascist Institute of Culture was inaugurated with Gentile as its first president.[57] In his inaugural address he urged intellectuals to adopt a more positive attitude toward Fascism, and Fascists to adopt a more positive attitude toward the intellect. With the intellectuals he pleaded: "Not all the manifestations of which this movement is the cause may be pleasing. But what matters is this: that there is a new spirit . . . a fundamental note . . . which fulfills an ancient prayer of those few Italians who did so much in the past to illumine with glory the history of their people." [58] While to the Fascists themselves he spoke in tones of warning, saying that if the new spirit was to bear fruit it must be governed by intelligence and not degraded into partisan

---

[56] B.838; for Gentile's speech at the congress see B.813, pp. 95–116. Croce wrote a Protest against this Manifesto, which publicly signalized the breach between himself and Gentile (see the note at the end of the present chapter).

The failure of Fascism to appeal to intellectuals can be judged from Gentile's remarks about the first organizations of Fascist teachers. Sacchetti organized the *Corporazione della scuola* in 1923; in 1925 it became the National Association of Fascist Teachers (ANIF); and in 1931 it was finally transformed into the *Associazione fascista della scuola* in which all teachers were automatically enrolled. Looking back at the time of this transformation, Gentile pointed out how essential it was that there should be a movement of new life against the dominant tendencies of socialism and masonry among the teachers if his reform was to become a living reality. He adds that at the university level there was no sign of such a renaissance; and "the hostility universally manifested among intellectuals in 1925 against Fascism" was sufficient to excuse in his mind the admittedly crude methods used to dragoon teachers into ANIF and the low caliber of its officials and publications (B.1033). His letter to the journal *Corporazione della scuola* (B.832 in B.818, pp. 163–66, or B.937, pp. 38–43) in 1925 should be read in the light of this later confession.

[57] From the beginning there was a battle among Fascist intellectuals over whether the institute was to be a 'Fascist institute' of culture or an institute of 'Fascist culture.' Gentile fought for and in name obtained the former. But there was always a tendency for the institute to become simply part of the machinery of Party propaganda, and when it moved to new and more imposing headquarters in 1936 the name itself was finally changed (cf. B.1149). What can be said is that thanks to Gentile's efforts it did always continue to advance the cause of culture, as well as the cause of Fascist propaganda (cf. the remarks of Schneider, *op. cit.*, p. 218).

[58] B.836 in B.937, p. 56.

prejudice. Fascism might be a religion, but that did not mean that those who held Party cards were the elect:

We are absolutely uncompromising inasmuch as we can never give a post of responsibility or authority to a man who is utterly opposed to the new conscience of Italy. But may I be allowed to state here and now that this is not the same as saying "to a man who does not hold a Fascist Party card," for on the contrary, there is no true intransigence that can be content with a card or a material distinction. But we are very willing to compromise where a cultural or other good that has an intrinsic value can actually be employed as a reliable instrument in the great work of construction, which is the mission of Fascism. A spirit of compromise which will become more pronounced day by day, progressively as, when the second term is fulfilled, the first term of the great Roman admonition appears ever more opportune and more just: *parcere subjectis et debellare superbos* ["to spare the conquered and war down the proud"].[59]

The object of Gentile's policy of conciliation, as the above quotation shows, was to preserve as far as possible the autonomy of culture. He argued strongly that there should be no attempt to impose Fascist doctrine in the State universities: like the Catholics they must have a university of their own until such time as the new spirit had so deeply penetrated the consciousness of the nation that State universities were Fascist because everyone in them already believed in Fascism.[60] And he declared in the senate that an intellectual dictatorship was a self-contradictory absurdity: "In the field of academic studies, science and critical thought, there can be no life without liberty and autonomy."[61]

Similarly in the sphere of popular culture represented by the press he insisted on the value and importance of an independent non-Fascist press alongside the official Party newspapers:

A precise definition of what the Fascist Press is has a significance on this condition: that the other Press is recognized as exempt from the obligation of becoming Fascist, and yet still capable of exercising a sane and useful function in the organism of Italian public life. . . . For there must sometime be an end to a certain form of systematic polemic against the journals that are not organs of the Fascist movement, a polemic which would tend to destroy every kind of expression of opinion which could not pretend to represent the thought of the upper hierarchies of Fascism

[59] *Ibid.*, pp. 61–62.

[60] B.818, pp. 100–105. It was, in his view, precisely because the universities could not—and should not be expected to—teach Fascism that a separate institute was necessary (cf. B.940, B.972). He resisted as long as possible the forcible impoَition of Fascist doctrine in universities (cf. B.975 and see pp. 195–97, 208, herein).

[61] B.877 (March 1926) in B.937, pp. 130–31.

or of the Government. This tendency is madness, since under the guise of the most heartfelt Fascist zeal, it resolves into a sordid and treacherous war upon the vitality of Fascism itself. For, when there remained no other thought, the thought of the Party and the Regime would itself die on the day when it had absorbed everything, and had no more difficulties to overcome or minds to persuade.

In conclusion, it may be not altogether superfluous to observe that, even within the ambit of the recognized and registered Fascist Press, both Fascists and non-Fascists should understand the duties of party discipline *cum grano salis*. . . .[62]

On the positive side, the conception of culture which Gentile defended as genuinely 'Fascist' was the same living, spiritual attitude which he had been preaching for years, in opposition to the traditional realism of the school which reduced culture to dead matter, a body of factual information. This contrast was the fundamental thesis of *The Reform of Education*, and since we have already examined it, there is no need to enlarge upon it here except to point out that it was an ideal which bore little relation to the facts, as can be judged from the more or less complete failure to produce any 'Fascist' literature worthy of the name. Some serious work was done (largely by Gentile's students) in economics and political science; but most of the books purporting to expound the Fascist philosophy and way of life contain nothing but dithyrambic nonsense unworthy of critical consideration. The *stile fascista* in practice was synonymous with empty bombast.

Paradoxically enough, in view of Gentile's claims about the 'Fascist' conception of culture, the most important cultural achievement for which the Fascists deserve credit was the publication of the *Enciclopedia italiana*. Gentile was the moving spirit in this great enterprise from the beginning. He first persuaded a millionaire fellow senator, Signor Treccani, to finance it, and later arranged for its transformation into an *ente morale* supported by a group of banking companies. On the scientific side he directed it from its inception until shortly before his death, and he deserves much of the credit for the fact that it was not completed in any narrowly partisan spirit, but objectively, without any other criterion than the professional competence of a potential contributor. This objectivity was not achieved, as Gentile himself declared at the time of his

---

[62] B.922 (February 1927) in B.937, pp. 119–20. Alas, when the party did absorb everything, Gentile discovered that it was not dead but more alive than ever because all thought is really *self*-criticism!

resignation, without a hard struggle. The history of the *Enciclopedia* was "tormented by dissatisfied and factious partisans of Fascism." [63] But it was in fact achieved, as even anti-Fascist exiles like Count Sforza bear witness; and as a result the *Enciclopedia italiana* is universally and rightly considered to be one of the best encyclopedias in the world.

This, however, was only the most obvious and most imposing of Gentile's achievements in the cultural field. Next to it must rank his work for the *Scuola Normale Superiore* at Pisa. He had himself begun his university career as holder of an internal scholarship at this institution, and it was one of his dearest wishes to increase the number of such scholarships; but if this was to be possible the school itself had to be enlarged. Gentile campaigned for this over a period of several years, and finally gained the ear of Mussolini, to whom, of course, he gave all the credit in his inaugural speech for the new buildings in 1933.[64]

He was also very active in an official way in the field of Risorgimento studies. He was a joint director of the national edition of the letters of Gioberti; member of the committee for the national edition of Mazzini; director of the national edition of Ruggiero Bonghi; and, as was only fitting for the greatest living Sicilian, president of the committee for the national edition of Giuseppe Pitré. In 1937 he completely reorganized the National Committee for the History of the Risorgimento [65] and in 1939 he inaugurated

---

[63] *Vita e pensiero,* IV, 25. On the general character and history of the *Enciclopedia* cf. B.1031 (in English); B.875 in B.937, pp. 110–15; B.1088; also the article by Gioacchino Volpe in *Vita e pensiero,* I, 335–62. Doubtless the struggle was fought out largely behind closed doors; but echoes of the battle can be caught in Gentile's newspaper articles on the *Enciclopedia* in 1931 (B.1032, B.1034, B.1037, B.1039). Bellezza, in his bibliographical review of Gentile studies (*Giornale di metafisica,* X, 1955, 125n11), gives references to some of the attacks on Gentile's policy by more militant Fascists. Gentile was perhaps rather rigid in his attitude to critics of all kinds.

After the Concordat the Church exercised censorship over articles on theological and religious topics; Gentile resisted this as far as he could but he was not always successful (cf. C. Sforza, *Contemporary Italy,* New York, Dutton, 1944, p. 323, and the example given by G. Salvemini in Keene, *op. cit.,* p. 127).

[64] The inaugural address is B.1084 (= 1067). For Gentile's campaign cf. B.976 bis, B.977, B.1019. In all of his articles and speeches on the subject he stresses the need for the scholar to be free from the hurly-burly of ordinary economic life. There is a distinctly nostalgic note about his evocation of his own youthful days in the calm of the academic cloisters (for this cf. also B.1132 in B.1139, pp. 183–203).

[65] B.1166.

the National Center for Manzoni Studies, another monument to his persistence in overcoming obstacles and persuading the banks to finance cultural undertakings. We should notice also that since it involved the compulsory transfer of Manzoni collections from other museums it could probably never have been achieved without authoritarian use of the powers of government.[66]

Finally, he was prominent in government agencies for international cultural cooperation, such as the Italian Institute for German studies [67] and the Institute for the Middle and Far East: [68] institutes of this kind were subordinate to the National Fascist Institute of Culture and one can sometimes detect motives of Party propaganda in their proceedings, especially in Gentile's own contributions in areas where he had no technical competence.[69]

The fact that Gentile's influence and activity spread over such a wide field can be taken as evidence of several things. First, and most obviously, of the tremendous force and energy of the man. The only thing comparable in Italian intellectual life to the range of his activity in the practical organization of Italian culture is the no less astounding range of Croce's scholarly and critical work. But secondly, one feels bound to ask whether there is not here an implicit tendency toward a cultural dictatorship. Gentile always vehemently denied that he had any such conscious aim; and his sincerity was demonstrated by the readiness of his sympathy for all kinds of cultural initiative. But the fact remains that he did love to have a finger in every pie, even where he had nothing of value to contribute to the making of it; and his enemies did not scruple to accuse him of setting up a cultural dictatorship of the crudest kind.[70]

---

[66] B.1207; cf. the obituary of Gentile by F[austo] G[hisalberti] in *Annali Manzoniani*, V, 1949, 405–7.

[67] Cf. B.1063.

[68] Cf. B.1089 (= B.1120) and B.1167.

[69] During the war, of course, this tendency was most marked, as for instance in the founding of the group *Amici dell'India* (B.1262; cf. also B.1243, B.1261).

[70] In 1931, while Gentile was away at the Hegel congress in Berlin, a whole series of accusations were thrown at him in his capacity as president of I.N.F.C. by the review *Roma fascista*. It was alleged that he used his official position to propagate his own philosophical gospel; to provide jobs and a forum for his disciples and to spread 'liberal' propaganda. Gentile's deputy in I.N.F.C. replied in a letter that as a matter of fact there were no 'Gentilians' on the staff of I.N.F.C. in Rome, or among the presidents of the eighty-six provincial sections; that the only institute publication by a disciple of Gentile was a small volume on economics by Spirito which had received the praise of Mussolini; that his school had its own organs and that its members contributed to *Educazione fascista* only rarely; that Croce seemed to find no 'liberalism' in any

Of course, the whole structure of Fascism in theory and practice, not to speak of the structure of Italian academic life both before and after Fascism, worked in favor of cultural imperialism. And this leads to one final reflection: the ubiquity of Gentile's influence is evidence, above all, of the cultural poverty of Fascism itself. Whatever truth there is in the claim that he was a cultural dictator is only the shadow of another more fundamental truth—that the only 'Fascist' culture worthy of the name was the creation of Gentile and his 'school.'

The Doctrine of Fascism

Volume XIV of the *Enciclopedia italiana,* which appeared in 1932, contained in its due place an article on "Fascismo." This was in two parts, "Dottrina" and "Storia," of which the second was written and signed by Gioacchino Volpe. The first part of the article was subdivided into "Fundamental Ideas" and "Political and Social Doctrines," and both sections were ascribed to Mussolini. But almost from the day of publication rumor pointed to Gentile as the real author of the first section. Writing in 1940, Mueller asserted categorically that it was by Gentile; and since the fall of Fascism his assertion has now been confirmed in Italy itself.[71] Nevertheless I do not propose to discuss the article here. Gentile wrote it *for* Mussolini and I think this affected the way he expressed himself. It

---

publication of the institute; and that Gentile himself accepted no salary for any of his official Fascist activities (B.1028).

Hegel congresses seem to have been moments of particular irritation to Gentile's critics, however, for in 1933, when the Hegelians came to Rome, F. Orestano, who as a member of the Italian Academy must, I suppose, be regarded as a leading light among Fascist intellectuals, began an even more violent polemic. The blind prejudice of his attacks reveals in a very graphic way that the impotence of Gentile's critics among Fascist intellectuals was innate, either in the individuals concerned or in the total social and political situation, and did not result from any cultural strangle hold established by the idealists (B.1091, B.1092, B.1093). The polemic was solemnly reported to American readers by a Catholic witness, in the *Personalist,* XV, 1934, 66 ff. Of course for the Catholics any stick was good enough to beat the idealist dog.

[71] *La pensée contemporaine en Italie,* p. 310n1. Minio-Paluello says "those who were closest to the 'philosopher of fascism' in his capacity as general editor of the *Enciclopedia italiana* are sure that no mistake has been made in attributing this section to him" (*op. cit.,* p. 123). Mueller's assertion must have been based on some such authority. Definite confirmation is now supplied by the *Bibliografia filosofica italiana* (1900–1950), Rome, Istituto di studi filosofici, 1952, II, 3.

is an open secret, if indeed it is a secret at all, that political leaders do not usually write their own speeches; this does not alter the fact that they and not their speech writers are responsible for what they say. Thus, what Gentile meant in this article is less important than what Mussolini thought that he meant, when he read it over before signing it. For this reason Herman Finer's commentary, which was based on the assumption that the document was an authoritative pronouncement by Mussolini, remains valid; and I do not think that I could improve upon it.[72]

We can afford to pass over the *Enciclopedia* article in any case, because Gentile spoke for himself on the topic in a book which reached its final form at about the same time. He published his first statement of the philosophy of Fascism in 1928; and at a philosophical congress in 1929 he proclaimed his discovery that the State must necessarily have a philosophy of its own. This would appear to be a retreat from the position he had adopted at the Bologna congress in 1925 where he had strongly and successfully opposed any attempt to formulate an official 'doctrine.' But the briefest summary will show that he did not really change his attitude very much; the only real difference that is detectable in 1928 or in any of his subsequent essays on the 'philosophy of Fascism' lies in his increasing recognition of the difficulties of his position.[73]

---

[72] See *Mussolini's Italy*, London, V. Gollancz, 1935, Part III. The analysis may seem to be vitiated by his 'discovery' of the influence of Alfredo Rocco in the article; for Rocco was an extreme Nationalist, who was certainly guilty of the 'naturalism' for which Gentile castigated the Nationalists in 1917 (see Chapter 5, p. 133, herein). In his "Political Doctrine of Fascism" (tr. by D. Bigongiari in *International Conciliation*, No. 223, October 1926, pp. 393–417) the Nation emerges as a sort of transcendent deity. But Finer's interpretations remain valid because in terms of objective content there is a tremendous overlap—amounting almost to a complete coincidence—between Rocco's theory and Gentile's. It is only the *meaning* which they attach to a common assertion that varies. Thus Gentile might write a sentence which, coming ostensibly from Mussolini's hand, should properly be understood in the sense that Rocco would have given to it, because that would be how Mussolini understood it when he read it over. For it is undeniable that Rocco's theory accords better with the actual policies of Fascism. Indeed, it must be said that Gentile himself often, though perhaps unconsciously, treats the State as an objective *transcendent* reality in his Fascist apologias rather than as a subjective *transcendental* one.

[73] "L'essenza del fascismo" (1928, B.948) forms the main body of *Origini e dottrina del fascismo* (1932, B.1104). Readers unfamiliar with Italian will find a condensed version in the American journal *Foreign Affairs* (VI, 1927/28, 290–304) under the title "The Philosophic Basis of Fascism" (B.941). For his essay on "Philosophy and the State" (B.980) see n34 in Chapter 7 herein.

The essay of 1928 treats the intervention of 1915 and the revolution of 1922 as the latest crisis in the great conflict between two Italies that had been going on since the Renaissance,[74] and in particular as a return to the religious patriotism of the Risorgimento exemplified in figures as different as Mazzini, Gioberti, Cavour, and Manzoni. The intervention in 1915 had not been decisive. It was necessary for the State to reassert its authority violently through the *squadristi* in order that the new vision of life, the new totalitarian spirit, might come to fruition.

There is still the insistence, as in 1925, that Fascism is not a philosophy in any ordinary sense of the word, still less a religion, because it has no *credo* or absolute dogmas. We have already pointed out that this amounts to saying that only Mussolini's interpretation of the new 'spirit' really counts for anything. Gentile himself now confirms and underlines this conclusion:

The truth, the significance of Fascism, is not to be measured in the special theses that it assumes from time to time, in theory or in practice. . . . Often, having set up a target to be reached, a concept to realize, a way to follow, it has not hesitated to change its course when put to the proof, and to reject that aim or that concept as inadequate or repugnant to its own principle. It has never wished to bind itself by pledging the future.

In 1937 he delivered a lecture for foreign students of Fascism in which the same theses reappeared unchanged (B.1168). But since his audience was not subject to the actual government of Mussolini he was able to concern himself even more exclusively with the 'ideal' aspects of Fascism. The result is perhaps the most attractive but also the most unrealistic of his political apologias. His last article on the subject written in 1941 (B.1246) exhibits the same consistency and the same defect (cf. Chapter 8, pp. 246, herein).

[74] The theory of the "two Italies" has its roots in Gentile's wartime essays (see Chapter 5, pp. 134–37, herein). He discusses the 'prehistory' of his Fascism from Machiavelli through Vico and Alfieri to Mazzini and Gioberti in various places (notably in B.828, B.837, B.921). I have not discussed this subject because what we may call the 'Gentilian' view has already been set forth, in English and in greater detail than Gentile ever expounded it, by Aline Lion in the first part of *The Pedigree of Fascism* (London, Sheed and Ward, 1927). Exposition would therefore be superfluous. Criticism seems to me hardly less so. Gentile's interpretation of Italian cultural history has a certain plausibility, perhaps even a certain validity, in relation to his ideal theory of Fascism. But, given the virtually complete divorce that always existed between that ideal and the actual practice of the Fascist government, it is simply irrelevant. Whereas his theory of the political history of Italy as a nation is of the first importance because, insofar as it helps us to understand Fascism, it must inevitably compel us to make a more critical evaluation of the Risorgimento. Even Croce shows himself uneasily aware of this; he seems to have been more influenced by Gentile's analysis than he would ever consciously allow (cf. A. R. Caponigri, *History and Liberty*, London, Routledge and Kegan Paul, 1955, pp. 249, 255).

It has often announced reforms, when the announcement was politically opportune, but it did not believe that it was thereby committed to their execution. The true resolutions of the *Duce* are those that are both formulated and put into actual effect.[75]

It is odd to see how Gentile takes this extreme opportunism, which certainly was characteristic of Fascism, as an application of the Mazzinian dictum *pensiero ed azione*. He is right when he says that Mazzini meant to castigate the intellectuals who divorced speech from action; Mazzini certainly held that a real conviction must produce positive action. He would have agreed, too, that it is the practical ideal that matters, and that in the pursuit of this ideal different policies might well be appropriate under different circumstances. But he would have condemned wholeheartedly the proclamation of a policy, unless and until circumstances *were* ripe, and one was ready to strain every nerve to put it into effect. Fascism, with all its boasted anti-intellectualism, would have received and deserved his censure as a movement swollen with rhetoric—if not something much worse.

Of course Gentile himself is quick to add that whatever some ignorant Fascists may believe, the anti-intellectualism of Fascism is not a denial of all value to intellectual culture, but a condemnation of the neutral attitude of 'pure' thought and 'pure' science. Fascism itself is action guided by intelligence; like all great spiritual realities, the political action of Fascism contains an immanent philosophy of which the central notion is, in one word, the *Nation*. And now again a qualification: the nationalism of the Fascists is not that of the old Nationalist party, who opposed the Nation to the individual. In the philosophy of Fascism, Nation and citizen coincide; the Nation is not conceived as a transcendent natural entity, but as a spiritual reality generated in consciousness.[76]

---

[75] B.948, p. 110, or in B.1104, p. 38; cf. B.941, p. 300. Finer gives a fairly lengthy extract including this passage, as a "luminous" commentary on the opportunism of the Fascist regime, and remarks: ". . . I am obliged to confess that, though I am sure Gentile would not joke about matters of such high importance, his remarks have the air of sly censure; and no one surely would regard them as complimentary" (*op. cit.*, p. 18). Unfortunately, any charitable interpretation of this kind is rendered quite untenable by the close connection that Gentile goes on to develop between this doctrine and the Mazzinian dictum.

[76] This familiar doctrine is the basis for Gentile's claim that Fascism is the highest kind of democracy. "The State exists inasmuch and for as much as the citizen causes it to exist" (B.941, p. 302, B.948, p. 115, or in B.1104, p. 49). But what evidence was there that the Fascists really held this view of the

This intimate awareness of community is maintained in the minds of the citizens by the corporate organization of the State. Furthermore, Gentile goes on, the corporations provide a sound basis for truly representative government. But he now shows himself much more aware than he was in 1925 of how difficult it is to reconcile these two ideals. He never admits explicitly that 'corporate' liberty can only be concretely possessed, or in other words consciously enjoyed, by a convinced Fascist. But he does say that the Party must inform the whole people with its spirit and he does admit that this will not be easy:

The problem is formidable and its solution creates infinite difficulties, because, for one thing, it is virtually impossible that the great masses, which only slowly, over a period of centuries, become educated and reformed, should become equal to the requirements of a party of elite, a moral avant-garde; for another thing, because of the dualism between governmental and Party action, which can scarcely be avoided, despite every effort and unity of discipline, when a party organization is enlarged to proportions almost equal to those of the State; or yet again, because of the risks that every power of initiative and progress runs, when all the individuals are caught in the meshes cf a mechanism which, no matter how enlivened by a single spirit at the center, cannot help letting all autonomy and liberty of movement languish and die, as one passes gradually from the center to the periphery.[77]

The Beginnings of Disillusion

In his assertion that Fascism was not really anti-intellectual, or antiliberal, or antidemocratic, but stood for a higher culture, a more profound liberalism, and a more real democracy, Gentile found himself increasingly alone as time went on. We have seen how, in the

---

Nation? Gentile thought that the attitude of the Party toward the monarchy was significant in this respect: it had never been sacred for them, as it was for the Nationalists. While it appeared that the king was ready to see the spirit of 1915 liquidated they had favored a republic; they only abandoned republicanism when the king showed himself conscious of his duty to the Nation by refusing to suppress the revolution. Of course, we have only to remember that the Fascists took their place on the extreme right of the chamber when they first entered Parliament in 1921 to see how questionable this is as an interpretation of Fascist policy. But it is important, nonetheless, because it helps to explain Gentile's decision to support the forlorn hope of the Fascist Social Republic in 1943.

[77] B.948, p. 115, or in B.1104, p. 49. Gentile shows himself here to be aware of the paradoxical way in which his personalism has to be interpreted in order to justify authoritarianism. The "single spirit" is the spirit of Mussolini so that it must inevitably remain at the "center" of a "mechanism."

cultural field, he was obliged from the beginning to fight for the preservation of the freedom of thought which had always until that time been taken for granted; in this area even he was obliged to recognize very rapidly how far removed his ideal was from the reality. In the field of politics proper, his attention was at first directed almost entirely toward the overt opposition to the new Regime, so that he was hardly conscious of the faults and excesses of Fascism except as things to be justified or explained away. But even in the early days, when he was busily insisting that the Fascists possessed all the real virtues to which the 'liberals' and the 'democrats' laid claim, he spared a moment every now and again to warn the Fascists themselves that their mission was an ideal and they themselves were erring human beings like their opponents. At the Bologna congress he challenged his audience thus:

Can we say that we have always remembered to do as we said, that we have always said no to our own interest when it was in conflict with that of our Country, that we have never yielded to the enticements of our own selfish instinct, that we have ommitted nothing that would make us worthier to hold the position we desire to hold?

And he went on to reply to his own question:

Here, I believe, we are all Fascists and can make confession among ourselves frankly. And if we are not all Fascists, it does not matter, we must make the confession: our intransigence is sometimes merely verbal. Not always do we do as we say; not always do we practice that absolute devotion to the ideal which we preach. Not always does that religious flame burn and glisten, in which we have resolved to purify the young Italian nation in order to create a *great* Italy. . . . We must confess it boldly, for only this confession, made in sincerity and humility, can give value to the faith for which we fight. Otherwise it falls away into rhetorical verbalism and shameful hypocrisy.

. . . Let us not vaunt ourselves, or set ourselves up in our own persons as superior to our adversaries: we also have a long way still to travel. . . . To say this and to feel it will not weaken, but rather strengthen us. Our adversaries will respect us the more; and what is more important, we shall respect *ourselves* the more, since to feel one's own defects is the primary condition for liberating oneself from them, and for acquiring the power required for such self-liberation.[78]

As organized opposition to Fascism disappeared, and Gentile found himself addressing what was, formally speaking, a completely Fascist audience, this note tended to recur more and more in his speeches and articles; and as Fascism approached the be-

---

[78] B.818, pp. 110–12.

ginning of its second decade there was even a note of desperation in his preaching. He began to look round and wonder whether he had not cut the ground from under his own feet in his enthusiastic tirades against 'pseudo' liberals and 'pseudo' democrats.

His disillusion developed gradually. He had joined the Party largely because of his enthusiasm over the educational reform for which Fascism had provided means and opportunity. But he soon found that "the most Fascist of the reforms" was still not Fascist enough for some of his Party colleagues. And he, who had continually preached the necessity for life and movement in the schools, and had exalted the Fascist regime as a "continual revolution," was obliged to become the defender of stability against the "gangrene of retouching" (*cancrena dei ritocchi*) with which every successive minister afflicted the new school system. Almost every year the timetables were revised; and gradually several of the main pillars of his reform were whittled away. The first principle to be sacrificed was that of limiting the numbers in the secondary schools. The limit on the size of classes was lifted almost immediately; and in 1926 provision was made for the setting up of *classi aggiunte* in special cases.[79]

The freedom of the teachers was likewise of short duration. Gentile had set up a commission to examine all textbooks published; this commission placed considerable emphasis on national patriotism, but it approved a wide variety of books and it showed "very little, if any, political bias . . . in the years from 1923 to 1927." Early in 1928 it was officially decreed that all schoolbooks must be in accord with the spirit of Fascism; and at the end of the year it was decided that official textbooks for the elementary schools must be issued.[80] These, when they arrived, were of the

---

[79] Minio-Paluello, *op. cit.*, p. 117. These facts make Gentile's attitude in his articles on "the Educational Policy of the Regime" (*Corriere della sera,* March 1929) appear somewhat ostrichlike. He speaks of the abolition of the *classi aggiunte* as "one of the most Fascist dispositions of the law of 30 May 1923" since only a government with its eyes fixed on the public good could have carried out such a policy in the face of so many protests! (B.973 in B.1057, p. 447). Presumably he was seeking to criticize the change of policy in a manner at once acceptable and forceful.

[80] Minio-Paluello, *op. cit.*, p. 171. I have not been able to discover that Gentile ever uttered a word on the subject of the *libro di Stato.* A compulsory textbook was something absolutely opposed to the whole of his philosophy of education. Some idea of the textbook commission's work in the period 1923–27 can be gained from the statistics and quotations from approved books given in Schneider and Clough, *op. cit.*, pp. 93–102.

poorest quality, since the only criterion of selection was the amount of Fascism in the work submitted.

Then too, a dualism between Party and State in the field of education rapidly and inevitably developed, which placed Gentile in somewhat of a quandary, since he had himself fervently proclaimed the Party's mission to educate the people. As we shall see, he chose to support the State, and preached patience to the Party enthusiasts. But here again he found that the 'continuous revolutionaries' paid no heed. The Party—probably rightly—regarded the intellectuals as among their worst enemies; and any action taken in the educational field by the State would have to be implemented by these same independent intellectuals.[81] So it was obliged to develop its own organizations for the indoctrination of the young.[82] In this way, too, the activities of the intellectuals could ultimately be controlled in the most effective way conceivable: the presence of a group of convinced young Fascists in a class would soon curb any expression of independent judgment. But the resulting encouragement of spying naturally had a disastrous effect on discipline and on the value of the teaching, especially in the universities—the level at which, in Gentile's view, freedom was most essential.[83]

Gentile made a strong, it necessarily a somewhat guarded, protest against the 'retouching,' the relaxation of secondary-school regulations, and especially against Fascist pressure groups in the universities, in a speech to the senate in April 1930—a speech which according to Finer displeased Mussolini because it received too

---

[81] The Protest against Gentile's 1925 Manifesto became the symbol of this alienation. Thus Gentile found that the reaction to his own intransigence had become the worst obstacle to his policy of pacification. In 1929 he pleaded that the Party's refusal to forgive and forget in the case of repentant signatories of the Protest was effectively preventing the penetration of Fascism among intellectuals, or at least disguising its extent; and he welcomed Mussolini's nomination of some of the signatories to the new Italian Academy as a sign that this policy of spiting one's face was at last being abandoned (B.975).

[82] Gentile naturally applauded the early decision to bring the work of the Balilla—the Party youth organization which concerned itself mainly with physical education—under the control of the Minister of Education. But he suggested that the absorption ought to be more complete; the Balilla ought not to remain in an ambiguous position of semi-independence (B.991 in B.1057, p. 454). In fact, however, the ambiguity was soon resolved in a contrary sense. When it was found impossible to combine State and Party functions, a new youth organization was established, under the direct control of the Party.

[83] It was only at the university level that this method was important; in the schools there were plenty of official, governmental, controls.

much applause.[84] The Fascists aimed to use the school system as a means for the transformation of the national consciousness. This was certainly in accordance with Gentile's general philosophy, but he was so convinced that they were trying to go too fast that in his appeal for patience and tolerance he went so far as to assert that it could not be done:

Gentlemen of the Senate, within the school you will find only the same life that exists outside of it: a new national life, a new public conscience may generate a new school. But if the former halts the latter too is arrested and stagnates. . . . Therefore I tell you that the problem of making the schools Fascist is just precisely the problem of making the nation Fascist. . . . The important thing is not to confuse faith with formula, the life of the spirit with the membership card. The great mass of the Italians today, if we consider only simple adhesion to the Regime, is Fascist; and the same can be said of the vast majority of the teachers. The famous Antimanifesto of 1925 belongs to prehistory. . . .

But the Regime is a banner, a program, a principle. Being Fascist means more than adhering formally to the Regime and moving within its orbit. It is only too evident that the "Fascist for fear"—and there are some of that kind too—is only Fascist with his lips, or at most in his outward behavior; but Fascism is rather courage, or even boldness. Discipline yes, iron military discipline; but discipline of soldiers, that is, men who have a conscience, a will, a character, and therefore do not give themselves up in a surrender in which . . . nothing is given! The Fascist must think and will, educate himself and do his share in the building of that newborn and mighty *Patria* which cannot be a mere word, no matter how loudly it is shouted, but must be a reality; and this reality can be born only from the sacrifice of men who devote themselves to an ideal.

Fascism is a new conception, or if you will, a new program of life, which, like every program, can only be realized gradually, as the intellectual and above all the moral conditions through which its realization is possible come into existence. And whoever has faith in the program must have patience, and wait serenely and securely for the slow ripening of minds. The school will become ever more Fascist, as the Italian people becomes ever more Fascist, destroying the old man within itself and educating the new one. All impatience is sterile and sets us further from our goal.[85]

---

[84] *Ibid.*, pp. 453–77; cf. Finer, *op. cit.*, p. 469.

[85] B.991 in B.1057, pp. 468–70. He had already used the same general argument in 1929 in criticizing the establishment of special faculties to teach Fascist doctrine and institutions in the universities. "It is not a matter of adding but of transforming." To the argument that the special faculties could be regarded as a temporary expedient for the purpose of making a beginning he retorted that the personnel were to a large extent academically incompetent and that students were rapidly coming to understand that the new disciplines did not have to be studied seriously (B.975). This was absolutely true, but such public plain speaking on the subject was extremely rare.

Possibly some pressure was brought to bear on Gentile as a result of this speech, for a few months later, in his inaugural address for the 1930–31 session of the National Fascist Institute, he recanted. In the course of a bitterly sarcastic attack upon Croce, who had taken the opportunity while receiving an honorary doctorate at Oxford to criticize the Fascist regime, he confessed that the policy of softness toward intellectuals which he had been advocating since 1925 was mistaken.[86] He even went so far as to advocate a purge of those who thought the dictatorship had served its purpose, thereby indicating that he was prepared to approve of the way in which his provision for an oath of allegiance in the law of 1923 was at last about to be implemented. The oath which he had originally envisaged was a simple pledge of loyalty to the king and the constitution; in the oath that was actually demanded of professors in the fall of 1931 a specific declaration of loyalty to the Fascist regime was added. Only eleven professors actually refused to take it, so that, on the surface, Gentile's earlier forecast that its administration would show that the antimanifesto of 1925 was dead and buried seemed to be vindicated. But the volume of protest proved the contrary, and the general sense of shame among those who took the oath showed that in fact the Party had won a victory over the hated intellectuals by making them feel self-betrayed and self-degraded.[87]

The Concordat

Gentile ended his senate speech in March 1930 with an apologia for his own 'Fascist philosophy' which was at that time under a cloud because of the recently concluded Concordat. The Lateran pacts of 1929 may be taken as marking the eclipse of 'Fascist

[86] B.997.

[87] B.975; Minio-Paluello, *op. cit.*, p. 163 (where the year is erroneously given as 1930). Ascoli (*op. cit.*, pp. 251–52, abridged in Keene, *op. cit.*, pp. 119–20) suggests graphically the way in which the professors, having made what they thought was a merely formal act of obedience, were inevitably led or driven into "more positive acts of loyalty" which "were categorically suggested, more and more exacting and detailed." Like many other authorities he gives the number of recusants as twelve. This is because of the ambiguity in the case of former Prime Minister Orlando who was included in the first list but later held to have resigned before the oath was imposed, so that his refusal to take it could not constitute grounds for dismissal. (See *School and Society*, XXXV, January 1932, 47–48, for a full list and the text of the oath.)

idealism.' In 1932 Gentile provided the most authoritative statement of Fascist theory.[88] But after 1929 it was impossible for him to nourish any illusion that he was a power in the land.

In his attitude toward the Church, Gentile remained true to the ideas of his liberal past throughout his career as a Fascist.[89] As Minister of Education he had tried to put into effect the policy that he had been advocating since the beginning of the century. But he soon found that the equilibrium which he had envisaged was not being maintained. The Catholics clamored that if dogmatic religion was true in the primary schools, it was true in the secondary schools; and Gentile's successors at the ministry did not understand the logic of his reply that precisely *because* it was true in the former it was not true in the latter.[90]

About the Roman question he was in somewhat of a quandary himself when the Fascists began to discuss conciliation openly. His primary concern had always been to preserve the sovereign autonomy of the Italian State; and for this reason he had always rejected any solution of the Roman problem based on international intervention or international guarantee. Since he had always conceived the aim of the clericals in these terms, he was nonplused when the idea of a bilateral settlement was mooted. Though still inclined to insist that no surrender of territorial sovereignty was possible, he rested his case mainly on the argument that it was contrary to the Church's interests to accept corporeal existence at the hands of a national State.[91]

But this, of course, was something for the Church itself to decide about; so that, although Gentile must have felt very unhappy

---

[88] Mussolini was quite ready to bring the idealist theory into the foreground again at a time when Fascism and the Church were at daggers drawn.

[89] On the one hand religion must have a central place in elementary education —"In this field also I did not wait for the March on Rome in order to think what I think" (B.832, 1925, in B.818, p. 163, or in B.937, p. 38); but on the other hand, "once the germs of a positive doctrine have been planted in the minds of the young, there is need for liberty: full and complete liberty of thought . . ." (B.942, 1928, in B.937, p. 199). And in the wider field of politics any attempt to resolve finally the conflict between State and Church would be contrary to the highest interests of both (cf. B.912, 1927, in B.937, pp. 182–88).

[90] B.944 (1928) in B.937, pp. 201–5. The Minister of Education had in effect surrendered the Gentilian principle some time before by permitting optional classes in religion to be held in secondary schools (see D. A. Binchy, *Church and State in Fascist Italy*, New York, Oxford, 1942, p. 450).

[91] B.912 and B.912 bis (1927), in B.937, pp. 182–95.

when the agreement was announced, he was able to regard the *Treaty* as a great achievement of Fascist diplomacy, because, in his view, by recognizing the kingdom and agreeing to a purely domestic settlement of the problem the Church had accepted in all essentials the authority claimed by the State in 1870. About the *Concordat* he spoke coolly, striking a note of warning. Taken literally, it was a direct contradiction of his whole philosophy of politics; he insisted therefore that it was not to be taken literally:

The Concordat . . . although it is inseparably conjoined with the Treaty, is an act of quite a different nature . . . a *program*, that will get the precise significance that it actually receives from the way in which it is put into execution; and the mere words therefore would tell little to one who did not begin by considering that on the State's side it has been concluded and will be executed by the *Duce* of Fascism, who is the most vigilant sentinel of the essence and the inalienable characteristics of the modern State. . . .

The Church was drawn . . . to the Treaty by the Concordat; and the State was drawn to the Concordat by the Treaty. From this the direction of our future ecclesiastical policy, which must give concrete content to the clauses of the Concordat, follows by logical and historical necessity. The juridical formula of the Concordat is not to be judged by the standard of the old liberal ideologies, which might persuade one to see the sovereignty of the State diminished in its most delicate and vital part therein. I am referring in particular to the clause concerning matrimony and its annulment, to that which concerns religious instruction with a program of which the State will not be absolute arbiter, and to other clauses, which some of the newspapers have reported. All of them are clauses which, in themselves and independently of the criteria and the spirit with which they are to be applied, are without significance.[92]

He spoke thus because, in his view, the Fascist State *could not* abdicate its sovereignty over whole aspects of the national life; such an abdication was contrary to the logic of history and could only lead to disaster. The stormy history of the *Concordat* in its early years proved him right—a fact which he was not slow to emphasize.[93] Nevertheless the teaching of religion was actually in-

---

[92] B.970 in B.1104, pp. 95–96.
[93] B.1027 in B.1104, pp. 98–103. In discussing the aftermath of the Concordat Professor Binchy writes: "Many Fascists began to feel somewhat ashamed of their early transports, and those who had already committed themselves in print must have regretted their excessive haste, as it gradually dawned on them that their masters had quite other ideas. Gentile, for example was chagrined to discover that he might have spared himself such an ignoble expression of servility as his article written immediately after the settlement, in which this arch-opponent of Reconciliation recanted everything that he had been preaching

troduced in the secondary schools and the teaching of philosophy
was brought into line with it. Thus the whole spirit of the reform of
1923 was abandoned.

In the brief honeymoon that followed the conclusion of the Concordat, the small group of 'Catholic Fascists' occupied the lime-
light, and Gentile with his idealist philosophy of Fascism, which
was anathema to the Church, was pushed into the shadows. This
was the situation to which he referred at the end of his speech in
the senate in April 1930. He protested against the general distrust
of philosophy in certain Fascist circles, admitting that Fascism was
a new spirit, not the philosophy of a particular school, but contend-
ing that in order to be an active power the new spirit must be determinate and have a definite doctrine and principle of its own.[94]
Hence it must be meditated upon and critically discussed.[95]

---

for the last three years" (*op. cit.*, p. 198). But this is a misrepresentation.
Gentile did not really recant anything. In view of the fact that the Lateran
Treaty was, by universal consent, a considerable concession to the Italian State,
he can hardly be blamed for abandoning some of his more extreme contentions
about national sovereignty and the Law of Guarantees; while toward the Concordat his antipathy was always clear. He reconciled himself to it only in an
interpretation that was quite unacceptable to the Church. He would not have
reprinted his article of 1929 alongside his triumphant 'I told you so!' of 1931
(the article referred to at the beginning of this note) if Binchy's view were
correct. The later essay refers back to the earlier in no uncertain terms: "We
were not among the enthusiasts of the Concordat, and we did not delay a day
to consider it as the condition by which the treaty of conciliation was made
possible, and to say clearly that it was not a point of arrival but a point of
departure. A popular proverb employed by good sense in the regulation of
private relationships tells us: clear contracts mean long friendship. One cannot
truly say that the friendship that was sealed in the Palace of the Lateran on
11 February 1929 has been very long. So then, the contracts were not clear"
(B.1104, pp. 100–101). Binchy might retort that it was only in the Gentilian
interpretation that the Concordat was not clear, and that the Fascists had no
right to sign it if they did not mean to execute its provisions. I agree. But the
point is that Gentile did not sign it, and never would have signed it. Faced
with a *fait accompli* he gave to it the only significance that such a document
could have for him. (It must be added that Binchy's account of Gentile's relations both with Fascism and with the Vatican is in general very accurate.)

[94] B.991 in B.1057, p. 472. Gentile's change of front on this point came about
because Balbino Giuliano, then Minister of Education, had taken a leaf from
Gentile's own book, and exploited the ambiguities of the dialectical method
against him by arguing that Fascism had no philosophy but contained all
philosophies within itself dialectically!

[95] Cf. his response to the *Osservatore Romano*, which attempted to urge Party
discipline as a reason for him to keep silence. They could hardly expect discipline to be sterner in the Party, he argued, than it was in the Church itself,
where the rule was *"in* necessariis *unitas"* (B.994).

He also protested that it was unjust to regard him as an anti-clerical. His record at the congress of secondary-school teachers in 1907 and ever since stood against the libel, and his opinions on the subject were still unchanged:

. . . We sincerely applauded the Treaty and the Concordat which made it possible and was meant to establish it ever more firmly in our minds. But we did not believe—and we were given the most solemn assurance of this both here and in the other branch of Parliament—that there could ever arise from those Accords any menace either to the State as it is nowadays understood by all, and especially by the Fascists, who have poured out their own blood in order to restore the consciousness of the Italian nation; or to culture, by which I mean knowledge or thought, which is the very fount through which the State comes to achieve its own consciousness. . . .

. . . the Catholic religion is . . . the profound religion of the Italians which it is right to revive and cultivate.

But this religion does not prevent us, nor can it ever prevent us, from revering at the same time our Country and living for it (living for the ideal that sums up all the highest ideals of our life). . . .

If in some of the forms of religion, in some of the attitudes of the Church through which it has life, we perceive that a need of this our moral life, the only life that is possible for us, is ignored, are we to submit or deviate from our course? The world has advanced because, whenever it has been necessary, all men have been ready to appeal from the external and visible Church to the invisible one, and from the God of the Church to the God of their own conscience.[96]

Vox clamantis

Whether in or out of favor, Gentile always continued to interpret the actions and policies of the Party in the most optimistic way possible, though at times this involved withdrawal from positions which he had previously maintained. It would be wrong to call him a hypocrite, however, or even to dismiss him as childishly naive, though that would be closer to the truth; for what he was really trying to do was to make Fascism its own critic. His policy was all contained in the motto *ex ore tuo, te iudico;* he hoped that by taking the claims of Party propaganda seriously he could persuade the Party to take them seriously likewise. This hope itself was certainly naive, but there was no childish or lazy optimism about it.

---

[96] B.991 in B.1057, pp. 475, 477. The concluding paragraph, which is in many ways typical of Gentile's attitude toward religion, makes the unfairness of many of his criticisms of Protestantism apparent.

Thus, for instance in 1925 Gentile had argued that a healthy opposition was vital to the well-being of the new movement; and from the beginning he had drawn a careful distinction between Fascism as a reality (the Party) and Fascism as an ideal (the Regime). When the Grand Council of Fascism was given a central position in the constitution of the State in December 1928, this distinction appeared scarcely tenable any longer, since the Party had become identical with the State. But Gentile neither condemned the new legislation nor abandoned the distinction. He argued that the organizational separation had been maintained in the early years because of the revolutionary character of the new movement; the Fascist leaders had recognized that the "Regime" would only triumph through a gradual conquest of the national life mirrored in a progressive "constitutionalization" of the revolutionary force.[97] This process was approaching completion because the unity of Party and Nation was now no longer virtual but actual, and it must therefore be explicit. "Not just the Party only but the whole of Italy is Fascist." [98] But on the other hand, the identification was not and could never be complete or the Party would lose its *raison d'être*. The great task of educating the mass of the people in the new spirit would have to go on; and a partisan interpretation of the meaning of this identity must at all costs be avoided. Now that the Party no longer faced criticism from without it was doubly necessary that it should be self-critical. The popular comparison of the Party to the Catholic Church should be understood in the sense of Gioberti's remark that there are as many Catholicisms as there are Catholics.[99] The Regime must be the common ideal: it could not be imposed.

The great Charter of Labor had already been promulgated in 1927; and from 1929 onward the Grand Council set to work to build the Corporate State on this foundation. In the process a rift was

---

[97] B.943 (February 1928) in B.1104, pp. 72–73n; cf. B.946.

[98] B.995 (1930) in B.1104, p. 83. He justified the replacement of the National Association of Fascist Teachers (1925–31) by the new Fascist Association for the School on the same grounds (B.1033; cf. n55 above). But he went on to point the same moral and to beg that the relations between Party and State authority in the new association should be clarified. He still insisted that the autonomy of the universities should be preserved so as to strengthen internal discipline. The Party should not interfere in matters of professional competence such as hiring and firing. Its influence should be 'spiritual' and the State (i.e. the Ministry of Education) should retain 'temporal' power (B.1035).

[99] B.976 (1929) in B.1104, p. 89; cf. B.837 (1925) in B.818, pp. 10–11.

revealed among the supporters of the Regime. On the one side there were the conservatives who defended the freedom of enterprise guaranteed by the charter; on the other, the syndicalists who had more than a dash of genuine socialism in their mental composition. The latter wished to make the corporations the real foundation of the new Fascist State, while the former desired to reduce them to purely technical and advisory bodies, simple instruments of the government. Gentile was definitely more inclined toward the conservative view; but some members of his 'school' were associated with the Fascist 'Left,' and he recognized himself that the Corporate State must be more than a mere façade.[100] Here again his principal concern was to persuade the Party leaders that the existence of this disagreement was healthy: it should be "watched over, but not suppressed or deplored." [101]

In his inaugural address to the Second [102] Congress of the Fascist Institutes in November 1931, he enlarged on this theme in quite a bold and trenchant manner:

The whole of the Italian people is Fascist; and the delayers have been swept out of the road on which the people is marching forward. Our people are certainly marching, but they can only march if they are disciplined. And there can be no real outward discipline if there is not also inward discipline; a discipline of hearts because it is in the first place a discipline of thoughts.

Just as baptism is not enough to make a Christian really a Christian, so the membership card is not enough to make a Fascist really a Fascist. He too needs the grace that is with him today and will be ready tomorrow and never desert him. I mean that he needs education, he needs self-education, the continual struggle for perfection through practice and reflection. For one disagrees with one's adversaries, and writes polemics against them, and one tries to be in the right. But there may be, and among men who are truly alive there is, and I should like to say that it is good that there should be, disagreement also among friends. Even among the most loyal members of the same Party there are differ-

---

[100] "On the one side there is a tendency to deny the ethical substance of the State, and hence the State itself; on the other a tendency to deny its economic content, that content which it is the merit of Fascism to have perceived and indicated clearly" (B.974 in B.1104, p. 86).

Because some of the syndicalists (e.g. Spirito) were known to be his pupils, Gentile was sometimes thought to have sponsored views more extreme than those which he actually held. While denying personal responsibility for the opinions of his younger disciples he readily supported and defended them against the charge of Bolshevism (cf. B.1073).

[101] B.976 in B.1104, p. 89.

[102] The 1925 congress at Bologna counted as the first.

ences of opinion; and one knows that not everyone can be right. It is necessary to discuss, to criticize what appears to us at the first glance to be true; we must hear the arguments of those who are doubtful and think differently. Through this discussion and criticism and mutual correction every one of us can succeed in really conquering himself and becoming genuinely Fascist. Here again to presume that we are what we want to be is to destroy in ourselves the living power to become what we would. Instead we must always doubt ourselves and feel ourselves always unworthy of the ideal to which we aspire and of the title which we wish to deserve.

These are not, certainly, strange truths; nor should I have the courage to pronounce them here at this moment if it were not perhaps appropriate [se non potesse tornare opportuno] to remember them just at this moment, as an antidote for the natural swelling of pride that always fills the hearts of the victors. For the victors, the masters of the field, are tempted to think of themselves as the Lord's anointed; but what wins the victory is always an idea, not men. And if the men are to stand for the idea, they must always, every day, every hour, every instant, rise above themselves. . . .

It is good to turn back continually to examine our own ideas and our own conduct in the light of them. And this is the business of culture, which . . . in part, insofar as it is a matter of general doctrine and fundamental outline, can and must be the task of our Institutes of Culture. Our Institutes therefore assume a high responsibility toward the Country and toward the *Duce*. And we, if your trust is with us, O *Duce*, will assume it, and fulfill our delicate duty, with humility and loyalty as party members, in the certainty that, walking in your footsteps, we shall be working for the fortunes of the Regime and the greatness of the *Patria*.[103]

But Gentile's plea for a measure of freedom fell on deaf ears; and for all his many tributes to the glorious achievements of the Regime in every sphere, he began gradually and reluctantly to admit

---

[103] *Educazione fascista*, December 1931, pp. 1071–72. The December issue contains a stenographic record of the whole congress. Gentile's speech was also printed separately. Both these items escaped the notice of Bellezza (they should be listed as 1028 bis).

On the heresy of regarding the *tessera* as an infallible sign of grace cf. also the article "Beati possidentes?" (B.1036). Before arriving at his peroration which is here quoted, Gentile dilated on the achievements of Fascism in the intervening years and on the greatness of Mussolini, through whose genius the whole fabric of the State had been transformed in all directions. He does not seem to have felt that there was any conflict between his almost worshiping attitude toward Mussolini, who was on the platform beside him, and his doctrine that "what wins the victory is always an idea, not men." Presumably he never saw the dry comment of Finer on this speech: "John Stuart Mill himself would not have been dissatisfied with the full implications of Gentile's arguments in favor of doubt and criticism. They do honor to Gentile; if they were in being they would scarcely give continued life to Fascism" (*op. cit.*, pp. 24–25).

that the revolution involved a break with the past in which something valuable had been lost—something which he himself represented. The Concordat and his senate speech in April 1930 marked
the turning point in his attitude. The brief emergence of 'Catholic
Fascism' made him realize for the first time that the trouble might
be a more deep-rooted one than mere impatience. He began to
feel that perhaps the virtues he claimed for the Fascists had really
belonged to their despised opponents and that the new elite was
inclined to overlook certain aspects of the truth which their predecessors had understood.

In March 1931 he wrote an article for the review *Politica sociale*
entitled "Current Ideologies and Easy Criticisms" in which his dis-
quiet was scarcely concealed. Granting that a political movement
must have its myths, since it is only as myths that its ideas can become forces, he emphasized that these myths should not be allowed
to ossify into dogmas. The Party must keep its critical faculty alive
and adapt its myths to changing situations.

By way of example, he cited the myth of the State and the "antidemocratic" myth; and in dealing with the former he took the
opportunity to point out that his 'Catholic Fascist' critics were more
disposed toward 'Statolatry' than he was, for although they de-
claimed against the "diabolic philosophy of the ethical State," they
accepted such current Fascist commonplaces as that

the State is everything and the individual nothing; or that the State
creates the individual and not vice versa as the contract theory and in-
dividualistic liberalism held; or at least that the State is prior and the individual comes after.

Whereas he, the diabolic philosopher, recognized this myth as a
half-truth that could become dangerous:

. . . after having conquered individualism we must still do it justice
and recognize the aspect of truth to which it directed attention exclusively. . . . if it is not true that the State is created by the individual, neither is it true that the individual is created by the State; and in
order to understand the truth of the matter we must ascend again from
the dualism of the two terms . . . to their unity, where both coincide
and the State is no longer that imaginary Leviathan which is above the
individual and swallows him up; but rather it is within him . . .[104]

For this reason dogmatic rejection of democracy was a mistake.
Not every form of democracy or self-government was foreign to

---

[104] B.1021, p. 169; cf. also B.999 (newspaper report of speech given in
March 1930).

Fascism, for the revolution was certainly not a return to the principle of divine right. It was a popular movement, and although it had reached a dictatorial form, it expressed the national will. In fact the Nation had never possessed such a degree of freedom and self-mastery before, being now "liberated from little plutocratic oligarchies and artificial social structures." Fascism set up the liberty of the Nation as the only real liberty, in contrast to the presumed liberty of individuals "not because one can deny the latter for the sake of the former, but because the true liberty of the individuals coincides with the liberty of the Nation." National liberty is not something factual but is realized in the hearts and minds of the citizens who serve it and represent it. The Fascists should understand this ideal source of State authority before condemning democracy out of hand. "So then we must revise certain concepts and not abandon ourselves without reflection to overfacile criticisms." [105]

The honeymoon with the Church was soon over. Gentile must have felt a new lease of hope as he penned 'Mussolini's' article for the *Enciclopedia* in 1932. Doubtless his short paean for the tenth anniversary of the revolution was quite heartfelt and sincere.[106] But the liberal values for which he stood were gone beyond hope of recall. Nothing brings out the ambiguous nature of Gentile's relations with the Party in the early years of his enthusiasm more clearly than his anxious protests against the revolutionary fervor of the first generation to emerge from the new schools. All his past arguments about the value of the religious spirit in education began to take their revenge on him. He discovered to his disgust that in the eyes of the 'Youth' to which Fascism so stridently appealed, he and his philosophy were part of the world that Fascism had left behind. The bitterness of this realization was sharpened by his recognition that his own polemic with Croce had in no small measure contributed to this result.[107] It seemed to him in 1933 that the younger generation had fallen a prey to two dangerous illusions.

---

[105] B.1021, p. 170.

[106] B.1064. His article for the eleventh anniversary is more apologetic in tone (B.1090).

[107] "Even the bitter polemics fought out in these last years between the leaders of thought [*maestri*] who prior to the War and the advent of Fascism had marked out a way for the new generations of the early twentieth century . . . have shaken the authority that is wont to be for the young the primary factor in deciding their choice of leaders and hence in the direction of their culture" (B.1085 in B.1139, p. 359).

One party wanted to jettison even the living past altogether and looked always forward to a culture that was to be really new and truly Fascist; the other sought to revive a past which Gentile regarded as decently dead and buried, through a return to the authority of the Roman Catholic Church and a fully 'religious' conception of life. For both parties the great idealist revival was already a subject of purely academic interest. Like a voice from the tomb Gentile prophesied that 'Fascist' culture could never be achieved without reverence for the past and an abiding belief in the free creative power of human reason.[108]

The Ethiopian war naturally drew his attention away from the Fascist policies at home, which caused him so much discomfort, to the world of foreign affairs. Here he saw nothing but good; [109] but even in the midst of a panegyric on Fascist imperialism he spared a few moments to utter some words of doubt about the general trend of educational policy and to give two fairly specific warnings. In the first place discipline must be voluntary and not coerced:

. . . if we do not take care, discipline, instead of being, as it ought to be, a free adherence to an authority capable of interpreting our own inward needs, may be converted into external formal obedience, a lie and a source of corruption, the fount of that vile hypocrisy which is the ruin of the character. This is a most serious danger against which it is by no means easy to guard in a rigid organization of great masses.

And in the second place the religious revival, if carried to extremes, would mean

subjecting the national culture once again to the routine mechanical observances of an outward religiosity and to the consequent limitations of inward spiritual liberty, from which the Italians have labored for centuries to redeem themselves. . . .[110]

---

[108] *Ibid.*, pp. 341–61. The beginning of a new era and the existence of the new 'Fascist' culture were signalized in 1934 by changing the title of the I.N.F.C. journal from *Educazione fascista* to *Civiltà fascista*. But the change was heralded by an unsigned editorial, "Camminare," in June 1932 (pp. 429–31); and after January 1933 the format and content are much more literary and there is much less polemic about matters of policy. In view of this speech in November 1933 it is hard to credit that in January 1934 Gentile really believed as he claimed, that the revolution had reached maturity and was ready to leave school (B.1115).

[109] See the following section, pp. 213–16.

[110] B.1144 in B.1139, p. 385. Notice in the first passage the echo of his remarks about the problem of political discipline in 1928, cited on p. 192 herein.

In 1936 another principle of the Gentile reform was abandoned: the autonomy of the universities was taken away and they returned to the sphere of direct ministerial control. Here at last Gentile's patience broke. He was convinced that in the universities at least freedom was of more importance than perfect discipline.[111] As we have just seen, he did not himself think that the situation in the universities was as good as it might be, but the suggestion that they could not manage their own affairs roused him to something very like wrath, and in 1937 he began to protest against the whole tenor of educational policy.

A series of brief communications signed "A. Z." and "Giacomo di Chabannes, signor de La Palisse" [112] appeared in *Leonardo*, a literary review edited by Gentile's son Federigo. Their real origin was quite apparent from the first, and at the end of his polemic Gentile acknowledged his authorship. In the first of these communications he attacked the new regulation of the universities. The State, he argued, should deal with special problems through an appropriate delegation of authority. In the sphere of the higher culture the universities themselves were the best guardians of its interest.[113]

The second short article, "Vox clamantis," although still primarily concerned with the university reforms, voiced his disillusion over the whole field of Fascist educational and cultural policy and defended the ideal of the reform of 1923:

After the reform, the counterreform.

A Fascist reform of the schools, the most Fascist of the Fascist reforms. But then a counterreform more Fascist still, superlatively Fascist: Fascist in content, not merely in form or method. For to listen to the authors and supporters of the counterreform, the programs at least of the first reform were not inspired by Fascism of the purest and most authentic variety. Indeed (and why not?) they might be considered worthy of a school that was more liberal than Fascist. A school liberal in its respect for all the forms of culture, and in its humanist character, which is the es-

---

[111] In 1933 he had protested strongly against a proposal to introduce compulsory curricula (cf. B.1087).

[112] Jacques de Chabannes, Sieur de la Palisse (*c.* 1470–1525), was a Marshal of France under Francis I, and accompanied the latter on his Italian campaigns. He was killed at the battle of Pavia in 1525. Shortly after his death his soldiers composed a song intended in his honor, which made his name proverbial as a purveyor of obvious truths or platitudes on account of the naiveté of two lines which survived: "Un quart d'heure avant sa mort/Il était encore en vie."

[113] B.1175.

sence of true culture; liberal in its respect for the spontaneous inclinations of the pupils in all kinds of schools, insofar as these inclinations are not accidental arbitrary preferences but a universal expression of human nature; and hence liberal in the freedom of study [nelle facoltà di studio] accorded to University students, and the freedom in organization of studies assigned to Universities; liberal in short in the limits imposed on the inspecting and controlling activities of the higher authority, which can and should watch over the school without upsetting it by its intervention. . . .[114]

In their eagerness to wipe out the shame of liberalism, the authoritarian reformers were falling into a formalism that was far more terrible. They were again reducing education to the satisfaction of formal requirements, the passing of examinations: [115] "the new system carried to its extreme implications may be Fascist, but its Fascism will suffocate life." We must have done with this reduction of discipline to outward obedience:

. . . And to begin with let us have done with the mythology of this insolent anti-Fascist Liberty: which is a stupid fable, like that of the notorious enmity between Fascism and culture, with which it makes a pair. Come now, a little extra understanding does harm to nobody. Myths, by all means; but let them be beneficial myths, not poisonous ones.

The reformers paid no heed; there was even talk of abolishing the separate organic units of the reformed secondary-school system and extending the weakness of the liceo scientifico by establishing a unified lower course for all secondary schools.[116] This was a serious threat to the classical ginnasio-liceo, and to the traditional humanism that had hitherto dominated Italian education. It seemed to Gentile that the Fascists, who had come to power in order to preserve the national tradition, were now about to betray it and revive the prewar Socialist ideal of a 'democratic' educational system.[117]

This aspersion did not pass unchallenged. The supporters of the unified school retorted, in the best Gentilian fashion, that it was the spirit in which a program was executed that counted—a scuola unica fascista was not at all the same as the scuola unica of prewar

---

[114] B.1176.
[115] He pointed out some of the fallacies and absurdities inherent in this reduction in a later communication (B.1178).
[116] Gentile remarked that, for his part, he would have set up a ginnasio scientifico if he had had the financial resources available to later ministers (B.1177, p. 119).
[117] Ibid.

years. Whereupon Gentile came forward as the champion of simple common sense and reported that, in the opinion of his friend, the Sieur de la Palisse, facts were facts and there was no getting away from them. One wonders what he would have said if his opponents had invoked the French nobleman against some of his theses.[118]

His opponents asked if he wished to remain forever wedded to the inviolable principles of 1923; and they challenged him furthermore to abandon the pose of anonymity and come forward openly. In reply the Sieur de la Palisse himself asked how there could be anyone in Year XVI of the Fascist Era

so naive as to pretend that we should still stand firm eternally on the immortal principles of the so-called Gentile Reform. For I have heard that this same Gentile, being busy with other business, is far, very far indeed, from the thoughts of time gone by; he never speaks of his reform, and never wishes to hear it spoken of; and when someone asks him his opinion on scholastic affairs, he shrugs his shoulders and excuses himself thus: —For the love of Heaven, *parce sepulto!* [119]

But in January 1938, under the heading "A declaration . . . worthy of La Palisse," Gentile finally acknowledged that the protests were his.[120]

Thereafter his criticisms ceased; and when Bottai's School Charter containing the principles of the new *Fascist* education was promulgated in 1939 he was once again ready and willing to make the best of things. He was still reluctant to give his opinion because, as he put it now, ". . . for several years I confess that I have made it my policy not to open my mouth again on this subject. In fact I have dedicated so many years of my life to educational questions that I can surely claim the right to think about something else in the years that remain to me. . . ." [121] But, having acceded to the invitation of the *Corriere della sera,* he proceeded to tell its readers that, when he was finally able to read the much-heralded charter, he was greatly relieved to find that the rumored reform *ab imis* had not materialized. "One should congratulate His Excellency

---

[118] B.1179. Two years later he managed to get away from the facts and back into the 'spirit' of the thing!

[119] B.1180.

[120] B.1190.

[121] B.1213. As an explanation of his policy of silence, the last sentence can scarcely be taken seriously. The Sieur de la Palisse was nearer to the truth —Gentile's silence was the silence of despair.

The text of the School Charter is given by I. L. Kandel in *Educational Forum*, IV, January 1940, 206–12. For a critical discussion see Minio-Paluello, *op. cit.*, Part IV.

Bottai . . . above all because his Charter, all things considered, had spilt little blood." According to Gentile it was, in fact, a continuation of the tradition of humanism.[122] The principle of rigorous selection for the classical lyceum and the 'academic' faculties of the universities was maintained, and the State's responsibility for the total moral and intellectual formation of its citizens was reaffirmed [123] in the provision for inspection of private schools, and the lengthening of the period of compulsory schooling. The spirit of the *Riforma Gentile* lived on in the new charter.

Taking a leaf from his opponents' book, Gentile was even prepared to regard the *scuola media unica* as being in accordance with this spirit, "at least in the purpose for which it is instituted." The introduction of Latin into the curriculum of all the secondary schools in 1923 was what had made it possible. Under the old system the differentiation of a particular type of culture took place gradually in a single institution dominated (at least ideally) by a single spirit. But that was a minor detail. The really bad thing about the old *scuola unica* had been that it meant the abolition of Latin; whereas the new Fascist version was founded on it.[124]

Again, in the matter of the *esame di Stato*, the principle was preserved and that was the essential thing:

. . . Nor am I inclined to despondency because the majority of the examiners is constituted, according to the Charter, from among the teachers of the same school in which the pupils are prepared. Everything, in fact, will depend on the seriousness with which the two members of the committee added by the Minister are chosen; for without doubt two committee members who are good, I mean capable and conscientious, will be worth a thousand times more than a whole committee of outside judges nominated at random. . . .

Good administration was ultimately more important to the school than good laws, for even under bad laws a school could prosper, given the right spirit in their interpretation.

---

[122] This is a very Pickwickian assertion. The primary novelty of the charter lay in its emphasis upon manual labor as an essential part of the curriculum in all schools. It may possibly have influenced Gentile's conception of what humanism really was, however (see Chapter 8, pp. 273-78, herein).

[123] As if that principle was ever threatened by any Fascist!

[124] It should be recollected that in 1909 Gentile had condemned the proposal of a *scuola media unica* with Latin—which he had later "virtually" adopted as he here says—as a compromise which was based on no principle, and only introduced confusion. It was "hybridism"—an attempt to serve two masters. His opinion then was that if it was admitted that Latin ought to be retained, the principle of the classicists was granted and there could be no grounds for excluding Greek (B.217 in B.813, pp. 137-38; cf. Chapter 3, pp. 54-55, herein).

All this was little more than the fox insisting that the grapes were sour; and even so, Gentile could not quite reconcile himself to the substitution of special entrance examinations for the different faculties of the university, in place of the former comprehensive 'maturity' examination. However good the intention might be, he felt that only a miracle could produce good results from this change. He also expressed a pious hope that the promised "experimental didactic centers" did not mean the resurrection of the old formal "pedagogics" which he had abolished.

About the new emphasis on manual labor—which was the most revolutionary thing in the charter—he expressed himself in a somewhat guarded fashion. Given "intelligent and discreet" programs and methods of execution, the idea of associating manual labor with intellectual education was an "excellent" one—it is apparent that he had grave doubts as to whether these preconditions would be fulfilled.

In the light of this article it is no surprise to find that Gentile voted for the institution of the *scuola unica* when the law implementing that article of the School Charter was proposed in the following year. In his brief speech on that occasion [125] he repeated all his reasons for regarding the new secondary-school system as a continuation of the traditional humanism. At the very beginning he emphasized that he was a staunch supporter of the new law. As a loyal Fascist he was bound to make this affirmation, since, as he said himself, it was only a particular application of the School Charter which had already been approved, and therefore could not be discussed. But it is embarrassing to see how he felt constrained to repeat it several times in a very short speech which contained only one or two minor technical suggestions and a hesitantly expressed doubt of the wisdom of trying to make the three-year course of the *scuola unica* an independent and autonomous whole from the administrative point of view. The abjectness of this speech provides a bitter contrast to the high hopes with which as Minister of National Education he accepted the *tessera* of the Fascist party in 1923.

---

[125] B.1232 (given in the form of an indirect report in G. Bottai, *La nuova scuola media*, Florence, Sansoni, 1941, pp. 88–90).

Fascist Imperialism

From the very beginning there was in Fascism a strain of romantic violence which was almost certain to lead to imperialist expansion in the long run. This prospect did not disturb Gentile. It was after all a cardinal tenet of his philosophy that the essential character of the spirit was only fully realized in the unrestricted activity of the Nation-State; to that end the individual must be ready to sacrifice everything. Though not in any ordinary sense a 'militarist,' [126] Gentile was always inclined to glorify war, because it brought home to the individual that this sacrifice was his highest moral duty, and therefore the supreme realization of his own moral personality; so that he willingly accepted and supported the Fascist doctrine of 'war-mindedness' as a means of keeping this consciousness alive. But words would not maintain it for long without deeds. In 1931 he declared that just as the ideal of nationalism led to the breakdown of empires, so the self-maintenance of the Nation when it came into existence necessarily led to the construction of new empires.[127] It was natural, therefore, that he should heartily support the war in Ethiopia.

Here for once he was at one with the general current of opinion, and no longer an unheeded Cassandra. He clearly recognized what seems to be an undoubted fact, that the war united the nation to a greater degree than at any previous time since 1922. He expressed this by saying that the war completed the Fascist conquest of Italy, and in the light of this great moral advance he felt justified in condemning as simple-minded the "Quakers and well-meaning members of societies" who had scruples about Italy's aggression.[128]

His natural desire to celebrate this new national solidarity and to

---

[126] The only sign of orthodox militarism in his writings is one rather remarkable book review of 1919 (B.537; cf. n42 in Chapter 5 herein).

[127] B.1023 in B.1139, p. 120. In general, however, military imperialism was not part of Gentile's conception of Fascism before the Ethiopian crisis. His antipathy to "the pacifist club of Geneva" was given free rein in his article for the eleventh anniversary of the March on Rome (B.1090). But in spite of his insistence on political realism he presented Italy as a "principal artificer of that world peace, which is disarmament of frontiers and of hearts, loyally and courageously willed, and hence made realistically possible" in his proem to Civiltà fascista in 1934 (B.1115; cf. B.1117). He quickly returned to this line of argument once the war was over (cf. B.1173, p. 143).

[128] B.1144 in B.1139, pp. 382–83.

exult in the triumph of Fascism over the opposition of the League blinded Gentile to the realities of the international situation. He forgot his own earlier characterization of the "pacifist club of Geneva," and when the war was over and an imperial crown placed on the head of Victor Emmanuel, he celebrated the event as a victory over "one of the most formidable European coalitions that history records." [129] Any opponent of Fascism who continued to cry for "formal and nonexistent democratic liberty" must now stifle his own feeling of pride first; [130] so that the founding of the Empire was really the making of that new Italy which Fascism had striven constantly if not always quite coherently to create. The attempt by supporters of the League, especially England and the Soviet Union, to draw a distinction between the people toward whom they claimed to be friendly and the government of which they disapproved was an insult which the Italian people had justly resented.

Realizing, perhaps, that there was something rather odd about viewing the opposition of the League as if it were a military alliance, and also about his reconciliation of militarism with the cultural mission of Fascism, Gentile met the difficulty by arguing that the Fascists knew their enemies would attempt to enclose them in a circle of steel eventually; hence they had prepared from the beginning for a war which *they* did not will, but which their enemies *would* have willed sooner or later.[131]

From *any* point of view this conception of the Ethiopian war can be shown to be a mistake. We can agree with Gentile that the 'juridical' attitude adopted by the League was only a cloak for hypocrisy. But when he argues that it was ridiculous to pretend that the King of Italy and the Negus of Ethiopia were equal members of one society, he forgets that this pretense was supported by Italy against all the protests of his archvillain England, at the time of Ethiopia's admission to the League. By leaving the League Italy cannot be said to have escaped from responsibility for the legal

---

[129] B.1145, p. 321.

[130] Gentile was probably thinking of Croce here; for even Croce confessed to a certain sense of national pride over the conquest of Ethiopia.

[131] *Ibid.*, p. 325. After dealing with the foreign enemies of the Fascist regime, Gentile proceeds by a more than usually confusing reversion from the 'external' to the 'internal' point of view, to brand the Roman Catholic Church finally as the archenemy of Fascism. There is no logical connection between this part of the essay (B.1145, pp. 327–29) and the earlier indictment of the League. Nor was there any connection at all that I can discern between the Ethiopian war and the relations of Fascism with the Vatican. Gentile simply took the opportunity to slip this pill of criticism into the sugar of his loyal enthusiasm.

situation she had helped to thrust League members into. The hypocrisy of the most prominent League powers lay not so much in their attitude toward Italy as in their attitude toward the League itself. They were quite sincerely, indeed almost desperately, anxious to retain Mussolini's friendship. But times had changed since the days when European diplomats could carve up the world as they chose; and in any case such arrangements had always been made with a minimum of publicity. Mussolini himself destroyed any possibility of a secret settlement by a policy of adolescent brashness and swashbuckling bravado which turned public opinion in the democratic countries decisively against him.

Gentile suggests that the Fascists forestalled a war by showing that they were in earnest. In saying that Mussolini's behavior turned public opinion against him I do not mean to suggest that on the contrary he made a war against Fascism inevitable. The ordinary people who supported the League were scarcely less hypocritical than their leaders. They saw the Negus as a defender of liberty, equality, and fraternity, and they protested; but they were not prepared to fight at his side. Their desire for peace was selfish; it was not even a militant pacifism. And so, when Mussolini had called their bluff they, like their leaders, would have been quite prepared to forget about it. The link that binds the Ethiopian triumph to the shame of 1943-44, the link that demonstrates the ultimate bankruptcy of Fascist foreign policy, is to be found in the perpetuated pretense that the Ethiopian triumph was really a military one. If instead of dressing up a diplomatic coup as a famous victory they had settled down to the peaceful tasks of empire building, Italy might perhaps have kept her empire till the day when, for her as for other imperial powers, it finally began to resemble Frankenstein's monster.

Gentile did often urge that the position of an imperial power was one of increased burdens and responsibilities, that it was a cultural mission for the advancement of civilization and so on.[132] But he must bear some share of responsibility for the mystique of military adventure which led Italy into the Pact of Steel and finally into the

---

[132] Especially notable in this respect is the lecture he delivered in 1936 (B.1152) at Cremona, the stronghold of Roberto Farinacci, the most extreme representative of Fascist activism. Farinacci was chairman of the meeting and many compliments were exchanged between host and guest. But the speech was an almost overt polemic against Farinacci's conception of Fascism.

second World War. The article discussed above ends with a long section on the development of the Western conception of human freedom from the time of the Greeks and Romans, and especially on the Italian contribution to that development from the Renaissance to the capture of Addis Ababa.[133] But we must not forget that Gentile began by treating the halfhearted economic sanctions of the League as "one of the strongest coalitions that history records" and speaking of a "war fought in Africa against two-thirds of Europe"; that he treated warfare as the ultimate test of national purpose; and that he gave countenance to the encirclement myth.

Addressing foreign students who had come to Italy for a course on Fascism in 1937 he tried to harmonize the cult of war with the ideal of universal human civilization thus:

. . . the Fascist feels and affirms that life lies not in inertia, but in movement, not in the peace dear to one who is well off and therefore content to sit still, but in war, sacred at all times to him who does not carelessly give way to instinct, but feels in his heart the justice that yet remains to be done, and sees the tears that ought to be dried; and in short conceives his life as the militant service of an ideal—not the ideal of selfish domination over others, but the ideal of a world in which all legitimate aspirations are satisfied.[134]

But if we ask precisely *what* aspirations *are* legitimate it becomes evident immediately that Gentile is perilously close to the blind activism of a quasi-Darwinian struggle for existence. The long and short of it is that we can only discover whether an aspiration is legitimate by fighting for it.[135]

---

[133] Gentile rejected Spengler's thesis about the "decline of the West." He thought it impossible there should ever be a *real* decline of Europe; for he held the typically Hegelian view that Asia had no history, and the rather less typical view that America—Hegel's 'land of the future'—could never do more than carry on the cultural tradition of Europe. Similarly Asia could only enter the stage of world history by assimilation of the European spirit (the revolutionary doctrine and influence of Gandhi, for example, was traceable to his English education—B.1042).

On the other hand, his whole attitude was conditioned by Italy's emergence as an imperial power, in spite of the opposition of the League. He did agree that the tradition which the League represented was declining. The true expression of the spirit of Europe was to be found in Fascism rather than in the decadent materialism of the industrial democracies or the militant materialism of the U.S.S.R. And Japan was the herald of the Asian renaissance because she recognized and accepted what was sound in Western culture (cf. B.1149, p. 774, B.1167, B.1261).

[134] B.1168, p. 19.

[135] The claim of the League of Nations to decide this on a juridical basis is rejected explicitly immediately before the passage quoted.

Summing Up

Gentile's adhesion to Fascism gave rise to a great variety of opinions regarding his character and his philosophy. Almost all of these opinions were erroneous in a greater or lesser degree, since they rested on a mistaken view either of his philosophy or of his Fascism—and sometimes of both. Nor is this surprising, for the truth is that Gentile understood politics hardly at all. He did not see what Fascism was because he did not want to see. Or rather, he twisted what he saw until it corresponded in some measure with what he wanted to see, and explained the result in terms of his speculative philosophy by means of a whole series of equivocations and ambiguities.

Because of these ambiguities there were not wanting those who followed Croce's lead and denounced his whole philosophy as rotten. Perhaps the oddest product of this school is the little cautionary tale in the *Autobiography* of R. G. Collingwood: ". . . Fascism was not capable of honesty. Essentially an attempt to fight Socialism with its own weapons, it was always inconsistent with itself. There was once a very able and distinguished philosopher who was converted to Fascism. As a philosopher that was the end of him. No one could embrace a creed so fundamentally muddleheaded and remain capable of clear thinking. . . ."[136] One can forgive Croce's rancor but not this, for Collingwood certainly read and profited from Gentile's *Philosophy of Art* for example, which was published in 1931.

Even the temperate Dr. Mueller was perplexed by the contradiction between Gentile's liberal affirmation in 1907 that although a definite philosophy should be taught in the schools it should not be a State philosophy but a free expression of the teacher's own conscience, and his acquiescence in the imposition of just such a State philosophy twenty years later.[137]

To understand Gentile's Fascism is to understand this *volte face.*

---

[136] R. G. Collingwood, *An Autobiography,* Oxford, Clarendon, 1939, p. 158. Even this verdict is moderate when compared with the shameful travesty produced by Herbert Marcuse in *Reason and Revolution,* New York, Oxford, 1941, pp. 402–9. Lacking, apparently, any knowledge of Italian, he set to work to force the doctrines of *The Theory of Mind as Pure Act* into agreement with his own polemical interpretation of the German translation of the *Origins and Doctrine of Fascism.* It is not thus that the rights of reason are to be defended.

[137] Mueller, *op. cit.,* pp. 317–18. The reference is to Gentile's essay "La filosofia e lo Stato" (1929, B.980); see n34 in Chapter 7 herein.

We have to remember that in 1907 he was one of a tiny minority who pleaded that a completely 'lay' school was no school at all; even then he felt that *any* faith, even an imposed authoritarian one, was preferable to no faith at all. When Italy entered the war he thought that she had found her way to faith in herself; Caporetto seemed to show that he was mistaken, that the long centuries of cynicism and pessimism had weakened the heart and spirit of the people— and he felt that the 'lay' school was ultimately responsible. But in her worst hour Italy found the power to resist, and the war ended at last with her first great victory as a nation. There followed four years of anarchy in which no one ever stopped to consider that debt to the City and the Laws which Socrates gave his life to repay. Gentile was not the only thoughtful and moderate person who saw in the Fascists the vindicators of the principle of authority, law, and order without which no community can exist. But his feelings were stronger because his hopes had been higher. As Minister of Public Instruction in 1922 he was still insisting that "every faith is sacred; but a faith there must be." [138]

He was not then thinking of a political faith; and no one has suggested that he himself would have done what later ministers did. He was ready, however, to justify what they did. The parallel he drew in defending the educational purge is instructive; he recalled De Sanctis' purge after the establishment of the kingdom in 1860. [139] In his view the Fascists had to make a clean start, just as the nation had done then. It is true that the Fascists went further than he thought was wise in their zeal for discipline; and he said so. But he remembered his Vico and reflected that they would grow wiser and more temperate in time. The alternative was anarchy. Even Croce, we should remember, was still prepared to give the government a vote of confidence during the Matteotti crisis.

But where Croce, despite his earnest desire for social order, drew the line at outright dictatorship, Gentile went on. He did this because, when he joined the Party in 1923, his action expressed something more than an agreement with Party policy. It was an act of allegiance to a 'Regime': something which was "above and beyond the Party" [140] as Socrates' City was above and beyond his accusers. His loyalty to the 'Regime' continued—perhaps indeed it was even

[138] B.668 in B.1057, p. 17.
[139] B.836 in B.937, pp. 62–63.
[140] Cf., for instance, B.1027 in B.1104.

stronger—in his years of eclipse. The Party made mistakes, but the Regime was an ideal; and only through absolute loyalty to the ideal could the mistakes be corrected.

There is one aspect of Gentile's loyalty to the Fascist regime that we have not hitherto considered. He was not simply loyal to the Nation as a purely ideal entity. He was personally loyal to Mussolini. He was a true Fascist in that he shared the faith of many less cultured and less critical minds that "Mussolini is always right"— *Mussolini ha sempre ragione*. He did not, perhaps, take the saying quite so literally as a bigoted Fascist militiaman; [141] but he certainly believed that Mussolini possessed the Mazzinian "privilege of genius." [142] He was "the great Captain"—*il Condottiero possente* [143] —of whom Machiavelli had dreamed. In Hegelian terms, Gentile was certain that the *Weltgeist* possessed him and spoke through him. In his own preferred terminology, Mussolini was simply *l'Uomo*, "the Man"—the one man, we might say, to whom Gentile's Fascist philosophy really applied, when stripped of all its equivocations.

This conviction, which accounts for his cheerful acceptance of the unprincipled opportunism which was such a marked characteristic of the Fascist regime, is eloquently summed up in an article of 1934:

. . . the major contribution of the personality of Mussolini to the ideas which he represents is the great moral force that emanates from him, his prestige, the fascination that he exercises on the individuals who come into contact with him, and the masses to whom he speaks in gatherings of many thousands of persons, such as were never before seen crowding together excitedly to listen to an orator. A moral force, which springs from the absolute faith which he, above all others, has in his own ideas and the providential mission that he is destined to fulfill for his country, and from the great humanity of his soul, closed to every individual interest and open only to the vast generous awareness of those ideal goods which transcend the individual and concern the *Patria* in its honor, its glory, its security and prosperity, and, therefore, in its power and its value in the history of the world. A vast awareness which is echoed in his forthright, nude, and powerful eloquence, which reaches the minds of the listeners as the immediate expression of that which they have always felt at the bottom of their hearts without thinking about it or forming a clear concept of it, so that they never knew how to express it to themselves clearly. [144]

---

[141] "I have never believed in the infallibility of anybody," he said in October 1925 (B.834 in B.818, p. 138).

[142] B.836 in B.937, p. 47; B.924 in B.937, p. 87.

[143] Cf. *ibid.*, p. 91.

[144] B.1117; cf. also Finer, *op. cit.*, pp. 301–2.

It was almost certainly his belief in the providential mission of Mussolini which turned the scale in his mind after he had gone into retirement in 1943, and caused him to become involved in the last mad adventure of the Fascist Social Republic, which led to his death.[145]

Because of this loyalty to an ideal personified Gentile went on to the end, trying within the framework of the Fascist State to correct and moderate the errors and excesses of various government authorities. It cannot be said that he was any more popular among the Fascists than among the anti-Fascists.[146] But it must be admitted that he was sincere, and that, if prejudiced, he was at least personally disinterested. If ever there was such a thing, he was a 'good' Fascist; indeed, his conscious moral uprightness was his worst fault in the eyes of both sides. The arrogance of innocence is a most infuriating thing in politics, especially when the innocence is not, or when one suspects that it is not, completely disingenuous.[147]

The fairest verdict on Gentile's political career seems therefore to be that of Dr. Minio-Paluello: "Gentile . . . and some of his followers, such as Codignola, who entered the Party, thought that they were giving Fascism an intelligent soul, which would lead the emotions along a good path. This marriage between philosophy and power was not very successful in the long run." [148] He did have

---

[145] C. A. Biggini, in his official obituary of Gentile, claimed that after leaving the audience with Mussolini, at which he gave his allegiance to the Fascist Social Republic, Gentile exclaimed, "Either Italy saves herself with him, or she is lost for several centuries" (*Civiltà fascista,* May 1944, p. 22).

[146] The attitude of the Party is well summed up by Ascoli (*op. cit.,* p. 252; not in Keene): "For the present ruling class he is too much of a philosopher, sometimes too outspoken—as for instance in his opposition to the Lateran Treaties—too ready to rescue fellow scholars from political difficulties. But no other Fascist intellectual can command such respect as he does. He is considered an irreplaceable nuisance that the regime must stoically bear."

[147] I have suggested above that Gentile enjoyed the position of dominance in the realm of culture which his allegiance to Fascism ensured for him. This is perhaps borne out by his desire to retain his official positions even after the fall of Mussolini (see Chapter 8, pp. 249–51, herein). But his undoubted enjoyment of power was only the shadowy side of his unstinting eagerness to serve the causes with which he had identified himself. He never sacrificed his conscience for the sake of power, and he always insisted that loyalty to Fascism could not involve such a sacrifice: "we are firmly convinced that Fascism does not want such sins and indeed does not allow them" (B.1149, p. 772).

[148] Minio-Paluello, *op. cit.,* p. 67. Cf. Finer (writing in 1935), *op. cit.,* p. 470: "Not the open free will idealism of Gentile has triumphed—he was squeezed dry and the peel thrown away—but the closed mind of the Fascist doctrine." ("The closed mind of the Fascist doctrine" is typified in Finer's view by Alfredo Rocco; cf. p. 166.)

some success in preserving the standards of culture against the worst excesses of dictatorial barbarism. In this his rigidity, his inability to compromise, which was often regarded as a fault, was perhaps his greatest asset. Nothing short of a religious conviction could have sustained him in a struggle against such hopeless odds. But, of course, if he had been more pliant, more conversant with the everyday weakness of ordinary 'empirical individuals'—himself included—he would probably never have become a Fascist at all.

Note on the Breach Between Gentile and Croce

After the maturing of actual idealism Croce and Gentile gradually drifted apart. It was not that either side wished it; each recognized the value of the *concordia discors* that existed between them. Gentile dedicated the second edition of his *Theory of Mind as Pure Act* (1918) in words which make this abundantly clear on his side; and as late as April 1921 Croce wrote a most friendly and perceptive Introduction to the English translation of *The Reform of Education* (B.659, pp. vii–xi, quoted in Chapter 1, p. 21, herein). Sprigge is therefore quite wrong in speaking of the open letters exchanged in *La voce* in 1912–13 (see Chapter 2, p. 23, herein) as a "quarrel, on which Croce maintains silence in his autobiographical sketch" (*Benedetto Croce*, p. 16). There was no quarrel; but Croce's attitude toward actual idealism continued to be mainly negative and when it began to attract disciples he was unwilling to accord to them the sympathetic consideration that he accorded to their master.

Hence Gentile was led to found a new review—the *Giornale critico della filosofia italiana*—as an outlet for the activity of his 'school.' He appears to have been rather hurt by Croce's virulently hostile criticism of some of his pupils' books, and he firmly declined to admit the distinction that Croce attempted to set up between master and disciples. But he continued to contribute to *La critica;* and on Croce's side, the very fact that he did try to make the distinction is evidence for the continued existence of the friendship.

Just before the March on Rome, the two philosophers were associated in the founding of the review *Nuova politica liberale* (cf. *Giornale critico,* III, 1922, 419). But by the time the first issue of that review appeared in January 1923 Croce seems to have withdrawn. It is very probable that Gentile's decision to join the Fascist party and his claim that Fascism represented the true liberalism was one of the most important catalysts in resolving Croce's hesitation about the new movement. After January 1923 Gentile's contributions to *La critica* ceased abruptly—an incomplete article being left hanging (B.768). We should not attach much importance to this, however, in view of Gentile's heavy ministerial duties at this time: virtually nothing from his pen—except a chapter from the second volume of the *Logic* which was probably written before October 1922—appeared even in the *Giornale critico* in this year; and the fact that the article in *La critica* was never reprinted suggests that probably it was never completed.

In 1924 Croce published his essay on the "Elements of Politics" in *La critica*, in which he stigmatized Gentile's theory of the Ethical State as a "governmental" theory of morality; and Gentile replied in a brief note in the *Giornale critico* (B.812). The tone of this exchange was hostile but impersonal (see Chapter 7, pp. 226–30, herein). The dedication of the *Theory of Mind as Pure Act* to Croce was still retained in the fifth edition published in this year; and in a very critical review of Gentile's *Logic* Croce emphasized that he and Gentile were still friends and collaborators despite their disagreements.

Croce's declaration in favor of the Liberal party in 1925, after nearly forty years of scholarly aloofness from politics, was the occasion that finally transformed the theoretical polemic into a personal quarrel. Gentile replied to Croce's praises of Liberalism as the party of culture (*Giornale d'Italia*, 18 March 1925) in an article published in *L'Epoca*, 21 March 1925 (B.830 in B.818, pp. 153–59). His tone was one of great respect and even affection for Croce, but he suggested that the whole of Croce's past and the Risorgimento tradition to which he belonged stood against his expression of sympathy with democratic liberalism: "the whole of Croce's philosophical education and the constant and most profound inspiration of his thought makes him a genuine Fascist without a black shirt. I am sincerely sorry to say something that at this moment may be displeasing to him, but all of us who love Croce and feel that he is alive beside us and within us cannot resign ourselves to abandon him to the past, where because of a certain taste for nostalgic yearning, scholarly yet instinct with inward emotion and inward aestheticism, he sometimes would like to take refuge from the tiresome events and persons that besiege us in the present" (*ibid.*, p. 154). Croce was in fact so displeased with this suggestion that he never forgot it, or forgave Gentile for making it; and in his brief reply (*Giornale d'Italia*, 23 March 1925) he even attacked Gentile's competence as a scholar. Gentile pointed out that the whole world knew that for twenty-five years Croce had been of a different opinion on that subject (B.831 in B.818, pp. 159–61; cf. B.945).

A few days after this exchange in the newspapers Gentile was commissioned by the Congress of Fascist Intellectuals at Bologna to write a Manifesto expressing their faith in the new Regime. In reply Croce published a Protest against the introduction of party politics into the world of culture, which was signed by a great number of prominent Italian men of letters. The original Manifesto was soon forgotten. But the Protest was long remembered by the authorities; it became known as *the* manifesto, and 'signatory of the manifesto' was a badge of shame in official circles. Thus the personal quarrel between Croce and Gentile assumed a national significance, and the breach became absolutely irrevocable.

Gentile's tone throughout the polemic of the next eighteen years was outwardly calmer than Croce's. He once stigmatized the personal tone of Croce's vendetta against himself as "obscene" when viewed in relation to the dedications of the latter's *Poetry of Dante* and *Bibliography of Vico* (1929; see B.982). Benedetto Gentile tells us that in private life his father always abstained from uttering a word against Croce (*Vita e pensiero*, IV, 20).

But Croce might well have retorted that the references to his *Aesthetics* in Gentile's *Philosophy of Art* were scarcely less than obscene in the light of many earlier tributes; and there was a note of self-righteousness even in some of Gentile's most placatory utterances which was in its own way quite as insulting as Croce's unreasoning outbursts of emotion. It may be noted that when Croce adopted the same tone in his reflections after Gentile's death, Gentile's friends were quick to resent it, while Croce's party in their turn could see nothing but perfect charity in the passage objected to (cf. *Croce, the King and the Allies,* tr. by Sylvia Sprigge, London, Allen and Unwin, 1950, pp. 111–12; Spirito, "Lettera aperta a B. Croce," *Giornale critico,* XXIX, 1950, 11, or *Vita e pensiero,* V, 267, or *Note sul pensiero di Gentile,* p. 74; Nicolini, "Brevi cenni sulla vita e sulle opere di B. Croce," *Nuova antologia,* CDLVII, January 1953, 15n).

VII

POLITICS AND ECONOMICS IN THE ETHICAL STATE

Croce and the Ethical State

Almost all of Gentile's important work after 1923—with the exception of the *Philosophy of Art* [1]—was influenced by his Fascist sympathies. It is by no means easy to decide where to draw the line between philosophy and political polemic in this period. This is not in any way surprising since Gentile himself insisted continually that philosophy and life, theory and practice could not be separated—indeed, it is his account of their indissoluble union that constitutes the essential core of his philosophy. We have several times said that his whole view of reality is fundamentally ethical, and by this time we do not need to point out that his ethics was fundamentally political; so that although a distinction can be drawn between his 'political writings' and his 'writings on political theory,' any attempt to treat them separately must necessarily be somewhat pragmatic. [2] Even the writings dealt with in the last chapter, in

---

[1] A political occasion has been suggested even there. Dr. Mueller writes: "j'ai eu l'impression qu'elle a été rédigée plutôt pour se substituer, dans l'enseignement secondaire en Italie, au *Bréviaire d'esthetique* de Croce, que pour satisfaire à une véritable exigence interieure" (*La pensée contemporaine en Italie,* p. 310n). But this seems to me a case in which his intuition is seriously at fault. Whatever one's opinion of the book as a statement of aesthetic theory, there is no doubt that the theory of 'feeling' on which it is based is a revolutionary development of the dialectic of the 'pure act' such as could only arise from a deeply felt "inward need."

[2] The pragmatic purpose of this chapter is to discuss those essays which Gentile specifically refers to in his Preface to *Genesis and Structure of Society* as anticipations of the doctrines there developed.

which the influence of nonphilosophical prejudices is most clearly evident, contain many pages of valuable reflection and speculation, often of a kind that would not be considered political in any *Weltanschauung* less totalitarian than that of actual idealism. While on the other hand the controversy with Croce concerning the nature of the State, which will here be treated on its merits as a philosophical discussion, clearly has its roots partly in the practical disagreement between the two men.

Even before the advent of Fascism, it was apparent that the two philosophers did not altogether agree about questions of political theory. In writing his *Ethical Fragments*—which appeared in *La critica* in the years following Italy's entry into the first war—Croce offered some pertinent and positive criticism of his friend's conception of the State, and showed why he could not accept it although he recognized elements of truth in it.

Politics, Croce argued, is a technical business: it is the special art of directing the economic selfish interests of individuals into orderly channels in such a way that their conflict shall not degenerate into a war of all against all. The politician is a kind of artist, detached from the passions of men, which are simply the material on which he works. It is not he, but the ordinary man, the good citizen, who recoils from the evil and corruption in the world. The good citizen recoils especially before the spectacle of corruption in public life, since the State, the rule of law, represents his only defense against universal barbarism—"the State, in the aspect here considered, is an ethical institution, the greatest of all ethical institutions, and virtually the sum of them all." [3] But his impatient demand for 'honesty' in public life demonstrates an inability to grasp the real nature of politics. We do not worry about whether a surgeon is 'honest' or not. "Political honesty is nothing but political capacity." Capability carries with it its own moral guarantee—"a man endowed with genius or real capacity may let himself be corrupted in everything else but not in politics, for politics is his passion, his love, his glory, the substantial purpose of his life." [4]

Being unable, except by a slow and laborious process of transformation, to alter the passions that provide his raw material, the

---

[3] *Etica e politica*, Bari, Laterza, 1945, p. 160 (English translation by Arthur Livingston with the title *The Conduct of Life*, New York, Harcourt, n.d., p. 240).

[4] *Etica e politica*, pp. 166–67; cf. *Conduct of Life*, pp. 251–53.

politician is often obliged to cheat and deceive them. He himself feels that this is 'wrong,' but he feels forced to do it nevertheless— which indicates that ultimately it is not wrong at all. He is the architect of the economic life, the world in which everyone recognizes that 'business is business' and no one feels guilty about it. But the fate of Machiavelli warns us that a candid acknowledgment on the part of the politician that *his* business is not run according to the strictest canons of abstract morality would be an irretrievable mistake. He must keep it a secret even from himself if possible.

Furthermore, in the performance of his duty, he is not bound by the ideals which govern personal life. States have no 'honor,' no moral ideal, they cannot acknowledge error or sin—"the State does not revolve in the circle of ethics." [5]

How can this conclusion be reconciled with the previous admission that the State is "the greatest of all ethical institutions"? We have to consider what it is that each of these assertions is meant to deny. Machiavelli and the sound political theorists deny that the State is "subject to the norms of Christian piety." Whereas those who declare that the State is an ethical value mean to assert its autonomy, its independence of the moral authority of the Church. They claim that the State itself is the true Church. In the two assertions 'the State' is taken in two different senses: "in a first moment as pure potency, pure utility; and thence it rises to morality —not repudiating its former character but negating it, that is, preserving it by transcending it." [6]

The real State, Croce concludes, is not identical *either* with 'power' *or* with 'morality.' These are only ideal tendencies within it. The State itself is simply the practical activity of man, and 'power' and 'morality' are the eternal forms of human practical activity.

It was not surprising that when Gentile began his polemical activities on behalf of the Fascist regime, Croce employed this critical analysis against him. In 1925 he published a little volume on the *Elements of Politics* in which the doctrine of the Ethical State, as held by Gentile, was denounced as a "governmental concept of morality." Political action, Croce now argued, is properly action undertaken from the politician's point of view—economic, utilitarian action. For the politician everything, even religion and morality, is

---

[5] *Etica e politica*, p. 177; cf. *Conduct of Life*, p. 264.
[6] *Etica e politica*, p. 182; cf. *Conduct of Life*, p. 274.

simply an economic instrument or obstacle. He employs great ideals like "Liberty, Equality, and Fraternity" as powerful weapons for securing political ends. But in the process of realizing these ends politics itself becomes moral—it is ethics that is built on a political foundation rather than vice versa. The priority and hence the amorality of politics is temporal and definite,[7] but politics is not a self-sufficient sphere of activity. When political action is governed by the moral conscience and directed to ethical ends, the simple utilitarian State is transformed:

. . . it is no longer a simple utilitarian relation, a synthesis of force and mutual consent, of authority and liberty, but an incarnation of the human ethos and therefore an ethical State or State of culture. . . . So it is, too, with the word "consent," which now becomes ethical approval and hence devotion to "force," but to the force which is the force of good, so that consent is not more or less forced, but becomes full and complete. . . .

From this point of view, that exaltation of the State which . . . still re-echoes in many schools today may seem unexceptionable though redundant.

The "exaltation of the State" is not really so unexceptionable, however, for

When "morality" is conceived as the "ethical State" and the latter is identified with the political State, or simply with the "State," we arrive at the concept (from which the theorists of that school do not recoil) that concrete morality lies wholly in those who rule, in the act of their governing; and their adversaries must be considered the adversaries of morality in action, deserving not only to be punished, with or without the sanction of the law . . . but also deserving the highest moral condemnation. This is, so to speak, a "governmental" concept of morality. . . .

And a " 'governmental' concept of morality" is inadequate because

the moral life embraces both the men who govern and their adversaries, the conservatives and the revolutionaries, and the latter perhaps more than the former, because they open the ways of the future better than the others, and bring about the advancement of human society.[8]

Gentile replied to this indictment in a brief but brilliant critical notice, arguing that Croce had simply misunderstood the theory of the Ethical State and that, moreover, his own position was fraught with difficulties.[9] The proposed definition of the "political" State, for instance, was an atomic, materialist conception which Croce

---

[7] *Etica e politica*, p. 228; cf. the English translation by Salvatore J. Castiglione under the title *Politics and Morals*, London, Allen and Unwin, 1946, p. 22.

[8] *Etica e politica*, pp. 230–32; cf. *Politics and Morals*, pp. 23–26.

[9] B.812.

himself was unable to maintain. How could he admit that the State was a "spiritual category" while he insisted in defining it in an empirical way? Or again, since he held that sovereignty subsisted in neither party to the sovereign-subject relation, but rather in the relationship itself, and that force and consent were correlative terms, the failure of either of which involved the destruction and death of the State, how could he hold that the State does not transcend the mere individual statesman?

Certainly the State is a force, Gentile goes on, and certainly it is individual. But it is a moral force, and its individuality is not the immediate individuality of the empirical individual but the imma-nent universality of the rational will. As for the argument that it is not the State but the total process of world history, in which in-dividual States are particular elements, that is ethical, the answer is that the State, apart from its actual history, is an abstraction.[10] The Ethical State is the State as determined within the complex of world history, so that no diminution of the State's ethical character is involved in the final appeal to it.[11]

Croce's fundamental argument that the individual is the prin-ciple of progress, through his power to oppose his will to that of the government, receives short shrift when Gentile finally gets to it: "This 'surpassing' seems to us to be a very easy victory over an imaginary foe: for the State does not leave outside of itself the

---

[10] *Etica e politica,* pp. 261–62; cf. *Politics and Morals,* pp. 55–56. In this respect, as Gentile points out, Croce is obliged to condemn his own concept of the State as abstract. Croce does in fact say that "History" pure and simple is "ethico-political," and that this ethico-political history includes "not only the State, the government of the State and the expansion of the State, but also that which is outside of the State, whether it cooperates with it or tries to modify it, overthrow it, and replace it: the formation of moral institutions, in the broadest sense of the word, including religious institutions and fancies, and myths that are practical in tendency and content. If, however, one wishes to consider the complex of this movement as the very life of the State, in its highest sense, we shall not object to the word, so long as it is interpreted thus" (*Etica e politica,* p. 279; cf. *Politics and Morals,* p. 73). According to Gentile, this *was* precisely what the supporters of the *Staatsgeschichte* that Croce con-demns meant.

[11] But Gentile himself uses this same argument against Hegel; cf. p. 241 herein. He never did really face the problem. The argument of the preceding note gives a formally satisfactory answer but it is not a genuine solution because Gentile never concretely conceived of rebellion, revolution, or spiritual exile as actual, morally respectable possibilities. If he had done so he might have stayed in retirement in 1944 (cf. the following note).

opposers of the government, but generates revolution within its own breast, the revolution which is not its annihilation, but rather its realization." [12]

The interesting thing about this argument is that each side appears to me to be both right and wrong. The 'economic' theory of the State advanced by Croce is surely as unacceptable as that of Machiavelli without being quite as consistent. The politician is not a technical expert chosen for his ability to deceive us for our own good. How could we choose him for such an ability? Politics, as opposed to diplomacy, is not a technical matter at all, but a moral one. It is not concerned with means but with ends. Unless the politician tells us honestly just what he considers the 'national interest' to be, we cannot decide whether he is a fit person to be looking after it. The national interest is not something that defines itself, in the way in which 'prosperity' in the economic world reduces to 'long-term monetary advantage.' Croce's theory of politics in the *Ethical Fragments* is essentially Platonic. The politicians may legitimately deceive everyone except the Guardians—the philosophers who are capable of thinking 'dialectically.' It is a measure of the success of Giolitti's regime in Italy that his spirit penetrated so deeply into the thought of a mind as acutely critical and as deeply moral as Croce's; but a careful study of Croce's theory will show why that regime was bound to break down.

The salvation of Croce's political thought lies in the barrenness of his 'economic' theory of the State. The fruitful concept in his

---

[12] B.812; cf. B.980 in B.1075, p. 182 (2nd ed., p. 164). Any attentive reader of the preceding chapter must surely agree that Gentile's theory of the Ethical State was not a "governmental concept of morality." Any critic of the State whose criticism is informed by good will is *ipso facto* included in the self-critical consciousness of the State. Whether or not a critic is a man of good will can be discovered in time of crisis. Gentile was elated over the popular response to the Ethiopian crisis because he felt it proved there were no irreconcilable opponents of the Regime left; and Croce himself, when faced with the problem of the second World War, eventually decided that his allegiance to the *patria* must come before his opposition to Fascism, thereby showing that, from Gentile's point of view, his moral life was part of the life of the State. But if he had decided, as he might have done had he been driven into exile, that the defeat of Italy was the only thing that could save what was valuable in the national tradition, his criticism would have been part of the action of world history upon the State from above, or at any rate from outside. It is the possibility of this choice by an Italian that forms the real weakness of Gentile's theory of the Ethical State as a complete account of moral life.

meditations on the subject is that of 'ethico-political history'—a history created by the moral conscience of one who is not deceived by the wiles of professional partisans. Vico and Machiavelli may have had important insights into the role of force and deceit in politics; but the importance of these insights lies precisely in the fact that they make it possible to overcome this force and deceit, by consciously willing in accordance with the "plan of Providence" or the "effective realities of the situation."

This 'ethico-political history' is identical with Gentile's 'Ethical State.' The danger implicit in Gentile's formulation, however, is that political action may degenerate into a servility to the "effective realities," which is thoroughly *immoral* and therefore much worse than the amoralism of Croce. All too often in Gentile's Fascist polemics the word 'State' obviously means 'Fascist government.' It can have moral value, therefore, only for the convinced Fascist; but it is obvious that Gentile means to claim for it authority over Fascist and non-Fascist alike. One can hardly escape the feeling that a view of the State which makes such equivocation possible is *ipso facto* inadequate as a moral ideal. An examination of history is not reassuring: the supporters of the ethical character of the State, from Socrates onward, have for the most part been extreme conservatives. It seems that the equation of 'State' with 'government' is not merely possible, but natural and indeed almost *necessary*—as Croce claims—in order to give definition and concreteness to the otherwise empty theory.

Economics and Ethics

Gentile was not content with a mere refutation of Croce's arguments. A few years later he carried the war into the enemy's country in an article on "Economics and Ethics" which, although in accordance with an unwritten law of the Fascist regime it did not mention Croce, was clearly directed at him.[13]

He began by stipulating that economics is only an 'abstract' science. Once this is admitted many philosophical or semiphilosophical polemics against it fall to the ground. But the fact remains that as an abstract science it stands in continual need of philosophical criticism. Therefore, although he admitted that he lacked the

[13] B.1107 in B.1139, pp. 271–93.

technical competence to provide a systematic critique, Gentile felt himself entitled to make some general comments.[14]

In the first place, he argued, economics is not a science of external objects but of internal desires. Its ultimate concern is the human will. The 'things' to which the will is directed are called 'useful' in virtue of the fact that it is directed to them: "The primary useful thing is the earth; but insofar as it is useful, it is precisely the earth that man occupies, and possesses, and makes his own, linking it ever more bindingly and rigorously to his own life, and incorporating his own labor in it to an ever greater degree." [15]

When this inwardness of economics was recognized, it seemed at first that economics had been given a philosophical foundation, through the discovery (sc. by Croce) of the new spiritual category of "economic value" (economicità). But the 'discovery' soon proved dangerously ambiguous; for the new spiritual category did not assist the understanding of the empirical science—which continued obstinately empirical—while from the philosophical point of view "it presented itself from the beginning as something fleeting, being immediately transformed into morality." The attempt to define "economic will" as "volition of the individual" failed because concretely the will wills only itself, the universal, the good or bad action. In itself and for itself, economic action exhibits the firmness, constancy, and coherence which are essential to morality. It is real and serious; [16] and its ends are only abstractly 'accidental.' Concretely the end presents itself always as necessary, that is to say it has the marks of an immanent universal, a moral value; it can only be adjudged 'particular' posthumously, through the application of a criterion external to the original act.

The recognition of this puts us in a position to solve certain vexed questions in political theory. It is obvious, for example, that the conventional distinction between public and private morality, which has been employed in discussions of Machiavelli, is baseless. It will not do to say that Machiavelli is a master of the theory of economic will, and that we are wrong to expect morality of him. If the State

[14] His only excursion into economic studies—if we may dare to dignify it to that extent—was an article surveying the statistics of trade between the countries of Italy's African empire and the Middle and Far East (B.1173). But we must remember that his pupils, notably Spirito, provided much of the economic theory for the Corporate State.

[15] B.1107 in B.1139, p. 273.

[16] "Far, far rather Cesare Borgia than Pier Soderini" (ibid., p. 276).

which is served by a Machiavellian Prince has a moral value, then so has his political theory and practice. In making the State the Prince acts as representative and interpreter of the community; the State's conscience is his conscience—a conscience which contains his private life and activity and is inseparable from it. The same holds for every adult citizen conscious of his civic responsibility. It is in the light of his consciousness of the State that he governs his conduct as a private individual. Political morality is not lower but higher, more concrete.

What then of the Machiavellian doctrine that the end justifies the means? The difficulty here arises from a false dichotomy: end and means are not concretely distinguishable. An immoral act can only tend to create an immoral State, a State without roots in the hearts of its citizens. But this does not mean that we have to agree with the abstract moralists against Machiavelli. The morality of a Prince's actions is not to be measured in terms of an ideal theory but rather by reference to the course of events in a time of crisis, and especially in war.[17] 'War' exists when some element in the world presents itself to the spirit as an obstacle. Within the State it is a sign of weakness, imperfection, immorality; but between States it is moral—though with a morality very different from that of peaceful civic existence. To kill a man in battle, says Gentile, is not murder because it is the State with its higher morality that is the real agent in this case, as likewise in the case of the judicial execution of a citizen who, "being estranged from the conscience of the nation, turns against the State, which is the living actuality of this conscience, like a stranger." [18]

There are two implicit suppositions here, both of which must be rejected as inconsistent with the fundamental principles of actual idealism. The first is the militarist presumption that the morality of war is higher than that of peace. It is true that to kill a man in battle is not murder. This significant fact about war shows that the State is an ethical institution, which we have an overriding duty to defend. But it does not alter the fact that the killing is an absolute disvalue, the reduction of consciousness to a mere thing, which is exactly contrary to the guiding principle of moral endeavor. The morality of war is morality reduced to its ultimate

---

[17] Cf. the argument of n12 above.
[18] B.1107 in B.1139, p. 284.

minimum, not raised to its highest intensity; it is the rear-guard action of the spirit in the moment of defeat. In 1914 Gentile seems to have seen this much more clearly than in 1934, for in his lecture on "The Philosophy of the War" he declared: "It is quite true then that the individual as such does not count; but the individual counts, he counts for everything, inasmuch as he is the reality of the universal; and when the individual is destroyed, nothing remains. Hence the absolute value of personality, *infinite in value even within the limits of its empirical particularity.*" [19]

Secondly, the implication that judicial execution is justifiable is contrary to the cardinal principle of Gentile's philosophy of punishment, which requires that the punishment be internal to the consciousness of the delinquent. We have seen how he inherited this principle from Spaventa,[20] who clearly understood and stated its implications in this respect; and the passage we have just quoted from his 1914 lecture is sufficient proof, if proof is needed, that Gentile accepted Spaventa's conclusions. But in reality we do not need to go so far afield, for the context of the present passage is sufficient. Gentile has argued that war within the State is moral weakness, whereas war between States is a necessity of moral life. The juxtaposition of these two assertions clearly implies that the killing of a native criminal cannot be justified by the same argument as that of a foreign soldier. To give the State the right of life and death in criminal justice is to allow it to make war upon its subjects; if this war is moral weakness it can hardly be backed by moral right. Furthermore, to call the exercise of any such right *moral* is to accede to the "governmental concept of morality." Analysis of Gentile's argument here shows, at one and the same time, how far he was from it in theory, and how near it he was prepared to come in practice.

Apart from this momentary descent into militarism and totalitarianism, however, Gentile's argument marches logically enough toward the complete resolution of economic activity into morality. If actions were really particular things strung out in series, the economic question "What *use* is that?" would be the only one we

---

[19] B.306 in B.497, p. 21 (my italics).

[20] See Chapter 3, pp. 41–43, herein. Gentile first betrayed a tendency to regress from the position of Spaventa to that of Hegel in one of his apologias for Fascist violence in 1925 (B.837 in B.818, p. 31). But cf. also Chapter 4, pp. 90–91, herein.

should ever need to ask. But in fact actions have value because they are expressions of a human personality. This is the clue to the correct distinction between economics and ethics. "Economic goods are not realizations but instruments of the human spirit. What is human is not useful; the useful is that which is a tool for man." [21] Utility is a concept applicable to things; it is not properly a category applicable to actions at all, though we may abstractly distinguish 'instrumental' or 'useful' phases in a complete (i.e. moral) act. Food, shelter, the land, these are properly speaking the 'useful.' A slave ceases to be useful when his master loves him, and does not merely 'set a value' on him. Whatever is regarded as external to the spirit can have only an economic value or disvalue. Thus in the end Gentile reverses the Crocean revolution and makes utility an external concept rooted in the material world.

This conclusion suffices to explain the empirical and mathematical character of economics. Economic goods are essentially material; they form an indefinite multiplicity of things comparable with one another. In short everything has its *price*. The things of the spirit on the other hand are always unique and incommensurable. *Niente di spirituale si scambia*—"there is no commerce in the things of the spirit." [22] For whereas economic activity divides men by sharing things *out*, the spirit unites them by enabling them to share *in* things.

If man were really an economic animal he would be condemned to a sterile pursuit of egoism. But as a creature capable of conscious thought he rises necessarily to a higher, universal, standpoint. The economic viewpoint is one that all must pass through, since all alike must recognize and build on the natural, material world. But the spirit returns from its self-alienation to a fuller knowledge of itself. In conquering nature man conquers himself. In the most primitive act of consciousness this conquest of nature is achieved—it is internalized, given spiritual value in the form of 'feeling.' [23] For a man

---

[21] B.1107 in B.1139, p. 287.

[22] *Ibid.*, p. 289. At this point, as in the concluding section of the paper, Gentile descends to frankly political polemic of the kind dealt with in the last chapter. For he accuses anti-Fascists, both liberals and Marxists, of accepting economic principles as universally applicable laws. Only Fascist corporative economists recognize the subordinate character of economic considerations!

[23] For a criticism of this argument cf. the remarks on pain and evil in Chapters 2 and 4 herein (especially pp. 32–33, 99–101, 113–16). All that it can legitimately mean is that the real problem is not the (morally indifferent) conquest of nature but the essentially moral conquest of self.

to remain at the economic level would be to renounce life: *sit diva dum non sit viva*. Economic science, therefore, has an important instrumental value but no normative powers; and economic life should properly be controlled and regulated from a higher, political, point of view.

On the surface, this conclusion appears to reduce Gentile's disagreement with Croce to a merely verbal quibble. If he is prepared to concede that the economic viewpoint is one that all men must pass through, it seems idle to make such a fuss about the contention that utility is not a spiritual category because it applies only to things and not to actions. Croce on his side was quite prepared to admit that economic life should properly be controlled and regulated from a higher *ethico*-political point of view. He distinguished almost from the beginning between *liberismo* as an economic program and *liberalismo* as a political ideal which might under given circumstances involve the abandonment of laissez-faire economics.

The disagreement is more than verbal, however. It appears to be no more than a quibble only because we have not got it clear at the verbal level. What is really at issue is the hoary old problem of whether the forms of the spirit are 'opposites' or 'distincts.' Croce claims that utility and morality are *distinct* categories of the spirit. Gentile's view, though he does not state it clearly, is that insofar as economics and ethics are distinct, economics is not a spiritual category; while insofar as it is a category of the spirit it is not distinct but opposite. What is unfortunate is that Gentile should have chosen to go on using the term 'economics' in both senses. His view would be much clearer if he used *only* terms like 'hedonism' or 'egoism' for the spiritual category, since it is really quite untrue that there is a purely 'economic' level in his theory of action. One cannot simply regard things as *useful;* they are always useful *for* something—of course, as actual idealists we ought rather to say for some*one*. And 'usefulness for me as an animal' (or as an 'empirical ego') is no nearer to the 'pure' usefulness of abstract economics than usefulness for the family, the tribe, the State, the transcendental Ego.

The difference between Croce and Gentile can be seen from another side by examining their conceptions of politics. They both agree unequivocally, to begin with, that politics is the category that includes all human action. But Croce proceeds to introduce an equivocation into his use of the term which is similar to the equivocation in Gentile's use of 'economics'; Croce does, however, explicitly recognize what he is doing, and indicates the *special* sense of the term by qualifying it as '*ethico*-political.' For Gentile such a qualification would be pleonastic. Politics is necessarily ethical and the ethical conscience does not supervene upon an existing activity. Thus for Gentile there can be no distincton between the point of view of the citizen and that of the statesman; and the Platonic notion of an aristocracy of the intellect, or of politics as a technique, is illegitimate. Politics must mean *self*-government, for it is only in that interpretation that it can be identified with ethics. Whereas for Croce politics can never be fully ethical because at best it is always the governance of others.

In the light of this analysis it may seem a little odd that it was Gentile, not Croce, who became a Fascist. Several things need to be remembered at this point. In the first place, Croce maintained the attitude of benevolent neutrality which he regarded as proper for the good citizen in his relations with the political technicians, until the Fascists, by establishing a dictatorship, transgressed the limit that separates politics from ethics in his view. Secondly, Fascism was a mass party proclaiming its mission to educate the people. Gentile could not but be sympathetic to their totalitarian appeal. He failed to see the essentially democratic implications of his own theory, because the existing democratic structure had become the preserve of the political technicians who had in his opinion led Italy to Caporetto; and because his own education in the tradition of aristocratic humanism made his conception of freedom too narrowly intellectual. Pellizzi was right to call Croce "the last of the bourgeoisie." Gentile *ought* to have been the 'first of the proletariat': his early study of Marxism leads through his Fascist essays to his final proclamation of the 'humanism of labor.' But his vision could never become a reality because in pursuit of it he sacrificed the only means to its realization, the absolute respect for free self-expression which Croce, despite his Olympian disdain for the masses, so gloriously preserved.

Politics and Law

It is interesting, and even important, to compare the theoretical relation between economics and ethics in Gentile's social theory with the practical relation between law and politics. We saw in Chapter

4 that he regards law as the abstract content of morality. He does not admit the existence of a purely juridical reality: law is simply the objective moment of volition, the moment in which the will is alienated from itself and does not recognize itself. It is "nature in the realm of the Spirit."

Hence he was bound to condemn Croce's conception of law as something which can subsist in ideal abstraction:

> We are committing a grave error therefore, when we attribute a kind of substantial existence to abstract laws in their imaginary universality, in accordance with the absurd logical theory of the pseudo concepts. It is not true that a law can be conceived as possessing its full legal value, apart from all the particular cases in which it is posited and meant to have legal validity. It can have legal validity on one condition: that it be the soul of all the particular cases in which it becomes actual in history . . .[24]

Law, like economics, is inconceivable except within the wider synthetic unity of life and action. The dialectic of this wider synthesis is politics.

The apparent parallel between law and economics, however, is largely specious. Law is not really reducible to 'nature' on account of its imperative character. We see this in political activity, when the moment of static alienation proper to law is overcome. It sometimes happens that the law that is thus realized in action is not the one which is "universally recognized." [25] In this event we have what is called *crime;* and it is necessary that the criminal's error be demonstrated. This necessity shows that if law is 'nature,' at least it is not morally neutral, as utility is, but morally positive. In crime the universality of the acting subject is at odds with the universal subject presupposed by the law; but through this divergence the law may itself be raised above the level of fact and endowed with spiritual life. The criminal may be obeying a higher law than that which is written (as in the case of Antigone); in such action the moral ideal is itself established as law in the most concrete form. The power of this new law is dependent partly on the strength of conviction, but also on what Gentile calls the "power of universality" (*potenza di universalità*) of the agent by whom it is affirmed; by

[24] B.989 in B.1157, pp. 122–23.
[25] *Ibid.*, p. 126. For an actual idealist this is a slightly loose and empirical way of talking. Strictly speaking the law that is realized never lacks universality —and 'universal recognition' has a ring of that "imaginary universality" of empirical concepts. For the criminal *his* law remains *the* law. Only when he makes the public law his own does it have a moral value.

this he seems to mean the extent to which the agent can call forth an echo of his feelings in the general conscience of the society faced with what would otherwise be simply a criminal action.[26]

The law as promulgated is meant to express the abstract essence of this general conscience. Politics, on the other hand, is the real active conscience of the community. Thus 'politics' coincides with 'the State.' The distinction between the two terms is purely verbal, like the distinction between 'will' as a substantive and 'willing' as an activity. The whole substance of the State is actually exhausted in its political activity; and political activity generally is not (as Croce claims) simply the sum of the activities of all the citizens but an organic system of activities informed by a single universal spirit.

None of an individual's actions are really private; that is what is meant by saying that man is a political animal. It is true that some men are better political animals than others; but the activity of the follower is not fundamentally different from that of the leader, and the will of every individual has an essential value in the will of the State: "The will of the inferior depends on that of the superior no more than the latter depends on the former, in the sense that each must take the other as its own norm; and we can even say that each in its own way has its norm within itself." [27] So that the best answer to the question "What is the will of the people?" is that which it receives from the conscience of every man who sincerely puts the question to himself.

From this conception of politics and law it follows that the dialectic of legal history is generated by the dialectic of political life. Law cannot, of itself, have any history, for it is a mechanical thing, fixed in formulas which are what they are. Legal history has to be looked for within the context of political (moral) history. The common objections to the identification of morals and politics arise from a tendency to take a legalistic view of morality as something which transcends the will and expresses itself in objective formulas

---

[26] It may be remembered that in 1916 Gentile exalted the attitude of Socrates in the *Crito* (cf. Chapter 4, pp. 121–22, herein). In 1930 he has advanced to a justification of Antigone. Factors contributing to this development are on the one hand his attempts to justify *squadrismo,* and on the other Croce's criticisms of the "governmental concept of morality."

[27] B.989 in B.1157, p. 129. How can such a conception of the political nature of man be maintained unless, to use another Aristotelian tag, we take turns ruling and being ruled?

like those of the law. History itself provides the proof that morality should properly be assimilated to the political activity that creates the laws, not the abstract form of the created product.[28]

Forward from Hegel

So far in this chapter we have been considering the crystallization of Gentile's final views as a result of his polemic with Croce. There is, however, one other important transitional essay in which Gentile settles accounts, not with his former friend and collaborator, but with his old master, Hegel. We may remember that in 1904, in his Introduction to Spaventa's *Principles of Ethics*, he defended the political theory of Hegel against certain views which he considered to be mistaken criticisms or misinterpretations. He showed then that he considered himself to be, in general, a loyal follower of the Stuttgart philosopher.[29] Twenty-seven years later, looking back after he had developed a systematic philosophy of his own, he took a much more independent and critical view of the tradition from which he had sprung. He was willing to recognize his enormous debt to Hegel but he clearly distinguished his own from the orthodox Hegelian position.[30]

He acknowledged, certainly, that it was Hegel who first formulated the concept of the State as he understood it. Down to Fichte the substantial character of the State went unrecognized because the individual person was the starting point of all political theories. So long as the individual was conceived atomically the State could be no more than an artefact. Only when man was conceived dialectically, as a historical process rather than as an atom, did the State

---

[28] Croce was at one with Gentile in this rejection of 'moral legalism.' But he went further than Gentile toward the conception of law as an *economic* category, not a moral one at all.

[29] Cf. Chapter 3, pp. 39–44, herein.

[30] B.1017 in B.1157, pp. 103–20. It is only fair to say that anyone who read this paper alone might well be left with the impression that Gentile's philosophy was less Hegelian than it really was. In 1904 he was concerned with persuading his readers that his own budding philosophy of immanence was the true interpretation of Hegel. In 1931 he advanced his theory rather as what Hegel *ought* to have meant. In the interim he had broken decisively with the 'encyclopedic' ideal in philosophy, and hence the material *separation,* in Hegel's system, of elements which are properly only ideal moments now appeared to him as a defect to be castigated and not merely explained away.

emerge as "ethical substance conscious of itself" (*sostanza etica consapevole di sè*).[31] This definition represented a great advance, since the State no longer appeared as the negation of liberty but as the universality through which alone liberty is possible. Hegel saw the universality of the will as something that develops gradually through the stages of the family and civil society to its full concreteness in the State. Authority thus becomes a force within the individual himself, and the opposition of liberty and law is at an end. As an actualization of liberty the State is essentially moral: it is a realization of the spirit "which will be more or less moral, but tends to be absolutely moral." [32] And in virtue of this immanent tendency it can be viewed as *ein Irdisch-Göttliches.*

Hegel then was the "herald of a new era." But the herald is one "who opens the way, but does not traverse it right to the end to which it leads." Hegel's concept of the State was vitiated by certain defects arising from the residuum of empiricism that still survived in his conception of philosophical method. He did not master the true method of idealism—the method of immanence; and as a result of this failure Gentile finds that his concept of the State, which being an ethical substance ought properly to be infinite, was limited under three aspects.

In the first place he conceived the State as one among others so that the will that is actually realized is not the will of the State, but the will of the World-Spirit which evolves in the process of *die Weltgeschichte.* Secondly, he assigned the State to a definite stage in the total evolution of the Spirit—the moment of Objective Spirit; it is flanked by the moments of Subjective Spirit which has not risen to its level, and Absolute Spirit which has passed beyond it. Thirdly, even within the objective moment it is preceded by the Family and by Civil Society which form the necessary basis for its existence.

If he had grasped the true method of immanence Hegel would have realized that the State as a spiritual reality is not a historical

---

[31] *Encyclopaedia*, para. 535. Gentile cites also *Philosophie des Rechts*, para. 257, but I do not find the phrase there.

[32] B.1017 in B.1157, p. 113. But in Hegel the internalization and hence also the morality may be very implicit and transcendent. We might say that Gentile is here developing the seeds of his own idealism in Hegel; but it would be equally true to say that he is doing violence to the theory of political ethics expounded in the earlier sections of this chapter by forcing it into the mold of an authoritarian intellectualism which happened also to be expedient for the justification of the policies of the Party to which he had given allegiance.

entity defined by geographical boundaries. Its history is not an unfolding panorama of which we can afford to be mere spectators. For the good citizen his own State is *the* spiritual reality, just as his mother is 'Mother' purely and simply. On this plane the other States have a place insofar as they are related to 'ours'; and thus they also are 'ours' since they are essential elements in the determination of our own history. In fact the real State coincides with *die Weltgeschichte.*[33]

Again, once the fundamental identity of individual and State is recognized, a purely subjective or purely objective phase of spiritual development is seen to be a mere abstract ideal. The Spirit is always absolute. If the State were purely objective it would remain eternally foreign to the conscience of the citizen; and if the Absolute transcended both alike it would be inconceivable. The State, like all other spiritual realities, is a form of philosophy.[34]

---

[33] When Croce made a similar objection to the theory of the Ethical State Gentile insisted that this view was common to the whole Hegelian tradition. And certainly Hegel did not mean to deny the identity of the State as 'ethical' with world history. The State, he says in one place, is "the march of God in the world"—a statement which can hardly be reconciled with the famous tag that he borrowed from Schiller ("Die Weltgeschichte ist das Weltgerichte") on any other hypothesis. But his notion of world history itself is certainly 'mythical' from the point of view of actual idealism. He regarded it as being literally a "march," or spatial progress (Orient-Greece-Rome-Germanic world) so that in a way his State was geographically limited. As a result of this limitation he was able to conceive the philosopher as a mere spectator of the "march of God." That is what Gentile here objects to.

[34] Gentile developed the consequences of this thesis in a paper on "Philosophy and the State," delivered at the Italian Philosophical Congress in 1929 (B.980 in B.1075, pp. 174–88): the proper philosophical attitude for the State is *nihil humani alienum.* But it cannot be agnostic; it must have a doctrine. The possession of such a doctrine is the foundation of its right to educate: "[the State] has the right to teach because it has a doctrine, it knows the end of the Nation, it knows the value of this end; and its knowledge is not an abstraction, but is related to the past and to the actual present, and to the living and perpetual forces of the nation, since *res sua agitur.* And always he who teaches has a right to teach: this is the essential law of the spirit, which has given and always will give authority and educative efficacy to the man who knows over the one who does not, and to the man who knows more over the one who knows less" (p. 184).

But this does not mean there is a State truth. The State—at least the legitimate State—is nothing other than the universal self-consciousness of the citizens. The truth that it inculcates must be the real truth which is not something fixed; it lives and grows, and it dies if this self-critical growing character is not respected. It must take critical cognizance of the views of independent citizens. The philosophy of the State must evolve through a dialectic of opposed views watched over by the State (cf. Gentile's plea for free discussion

Finally, if the State is the universal moment of individual consciousness it is obvious that lesser communities like the family, or what Hegel calls Civil Society, are only empirically or abstractly distinguishable from it. The conception of a merely economic association of families in civil society is a pure abstraction, an imaginary situation that never actually exists in any community, however rudimentary its organization.[35] And if the family itself is not equally abstract, that is because "In its spiritual actuality the family is State and the State is family." [36] The family constitutes the whole ethical world of its members when they act as its members; while for the good citizen the State absorbs the family completely. The fact that they have different natural bases is irrelevant since in moral action the 'natural' character of both is annulled.

Gentile's rejection here of the 'outward' moment in Hegel's dialectic of society follows naturally from his general view of the relation between economics and ethics. In his own 'social triad' Civil Society is replaced by the School. But his refusal to allow a distinction between the family and the State is not quite so easy to follow, since we know that he himself has elsewhere treated the family as an immediate natural basis for community life.[37] We must of course remember that he always insisted that family life is only quasi-natural and *relatively* immediate. In calling it 'natural' and 'immediate' he was speaking from the point of view of a member of the more inclusive community—the State. But it is much more important to realize that his whole conception of the relation of thought and feeling changed as a result of his meditations about the philosophy of art. As he was now convinced that *all* phases of conscious ex-

---

within the Fascist party "watched over" by the leaders in Chapter 6, p. 203, herein). The thought that triumphs in the struggle is the real philosophy of the State.

Thus the contrast between this paper of 1929 and Gentile's resolute opposition to anything in the nature of an 'official' philosophy in 1907 (cf. Chapter 3, pp. 69–71, herein) is much more apparent than real. As early as 1902 he was saying that only the possession of a philosophy could justify any State effort to make laws or to educate (B.70 in B.813, pp. 27–28). In 1907 he merely insisted that the State philosophy must be the work of the teaching profession and not of the government.

[35] Hegel himself recognized that historically the State is usually established before the economic differentiation that is typical of civil society develops. But he insisted nevertheless on its logical priority. In this matter Croce is a more orthodox Hegelian than Gentile.

[36] B.1017 in B.1157, p. 120.

[37] Cf. Chapter 4, pp. 81–84, herein.

perience have an emotional aspect the family could no longer be considered peculiar in this respect: "We cannot say that the family is 'immediate or natural spirit' (as Hegel does in *Encyclopedia,* 517); nor is it true that the spirit *ist als Familie empfindender Geist* (*ibid.,* 518). The same *immediacy,* the same *feeling* [*sentire*] is found also in patriotism or the political sense insofar as it is purely emotional." [38] His complaint against Hegel was that the systematic rigidity of his theory involves an illegitimate separation of two aspects of reality which in actual experience form a dialectical unity. What is here tucked away in a footnote is the crucial step in his own thought by which the apparent gulf between his 'idealism' (or 'logic') and his 'actualism' (or 'phenomenology') is bridged. The 'pure act of thinking' can no longer be mistaken for an 'act of pure thinking.'

---

[38] B.1017 in B.1157, p. 119n2.

VIII

THE GENESIS AND STRUCTURE
OF SOCIETY

Biographical and Historical Background

Gentile's last work—which despite its comparative brevity deserves to be counted among his greatest—was written during a period of personal and political crisis. Like most of his other systematic treatises it was based upon a course of university lectures. He completed the manuscript in the space of four or five weeks in August and September of 1943; and although he lived to review both typescript and proofs he made no corrections at any stage. He was dead before the book went to press, and it was not actually published until two years later in 1946.

In his brief Preface he tells us that the work was written "as a relief to my mind in days full of anxiety for every Italian, and to fulfill a civil duty, since I saw no other course open to me in my concern for that Italy of the future for which I have labored all my life." It forms a sort of epitaph on his life as a Fascist and, as Dr. Mario Rossi has suggested,[1] it goes some way toward explaining why he joined in the last mad attempt to bring Fascism back to life. Thanks to his son Benedetto, we are now able to understand fairly clearly just what was in his mind during this period.[2]

The Rome-Berlin axis came into existence late in 1936. I have not been able to find any reference by Gentile to the military alliance, but it is certain that he must have viewed with discomfort, if not

[1] *Journal of Philosophy*, XLVII, 1950, 217.
[2] *Vita e pensiero*, Vol. IV: *Dal Discorso agli Italiani alla morte*, Florence, Sansoni, 1951.

positive alarm, the gradual growth of German influence, which resulted in the promulgation and at least partial implementation of a series of racialist measures which were completely inimical to his ideal of Fascism.[3] He had earlier befriended Jewish scholars driven out of Germany, and as the war clouds gathered he helped some of them to escape again, this time from persecution in his own country.[4] It is notable that when war broke out in September 1939 he did not greet it with a philosophical pronouncement as he had done in 1914, and that he remained silent still even when Italy invaded France in 1940.

On the home front he made his rather obsequious speech in support of Bottai's reform of the secondary schools in June of that year.[5] But he more than redeemed himself a few months later at the national Congress of Philosophy in Florence. It was, as he said, the first time that he had appeared on the platform of the congress for ten years; his speech was for the most part a witty though somewhat arrogant defense of his own idealism against various critics. But at the end he adverted briefly to the political situation:

Intellectualism! That is the defect that the politicians scent in philosophy today. And therefore they more or less distrust philosophers as people who are ready enough to accept the Party card, but never want to compromise themselves more than is strictly necessary, despite the fact that acceptance of the membership card, which the Fascist Party meant to be regarded as a sign of the adhesion of the Italian citizen to the revolution that it is bringing about, involves the most compromising oath that one can think of. And the truth is that for obvious reasons, which there is no need to analyze here, there are far more Party members than Fascists; the deplorable distinction that is a consequence of this has made a great breach in the spirit of the Italians. *Intus ut libet* etc. Speech is one thing and practice another. This is precisely the opposite of what the Fascist doctrine was meant to inculcate; and by digging a ditch between the science and the man, it separates philosophy from the soul, which should be wholly poured forth in it, to seek, or in other words to construct its own world. . . .

. . . On the one hand, abstract philosophy without a hold on practical

---

[3] ". . . our culture is not a crude racialism, nor is it narrowly, that is, geographically, Mediterranean, but intelligently universal and human" (B.1144, February 1936, in B.1139, p. 384). In 1941, when the racialist campaign was in full swing, he paid tribute to the memory of his Jewish teacher Alessandro D'Ancona in a way that left no doubt that his feelings on this point were unchanged (B.1269).

[4] Cf. the obituary of Gentile by F[austo] G[hisalberti] in *Annali Manzoniani*, V, 1949, 405–7.

[5] B.1232; see Chapter 6, p. 212, herein.

life; and on the other, practical life which vindicates itself by reacting from without and smashing the liberty of the spirit that is disposed toward intellectualism. Hence moral effects that are far from happy, and lead to that absence of seriousness, that sterility of philosophy to which we have repeatedly alluded. On one side a demoralizing byzantinism; on the other an ostentatious passion that is hypocrisy and corruption of character, and may make of the philosopher a socially insignificant figure to be chased into the attic along with the owls, instead of the master of life that he ought to be.[6]

For ten years he had been hinting that a discipline based on fear would destroy all inward sincerity. Now, when Italy was at war, he at last chose to admit that this had in fact happened. This was an action that required some courage. But according to Gustavo Bontadini, who was present at the congress, he went further: "It was Gentile, I remember, who declared at the philosophical congress of October 1940 in Florence that he preferred the man who refused the Party card to save his conscience to the man who made the opposite refusal. I did not find these words in the speech as printed; but still the fact remains that to have said this then—the campaign in Greece had not yet begun—constituted at once an act of courage and of foresight."[7]

In December 1941 he preached sermons on a similar text at the First National Convention of Philosophic Studies in Rome. Here he made a passionate plea for the freedom and autonomy of the universities which he had always supported.[8] I do not think that his pleading was of any avail. He scarcely even expected to be listened to by this time.

The article on "The Philosophy of Fascism," which he published rather oddly in a bibliographical review during 1941,[9] contained nothing new and was chiefly remarkable for its silences. It did not mention the German alliance, the race policy, or even the state of war that actually existed. In view of Gentile's romantic attitude toward war, and his frequent insistence that philosophical speculation must spring from and return to the concrete historical situation, his silence is revealing. When at last after Pearl Harbor he publicly declared himself, he did not hide his doubts about the future, but simply urged that everyone should concentrate on the immediate

[6] B.1241, pp. 48–50.

[7] Vita e pensiero, I, 119.

[8] B.1272.

[9] B.1246.

present task of winning the war. The entry of Japan and the United States into the conflict seems to have comforted him somewhat because it proved that Italy's involvement was not a mere matter of individual caprice. He felt that the recognition that the war was a universal struggle between two opposed conceptions of life would cause hatred for the enemy to be replaced by a "flame of universal compassion" for the adherents of both sides, who were simply fulfilling their destiny; and he insisted that respect for the enemy and the desire not to prolong the struggle beyond necessity would not weaken morale but be a gain for all concerned.

Since he could not make the official Axis picture of the 'New Order' consistent with his own ideals he tried to argue that it did not really matter. The new world would emerge only gradually so the only thing to do was to wait and see: "A sane mysticism, which is the austere conception that we ought to have of the war, as likewise of the whole of life, will give us the patience to wait with quiet confidence." [10]

This retreat to mysticism is an ultimate confession of defeat; for like the mysticism of theologians faced with the problem of evil it is a tacit admission that the facts cannot be made to harmonize with the proposed theory. But it gave Gentile enough "quiet confidence" to come forward and reaffirm his faith—just as he did after Caporetto—at a time when others were drawing back. In June 1943, when the Allied invasion of Italy was already close at hand, Carlo Scorza, Secretary of the Fascist party, invited a number of prominent Italians to address a great public gathering in Rome. Gentile alone accepted the invitation—despite anonymous letters threatening his life.

The *Address to the Italians* which he delivered was primarily an expression of faith in Italy as a nation, and an appeal for national solidarity in a moment of mortal crisis. He emphasized at the outset that he was not speaking merely as a partisan of Fascism:

This discourse is addressed to all Italians who have Italy in their hearts: an Italy that is not a matter of empty rhetoric, but something living and working in their thoughts and wills. I speak as a Fascist, and I am proud of it because I am profoundly conscious that I am an Italian, and therefore I speak first of all as an Italian who has something to say to all Italians, Fascists and non-Fascists, Fascists of the letter and Fascists of the spirit, Fascists of the Party card and Fascists of the faith. I say Fascists

---

[10] B.1261, p. 12, col. 2.

of the Party card and Fascists of the faith, because I have always held
that the distinction was necessary in order not to confuse the ideal
principle . . . with material deviations. . . . And I have always held
that Party members and nonmembers alike could all be Italians, agreed
about essentials even though dissenting about forms of political discipline: all Italians and therefore all virtually Fascists, because sincerely
zealous for an Italy that shall count in the world, and be worthy of her
past.[11]

He admitted that there had been many bad Fascists; but he felt
that the ideal of the revolution was something above personalities
—something to which many honest men who disdained to join the
Party had been faithful. It was this ideal that he claimed to serve;
and he recalled how he had written after Caporetto that "an Italy
destined to perish as a result of a military defeat would no longer
be worthy to live." [12] The Fascists had grown up in that faith. It
was true that they had destroyed "that false, that bastard tyrannical
liberty that was the liberty of the parliamentary regime." But they
had put in its place a more concrete form of liberty—the liberty of
the Corporate State. Even the self-styled 'democracies' had abandoned the old-style liberalism—"liberty in those countries has fallen
to the ground, and there can be no salvation for it except in a
Corporative organization." [13]

Fascism had stood and still stood for the national tradition and
the national spirit. Italy had found in the voice of Mussolini a powerful expression of her existence as a nation. Now the enemy was
at the gates. This was not the time to stand aside and wait on
events:

No Italian has today the right to say:—This is not my war; I did not
will it—. There is no one in Italy who takes a more or less active part
in the life of the nation who has not willed the war in which our Country is involved. He will have willed it indirectly if not by direct decision. . . . For a war such as this . . . is not conceivable as the arbitrary
resolution of one or more individuals. . . . A much higher agency is at
work, an agency that is human, but which makes one think of God . . .
Fata trahunt; and all recrimination in a moment of peril is baseness. The
desire to stand aside, while the fire rages and it is the duty of all to help
in quenching it, is cowardly.[14]

---

[11] B.1265; reprinted by Benedetto Gentile in Vita e pensiero, IV, 67.
[12] Ibid., p. 69. Cf. B.384 in B.497, p. 62, cited in Chapter 5, p. 135, herein.
[13] B.1265; Benedetto Gentile, op. cit., p. 71.
[14] Ibid., pp. 76–77.

It will not have escaped the reader that the direct quotation from *War and Faith* is not the only echo of the first World War in this speech. The situation in Italy was not dissimilar. In both cases the war was 'political'—undertaken by the government in power for the sake of immediate advantage, and not out of a necessity recognized by the people as a whole. Gentile strove hard to persuade his audience that this was a mistaken view; but the facts were too much for him—one feels all the time that he could scarcely even convince himself.

The objective likelihood of victory or defeat seemed to him irrelevant. Victory would ultimately depend precisely on the efforts of those who were trying to calculate the chances. In any case, calculation of this sort involved the worst of sins—forcing the free life of the spirit onto the procrustean bed of natural science. The essential thing was to have faith in victory—to conquer one's own self: "I have always been, and I boast of always being, an optimist. But the optimism that is sane and legitimate does not concern the events that are in the hands of God, but radiates from within our own conscience and our own personality: it is the optimism of one who believes, and by his faith creates the good to which he aspires. . . ." [15]

In July came the invasion of his native Sicily; on the fifteenth he left Rome to spend the hot summer months at Troghi near Florence. On the twenty-fifth Mussolini was deposed by a conspiracy hatched in the palace and involving several prominent Fascist leaders. This turn of events came as a terrible shock to Gentile, but he loyally declared his readiness to obey and cooperate with the new government of Marshal Badoglio. There followed a nasty little incident in which his loyalty and trust were betrayed, and his offer of cooperation rudely rejected. Severi, the new Minister of Education, was an old colleague and subordinate of his. Gentile sent him a letter of congratulation and received a cordial reply. Then, only four days later, a personal letter from the minister to Gentile appeared in the newspapers (6 August). Severi 'thanked' him for three letters of 'advice' but informed him that it was unacceptable:

. . . I cannot accept Your advice because from 1924 right down to the unhappy address of 24 June of this year You did not hesitate to put yourself at the service of tyranny—and what tyranny—and with the authority

---

[15] *Ibid.*, p. 78.

of Your name, at that time beyond discussion, contributed more than so many others to reinforce it. The young, learning, the truth, were so far betrayed that a Minister of National Education in a government that is reviving liberty can no longer have You among his counselors.[16]

This letter gave the signal for a general attack on him by the national press. The *filosofia del manganello* returned to plague him in the pages of the *Giornale d'Italia* which declared: "He broke the united front of culture which ought to have been the front of liberty and human dignity, not so much with acts of servile surrender which would perhaps have deserved pity as the results of a weak temperament, as with acts of deliberate corruption and perversion of intellectual and moral values, which gave a false appearance of liberty to servitude, of national dignity to party faction, of high educational value to the brutal use of the blackjack." [17] While on the other side the Fascist Republicans assailed him a little later as a turncoat who had offered his services to the betrayers of Italy. For them he was a *funambolo* ("rope walker").

Just what was in the three letters to Severi we shall probably never know; but in a letter to Biggini (Mussolini's last Minister of Education) Gentile later explicitly denied that he had offered his assistance to Severi, and declared that he had merely made one or two recommendations of an administrative nature, especially concerning the *Scuola Normale Superiore* at Pisa of which he was at that time director.

Publicly he preserved an absolute silence. In his private reply to Severi he angrily rejected the charge of betraying Italian culture, and rightly stigmatized the whole letter as a deliberate attempt to place him in what its author knew to be a false light. He resigned all the offices that he held under the ministry, and ended with a declaration that in obedience to the royal proclamation at the time of Mussolini's fall, he was resolved not to engage in polemics and recriminations about the past.[18]

---

[16] *Ibid.*, p. 22. (I have capitalized the personal pronoun where *Lei* is used in the Italian text, in order to indicate as far as possible the tone of ironic politeness by which this letter adds insult to injury. The Fascists had prohibited, or attempted to prohibit, the use of *Lei;* Gentile used *Voi* in his private reply.)

[17] *Ibid.*, p. 23.

[18] *Ibid.*, p. 25. We have referred earlier to his remarks about the *Enciclopedia Italiana* on this occasion (cf. Chapter 6, pp. 185–86).

Severi's position later was none too secure: certain people appealed to Gentile to allow his reply to be used in political maneuvers against him, but

In view of his previous record it was impossible for the new government to continue to employ him in any public post. That much may be granted. But the unforgivable rudeness and cruel malice of the Minister of Education, which made Gentile a natural target for everyone who wished to demonstrate his newborn anti-Fascist fervor, stands in sharp contrast to the courtesy with which the foreign minister handled the same problem. From the time of its foundation in 1933 Gentile had been President of the Italian Institute for the Middle and Far East. He wished now to resign this post, but his friends persuaded him to leave the onus of decision on the government, so he contented himself with a letter of inquiry as to official intentions. The minister replied: "While I am very sorry that present circumstances lead us to provide for your replacement as President of the afore-mentioned Institute, I desire to express to you, on behalf of my ministry, the most lively thanks for the work you have performed." [19]

The Existential Problem of Coexistence

Such were the cares from which Gentile sought to distract his mind by working on his last book during the brief hiatus between the fall of Mussolini and the proclamation of the Armistice. As a result the book exhibits here and there some of the characteristics of an *apologia pro vita sua*. But his political and personal situation will hardly account for the major oddities of the work, which begins with problems of traditional ethics, passes to political theory and the philosophy of history, and ends with a long meditation on death and immortality. In the Preface Gentile directs our attention to his account of 'transcendental society' as the main novelty in the book; and a careful reader will perceive that this doctrine is also the theme by which the discussion is unified. But the choice and arrangement of topics is largely conditioned by certain polemical undercurrents whose presence requires some explanation.

---

he steadily maintained his refusal to publish it. Various factions published apocryphal versions suited to their own desires but even of these he took no public notice. Only once, and then privately, he wrote to the editor of a Fascist Republican newspaper to protest against the employment of this abuse even by the party which he was supporting (this was in November).

[19] Benedetto Gentile, *op. cit.*, p. 30. Here Gentile's desire to remain in a position of influence is fairly clear. His friends may have advised him wrongly. But doubtless they gave him the advice that they knew he longed to hear.

Chief among them is the attempt to prove that actual idealism can provide for the basic exigencies of existentialism. It seems clear that Gentile never seriously studied the existentialist tradition; and he felt that the attempt to transplant it from Germany to Italy was a mistake. But unlike Croce, he did not take a completely negative view of it. In his address to the national congress in 1940 he admitted that the existentialists at least offered something fresh in place of the stale controversies of his other adversaries. Nonetheless it was his opinion that "the speculative need to which existentialism answers, the need of the moment of individuality in the universality of the spirit, was previously recognized by actualism and satisfied more fully than that doctrine is able to satisfy it." [20] He repeated and elaborated this claim when he was invited to contribute to a series of articles on existentialism in the magazine *Primato* in 1943. He was willing to allow that, despite the common emphasis on the need for self-transcendence, there was a sharp contrast between the existentialist insistence on the singularity of the human individual and the idealist insistence on his universality. But he held that this was just where the existentialists were mistaken: Abbagnano's appeal to the facts of *birth, death,* and *coexistence* as inescapable limitations of human existence was "an improper recourse to the empirical representation of spiritual reality." [21]

Abbagnano retorted that for all its dialectic of self-transcendence the act of thinking remained self-imprisoned, knowing nothing of the community between one finite individual and another. He added that for his part he could not regard his own birth, his own mortality, or the birth and death of anyone dear to him, as something of merely empirical significance, and that he did not believe Gentile could do so either. In any case surely one must be able to account for the possibility of these aspects of experience. His challenge struck home in the existentialist as well as in the Kantian form.[22]

The problem of immortality was posed from a different quarter as a result of a lecture of 1942 in which Gentile professed to be, after his own fashion, not merely a Christian but a Catholic. He

---

[20] B.1241, pp. 45–46. The validation of this claim seems to be the task that Bellezza has taken for his own (see especially *Vita e pensiero,* Vol. VI).

[21] B.1268 (*Primato,* 15 March 1943, p. 102).

[22] N. Abbagnano, "Repliche ai contradittori," *Primato,* 15 March 1943, p. 104. It should be remembered that Gentile's son Giovanni died in 1942. This was another factor that doubtless inclined him to take the problems of death and of survival seriously.

was challenged by a friendly Catholic critic to state his views about the possibility of a future life. The critic, Antonio Bruers, argued that belief in a future life was the touchstone not merely of Christianity but of any genuine religion, because without a future life there could be no divine judgment and hence no divine justice.[23]

These challenges were very much in Gentile's mind when he set to work to summarize his latest course of lectures. He began, of course, with the fundamental criterion of his method of pure immanence: the moral law must be immanent in moral action and cannot be conceived as transcending it. "Virtue is its own reward" translated into actual idealist terms becomes "The object of human creativity is man himself." [24] Immorality is ultimately laziness, the arrest of this creative process; and the creation of self is synonymous with the conquest of the natural otherness of the world.

But if a plurality of real selves is admitted, this concept of self-creation through conquest of the natural world can only lead to a war of all against all. We are obliged therefore to admit that the real subject of this self-creative activity is 'the Whole'—or 'Man' with a capital M. The individual man is a member of society, a political animal; but this does not mean that he is one atom among others. He is conscious of his status in society, that is, he makes himself one with it. The symbol of this unity is language—the heritage of his community which is so intimate to his own being that he would not be an individual, a creature capable of saying "I," without it. Because of the essential universality of his thought and action he seeks public approval from his fellows. This is the root of the human thirst for glory and fame; but only a weak spirit regards the outward agreement of his fellows as the final test of his thought and action. *Vox populi vox Dei,* but only in the end. The really universal tribunal to which man appeals is found in his own conscience. Within him speaks the voice of an ideal community, and it is only in virtue of his membership of this community that he is able to enter any empirical society. This inner community is founded on a primitive *feeling* of unity (the 'brotherhood of man'); in actual experience it is the community of culture and is developed through the study of the human heritage.

When the eternal act of consciousness is conceived thus, as moral

---

[23] B.1264 and B.1277 (now in *Complete Works,* XXXVII, 121–44); Antonio Bruers, *Il cattolicismo e Giovanni Gentile,* Rome, Edizioni Stella, 1943.
[24] B.1288 (now in *Complete Works,* Vol. IX), p. 6; translation, p. 73.

membership of an ideal society, the notion of 'character' takes on a new significance. It is no longer seen as a complex of habits formed by repetition of actions that satisfy some external standard, but as the unity of the present with this ideal past in a single act. Character is not the repetition of the past but its actual living presence. Even the ancients recognized that it was a property of life as a whole. But they conceived the wholeness as something material and expressed their conclusion in the famous adage of Solon: "Call no man happy until he is dead." The truth is that spiritual wholeness or integrity is realized, if at all, in the dialectic of the individual and his conscience within the eternal present. No man can display publicly a firmness of character which he does not possess in his own mind.

Thus far Gentile has developed the theory of morality which he held even before he had developed his own systematic outlook. But this is not sufficient; for, according to his own criterion of absolute immanence, the distinction between 'ideal' and 'empirical,' the inward and the outward, is itself a crude and dangerous empirical one. The individual does not form a society simply with his conscience, or with the tradition of humanity as he understands it, but with other individuals, men like himself, but men who may not understand this tradition quite as he does. Gentile's speculative account of morality will fail to meet the existentialist challenge, unless a 'spiritual' interpretation for these relations can be found.[25]

To meet this need he introduces his final exposition of society *in interiore homine.* Briefly, society is immanent in any real individual because there is no Ego that does not contain an 'other' which is its essential 'associate' (*socius*)—an object which is not simply a thing, but a subject like the Ego itself. The real subject is the dialectic of the act which posits the particular subject and object as distinct.[26] If we take the distinct moments as independent they lose their distinctness and grow vague to the point of complete dis-

---

[25] It cannot be too often emphasized that, in Gentile's view, his ideal explanations are what constitute the very reality of the real. They constitute the *meaning* of reality for consciousness—and a reality without a meaning is nothing. This is the point at which he differs most radically from the American tradition of Peirce, Royce, and Mead. (Cf. B.890, which is his retort to a critic who tried to draw a distinction between the State *in interiore homine* and the State *inter homines.*)

[26] Cf. on this point B.409 in B.561, pp. 195–96; but see also the critical remarks herein, pp. 260–61.

appearance. Without consciousness the world is nothing, as consciousness is nothing without the world. This absolute nothingness, however, is not thinkable since thinking it concretely would involve the denial of thought.[27]

Since the reality of the subject consists in its unity with the object, the latter cannot continue in the negative opposition in which it first presents itself. In one way or another the duality must be resolved. Hence the child and the poet personify everything: since the subject speaks the object must speak also. This primitive resolution of the opposition in a synthesis, through the direct transformation of the object into another subject endowed with full life and liberty, may be naive; but the transformation is essential since "in order to be itself [the subject] must of necessity renounce its solitude." [28]

Roughly speaking, we may say that this 'renunciation of solitude' is the great novelty of Gentile's last work. Even the second volume of the *Logic*, in which the theory of the *alter* as *socius* briefly appears,[29] is dominated by the contrary doctrine of the "eternal solitude of the Spirit." [30] We must take care, however, not to treat the new doctrine as a direct contradiction of the old—the 'unity of the Spirit' remains the alpha and omega of Gentile's idealism. It is *because* of this underlying unity that the object is bound to be assimilated to the subject; but since this assimilation and the resulting explicit unity are always social in character the unity does not imply solitude.

The maintenance of this transcendental society is quite independent of the accidental presence or absence of other people, because all conscious activity has the character of the conversational partnership which the child naively externalizes. In thought we talk

---

[27] This is Gentile's account of the existentialist *Angst*. His whole case against the existentialists is that they stop short at the *Angst* of the spirit over its own non-being and do not grasp the actuality, the positive aspect of their own position. "*Angst* itself is defeated by *Angst*: for even *Angst*, though turbid and heavy, is still consciousness; it is an act which frees the Ego and the world from non-being" (B.1288, p. 35). But this is only a restatement of his theory of pain in the *Summary of Educational Theory*, criticized in Chapter 2, pp. 32–33, herein. One can scarcely grant its force against existentialism because it is purely formal. It is true, however, that the very least an existentialist can do is to express his *Angst* in artistic form (e.g. in a novel), which is a *creative affirmation* of the human predicament. (Translation, p. 100.)

[28] B.1288, p. 36 (translation, p. 101).

[29] B.1250, p. 110; cf. Chapter 4, pp. 110–11, herein.

[30] B.1250, pp. 21–22 for example.

to ourselves, even when we are thinking silently; when we write, we also read what we have written; in dreams the internal society is externalized and presented as an empirical fact. Society, in the ordinary sense of the word, is rooted in this transcendental dialogue. The gregarious animals such as sheep and wolves have no society; nor, for that matter, do the so-called 'social' insects, ants, bees, etc. For no one supposes them to be possessed of this internal social consciousness.

The 'otherness' involved in this internal society is not less real or easier to overcome than that which is involved in ordinary social relations. Indeed all external relations are mediated through it; and this process of mediation is not by any means always as difficult as the familiar task of making up one's own mind. The desires and passions that we must conquer in ourselves have each of them a personal voice to which we must give heed. We may even find it difficult to understand ourselves, but here we have a duty that we cannot evade. The 'other' within us *cannot* remain an enemy whose common humanity we do not recognize, though Gentile still seems to think that it is best if we begin from enmity and conflict:

What a distance there is between the law *contra hostes aeterna auctoritas esto* ["against enemies let there be always authority"] and the Christian love of one's neighbor! The *auctoritas* knows nothing of the man behind the enemy; while our neighbor on the other hand is completely one with us. But the *hostis* is always with us; and no love is more firmly and solidly based than that which is conquered through an apprenticeship in which the bond of conquest between us and the other passes over into the bond of brotherhood.[31]

We saw earlier that the first appearance of Gentile's doctrine of *societas in interiore homine* was marred by an undue emphasis on the moment of conflict.[32] It seems to me that even his final statement of the argument still shows traces of the same error. In personal self-discipline it is often the case that a particular desire must be absolutely denied until it can be redirected. But in normal social relations it is the unity rather than the duality that is, or should be, primitive. The enemy who is not human and has no rights is not a person; society—even transcendental society—cannot exist at all unless some rights are conceded to him. The truth is not that enmity is a necessary element in society, but rather that society involves

---

[31] B.1288, p. 40 (translation, p. 105).
[32] Cf. Chapter 4, pp. 102–7, herein.

at least an ideal conquest of enmity similar to the conquest which Gentile speaks of in his theory of pain and evil. Even Nature, the realm of mere things, can only be mastered if her integrity is respected—as the sculptor, for instance, respects the character and quality of the stone on which he works. The phenomenon of mutual respect deserves far more emphasis in Gentile's theory than it receives. The main weakness inherent in all forms of Fascism lies in the failure to recognize the necessary priority of this mutual respect in all social relationships.

Gentile's claim that his doctrine of transcendental society has never been stated by anyone else may well seem rather extreme.[33] The view that the conscious individual is a kind of society is a commonplace in the philosophical tradition. One thinks immediately of Plato's account of thought as an internal dialogue, of Aristotle's careful examination of the sense in which a man can be friends with himself, of Augustine's 'inner man' and 'inner Teacher,' of several aspects of Hegel's theory, most notably perhaps his analysis of "lordship and bondage" in the *Phenomenology*.

Gentile is not ignorant of this tradition and frequently acknowledges his debt to it. He refers quite often to Augustine, and several times to Plato and Hegel. What we have called the undue emphasis on the moment of conflict in his theory, for example, is part of his explicitly recognized debt to the latter.[34] He insists on the novelty of his view, however, because he feels that no one, not even he himself, has ever previously taken the social character of individuality seriously enough or interpreted it strictly enough. He is very anxious that we should realize how seriously and strictly he interprets it: "I hope that the importance of this concept will escape no one, for it is in my judgment the keystone of the great edifice of human society. And it is to be hoped that no one will come around to the view, which has hitherto been commonly received, that the fact to which I have drawn attention has only a metaphorical significance. . . ."[35]

There are, however, three American writers who took the social character of individuality as seriously as Gentile himself. None of

[33] It was challenged, for example, by G. R. G. Mure in his review for the *Philosophical Quarterly* (I, 1950, 83). He cites Plato and Hegel and argues that the theory is fully explicit in the latter. But it seems to me that this claim shows that he has missed the full force of Gentile's position. These two thinkers are almost the last people whom Gentile would be likely to forget.

[34] Cf. B.1288, p. 131 for instance (translation, pp. 187–88).

[35] *Ibid.*, p. 39 (translation, pp. 103–4).

them gave the Platonic "dialogue of the soul with itself" the 'transcendental' significance that he does, but each of them regarded it not as a metaphor but as a real process which constitutes and exhausts the whole nature of the soul. Of course, Gentile's 'transcendental' interpretation springs directly from his 'method of absolute immanence.' So that, if we are not to reduce his claim to triviality by interpreting it so strictly that only one of his own students could possibly have anticipated him, we must say that these three, Peirce, Royce, and Mead, did anticipate him. But, leaving aside any invidious considerations of priority (since he was almost certainly ignorant of their work as they were of his), one of the best ways to appreciate what is unique about Gentile's position is to examine the very different way in which the social analysis of individuality functions in the American theories. For this purpose Peirce and Royce can be taken together, while Mead must be treated separately.

As long ago as 1867 C. S. Peirce advanced the thesis that the self is not directly intuited but becomes known through practical contact with others. The individual comes to recognize himself as a particular person primarily through the discovery that his interpretations of experience are fallible in relation to commonly accepted interpretations presented in the testimony of his fellows. Royce, in the second volume of his *Problem of Christianity*, took this notion along with Peirce's theory of reasoning as a triadic relation in which two terms are mediately connected through a third (the "interpretant") and developed from them an ethical theory which Peirce had barely hinted at. He used Peirce's discovery that self-consciousness is ultimately dependent on membership of a community to justify his own ethical contention that "we are saved by the community"; and he perceived that the process of self-knowledge is "outwardly embodied in the whole world's history. For what we all mean by past time is a realm of events, whose historical sense, whose records, whose lessons we may now interpret in so far as our memory and the documents furnish us the evidences for such interpretation." [36]

This definition is not far from the Gentilian identification of *res gestae* and *historia rerum gestarum*. Yet in spite of this resemblance,

---

[36] *The Problem of Christianity*, New York, Macmillan, 1913, II, 145. For the early papers of Peirce that are here referred to see the *Collected Papers*, Vol. I, secs. 545–67, and Vol. V., secs. 213–357.

and of all the others that could be pointed out between these two 'philosophies of Christianity,' Royce and Gentile remain poles apart in metaphysics. For Royce ultimate reality was always an objective totality (that is, from the Gentilian point of view, a transcendent or presupposed logos); his philosophical development shows an advance from the idea of a unique absolute consciousness that perceived 'all at once' to that of an infinite and perfect 'system of interpretation.' While Gentile, on the other hand, moved from a dialectic of eternal moments to a transcendental dialogue of ideal persons.

In both cases the transformation occurred because the parties recognized that "interpretation is a conversation, and not a lonely enterprise. There is some one, in the realm of psychological happenings, who addresses some one." [37] But the problems they were seeking to solve were quite different. Royce (and Peirce also, for that matter) began from an accepted plurality and strove toward the establishment of a *systematic* unity; theirs was the problem of dynamic order, the problem that Leibniz bequeathed, of how to supply the monads with windows. Whereas Gentile began from the actual unity of consciousness and strove to derive from it all the multifarious determinations of historical experience; his was the problem of the *growth* of consciousness bequeathed by Fichte's interpretation of Kant, and clearly formulated by Spaventa's interpretation of Hegel. Peirce and Royce anticipated Gentile's analysis of the social character of self-consciousness, and developed it in greater detail and with more precision than he did. But from his point of view they erred by stopping short at a half-truth. They saw that all self-consciousness is social; but they failed to see that all consciousness of society is therefore self-consciousness.[38]

Peirce certainly, and Royce possibly, would retort that what they had shown was precisely that an impersonal state of social consciousness was more primitive than self-consciousness, and hence that the objective totality was more fundamental than the subjective apperception. It is interesting to speculate on how Gentile would have disposed of this claim. Certainly he would have argued that the distinction of 'myself' from 'other selves' can only emerge from

---

[37] Royce, *op. cit.*, p. 148.
[38] One might object that Royce did perhaps hold that all consciousness was self-consciousness. But the self to which he referred the totality of consciousness was transcendent; and therefore the consciousness of the 'Great Community' is not 'self-consciousness' in Gentile's sense.

a more or less impersonal awareness of the world because that 'impersonal' awareness is implicitly 'mine' from the beginning. Thus the empirical discovery of 'myself' as an individual, which results from my growing awareness of the special ways in which 'others' behave toward me and expect me to behave toward them, is simply an advance toward the *possession* of the 'self'—i.e. the world—that always properly belonged to me. In ethical terms we might express what happens when we discover ourselves as individuals by saying that this is the point at which the Gentilian Ego ceases to be a spectator of its own reality and accepts the full responsibilities of 'self-constitution' (*autoctisi*).

Gentile and Royce agree completely that "he who would save his soul shall lose it." But for Gentile, although he has more sympathy for the moment of transcendence in his last period, the truth is more accurately expressed by saying "Christ liveth in me" than by saying "in God we live and move and have our being." [39] Gentile was ultimately an ethical thinker, as Royce was ultimately a religious one. He could never say, like Royce, "we are saved by the community"; he had to say, rather, that we must work out our own salvation by saving the community. If he could have agreed with Royce on the theoretical issue, then allowing for his complete secularization of the religious impulse, he would have been a lot happier preaching Fascism. His plaintive criticisms of 'Fascist myths' and his indignant rejection of the charge of 'Statolatry' all depend on his demand for absolute immanence. Nevertheless, it is a pity that he did not know about the Peirce-Royce 'community of interpretation,' for a critical response to it on the lines indicated above would have provided him with a much clearer account of the spiritual meaning of the individual's 'being born'—one of the problems that Abbagnano set him—than the rather vague and unsatisfactory theory of "political feeling" which he derived from the Greek tradition.[40]

---

[39] He does quote this text but he applies it to the relation between 'the State' (i.e. the transcendental society within the individual) and the empirical community (cf. B.1288, p. 110; translation, p. 169).

[40] *Ibid.*, pp. 125–26; cf. pp. 121–22. When Gentile discusses the 'beginning' of consciousness in 'feeling' (*sentimento, sentire*) he always seems to be faced with a dilemma. Either the feeling is only 'relatively' immediate, and then it is not *really* a beginning, or it is 'absolutely' immediate, and then it is *non*-actual, i.e. is not a beginning of *consciousness*. He shifts continually from one horn of the dilemma to the other according to the needs of his argument; but neither is ultimately acceptable. That is what Abbagnano's demand for a

Moreover, the explicitly 'triadic' or synthesizing character of the process of interpretation in Peirce and Royce would have shown Gentile how the apparently dyadic character of the 'transcendental dialogue' was to be reconciled both with the unity of the transcendental Ego and with the triadic dialectic of the 'act of thinking.' He insisted to the end on the dialectical unity of consciousness, but when in his last book he finally did justice to the actual experience of social intercourse between morally autonomous persons, he did not manage to articulate clearly how the 'dialectic' and the 'dialogue' are to be integrated. This can be done in terms of the 'community of interpretation' by identifying the 'act of thinking' with Peirce's "interpretant" or "mediating representation"—which, although Peirce talks of it as if it were simply a new kind of sign, is really the *act* whereby signs are so related as to become significant; and by identifying the 'transcendental Ego' with Royce's 'Spirit' of the community, or more specifically with the "real interpreter of the ideas which [the other's] deeds suggest to me." [41]

The parallel between Gentile and G. H. Mead is even more striking because of the *prima facie* opposition between them. Whereas Peirce (at least at the time of which we are speaking) and Royce were self-acknowledged idealists of a sort, Mead was a pragmatist, an empirical psychologist, even a behaviorist. Yet both he and Gentile were self-styled 'philosophers of the act,' and they provide an interesting example of how opposed programs will tend to coincide if they are genuinely opposed and if they are carried out to a logical conclusion. Mead explicitly declares that the historic pro-

---

philosophical account of 'birth' brings out. The logical difficulties here are beautifully dealt with in Peirce's proof that there is nothing immediate in consciousness (*op. cit.*, V, 259–63, 283–94). See further the discussion of the 'beginning' of the dialectic in Chapter 9, pp. 294–300, herein.

[41] Peirce, *op. cit.*, I, 553; Royce, *op. cit.*, II, 319–25. Royce actually says that the *other* self is the interpreter ("*You* are the real interpreter of the ideas which your deeds suggest to me"); but this is an elliptical inaccuracy resulting from the fact that he is here using the theory of interpretation to account for our belief in 'other minds.' The ellipse is possible because the process of interpretation *begins* from the other mind as, in Peirce's example, comparison of *p* and *b* must *begin* from one or the other in order to turn it upside down and superimpose it, etc. Actually the interpreting mind cannot be either *your* mind or *my* mind *immediately*; but it must *begin from* your mind and it must *become* mine if there is to be successful interpretation. The suggestion in the text, therefore, leaves only a very subtle 'distinction of reason' between the Ego and the Act. The Ego is the organic whole or 'community of interpretation,' which is at once postulated and validated by the Act or living process of interpreting.

gram of psychology which he is carrying on has been to approach the contents of consciousness "from below (that is naturalistically) rather than from above (that is transcendentally) by a study of the physiological processes of the central nervous system"; but he goes on to insist that "the patterns which one finds in the central nervous system are patterns of action—not of contemplation, nor of appreciation as such." [42]

We can thus characterize his program as an attempt to push the study of the empirical genesis of consciousness back past the impersonal social awareness of Peirce and Royce to the level of unconscious behavior. As a *social* psychologist he does not in fact concern himself with behavior in the nervous system, but with the gestures of the bodily organism. He finds the origin of society in what he calls a "conversation of gestures"; but the term "conversation" is misleading, for, as against Peirce's claim that "Man is an external sign" or Gentile's that "the body is all a language," he insists that the gestures, though they can be and are interpreted as signs, and are thus the preconscious source of the "communicative function," are not originally *intended* as such. There is a great difference between the man who *is* angry and the actor who *portrays* anger.[43]

In the "conversation of gestures" we have the most fundamental form of Gentile's transcendental society—the relation of soul and body. As Mead proceeds in his analysis of the social genesis of the self, several of the other forms of the theory which we have already found in Gentile emerge, often in a more developed form. Thus he leads up to his theory of the "generalized other" by distinguishing two phases in the child's activity, "play" and "the game." In the 'play' period the roles that the child takes up are not at first organized into a personality. This organization occurs necessarily when he begins to play 'a game,' for a game is a unified system of mutually implicative roles. This ingeniously shows how, from the 'alienation' in which consciousness of the self first emerges accord-

---

[42] *Mind, Self and Society,* University of Chicago Press, 1934, pp. 23, 26; cf. p. 21: "all that takes place in the body is action," or again, "Everything that took place in the body was part of an act." On the impossibility of reducing 'action' to 'motion' see, for instance, *Philosophy of the Act,* University of Chicago Press, 1938, pp. 412–20 (notice on p. 414 "We may perhaps say that all predictions are in an implied past").

[43] Peirce, *op. cit.,* V, 314; B.1288, p. 169. Mead, *Mind, Self and Society,* pp. 16–18 (the actual contrast drawn is with Darwin). (Translation, p. 222.)

ing to Peirce and Royce, the rebellious personality is able to return
to social activity. For Gentile it would provide a link between the
child's play as 'art' and the child's play as 'work.' [44]

Finally, Mead's theory of conscious thinking agrees almost to the
point of verbal echoes with the theory of the 'transcendental dialogue' as we find it in *Genesis and Structure of Society*. Thinking is the internalization of the so-called "conversation of gestures"
which occurs when we deliberately take account of the response of
others to our gestures. Thus it is the first genuine conversation:

It is the conversation that goes on within the self. This is what *constitutes*
[the individual's] mind. Now that thought . . . is only the importation
of outer conversation, conversation of gestures with others, into the self
in which the individual takes the role of others as well as his own role.
He talks to himself. This talking is significant. He is indicating what is
important in the situation. . . . It is this process of talking over a problematic situation with one's self, just as one might talk with another,
that is exactly what we term "mental." [45]

The way in which, in Mead's work, different phases in the development of Gentile's theory of society *in interiore homine* appear as
mutually complementary is bound to make us ask ourselves whether
there is really anything so very novel about the statement of the
theory in Gentile's last book as compared with his own earlier
work. The doctrine is, after all, a natural development of ideas and
theories hammered out years before. Two elements, at least, can
be traced back to the earliest stage in his thought: the theory of
language as inherently communal or universal, and the argument
that an empirical duality is irrelevant to the process of communication. For the rest, the conception of the dialectic of subject and
object as constitutive of individuality was developed in the period
of the great systematic works; but it is there inextricably interwoven

---

[44] Mead, *Mind, Self and Society*, pp. 150–64; *Philosophy of the Act*, pp.
374–75; B.1225, pp. 33–54, 65–81; B.1288, p. 127. Cf. Chapter 4, pp. 79–81,
herein. Children's games and family life are brought together in a way reminiscent of Gentile, but with an interesting Crocean variation on the relation of 'art'
and 'play,' by H. J. Paton in *The Good Will*, London, Allen and Unwin, 1927,
pp. 239–44.

[45] *Movements of Thought in the Nineteenth Century*, University of Chicago
Press, 1936, p. 385; cf. *ibid.*, pp. 375–76, 380–81; *Mind, Self and Society*,
pp. 140–42, 167, 173, 178–92, etc.; *Philosophy of the Act*, pp. 75, 150, etc.
I assume that Gentile would not challenge the occurrence of this "importation"
as a natural fact of human evolution (i.e. viewed "from below"). For what
he might say about it viewed "from above" (i.e. transcendentally) see pp.
259–60, herein; see also the Introduction to my translation of B.1288, pp.
48–50, for further criticism of Royce and Mead from a Gentilian point of view.

with the moral dialectic of universal will and particular inclination. This seems to be the key to the originality of Gentile's last work; for in it the "manifest authority" of the moral law is something that arises in a context of genuine social cooperation. The dialectic of ideal moments is replaced by a dialogue of persons who are neither empirical nor merely ideal but genuinely individual. 'Society' in earlier versions coincides immediately with 'the State'; now the coincidence is mediated so that the terms 'society' and 'State' are in a sense distinguishable—just as the duties enjoined by the two great commandments are distinguishable though not separable.

The State, as we know, has its transcendental ground in the relation of the individual to his conscience. The absolute obligation to follow one's own conscience is what is enshrined for Gentile in the First Commandment. That is the feat of interpretation achieved by his earlier accounts of society *in interiore homine*. What is accomplished in his last work is a transition from the First Commandment thus interpreted to the Second, similar to the transition which is argued in the fourth chapter of the First Epistle General of St. John. To have a conscience is now no longer to have a 'judge' but to have a 'brother' whom one is bound to love as oneself, since he is part of oneself. The moral command to love our neighbor as ourselves means simply that we must recognize him as this 'brother.' In order to recognize him as a neighbor at all, in order to communicate with him in any way, we must reduce the material external otherness to the internal spiritual otherness of our own thoughts. Hence we can measure the understanding that we achieve by the sense of inwardness or the sympathy that we feel. "Love is not the consequence but the conclusion and perfection of knowledge." [46]

Error and sin and all the spiritual disvalues are failures to achieve this inner community in which selfhood consists. Hence they produce *Angst*, awareness of a void in the depths of our own being. As soon as this consciousness of the void becomes reflective, the negative, absolutely *past* character of all evil and error is apparent. Sin and evil are only real as moments of the process of repentance and amendment: once we have grasped the fundamental unity that exists between ourselves and others, we recognize that the evil which seems to deserve condemnation in the activities of these others is our responsibility also, and therefore requires both repentance and amendment on *our* part. The eternal need for this redemp-

---

[46] B.1288, p. 47 (translation, p. 112).

tion from the past is the meaning, for Gentile, of the doctrine of original sin.[47]

The State

When we turn to consider how this new interpretation of the Second Commandment affects Gentile's earlier interpretation of the First, we find, alas, that his account of the coincidence of individual liberty with the power of the State is as unsatisfactory in this last book as it was before. He admits once more that the 'government' is only an abstract moment in the dialectic of the actual will which constitutes the State. But he virtually destroys the value of this admission by first claiming that "every opposition of government and governed vanishes in the consent of the latter, without which the government cannot stand," and then adding that the extent to which coercion is justifiable in procuring consent must be decided by the intuitions of a statesman—i.e. by the government in power —not by reference to abstract principles.[48]

He goes on to argue, fairly enough, that there can be no freedom for the citizen unless his community possesses real independence of action, and that no revolution is really anarchic. But he adds in a footnote that external independence involves war, and hence a limitation of liberty within the State. This one remark is enough to indicate that some appalling ambiguities are concealed in his conclusion: "So then, only the individual in the free State is free. Or better still the free individual is the one who is the free State. . . ."[49]

The position is somewhat clarified later, for in Chapter 10 Gentile elaborates on the thesis that external independence involves war. The problem of the empirical plurality of States is, of course, analogous to that of the empirical plurality of individuals. But he does

---

[47] Cf. *ibid.*, p. 55. Here again it is interesting to compare Royce's interpretation of the Pauline doctrine as a condemnation of ethical individualism (*op. cit.*, I, 156–59). Gentile's doctrine is much more abstract but that is because the terms of his problem are much stricter. The practical significance of the two theories is virtually identical (cf. pp. 280–81, herein).

[48] B.1288, pp. 59–60. Gentile does recognize that his theory logically involves the minimization of coercion as an ideal. But in the next sentence he treats this ideal as one of the extremes between which a mean must be found. For a more detailed analysis of the error in his argument see the notes in my translation *ad loc.* (pp. 123–24).

[49] B.1288, p. 66 (translation, p. 130).

not push the analogy as far as he might, and as far as I believe he should. Other individuals are freely recognized within the synthesis of self-consciousness, and thereby unified with the subject who remains singular. To understand these others in their otherness we have to put ourselves in their shoes, which is not altogether possible. In the same way every man has one *patria,* and others only exist for him so far as they are recognized, or in other words so far as there is a unity of will between his own State and these others. The realization of this unity is mirrored in systems of treaty obligation and in the growth of international law. But it can never be complete; and this leads Gentile to deny the possibility of world unity:

For if this tendency could be perfectly fulfilled (in a confederation, a single center of power, a society of nations, etc.) the result would not be the absolute realization of the State but the end of it. For the State—despite its name!—is not something static. It is a process. Its will is a synthesis which resolves all immediacy. If the State presented itself to us all fine and finished, if its uniqueness were simply an immediate datum, a matter of fact, and there were no further otherness to conquer, since the dream of *perpetual peace,* the eternal heart's desire of humanity fleeing from the horrors of war, had come true, then the movement which constitutes the life of the State, the life of the spirit itself, would come to a stop. And instead of the very best of States we should have the death of all States.[50]

This seems to me to be nothing but a very illiberal prejudice masquerading as a philosophical argument. There are no grounds in the theory of actual idealism for a belief that interstate war is essential to the spiritual life. The argument is only rendered plausible by a misrepresentation of the situation that would exist if an international order were established, and by a crudely material interpretation of the ideal character of the State. It is simply false that if (to take the most extreme case) a single World State were established all political strife would cease. The World State would no more exist "all fine and finished" then than the national State does now. It is fundamental to the theory of the Ethical State that, in its 'ethical' aspect, the State remains *always* an ideal to be achieved. By Gentile's own admission, Italy was not finally 'made' in 1870 or even in 1915 or 1922. But to suppose that this ideal incompleteness of the existent empirical State has anything to do with the empirical existence of other sovereign States would mean

---

[50] *Ibid.,* p. 103 (translation, p. 164).

that we must either abandon the whole theory of an 'internal' society, and fall back into the position of Hobbes, or at least abandon the 'transcendental' interpretation of internal society, and accept the evolutionary naturalism of Mead as a complete account of it. The State is no *more* dependent on other States for its ethical life than the individual is dependent on other individuals in his philosophical thought.

One of the principal reasons why most people feel, and will continue to feel, that the doctrine of the Ethical State, whatever elements of truth it may contain, is an inadequate account of morality, lies here; and it arises merely from a serious imperfection in Gentile's interpretation of his own doctrine. For he recognizes quite clearly that the ideal State, above and beyond the empirical multiplicity of existent States, is identical with the totality of political history so far as it concerns the citizen and his community. World history, mediated through the thought of the individual historian, is the history of the united moral enterprise of humanity. As the concept of this enterprise 'the State' involves the ideals for which men have striven and which will continue to guide their efforts. It is never completely actual; there is always a transcendent element involved in ethical life, an element which provides a sufficient ground for distinguishing the divine from the human, if one wishes to assert that the State is 'divine' without being guilty of 'Statolatry.'[51]

Because of this transcendent ideal element the life of the State is a continuous revolution. Constitutions and laws provide an essential element of structural permanence in what would otherwise be a sheer flux. But they are continually evolving and there is clearly no point at which this evolution must or even can legitimately cease. The unity of humanity's moral enterprise requires the establishment of a system of law and mutual respect between nations, which can never be made effective until ordinary citizens

---

[51] Cf. *ibid.*, p. 107. There is no really compelling *speculative* reason for using religious language in talking about the State, because, although Religion is an eternal moment in the dialectic of the pure act, it is transcended by Philosophy, and the State is properly a 'philosophical' institution. From the theoretical point of view the meaning of assertions like "the State is the march of God in the world" or "the State is a kind of earthly God" is much more clearly expressed by saying that it is an ethical ideal. Gentile's reasons for wanting to talk in a religious mode were in part personal (his own religious temperament) and in part pragmatic (the ever-present shadow of the Catholic Church as a rival for the ethical allegiance of *Italian* citizens). (See translation, p. 167.)

recognize a higher loyalty than that which they owe to their particular national communities. In terms of the analogy which Gentile
himself draws we might say that war is no more essential to the
moral health of nations than dueling or the vendetta was to the
moral health of individuals and families, though individuals, families, and loyal patriots like Gentile may be unable to recognize the
fact. In fact, as long as war continues to be a legitimate "continuation of policy" we cannot grant that 'the State' contains even its
enemies; this will not be true until *all* war is equally regarded as
'civil' war. Gentile's final conception of ideal society merely makes
clearer the inadequacy of the views that he always held about
international relations.

Economics and Politics

This is not the case in his discussion of internal affairs. The account of economic life in Chapter 7 of *Genesis and Structure of
Society* is an interesting development of the thesis about economics
which we examined in *our* seventh chapter. The rigid distinction
between act and fact, concrete and abstract 'logos,' moral *action*
and economic or useful *thing*, is now subjected to the moderating
influence of the theory of transcendental society. The subjects of
the social relation here are 'soul' and 'body,' which are the terms
implicit in a primitive life-feeling that is at one and the same time
a sensitive activity (the soul) and an object sensed (the body).
Through our immediate sense of the body we master it and make
it obedient to our will. If we consider it in abstraction from the
conscious activity of the soul it is not human but subhuman; and
the same can be said of the whole of 'nature,' the totality of all
possible contents of the conscious activity of the spirit, within which
the whole realm of economic science falls.

Regarded concretely as the point where nature and spirit meet,
the body is a battleground. The various natural impulses constitute
a negation of the will of the spirit; they are, so to speak, a 'will of
the body,' which has an instinctive character about it because it is
the common heritage of man and the lower animals. Here Gentile
rather misleadingly appears to be accepting Croce's characterization of action guided by the impulses of nature as 'economic action'; and he argues that the intelligence exhibited in such action
differs only in degree from animal cunning. The argument is mis-

leading because he does not admit that there is an economic will which is logically prior to the moral will. The corporeal will is essential to the total dialectic of the spirit but it has no independent actual existence; it enters into actual consciousness only as the non-being of the moral will. It is a limit—an ideal entity whose actuality is constituted by the moral will of which it is the limit. So-called 'economic action' therefore is in an absolute sense not prior but posterior to morality.[52] This explains why even the 'utilitarian' and 'hedonistic' conceptions of life are able to assume a genuinely moral form in, for example, J. S. Mill or Spinoza.[53]

The State must concern itself with the "subhuman life of man" as material to be remolded into the free life of humanity. The theorems of economic science have an instrumental but not a normative value in this remolding, for concretely man is not an animal but a living spirit. Before we can examine the political process by which humanity is created, however, we must consider briefly the other 'higher' values of religion and culture that have to be included in an integral conception of politics as the human art.

Unlike economic advantage, religious salvation is not an instrumental good. The statesman who endeavors to make political capital

[52] One might object that Gentile's theory of 'corporeal will' makes the description of selfish egoism as 'economic action' (to which we objected in Chapter 7, p. 235, herein) legitimate. But then one would have to add that after all the Pauline "law of the members" is an extremely active and powerful force and not merely a limit; and to this Gentile's reply would be that so far as such forces are unconscious they are mechanisms, brute facts, not acts at all. An involuntary act is no more a genuine act than is an earthquake—which is certainly an economic *event* of some importance. It is in this sense that 'corporeal *will*' and 'economic *action*' are limiting notions, and for this reason Gentile felt able to dismiss the work of modern psychologists on the theory of a dynamic unconscious as having no philosophical interest. Of course he was mistaken in so doing, for what modern psychology reveals is the extent to which the "law of the members" is able to clothe itself in the garments of the spirit. This would be the conquest of nature over self, that we should act mechanically, and believe, like Spinoza's imaginary stone, that we were acting freely. The eternal and inevitable possibility that this may be the case is the main reason why we cannot adopt such a negative attitude toward the "subhuman life of man" as Gentile proposes in his seventh chapter. The 'humanism of labor' of Chapter 11 is a much more adequate working out of a transcendental society between soul and body. But it must be extended even to 'unconscious' needs and activities.

[53] Gentile himself gives Spinoza as an example of the 'higher hedonism' (B.1288, p. 84). He mentions no names in his paragraph on utilitarianism, but this is only another example of his inveterate prejudice against all things English. No one, surely, exhibits better than Mill the ambiguities of a genuinely ethical theory that strives to be strictly 'economic'? (See translation, pp. 145–46.)

of it is inevitably doomed to fail, since his religion is a hollow sham in which he does not himself believe; and this emptiness will ultimately become apparent. Religion is the source of that quality of absoluteness which attaches to all the actions of life that present themselves as duties. The State therefore has an essentially religious character because no man can give his allegiance to its institutions or representatives unless he has a religious sense of its law as an absolute limit on his own will; and without the allegiance of its citizens the whole structure of the State would be only an empty shell. The contrast here between economics and religion can be expressed in terms of the eighth chapter of the Epistle to the Romans. In the life of the State they are both 'limits'; but the religious limit is an ideal and hence a spiritual reality (the "inward man" who "delights in the law of God"); whereas the economic limit is a natural fact and hence a spiritual nullity—("the body of this death"). Politics moves between these limits and the whole process of life consists in the substitution of the former for the latter.

Thus politics—the life of the State—coincides ideally with philosophy—the critical consciousness of human culture. This explains why philosophers who claim to stand absolutely apart from political life, as Spinoza or the Roman Stoics did, are inevitably suspect in the eyes of the political authority. Some measure of suspicion would appear to be inevitable, for both philosophers and politicians are essentially concerned with the education of humanity, and the philosopher's task in politics is essentially a critical one. He must be "always the apostle of the ideal, never the patron or defender of the achieved fact" [54]—spurring on the politicians of his party like a gadfly. But there is no reason why his party should always be the opposition and never the government.[55] His criticism will have value, in any case, only insofar as it becomes the self-criticism of the State authority. Even when in opposition, therefore, he should always recognize the positive value of the actual policies that he opposes. We ought not to forget, concludes Gentile, that the practical politician has his own philosophy and his own ideal of the

[54] *Ibid.*, p. 98 (translation, pp. 158–59).
[55] "Or are we seriously to believe that Plato was moved by a private interest when he wrote his letters to the King of Syracuse?" (*ibid.*, p. 95). The irony of this classic example appears to have escaped Gentile. One would have thought that Plato's relations with Syracuse were an eternal object lesson of the dangers of a close association between philosophers and politicians—especially dictatorial ones. (See translation, p. 156.)

State, and that these are the really important things so far as he is concerned. Philosophy is not something produced only in the study.

In any case, philosophical self-consciousness is only the aim and end of political life. The knowledge of one's political status, of being a citizen, cannot *initially* be philosophical. It must be felt. Politics is everywhere present in human experience, and it has its root in the emotional life of man. The child is almost by instinct a citizen in his own tiny commonwealth—which includes his family and his playfellows. The artist forms a sort of society with his own creations, which have a nature of their own that calls forth his respect and sympathy, even though they represent tendencies that he wishes to see abolished.[56] His creations would have no life if he remained coldly aloof from them. The scientist and philosopher form a society—completely internal but nonetheless a real society— with their own thoughts and with the past history of their problems.[57]

Even in man's relation with God Gentile finds an immanent politics. In actual idealism 'Religion' is the moment of self-alienation, the 'mystical' moment in which reality presents itself as a completely objective whole, and the subject is aware of his own nothingness. The 'logic' of this moment is symbolized in the posture of prayer. But even the mystic is not forever on his knees; he rises to proclaim his vision and to become, however inadequately, the mouthpiece of God. From this humanization of God springs the Church as an abiding order which represents His Will. The solitude of the hermit is an impossible ideal; once the possibility of man's

---

[56] *Ibid.*, pp. 128–29. As usual Gentile's example is drawn from Manzoni's *Promessi sposi;* he is careful to emphasize, however, that not only fictional persons but also material objects can have an individuality in the eyes of the artist. (See translation, pp. 185–86.)

[57] Here, in his own field, Gentile is less emphatic about the element of conflict immanent in transcendental society than he was earlier (cf. p. 256, herein). The scholar "moves always, by way of opposition and struggle, from a nonactual unity toward the actual realization of another higher unity which is alone effective." But "it should be noted that this opposition and struggle does not always develop in a hostile fashion as a conflict of individual adversaries, each desiring to annihilate the other. Indeed, properly speaking, there is never this desire: for if the other were annihilated he would no longer be the other whom the subject needs, to bear witness to his own universality, by reuniting with him in the self-consciousness which creates the other as an opposite precisely in order to realize itself as a unity of the opposed terms" (B.1288, p. 131; translation, p. 187).

speaking with God and for God is granted, a religious society becomes essential. No man's judgment in religion or anything else is
really private, for if it were, his zeal to spread the faith would be
incomprehensible. Truth will out because all thought is essentially
universal in import. Hence the intolerance of all religions. To be
certain of the truth is to be unable to admit any disagreement. The
dogmatic certainty of the missionary is, of course, an error; but so
is the skepticism of *chacun à son goût*. It is not because there is no
answer to Pilate's question that intolerance is wrong; but rather
because the truth cannot be formulated once and for all.

In short, it is impossible for any man to escape in any field the
responsibility of membership in some society. His ethics is bound
to be social; it is bound to have political roots and political implications. For if his community is an essential element in his own personality there can be no distinction of his own private affairs from
the sphere of public policy and the public good. Those who have
tried to set limits to the State in its relations with the 'private'
citizen have simply ignored the fact that any limitations they may
advocate can only be advocated legitimately as matters of public
policy, and only have effective reality through a decision taken in
the public interest, that is, a decision of the State which thus asserts
its sovereignty even beyond the limits it assigns.[58]

Certain important consequences follow for the theory of political
rights. Briefly, the right of the citizen is his right only because it is
first of all his duty. Everyone recognizes, of course, that *his* right is
something which *others* have a duty to respect; what we have to
remember is that, at bottom, this is only the distinction of 'self'
and 'other' within our own consciousness. If the child has a right to
be educated the father has a duty to educate him; and the root of
this reciprocal relation lies in the sense of community between them,
through which they are not two but one. Right and duty are always

---

[58] *Ibid.*, pp. 119–21. This argument is almost a Trojan horse for Gentile's
opponents. Whenever he tries to make use of it in practice, any cogency that
it may seem to possess arises from a purely terminological disagreement. For
instance, he offers it as a criticism of the Catholic defense of private initiative
in education. But any Catholic less bigoted in his attachment to a particular
form of words than Gentile himself could easily answer that he was far from
denying the paramount importance, in all matters, of the common good of
humanity. If Gentile chose to call that 'the State' he was at liberty to do so.
Only let him understand that in the Catholic view, the interests of 'the State'
required that 'the government'—quite a different thing—should at the very
least leave certain schools alone. (See translation, pp. 178–79.)

similarly correlative. The right to take part in politics belongs to every man because every man has the fundamental duties of a citizen.

The 'Humanism of Labor'

The ideal of democracy, as Gentile says, has always been to educate the individual citizen in the sense of his responsibility as the conscious focus of the total process of world history; whereas absolutism always stood for the reservation of political power and responsibility in the hands of a minority. In terms of this dichotomy Gentile considers himself a democrat; but he does not agree that democracy is properly synonymous with a certain system of institutions:

Parties and parliaments are abstract forms that derive their efficacy from the customary political life which they may favor and promote, but not create. And they will *mis*educate the people out of every real and healthy concern for the public good, as long as they remain artificial forms, corresponding to merely conventional principles, rather than to those tendencies and needs of individuals which accord with their effective interests.

This was the aim of the recent Italian political movement; and its constitutional experiments, though they were vitiated in their provisional forms of application by the transitory necessities of the political situation (internal and external), cannot go to waste, for they answered to that need for a more organic representation that had already been coming into its own for half a century in the most enlightened current of conservative liberalism.[59]

The Fascist Corporate State represented, in his eyes, a closer approach to the democratic ideal than the system of liberal parliamentary government, because parliamentary government belonged properly to an era in which political rights were the prerogative of a minority who had been educated in the humanism of the classical tradition. Education for citizenship is no longer conceivable simply in terms of that tradition:

To the humanism of culture, which was indeed a glorious step in the liberation of man, there succeeds today or will succeed tomorrow the humanism of labor. For the creation of great industry and the advance of the worker onto the great stage of history have profoundly modified the modern conception of culture. The word used to mean intellectual culture, and especially art and literature; it left out of account that vast

---
[59] *Ibid.*, pp. 110–11 (translation, p. 170).

segment of humanity who do not raise their eyes toward the free horizon of the higher culture, but work at the foundations of human culture, where man is in contact with nature, and *labors*.[60]

All labor, physical as well as intellectual, must be viewed as a conquest of otherness, a spiritualization of something material. It is labor that makes man truly human, for through it he creates a world of his own instead of simply drifting. Labor is therefore the only valid passport to active citizenship: the modern State must be a 'workers' State,' and the notion of 'culture' must be extended to cover all of the activity through which humanity is created. The Corporate State was simply the logical extension to this wider field of the organic principle which Gentile upheld in the narrower realm of academic culture. Just as he wished there to see pupils organized in schools dominated by a single aim, so, in his opinion, this new and wider ideal of culture should be articulated through the organization of workers in categories that corresponded to their special aims. The State must therefore respect the *family*, which is the focus of a man's work, the objective representation of his immortality, and the principle of *inheritance* through which the abiding unity and continuity of the family is preserved. But also it must respect the different worlds in which men live and work beyond the boundary of the family. The citizen can be defined as *the member of a family who works in a definite environment*; and if an individual is to accept the responsibilities of citizenship he must be able to see that his real interests, as defined by this environment, receive due consideration. Hence the State must be corporately organized.

Ugo Spirito finds the root of this 'humanism of labor' in Gentile's early studies of Marx.[61] His interpretation of the Marxian dialectic between man and his socio-economic environment as an essentially *educational* process certainly influenced his own later conception of human life as a progressive spiritualization of Nature—his boasted *concezione umanistica del mondo*; and Gentile himself refers at this point to the important part played by the Socialists in the trans-

---

[60] *Ibid.*, p. 111 (Gentile's italics). (See translation, p. 171.)

[61] *Vita e pensiero*, I, 331–34 (*Note sul pensiero di Gentile*, pp. 45–51); cf. Chapter 3, pp. 45–51, herein. It seems quite possible that his rereading of the early essays on Marxism in 1937 did influence his thought in his last period. At about the same time, we may remember, he had to reconcile himself to Botttai's School Charter which introduced manual labor into the regular school curriculum (cf. Chapter 6, pp. 210–12, herein).

formation of the traditional idea of culture.[62] But his explicit recognition of this transformation is one of the more surprising novelties of his last book. In discussing his educational theory we remarked earlier that although he seemed to feel that culture, being personal, *ought* to be a total conception of life, Gentile's own conception of it was essentially limited to what is vulgarly called 'book learning.'[63] He even tried to provide a speculative basis for this limitation in a speech on "Labor and Culture" at the inauguration of a School of Social Culture for the workingmen of Rome in January 1922.[64] He made a sharp distinction at that time between manual labor, directed toward material economic goods, and the labor of thought, which is directed to the universal values of the spirit. The assimilation of manual to intellectual labor seemed to him then to involve a dangerous equivocation. It was true that labor was the only source of value; and that in subjecting Nature to his will, man gave to it a human quality and hence a universal spiritual value. But for all that, Nature remained always obstinately material; and the continual effort to conquer this materiality involved a sort of abasement of the spirit. In part Nature was assimilated to man, but the price was a partial assimilation of man to Nature:

Hence by way of manual work, man assimilates himself to nature. The man who works is always in a way the slave of the soil; he resolves his own work, which is always human energy, into something physically and materially there: he plants the work of his hands in a determinate spot on the earth, from which it cannot be separated. And he himself remains always chained to it as to his own life. Human labor penetrates into nature, so to speak, and founds itself upon it; it is grafted onto it so as to prolong in a certain sense its own course, its own process. For certainly, nature unworked is very different from nature as it changes little by little and becomes transformed and transfigured through human efforts; but as this transformation produced by human labor gradually takes place, it absorbs all the labor into itself, assimilates it, and, in the common phrase, stores it up, so that man disappears and nature remains; man as an individual, as worker, vanishes, and nature is left, transformed and different, but always nature.[65]

Manual labor, and everything connected with it, the whole search after riches, binds man to his own lesser particular self. It is a heap-

[62] B.1288, p. 112; translation, pp. 171–72.
[63] Cf. Chapter 4, p. 129, herein.
[64] B.658 in B.937, pp. 16–37.
[65] *Ibid.*, pp. 26–27.

ing up of treasure on earth. Therefore Gentile expressed the hope that the administration of the new school would

be led by the essence and the logic of the culture that the workers need to broaden its scope, so as to include, in addition to those kinds of knowledge that are useful for the purposes of labor and its economic and legal organization, and necessary for the understanding of the world in which the worker operates, that higher disinterested culture, which is the true culture, the culture that makes man really human in the universality of his interests, the value of his ideals, the liberty of his intellect open to all the voices of the human heart. . . .[66]

The change in his attitude and the broadening of his outlook came about mainly through his interest in the theory behind the constitutional innovations of the Fascist regime. We have pointed out the similarity between his view of the Corporate State and the ideal of organic unity that dominated his reform of the secondary schools; and I believe it was this analogy that made him take manual labor more seriously as an educational process productive of real culture. But on the theoretical side it was his concern with the philosophy of art, and especially with the relation of art to practical life, that provided him with the means to answer his own objections. Some readers may have observed that whereas Gentile's theory of education rests on the triad art-religion-philosophy, his theory of politics is founded on the triad economics-religion-philosophy. The 'humanism of labor' overcomes this divergence by reconciling art with economics, and viewing economic life as a process of self-formation having its own aesthetic and moral value. Even as early as 1923, while he was still Minister of Public Instruction, Gentile referred briefly to the need for this reconciliation in a speech at an exhibition of the decorative arts. Industry and art had gone hand in hand during the Renaissance; under Fascism they were to go hand in hand again.[67] Six years later, while he was writing his *Philosophy of Art*, he lectured more formally on the same topic; and what he said deserves to be remembered when we are faced with the complaint that his aesthetics is mere romantic sentimentalism.[68] Having set up a conceptual opposition between 'labor' as willing subjection to nature and 'art' as the free play of imagina-

---

[66] *Ibid.*, pp. 34–35.

[67] B.719 in B.1057, pp. 103–7.

[68] B.968. There are many echoes of this lecture in his last book. It is one of the simplest and most persuasive expressions of Gentile's humanism, and it is greatly to be hoped that it will soon be reprinted.

tion escaping into an ideal world, he went on to show that they were reconciled in the actual process of self-conquest. In the history of the individual, self-conquest begins with the child's achievement of mastery over his own body; for unless he has control over his eyes and hands he cannot be a little artist, a dreamer immersed in his own world, even though his parents and guardians do take care of his 'economic' needs. While on the other hand, in the history of the race, the primitive man who is wholly absorbed in his economic struggle for existence expresses his growing mastery over the economic environment by setting his own artistic seal on the tools he discovers.

In 1929, however, Gentile still did not perceive that this revaluation of physical labor made a revision of the concept of 'culture' necessary. He still thought of the economic life as something that must be left behind in order to enter the realm of true culture. Aesthetic education, he concluded, "creates in man the faith that he can rise above instinct and the needs that press on him from within by way of the flesh—he feels the immense value of the ideal, falls in love with it and has faith in it all his life."

There is no doubt that the reconciliation of soul and body, art and economics, through the theory of transcendental society, was a great advance; it supplies in itself a sufficient answer to critics who, like Minio-Paluello, describe actual idealism as "an exalted intellectualism." [69] There is no question that in Gentile's personal experience as a professor and teacher "exalted intellectualism" is precisely what it was. But it is intended as a working philosophy of life; and as such it has possibilities of application in realms where any ordinary rationalism or intellectualism would have no meaning.

In breaking the barrier which his own missionary spirit as an educator led him to erect in 1922 between the ordinary workingman and the scholar or the artist, Gentile recognized this. But of course he never meant to abandon his earlier argument altogether. All his life he held that no man was worthy of the name who renounced all interest in the problems of life and death, and all concern for the universal human values of art, religion, and philosophy.

Unfortunately the Fascist Corporate State was not a very effective expression of the 'humanism of labor' in practice. It is as hard to see how a sense of the universal problems and values of humanity

---

[69] *Education in Fascist Italy*, p. 71. It is only fair to add that he does qualify this judgment as true "in one sense."

can be preserved in a social system in which the political activity of the individual is legally confined to the sphere of his own particular economic interest as it was to understand how the spirit of spontaneity which is the heart of Gentile's educational theory could ever flourish in an educational system as rigid as that which he envisaged. It is undeniable that "the advance of the worker onto the great stage of history" has posed a new problem in the theory of representative government; and certainly the organization of the mass of the people in great corporate bodies is a phenomenon that it would be foolish to ignore. But when these bodies are employed directly as organs of the State, the State becomes simply the moment of authority against which the individual feels himself driven to rebel. Hence a Corporate State tends necessarily toward dictatorship, on pain of ceasing to be a State altogether; and Gentile's claim that corporate institutions represent a more concrete realization of liberty and a higher form of democracy is ludicrous not merely in the light of fact but in the light of logic. The "necessities" which "vitiated" the constitutional experiments of Fascism were not "transitory." They were involved in the philosophy behind the experiments—or in Gentile's terminology they were 'eternal.' Here, as in the educational field, we can profit from Gentile's speculations only by neglecting his practical program—though in this case we must in fairness recognize that the practical program preceded and stimulated the development of the theory.

Life and Death

Gentile always insisted that all philosophy should be directed toward the ultimate problems of conscious existence.[70] It is very fitting, therefore, that his last work should end as it does with a meditation on "Transcendental Society, Death and Immortality." From the beginning he makes it clear that he cannot accept the thesis of Antonio Bruers about the logical relation between religious faith and belief in immortality: "It is not religion that is the principle of which the dogma of immortality is the corollary; it is the need to be able to rely on immortal life that makes us seek religion as the pillow on which to rest our weary heads at the end of the day of toil." [71]

---

[70] Cf. B.1250, pp. 252–60.

[71] B.1288, p. 139 (translation, p. 196); cf. pp. 252–53, herein.

Men yearn for immortality not because they want to see God's justice fulfilled but rather out of a desire for perfect happiness—happiness that will last. The existence that they wish to continue is a social life with their family and friends. The people most closely concerned in our lives are so much a part of us that we never expect their death any more than our own. Death breaks the pattern of life in such a way that it can only be restored by anticipation of a future in which there are no such irrational interruptions. This anticipation follows logically, in a sense, since man "lives in tomorrow." [72] The past is irrevocably lost but the future is an abiding possession in which all men, even the pessimist, confide—for even the pessimist looks to the future to vindicate him.

But how can this eudaemonism be made consistent with the mystical moment of self-denial which Gentile always treats as the essence of religion? In ordinary experience the two tendencies are harmonized through the conception of man's redemption from sin. Even the sinner with all his personal weaknesses can picture himself as traveling on this road.[73] On this pretext the high contemplation of the ascetic is transformed into the more worldly prayers of the ordinary man—or the woman who prays for the preservation even of the family pets. Christianity at its best is an almost philosophical doctrine of the suffering and death of the lower personality (the flesh) in order that the higher (the spirit) may attain eternal life. It is true that even here we find the notion of a resurrection of the body; [74] but at least there is a clear recognition that it is the divine element in man that is to be saved—he must surrender his worldly goods and interests.

---

[72] B.1288, p. 141. This thesis also was one that Gentile began to emphasize at about the time that he completed his *Philosophy of Art* (cf. B.1020).

[73] Sin, however, is also eternal. Hence Hell, the realm of immortal death. According to Gentile, Hell represents a logical working out of the theory that gives to evil a positive instead of a privative and dialectical character. Immortality becomes a natural property belonging to a 'thing' called the 'soul' or the 'spirit.' Whereas in his view the privative theory of evil, which is basic to the Christian tradition, should lead rather to the recognition that sin is eternal as a negative moment, or as the servitude which the spirit conquers and escapes. But if Heaven is a mythical expression of hope for the future, surely Hell is equally a mythical expression of despair for the past (cf. Royce's "hell of the irrevocable," *op. cit.*, I, 259 ff.).

[74] Gentile comments that the error of this belief lies more in the concept of the body that is to be made immortal than in the belief in its immortality. The body which is truly immortal is the body that forms an essential moment of the spirit, the universal object which is the content of all feeling. Considered thus it is freed from all particularity and spatiality.

Gentile prefers to defend his philosophical conception of religion, however, by arguing that the whole notion of immortality, whether in popular desire or in the religious visions of reality, is a perversion of religious truth because it involves an illicit contamination of eternity with time. It is *perpetuity* that we seek to guarantee for ourselves; and this is impossible. In any case perpetuity is a bastard idea—a concept which will not satisfy man's spiritual needs— because it is merely indefinite, not infinite. The eternity that really matters is the eternity of truth; and this is not something that depends on its temporal endurance in the memory. Nothing can destroy the value of a thought even when it is completely forgotten. This is the eternity of the act of consciousness for which there is no 'before' or 'after.' The eternal act is a living moment which may embrace only a single word or contain the whole history of a nation.[75] It is always a spontaneous creation, always unique, and does not endure through time. Time comes to birth only within the eternal present; and the human longing for immortality in the popular sense is simply a shadow cast by the spirit's struggle to realize itself and attain to the truth which is eternal.

Belief in the immortality of a *substance* is a delusion; so also is belief in personal immortality as long as the idea of personality is infected with the heresy of individualism. Did not Jesus say that he who would save his soul shall lose it? The personal immortality of popular belief "is what we might call the 'democratic' idea of immortality. It is the most irreligious, immoral, and illogical illusion in which men swaddle themselves, in their longing for immortality and their yearning after it as a comfort for life." [76] The Kingdom of Heaven is not something that exists already perfect elsewhere; it is our own future responsibility. Certainly it is "not of *this* world" —but yet it is "within."

Thus, in the end, Gentile comes down firmly against the 'logic' of a future life. Life and death are not things or events that can be separated: death is a moment of life. We reverence the dead because with them a part of us dies; and the fear of death arises from this sense of an abyss in our own being. The fear of this ulti-

---

[75] In general all of Gentile's examples of the eternity of the act are drawn from the world of art—especially poetry (cf. B.889 in B.1075, p. 269; 2nd ed., p. 244). In the chapter we are now discussing he finally settles on "the poetic world of Ariosto" (B.1288, p. 153). This is one of several echoes of the discussion of art and spiritual immortality in B.968. (See translation, p. 209.)

[76] B.1288, p. 158 (translation, p. 212).

mate nothingness is the root of all the arguments of pessimism. But it can have a positive value, in that it should bring home to us the fact that we are not sufficient unto ourselves and, conversely, that our personal existence does not belong to us alone.

Actually, we have no concrete (direct) knowledge of death. The 'other' within us who dies survives in memory. Here is the reality of immortality, in the feeling of inward presence, that common sense regards as illusory; whereas the immortality of common sense and popular belief is the illusion. We have to recognize that this subjective life in which the other does *not* die is "the real principle and the solid and absolute foundation of the world itself." [77] At first everything presents itself to consciousness as foreign. The quest for immortality is an attempt to find in this foreign world of objective nature the reality that belongs to the subject itself. To recognize this truth is not to commit the sin of Lucifer but to accept moral responsibility. For responsibility implies freedom; and freedom cannot be limited.

But do we not have something like an actual experience of our *own* death in the experience of falling asleep? Sleep provides an awkward problem for a philosophy that takes its stand on consciousness. Gentile is unguarded enough to approach it almost empirically. He produces what looks like a piece of 'probable' reasoning in defense of an a priori position, arguing that we dream continuously, and hence we are conscious all the time, but that we remember some of our dreams more vividly than others.[78] Rather than make this quite gratuitous assumption, he ought to remain firmly in the eternal present and content himself with saying that a sleep of which we remember nothing is indeed like death, and precisely for this reason it is not part of experience.

Death itself is not part of experience because it is the dissolution of the transcendental society. It is a limit which we perceive from afar but never touch. In its actuality death is a social fact. There would be no meaning in death for an absolutely solitary being. He cannot die; for to die is to become nothing for others. Man dies a 'civil' or moral death when he becomes a social outcast, no longer a human being but a mere dead object, in the eyes of his neighbors.

---

[77] *Ibid.*, p. 165 (translation, p. 218).

[78] *Ibid.*, p. 167. Contrast the attitude toward sleep that is implicit in the description of the universe as "the great Sleeper" before the emergence of man (p. 43). (See translation, pp. 220–21 and p. 107 respectively.)

In the gradual approach of death through paralysis—which brings the individual as near that ideal limit as it is possible to come— this is what happens to the body. But since the body is an essential partner in the transcendental society, that society itself, for which alone death would have a meaning, is at the last annihilated. And hence death is not, and never can be, an experience. Thus the doctrine of transcendental society provides, in the last analysis, a new and perhaps a more cogent way of formulating the traditional Epicurean doctrine that "death is nothing to us."

Final Evaluation

Early in September 1943 Gentile came from the country to Florence, where he showed the manuscript of *Genesis and Structure of Society* to Mario Rossi, who was opposed to Fascism, and told him, "*Your* friends can shoot me now if they want to. My life work is finished"; Rossi was naturally horrified and expostulated with him, saying that of course no one wished such a thing.[79] But since Gentile's remark proved to be prophetic, we must consider whether his sense of final achievement was well founded.

Genesis and Structure of Society is a short book—a mere 170 pages—and it covers a remarkably wide miscellany of topics. Yet stylistically it is subject to criticism not merely for the gnomic brevity and well-nigh oracular arrogance of some of its pronouncements, but for the prolixity and apparent inconsistency of other parts. An ill-disposed reader might therefore be tempted to set it aside as the apologetic meanderings of a has-been. But this would be a mistake. The book bears the marks of the haste with which it was composed, and of the weariness of the author; and for both reasons a very considerable knowledge of Gentile's career and of his earlier writings is requisite if one is to understand it fully. Nevertheless it is a unity, and the conception that unifies it is one that has a revolutionary importance not merely for Gentile's own thought but for the whole tradition of post-Kantian idealism. The

[79] M. M. Rossi in the *Journal of Philosophy*, XLVII, 1950, 217. Dr. Rossi says that this encounter took place at the beginning of *August;* but this must be a slip, for we have the testimony of Gentile's son and his publishers that the book was written in August and completed in the first days of *September.* (Cf. *Vita e Pensiero*, IV, 29, for a letter written on 20 August containing the remark: "I am writing a book, which gives me much satisfaction"; also B.1288, Avvertenza, n.)

theory of 'transcendental society' is the foundation stone of the whole work; and it involves the substitution of 'dialogue' for 'dialectic' over the whole compass of philosophy. It was because he wished to make clear how far-reaching the consequences of the substitution are that Gentile tried to cover so much ground, however sketchily, in one short book. The obvious critical rejoinder here would be, I suppose, that he tried to push the new theory too far. One might say that even if the self *is* a society in more than a metaphorical sense, this transcendental society becomes nothing but a metaphor, and a very strained one at that, when it is extended to cover man's relation to inanimate nature and the scientist's relation to his problems.[80] This objection misses the whole point. The theory of transcendental society is at bottom a new account of the relation of soul and body. If we deny that the body is really a term in a social relation the transcendental dialogue becomes indistinguishable from the Platonic "dialogue of the soul with itself" from which the whole conception of dialectic began. This is the "merely metaphorical" interpretation against which Gentile protests. The "dialogue of the soul with itself" is just what F. H. Bradley called Hegel's Logic, "a ballet of bloodless categories"; whereas the Gentilian dialogue of the soul with the body is 'the humanism of labor,' and involves ultimately the humanization of the whole natural world. Gentile cannot therefore allow the scientist to regard his work in a completely impersonal way. His results are not to be regarded as the fruit of a dialectic of pure reason even if they take the form of mathematical equations expressing universal laws. To put the point in a positive way, unless he thinks of himself as investigating *his own* nature and its potentialities, that is to say engaging in Gentile's transcendental dialogue, the scientist's experience of nature is not richer but poorer than that of the meanest peasant.

We may agree, therefore, with the verdict of Rossi himself: "It must be averred that the *Genesi* is indeed the crowning of Gentile's system, and even that it is the ultimate expression and best possible solution that can be given to one of the basic problems of idealism in general." [81] But we must add that Rossi does not seem to have realized just how basic the problem was. It was not simply the

---

[80] Cf. Holmes, *The Idealism of Giovanni Gentile*, p. 170. The passage is cited and discussed in n84 in Chapter 4 herein.

[81] *Journal of Philosophy*, XLVII, 1950, 218.

problem of community membership but the problem of self-formation that Gentile was trying to solve—here as in all of his earlier
works. And therefore Rossi's claim that "No theoretical difference
or inconsistency can be found between Gentile's first theoretical
statement . . . and this *Genesi,* composed thirty years later" needs
to be interpreted with some caution. There is, perhaps, no "inconsistency"; but there is a "theoretical difference" of the first importance: Gentile did here finally achieve the 'humanistic conception
of the world' at which he was always aiming.

Aftermath: The Fascist Social Republic

On 8 September, while Gentile was visiting Rome, the Armistice
was announced. It was a terrible blow to him, since he felt that
national honor required the continuation of the war to the last.
There was no word for it but betrayal; yet it was the act of the
king's government, and his loyalty to the Nation had always been
inseparable from his reverence for the Monarchy as symbolic of
the national tradition. He returned to Troghi, resolved to take no
further part in public life; and in October he moved to Florence
for the winter (rather than return to Rome). The Fascist extremists
had joined in the attacks on him immediately after the Armistice.
He complained of this to Biggini, who was a minister in Mussolini's
last cabinet; and again to the (Fascist) Prefect of Florence—and
because of these attacks he refused to accept even a reappointment
to the directorship of the *Scuola Normale Superiore* at Pisa from
the Fascist Social Republic.

But in November Biggini suggested that Gentile ought at least
to have an interview with Mussolini. This he felt he could not
refuse, and as a result he was led to accept the presidency of the
revived *Accademia d'Italia.* As he explained it in a letter to his
daughter:

Some time ago a friend who is a Minister came here to seek me, and I
told him frankly the personal and political reasons for which I desired
to remain in retirement. But he assured me that of course I could remain in retirement; only I ought to visit my old friend who desired to
see me and was distressed about certain recent manifestations of hostility
to my person. To deny this visit was impossible. . . . On the 17th I
had a conversation lasting almost two hours that was very moving. I
spoke my whole mind, and made many observations, of which I begin
to see some salutary effects. I think that I did much good for the country.

He asked nothing of me and he offered me nothing. The conversation was between the two of us alone. The nomination was arranged afterward with my friend the Minister; and brought to me here by a Director General. Not to accept it would have been a supreme act of cowardice and the demolition of my whole life. Enrico well knows that on June 23rd–24th I did not give way before threats of death. And then too I profoundly desire that we should win; that Italy should arise again with her honor; that my own Sicily should be at my death that supremely Italian island in which I was born and in which my parents are buried. To wait shut up in one's house, until events grow ripe, is the surest way to compromise them. One must go forward according to one's conscience. This I have preached all my life. I cannot give myself the lie now I am on the verge of the end. God will aid us. . . . [82]

In the obituary that he wrote for *Civiltà fascista*, Biggini stated that when Gentile emerged from his interview with Mussolini he exclaimed with great emotion, "Either Italy saves herself with him, or she is lost for several centuries." [83] His letter to the *Duce* accepting his new appointment was full of expressions of personal loyalty and trust. But he ventured one word of advice that sums up his whole purpose in returning to political life, and gives some idea of the 'good' that he believed he could do for his country: ". . . I am certain that you will want to proceed frankly to use the authority that you have to lead the Republic to a stable settlement and toward a pacification of hearts [*pacificazione degli animi*]." [84]

Gentile was tormented at this time by anxiety over the fate of one of his sons who had been deported to Poland as a prisoner of war. Shortly afterward another one fell mortally ill—though he survived his father by three months. Only in his new task, laboring always for the "pacification of hearts" (at least within Italy), did Gentile find any peace or comfort. Despite his nostalgic feelings about the Monarchy "in whose shade the Italians were born and thought to die" [85] he was convinced that the Fascists had obeyed the call of duty in rejecting the Armistice. But his main concern, even in the article which proclaimed his allegiance (*Corriere della sera*, 28 December 1943) was to plead that the Fascists should exercise the power they had seized "in a broad-minded spirit of pacification and construction," and not sacrifice the interest of the

---

[82] *Vita e pensiero*, IV, 39–40.
[83] *Civiltà fascista*, May 1944, p. 22.
[84] *Vita e pensiero*, IV, 41.
[85] B.1274; reprinted in *Vita e pensiero*, IV, 85.

Nation, which was something far above factional squabbles, to the demands of vengeance and abstract justice.

In January 1944 he became editor of *La nuova antologia*. In accepting the post he made certain stipulations. His task, as he saw it, was to re-establish the spirit of peaceful cooperation in Italian culture, and he proposed to "set aside the political discussions which today divide unduly the Italian people." He insisted, therefore, that he must be free to choose non-Fascist collaborators provided that they were thoroughly loyal to the Nation.[86] In the first issue under his editorship he set forth his aims in terms which recall the closing paragraphs of his lecture on "The Philosophy of the War" in 1914. The "infinite disaster of today" was not the invasion and the material devastation but the internal discord, which made Italians unable to recognize or understand themselves. In the universal values of culture all parties might find a firm basis of agreement:

Not that I am still under the delusion that there can be an indifferent culture that does not involve political tendencies or contain echoes of the practical personality. But I know that to things of beauty all men turn their eyes with a joy and admiration that makes them brothers. . . . All culture is like language, which is always individual and so acquires a personal stamp in every writer, but is yet the ideal chain by which men are linked together and form one single humanity. It is good to appeal to this culture as an instrument for the fusion of spirits when the moral unity of men is broken and seems to dissolve.[87]

He did not flatter himself that the "miracle whereby Italians would recover Italy" could be brought about by this means alone, but he trusted that at least "the desire and hope for such a miracle" might be aroused.

But although he pleaded for a moderate, conciliatory attitude toward those who were not positively and actively opposed to the Fascist Social Republic, he did not hide his contempt for the fence-sitters who simply waited on events. He was certain that no one could stand aside with an easy conscience: "To wait? That is the part of the lazy, the egoists, the cowards; but not without an internal gnawing dissatisfaction and a suspicion that waiting is a betrayal. A betrayal of one's Country, that is, ultimately of oneself. . . ."[88]

He made his own position unequivocally clear in a speech at the bicentennial celebrations of the death of Vico in March—a speech which was, possibly, not unconnected with the decision to

[86] *Vita e pensiero*, IV, 44–45.
[87] B.1282; *Vita e pensiero*, IV, 92–93.
[88] B.1285; *Vita e pensiero*, IV, 97.

assassinate him. Pouring scorn on the 'liberators,' he claimed that only Mussolini's voice had given back to the Nation a real consciousness of itself at a time when it was "as if the dishonor of a gesture had canceled twenty-five centuries of history brilliant with genius, virtue, labor, and endurance." [89] Even the German intervention he welcomed:

The resurrection of Mussolini was necessary like every event that enters into the logic of history. The intervention of Germany was logical, though the traitors had disowned her, because *quos Deus vult perdere dementat;* but her loyalty and power and audacity were always recognized and held in mind by the Italy of Mussolini. And so that Italy was suddenly found again through Mussolini, and aided in her resurgence by the Captain [*Condottiero*] of the great Germany that Mussolini's Italy looked for at her side, which was her post for her own honor and destiny, making common cause in the tremendous fight to save Europe and western civilization for her brave, tenacious, and invincible people.

And sadly but resolutely he surrendered his faith in the Monarchy:

. . . we have no longer the heart to seek out our King in that shadowy no man's land between the imprecations of a people betrayed and the ironic smiles or haughty disdain of the foreigner—our King, who was of old at the highest peak of our thoughts, because in our eyes he symbolized in his person our Country, which we would never have suspected that *he* could have handed over to the enemy.[90]

The marked political intransigence of this speech—made on an essentially cultural and academic occasion—was designed to silence the fanatical critics among the Fascist Republicans who regarded Gentile's desire for moderation and pacification as evidence of political unreliability.[91] It did not silence his Fascist critics; but it did arouse new ones among the anti-Fascists. The foreign service of the British Broadcasting Corporation replied to his announcement of the rebirth of Italy by listing some of the reprisals of the Fascists against Italian partisans, and commenting: ". . . this alone, the great suffering of a people is the monitory force of the present hour, the true voice of Italy in mourning and in arms. And the rest, all the rest, is silence." [92]

Benedetto Gentile finds in this broadcast a "clear invitation to

---

[89] "L'Accademia d'Italia e l'Italia di Mussolini," in *Vita e pensiero,* IV, 101.

[90] *Ibid.,* pp. 102–3.

[91] Cf. *Vita e pensiero,* IV, 52 (letter from Gentile to his son Benedetto); also B.1286, *ibid.,* pp. 87–88. Even on this occasion he managed to work in a condemnation of factional bitterness. His eulogy of Vico ends thus: "From Vico the Italians will always learn to disdain factions" (B.1283 in *Vita e pensiero,* IV, 119).

[92] *Vita e pensiero,* IV, 55.

violence" and connects it with strong rumors that British liaison officers aided and abetted the Communist resistance movement in Tuscany in planning the assassination. It is hard to see how the truth or falsehood of these rumors can ever be established; but it is surely unfair to find in the broadcast any more than an entirely natural rejoinder. Considering the situation that existed in Italy, the patriotism of a sincere supporter of either government—or of neither —was bound to appear nothing but a horrible blasphemy to his opponents, and any reference to ideals on one side was sure to be answered by an appeal to the facts on the other.

After this expression of his loyalty Gentile made only one more public utterance. This was an article published in *Civiltà fascista* a few days before his death entitled "The Sophism of the Prudent." In it he returns to his earlier attack on the "prudent" people who sit on the fence waiting to see what will happen. He now admits that they may be sincerely in doubt, that they may be hoping, at least, not to make matters worse; but he still insists that they must come to terms with the reality of the situation. At a moment of moral crisis those who continue to demand time for reflection and exam-ination of the situation are thieves living a stolen life and refusing the responsibilities involved in their own continued existence. They cannot escape moral responsibility whatever happens, because the spectator must accept responsibility for his failure to act:

Is it not evident that the spectator as such remains always an element in the reality he observes? He will be a dead weight; but precisely as such, he will weigh on the constitution of that reality which he says he wants to take account of. He will likewise be a part of that society in which he is not a combatant but a deserter, and as such responsible for the events which overtake his society. For society is never anything that can be represented objectively, like a spectacle which the individual can stand back from in order to observe it, and remain outside it with his own powers of action and hence his own policy determined by these powers. Society is what we make it; and we are always actors and never spectators.[93]

This is the essential text of the chapter on politics in his *Genesis and Structure of Society*. It is the fundamental premise of Gentile's political thought and action, and can be traced back explicitly at least as far as the article of 1918 on "Politics and Philosophy." Gen-tile there derived it directly from his conception of the history of Western philosophy as the gradual assertion of 'spiritual' realism—

---

[93] B.1284 in *Vita e pensiero*, IV, 125.

the Christian, creative view of the world—against 'intellectual' realism—the classical, contemplative attitude. Thus it expresses the very essence of actual idealism—the union of theory and practice in the act of 'self-constitution.' The real significance of the paradox of *autoctisi*, which seems so outrageously contrary to experience, lies simply in the duty of a conscious being to accept moral responsibility for the whole world of which he is conscious—a doctrine that seems to me to be the heart of Christian ethics. This brief article forms therefore a fitting close to Gentile's career as a philosopher.

And he lived his philosophy to the end. On the very morning of his death he went to intercede with the local authorities on behalf of certain persons who had been arrested as politically suspect; he was on his way home from this errand, and in fact his car had stopped at the gateway of the villa in which he was living—which stood in a park on the outskirts of Florence—when he was approached by two complete strangers, one of whom inquired whether he was Giovanni Gentile. On receiving an affirmative reply they shot him and then escaped on bicycles, together with two other men who were covering the action. Gentile must have died instantly as one of the bullets pierced his heart.

The assassination was publicly deplored by the moderate wing of the Partisan movement, and a rumor spread that not the Partisans but the Fascist extremists were responsible for it. The suggested reason was a proposed visit of Gentile to Mussolini in order to plead for the adoption of a more pacific and moderate policy.[94] The rumor was quashed, however, by the open admission of the Communists that they were responsible for what they described as "one of the boldest and most risky undertakings of anti-Fascist youth." [95] The Fascist authorities imprisoned three well-known anti-Fascist professors by way of reprisal; but the Gentile family, rightly judging that there could be no honor to the dead man in an abandonment of his policy, interceded and obtained their release.[96]

For more than two months the body remained unburied while the government deliberated on a proposal to inter it in Santa Croce.

---

[94] He did have occasion for such a visit in order to discuss the official business of the Academy. That he would have used such a fair opportunity to make some such plea can hardly be doubted.

[95] *Vita e pensiero*, IV, 55.

[96] Rossi, *Journal of Philosophy*, XLVII, 1950, 218; cf. *Vita e pensiero*, IV, 60.

Eventually the sons appealed to Mussolini, and he intervened with a personal order to the provincial authorities. The decision to lay Gentile's bones near those of Michelangelo, Machiavelli, and so many other great Italians is certainly one action of the dictator for which Italy need never feel ashamed.

IX

THE REAL AND THE IDEAL

Amicus Plato sed magis amica veritas

Thus far this study has been in the main a contribution to the history of philosophy rather than a contribution to philosophy. In this chapter I shall no longer be concerned primarily with the views of Gentile himself, but with the value of his theories in the solution of present problems. But the dividing line between the history of philosophical ideas and that criticism of them which constitutes a new philosophical activity is not hard and fast; indeed it is very doubtful whether it can be drawn at all, and perhaps it does not even exist. It is not as if I were now abandoning the role of apologist for that of critic. Throughout the preceding discussion I have not hesitated to criticize wherever criticism seemed called for. Such criticism is an essential moment of the process of understanding; and, on the other hand, the important point in the famous tag at the head of this section lies not so much in the *magis amica veritas*, which has always attracted attention, as in the neglected premise *amicus Plato*. Only a critic who can honestly claim to have studied his subject with a maximum of sympathy can legitimately adopt Aristotle's excuse for his criticism. In short, only a critic who can find the 'truth' in 'Plato' has any right to prefer *it* to *him*.

This sort of approach is, moreover, the only fruitful one in dealing with actual idealism. Gentile's philosophy has something of the character of a religious faith [1] in that unless one accepts it one can hardly hope to understand it; and that is why although it has

---

[1] We shall later see that to regard it simply as a religious faith is the error that produces Fascist idealism. We might perhaps call it a 'philosophical' faith; but the reader must have patience for a little until we are in a position to explain the distinction.

aroused hosts of 'outside' critics they have in general contributed but little to its development.[2] What will be attempted here is a criticism from within, an application of the method of absolute immanence to the work of Gentile himself; and the aim of the critique will not be merely negative. For if all that we could show by this method was that actual idealism destroys itself, we should only know that there was something wrong *somewhere*—we should not know whether the theory is completely corrupt or whether we had merely used what is evil in it to corrupt what is good. Our aim must be to use the good against the evil; and we can only be sure that we have succeeded if by our chosen method we can reconstruct as we go along whatever we are obliged to demolish.

During the last twenty-five years of his life it was one acknowledged aim of a great many Italian academic philosophers to 'overcome' Gentile. As a result, a large number of 'critical reconstructions' of actual idealism were presented to a perhaps unduly patient public. But we do not need to consider this literature, for the significance of the line of interpretation that I shall here put forward can best be appreciated by contrasting it with the two main schools of interpretation that can be distinguished in the exiguous literature on the subject in English.

First, there is Roger Holmes, who uses what we may call a 'canon of theoretical coherence' by applying to Gentile's own system the standards which Gentile uses to exhibit the failures of his predecessors.

Secondly, there are those who use a 'canon of practical coherence,' the canon expressed in the text, "By their fruits ye shall know them." For this school the most significant thing about actual idealism is the fact that it issued in Fascism. The critical comments scattered

---

[2] A partial exception must be made in the case of Bernard Bosanquet. In his last book, *The Meeting of Extremes in Contemporary Philosophy* (London, Macmillan, 1921), he adopted an extremely negative attitude toward actual idealism. Yet in his reviews of several of Gentile's books (*Mind*, XXIX, 1920, 367–70; XXX, 1921, 98–101) he gradually recognized that Gentile's transcendental Ego is "the mind and institutions of a group" and he argued that because of this Gentile remains dependent on the Platonic doctrine of 'participation.' This was a mistake. But it did draw attention to the problem that Gentile finally solved in *Genesis and Structure of Society.*

It should be added that the argument of this section cuts both ways. Gentile's criticisms of Kant and the post-Kantian idealists are of much greater value than his comments on the Graeco-Christian tradition or on modern empiricism.

throughout Croce's writings belong to this category, and Croce must be regarded as the founder of this school of interpretation. But the same canon is used by Angelo Crespi, who criticizes Gentile from an essentially Catholic point of view, and by George Boas, who does not seem to have any particular ax to grind.[3]

Each of these schools could legitimately claim that Gentile is its 'friend.' For on the one side the appeal is to the 'method of absolute immanence' and on the other to 'the unity of thought and action.' Gentile would not have wished to surrender either of these tenets. Yet the results on both sides are so unsatisfactory as almost to amount to a *reductio ad absurdum*. Holmes finds that the method of absolute immanence requires the elimination of the personal ego from Gentile's dialectic, which makes it hard to understand how Gentile can have any ethics at all, or how his philosophy can have *any* practical implications. While from the other side Croce denounces it as irrational activism, and Boas describes it more temperately as "the completest expression of lyricism" and speaks of the "headstrong creativity of Gentile's *atto del pensare,* which makes its own laws as it goes along and takes no heed of precedent or consequent." [4] Not merely is each of these conclusions unacceptable in itself, but each contradicts the basic premise of the other. On the one side Gentile's claim to have produced a 'system of logic' is taken seriously, and the conclusion is that any notion of an ethically autonomous individual must be surrendered; on the other the proposed ideal of ethical autonomy is taken seriously and the conclusion is that all pretensions to logic must be given up.

Since Gentile regarded the 'method of immanence' not merely as the logical condition of any absolute or philosophical knowledge, but also as the condition of any real or absolute freedom, the acceptance of either of the above interpretations is tantamount to a declaration that his philosophy is not viable, and that either his conception of absolute knowledge or his conception of absolute freedom must be abandoned. Any effective defense of actual idealism must therefore begin by refuting both of these interpretations.

---

[3] Crespi, *Contemporary Thought of Italy* (especially Chapter 4); for the views of Boas see "Gentile and the Hegelian Invasion of Italy," *Journal of Philosophy,* XXIII, 1926, 184–88, and the reference in the following note. For a full account of earlier discussions of Gentile in English see the Introduction to my translation of B.1288, pp. 7–41.

[4] *The Major Traditions of European Philosophy,* New York, Harper, 1929, pp. 427–28.

'Logocentric' Idealism and Positivism

We shall take Holmes first because of the logical priority that we have just accorded to the 'method of immanence.' In the first section of Chapter 2 we mentioned his conclusion that "what Gentile should endeavor to stress is the *thinking* and not the *personality*, for it is the thinking that is essential to his doctrine." [5] We now wish to maintain that this criticism of the Gentilian Ego rests on a mistake; but it must be admitted that the mistake is not a simple one to analyze. Holmes has not overlooked Gentile's argument that a 'person' *is* by not being, and he is quite well aware that Gentile's 'person' is not a presupposition. But he feels that the word does imply a substantial existence which is foreign to the basic tenets of actual idealism. His basic complaint is expressed thus:

The use of the Ego to initiate the dialectic leads necessarily to one of two insuperable difficulties. Either one starts with an Ego which is pre-supposed as it must be if it is the beginning of the series; or one begins with a pseudo-Ego (as Gentile does) which by the act of creating the Not-Ego creates a new Ego which is the only real one. In the first in-stance one violates the conditions of a presuppositionless logic; in the second, one commences with an unreal entity, hence invalidating meta-physically the argument by which one arrives at its destruction. Either path is fatal to the Gentilian idealism. . . .

And for this reason he maintains that

If Gentile means more by "Ego" than *pensiero pensante* connotes, or more by "Not-Ego" than *pensiero pensato* connotes, his derivation of the logic of the concrete is in error. If he does not mean more in either case he should not employ "Ego" and "Not-Ego," for certainly the con-notation of the latter words are different from those of the former. [6]

The first question to be asked is what can possibly be meant by the 'initiation of the dialectic.' Since the 'pure act' is not in time we are not dealing with a temporal beginning; but since the 'pure act' is first and foremost the generation *of* time we are not dealing with a merely logical priority either. We are facing, like Augustine, the problem of the first verse of Genesis, the problem of the begin-ning of time itself. The most basic error in Holmes's analysis is precisely that he assumes he is analyzing a *merely* logical process. He treats the whole problem of the relation of *pensiero pensante*

---

[5] Holmes, *The Idealism of Giovanni Gentile*, p. 171.

[6] *Ibid.*, pp. 157–58.

and *pensiero pensato* as a logical problem of the relation of concepts. But it is not really that at all: it is something much more concrete. Gentile may sometimes have given the impression—especially
in the central sections of his *Logic*—that he was offering a logical
demonstration. But what he was really doing was exhibiting in a
very abstract form the logical structure of a conscious process. Justice to Gentile's *Logic* requires that we should not accept the view
that his philosophy is pure lyricism or activism. But justice to actual
experience requires that we should insist that the 'logic of the concrete' is not all there is to concreteness. The whole essence of Gentile's philosophy lies in its emphasis on actuality. It must be *lived*.
Its categories should never be divorced from the actual process of
experience with all its determinate content. When we translate the
extremely abstract arguments of the *Logic* into concrete terms we
can see immediately that in actual experience there is no passage
from an 'unreal' Ego to a 'real' one. There is, on the contrary, a
dialectic within a real but limited Ego, which through the recognition of its own limitation is led to deny itself in order to realize a
higher, ideal Ego. Reality in Gentile's philosophy is not a logical
category but a value concept. To suppose that the limited Ego
provides the metaphysical validity of the ideal one is to misunder-
stand Gentile's conception of truth. It is not the 'false,' limited, ego
which is the norm of the true, but always the true which is the
norm of itself *and* of the false (*verum norma sui et falsi*). The
passage to the ideal Ego takes place only when it is recognized as
'true' or 'concrete'; and if it is recognized, that means that *ipso facto*
it validates itself and invalidates the ego which recognizes it. But
still it seems that the act of recognition becomes a logical paradox:
and if we admit that we shall have to bow before the accusation
of mysticism.

The genuinely mystical expression of the paradox can be found
in Jesus' oft-repeated statement, "whosoever will save his life shall
lose it: but whosoever will lose his life for my sake, the same shall
save it." But here, although the promise is ambiguous and difficult
to interpret, it is saved from ultimate *logical* paradox because the
saving power of Jesus is not constituted *by* the faith of the believer,
though it may in some sense be dependent on it. It is a presupposition of salvation just as God's existence is the presupposition of
creation in Genesis. It is easy to see, therefore, why so many of

Gentile's followers who wished to preserve his *Logic* ended by being reconciled with the Church and abandoning the requirement of *absolute* immanence.

In point of fact, however, there is no need to have recourse to such a desperate remedy, since the act of recognition is not really paradoxical; it does *not* invalidate the recognizing self but only *some specific limitation* of the recognizing self. The limited Ego recognizes *itself minus this limitation* in the ideal Ego; and it is in virtue of this substantial identity between them that the ideal Ego has the saving power to overcome the limitation.

We have now gone at least as far toward a solution of the problem as Holmes himself was able to go with his 'purified' terminology. He proposes alternative solutions:

It may be said on the one hand that one commences with *pensiero pensato,* without being forced to characterize it as presupposed. It *is* that with which one commences. Or it may be said on the other hand that one starts with a *pensiero pensante* which creates a *pensiero pensato* and hence leads to the creation of a new *pensiero pensante.* With this latter choice of terms the primary *pensiero pensante* is not a pseudo concept in the light of the later one; the series is simply expressive of thought as development, the act of thinking being real in the moment of action and being superseded by the new act.[7]

The choice that is offered here is not a genuine one since, whatever Holmes may imagine, we cannot begin with *pensiero pensato* without presupposing it. To 'begin' with it *means* to presuppose it. Over and over again Gentile identifies *pensiero pensato* with 'nature.' It is true that he also identifies it with other things, for instance with 'evil' and with 'law.' But these other identifications are merely very special and limited cases of the general, relatively neutral, identification with 'nature'; and to begin the dialectic of the spirit with 'nature' would be to return directly to Hegel and to undo Gentile's 'reform of the dialectic' altogether. On the other hand we cannot begin with *pensiero pensante* alone either. There is no such thing as an 'act of thinking' that is not an 'act of thinking something.' Actual thought is always *pensiero pensante un pensato;* and this *is* all that 'Ego' connotes in Gentile's logic, just as *pensato is* all that 'not-Ego' connotes.

So we come back necessarily to the solution as we have given it in terms of a real and an ideal Ego. Instead of saying, as Holmes

---

[7] *Ibid.,* p. 158.

does, that *pensiero pensante* "creates a *pensiero pensato* and hence leads to the creation of a new *pensiero pensante*" we must say that *pensiero pensante un pensato* turns itself (its old self, the soul that it 'loses') into a *pensiero pensato* by rising to the perspective of the new *pensiero pensante*.

We can now see that there is *no* 'beginning of the dialectic' in the sense of 'first term of the series,' because everything that can be a term in the series at all has to play *all* of the roles in the dialectic process in turn. That is why Gentile insisted that the act of thinking was an a priori *synthesis*. But there is a genuine problem about something which we might call the 'beginning of the dialectic' in another sense, for anything which can play the different roles or exhibit the different aspects required by the dialectic must have a very special primitive character. Or to put it in yet another way, there is a problem about the 'matter' that passes through the pure forms of the dialectic, and about the will power that transforms it or through which it transforms itself. Gentile scarcely considers this aspect of the problem in the central sections of his *Logic*, but we must never forget that his 'pure act' is an act of thought that is *at the same time* an act of will. Holmes's 'clarification' of Gentile's terminology clarifies out this volitional aspect altogether. The problem of the *beginning* of the dialectic is the problem of where the common root of thought and action lies. It is not a logical question simply, but a psychological one of how 'self-formation' or 'self-education' begins.

As we pointed out in the second chapter of this study, Gentile produced a theory of human experience in the first part of his *Educational Theory* which seems scarcely consistent with the apparently unsullied intellectualism of the subsequent theoretical works in that it begins not from 'pure thinking' but from 'sensation' as an experienced unity of subject and object. Reflection on the apparent contradiction between his two starting points led Gentile to a new theory of 'feeling' as the ideal origin and boundary of actual thinking; and this new insight was set forth at length in his *Philosophy of Art* in which as he himself said, "my philosophy . . . emerges somewhat changed in aspect." [8] The change consists precisely in a reaffirmation of the *personal* character of all thinking. Holmes recognized that even in the *Logic* Gentile insists on the

---

[8] B.1012, Preface.

voluntary character of the act of thought. Even the affirmation of a truth, says Gentile following Rosmini, is a voluntary act. In the *Philosophy of Art* the heritage from Rosmini is even more stressed, for the original content of the act of thought is identified as the fundamental feeling or mental intuition of the body. If Holmes had given the *Philosophy of Art* the attention that it deserves as a counterweight to the *Logic,* he would have seen that Gentile had anticipated his criticism and offered a solution substantially identical with his own.

But he might also have seen that his criticism was better justified than he realized because the solution fails. By identifying the original terms of the synthesis of actual thought as 'soul' and 'body,' Gentile may seem to have given the required existential reference to his *Logic,* and at the same time to have preserved the 'personality' that Holmes wished to banish. For the definition of an 'ego' as 'a union of soul and body' is traditional enough to be unimpeachable on grounds of usage. But in reality the new formulation conceals the same old paradox; for the *feeling* from which the whole world of creation is made to emerge, and from which the dialectic begins, is at the same time declared to be *non*actual—i.e., if we apply the method of immanence strictly it must be identified with that 'nothing' out of which God created the world. We say that experience begins with a 'fundamental feeling' which is identified as Spinoza's *objectum mentis,* the body. This is tantamount to Holmes's suggestion that the dialectic begins with *pensiero pensato.* But since we have already criticized this suggestion above we have some idea of what must follow. Holmes himself said that beginning with it must not mean presupposing it. Thus we are led to deny the 'actuality' of this feeling. What is actual, we immediately declare, is always the body as the mind is conscious of it. Thus from Holmes's first suggestion we are driven to his second. Or rather we are driven to put both the suggestions together; for we do not now begin with *pensiero pensante* but with *pensiero pensante un pensato.* Thus the nonactual primitive feeling turns out to be actual after all. In theological terms, it is as if we said that in order to create the world God had first to treat the 'nothing' as if it were something.

We are compelled to begin with the Ego. But then why should we speak of self-constitution rather than of 'remolding a self that is initially given'? The answer is easy. Nothing that is simply *given* can ever be a self. At least a part of what we mean by saying that something is 'given' is always that it is 'objective,' or 'independent of the self,' that it is in Gentilian terminology the 'non-Ego.' We cannot therefore regard the Ego as a presupposition without destroying it. The act of thought begins *with it* in the sense that it begins by positing itself as a particular ego. Thus the solution of our problem requires that the body, the 'fundamental feeling,' be accorded full concreteness as a true and genuine primary self. In the *Philosophy of Art* both the primary object of awareness, the body, and the primary subject, the creative freedom of the artist, are declared to be 'nonactual' limits. *Both* of these limits are identified as 'feeling.' Thus we are entertained by the odd spectacle of a world created out of nothing by an unreal creator. This "shadow of a dream," to use one of Gentile's favorite tags against him, is only dispelled when we recognize that the two limits *are* both 'feeling' because they are the twin facets of the fundamental feeling which is not simply 'the body' but the primitive awareness of the body. If we take both aspects of this 'feeling' together it is no longer an ideal limit concept. It becomes a concrete *sensation*. 'Feeling' in this *actual* sense is the required 'first' term of the dialectic. It is an Ego which reflects upon itself and through this objectification of primitive awareness is enabled to act appropriately. In order that this appropriate action should take place there must be a partial rejection of the feeling, it must be treated as a not-self. A man who 'feels warm' must somehow identify the warmth as *not* belonging to himself before he can do anything about it such as moving away from the fire, turning down the thermostat, or taking off his coat. The child begins to emerge from pure feeling into full selfhood when it discovers that the two aspects of its consciousness, the felt need, e.g. hunger, and the response, e.g. crying, are not indistinguishably confused together, or even mechanically related, but are separable. In other words, even bare consciousness involves a self because it is an implicit unity of act and fact, *pensiero pensante* and *pensiero pensato;* and *self*-consciousness involves *two* selves because it involves the reflective distinction of the implicit moments in the primitive unity.

If there is to be an absolute knowledge, a knowledge that is indubitable because self-validated, which is what Gentile's *Logic* demands, it must be the knowledge of a being which the knowing itself constructs; but if there is to be a constructive activity at all it must have material to mold. These two apparently conflicting requirements are met by the theory, expounded in Gentile's last book, that the dialectic of consciousness begins with a 'sense of self.' In the process of 'self-constitution' this self-sensation is treated in part as if it were an object, the not-self, the body. But this ignoring of its substantial identity with the self can never be complete. We soon learn that we cannot treat the body as if it were a lump of stone and we go on to learn that we cannot treat our parents that way either. Eventually we shall discover that there are occasions where for our own sakes we must even respect the individual character of the lump of stone.

It may still be objected that if the initial 'sense of self' is truly concrete and not nonactual, as Gentile always seems to say, then although there may be no sense in speaking of the self as a presupposition because thinking means *constituting myself* by recognizing a feeling as *my* feeling, a body as *my* body, another body as *my* father, mother, child, teacher, etc., and a community as *my* State, yet there is still something peculiar about all this talk of 'creation,' since the thinking does not *create* the feeling. This is true; and if we reflect we shall see that this is because the requirement of absolute freedom precludes absolute creation. The 'creative' act is eternal, which is as much as to say that *at no time* can we conceive the beginning or the end of it. Gentile's frequent use of the verb 'create' and its cognates is unfortunate, because at bottom his theory is a solution of Kant's antinomy, an attempt to mediate between the doctrine of creation and that of an eternal world. His fundamental concept *autoctisi* should be translated, as I have translated it throughout, by 'self-constitution'; and he would have been well advised to restrict himself far more than he did to the more neutral terminology of 'positing' and 'constituting.'

Holmes's critical reconstruction of Gentile's system is unsatisfactory because, considered simply as a logical category, *pensiero pensante* is as abstract and unreal as *pensiero pensato*. This is the truth in Gentile's claim that 'feeling' is nonactual whether we regard it as the pure spontaneity of the subject, or as the pure intuition of an object given. The reality, the very actuality of the act of thought lies in the synthesis of *pensante* and *pensato*. This union of both aspects of feeling is precisely that determinate existence which is called individual personality. The Ego and the non-Ego are able to sustain the apparently contradictory relations of equivalence and difference that are ascribed to them in Gentile's *Logic* because each has this personal character.

It would be unfair to urge against Holmes considerations drawn from the conception of the 'pure act' as a 'transcendental dialogue,' expounded in *Genesis and Structure of Society*, which did not exist when he made his study. But a more careful examination and fuller appreciation of the *Philosophy of Art* would have saved him from the purely 'theoretical' interpretation of the *Logic* into which he fell. He had a right to pass over the earlier formulations of the system in favor of the *Logic;* but Gentile gave clear warning that the *Philosophy of Art* was not merely a special application of his logical theory but a reformulation of it.

In any case, in the light of Gentile's career and of his constant insistence that his ideas arose in the schoolroom from his actual experience as an educator, it is a little surprising and disappointing that Holmes should have regarded the *Logic* as the ultimate court of appeal. It is not logically incorrect, but it is misleading, to say as he does that "No man as an individual, not even Gentile, is real. It is only the act of thinking that is real." It would be better to point out that for Gentile the act of thinking *is* Gentile; it is actual as Gentile, and it would not be actual if it were not Gentile. But 'Gentile' here means the whole world that is posited in the act, including other selves; and the existence of these other selves is essential to the doctrine. Holmes points out very acutely that there is nothing in the schema of actual idealism presented in the *Logic* to show that the existence of other selves is necessary a priori. But Gentile's refutation of egoistic solipsism (that the Ego alone in a world of things would itself become no more than a thing) proves that he was always conscious, like Royce, that the existence of other selves was a *moral* necessity; and his successive formulations of the theory of society *in interiore homine*, in the *Philosophy of Law*, in the *Prolegomena to the Study of the Child*, and even in the *Logic* itself, show that he always intended to buttress this moral necessity with a logical or 'transcendental' demonstration.

This deliberate harrying of the author of what is probably still the best critical study of actual idealism yet written, by one who has all the advantages of hindsight, may seem ungracious. If it does, I can only plead that my criticism is not really aimed at Holmes so much as at Gentile himself. I must emphasize that I am arguing on behalf of *actual idealism,* not on behalf of 'the ideal-ism of Giovanni Gentile,' about which Holmes wrote his book. I maintain that the concrete unity of the transcendental Ego, which is the aim and end of actual idealism as a philosophy of life, is not a logical truth intuited by the intellect, but an ideal of duty pursued by the will; and I have no doubt that Gentile would agree quite indignantly with this interpretation. But this does not alter the fact that he often spoke and wrote as if his idealism were the purely logical doctrine that Holmes says it is; and in thus making it 'logo-centric' rather than 'ego-centric' he surrendered the priceless ideal of the Ego for the worthless reality of the logos.

Let us consider an example of what I mean. In the first volume of his *Educational Theory* Gentile expounded his theory of sensa-tion as a concrete unity in which both subject and object are pres-ent merely as implicit aspects, side by side with his theory of pain as purely negative and hence nonactual. In the account of pain only the objective aspect is considered, and the pure 'givenness' of the sensation is shown to be a mere limit. The logic is impeccable. But it will not dry the tears of a child whose toy is broken; and anyone who tried its effect on a man with the toothache would get no more than he deserved if he received a black eye and so learned something about this astonishingly potent *non*actuality.

Gentile might have seen his own error, by considering the case where the pain becomes so excruciating that the patient loses con-sciousness, or the grief so unbearable that he suffers a mental break-down and 'forgets' it. Here it makes sense to say that pain is the 'non-being' of the spirit. But the existence of this limiting case shows the falsity of Gentile's claim that "when I am aware of suffering, it is not I who suffer, because *I* am rather the one who is aware of suffering." [9] Pure awareness, *pensiero pensante* in isolation, is not 'I' at all. In order to suffer I must, indeed, be aware; even passive endurance requires active acceptance. But where the suffering is extreme, this acceptance may be the *only* way of being 'active' that is open to me. What are we to say then of the vaunted freedom of the spirit? If the condition of suffering is awareness, the price of awareness is also suffering; and the price must be paid—or in other words pure awareness is as unreal as pure suffering. If there is to be a real 'overcoming' of the suffering, the awareness of the suffer-

---

[9] B.1251, p. 37.

ing must be regarded as a single term in the dialectic of actual consciousness rather than as two terms. Instead of saying as Gentile does that pain is the 'negation of sensation' we should say that it is the 'negating of sensing,' for this makes clear that it is not just the sense of 'non-being' but the sense of 'being in retreat,' the sense of an encroaching dissolving *force*, which may so absorb our energies and darken our horizon that at last, finding nothing anywhere but defeat, the spirit cries out, as in the case of Job, for oblivion. When this stage is reached, when there is nothing but the awareness of suffering, we have no longer the pure act of thinking for we have no longer a transcendental society. The awareness is imprisoned by the suffering, and can no longer objectify it so as to be free to conceive remedies or at the very least distractions. This is the situation in which physicians have recourse to drugs which diminish the suffering by diminishing the awareness; and the interdependence thus revealed shows the conditional character of the freedom enjoyed by thought at all times. The 'free' thought of a person in pain must be concerned either with remedies or with distractions. When he seeks remedies, then in terms of the transcendental society he is trying to meet a demand made on him by his 'partner,' or to get it modified by changing some of its premises; when he seeks distractions he is trying to shut out the demanding voice by attending to others that he is better able to satisfy.

Suffering or pain therefore is not simply negative; it is the protest of something positive against being negated. It is not simply the sense of a limit, but the awareness of a bond that defines the limit. This bond is the bond of transcendental society, which Gentile generally pictures either as a bond of love and voluntary commitment or as a bond of outright hostility, but which in fact usually reveals itself to us at least initially as a bond of inescapable common suffering. The burned child fears the fire because he has learned that the comfort of his fingers is too much a part of his own happiness to be lightly sacrificed to his desire to possess and play with the flames. Nothing can cause us pain if it is not in some way essential to our pleasure; and nothing can cause us grief except it be already an object of our love. That is why we cannot accept a merely logical triumph over pain and grief. The awareness of suffering contains, implicitly or explicitly, the *possibility* of and hence the *moral responsibility* for its overcoming. It would indeed be no suffering of ours if we were not responsible for its healing.

This acceptance of responsibility is exactly what distinguishes *actual* thinking from merely abstract theorizing in Gentile's view. But when he passes from the true premise that pain, error, evil, etc. are negative to the false conclusion that *therefore* they are not actual, he is himself guilty of abstract theorizing. Arguments of this sort are not merely 'theologizing philosophy' but something worse. For the traditional theology merely sought to relieve *God* of responsibility, whereas what we have here is rather Cain's attempt to evade his own guilt: "Am I my brother's keeper?"

We need to consider one further example, for when Gentile moves from the hedonistic to the moral plane his insistence on the positivity of the pure act leads to a moral evasion of quite the opposite type, an evasion which is more difficult to detect because it puts on the mask of perfect Christian charity. A member of Gentile's entourage remarked to Dr. Mueller one day: "If, for example, one asks him [Gentile] whether such-a-one, in such-and-such a situation, acted rightly, he will reply that the *Spirit* always acts well." [10] As Mueller says, the story illustrates a salient feature in Gentile's character, and a multitude of passages might be quoted from his writings in which he adopts just this attitude. The response is, from his point of view, logically correct, but it is practically absurd in that it would seem to imply that we ought to adopt an attitude of moral approbation toward *anything* that anybody does. Hence we must either say that Gentile's logical theory is morally untenable, or else that he has misused it.

At this point we can see the substantial identity of the two apparently contradictory lines of interpretation indicated in the preceding section. If we begin from the logical theory we appear to preserve moral autonomy in its full perfection,[11] but the result is that moral judgment becomes impossible. Whereas if we begin from our own experience of moral autonomy, we find it necessary to decide for ourselves what is good and what is evil, and the conflicting moral judgments of the various egos produce logical anarchy, from which only the *will* of a sovereign power, standing in the place of right reason, can rescue us. The only 'logic' possible appears to

---

[10] Mueller, *La pensée contemporaine en Italie,* p. 214.

[11] But notice how delusive the appearance is, for it is not "such-a-one" but "the *Spirit*" which "always acts well." This 'logocentric' interpretation really leads to the complete dissolution of personal autonomy. On the other side the 'lyrical' interpretation leads to the complete abolition of moral law.

be the logic of the blackjack. In both interpretations the fundamental propositions of Gentile's philosophy are revealed as an inconsistent triad.

We can only escape from this impasse by modifying the members of the triad; and it is not difficult to see what modification is needed. The vital requirement of 'concreteness' seems to have been ignored in both the 'logocentric' and the 'lyrical' interpretations of actual idealism. The hypothetical reply of Gentile to his supposed questioner would be logically correct, but only in an abstract sense. Its emptiness reveals its abstractness, and in terms of concrete ethical judgment it amounts to no more than a denial that the question itself is properly formulated. Gentile would never have said "the Spirit always acts well" in defense of one of his own actions, or the actions of his children or his pupils. He did, alas, say it in defense of his Party and his country, and in general in defense of those whom he regarded as fellow workers for causes to which he was himself committed, for instance the *squadristi* and later the Germans and Japanese. In this last case of the Germans and Japanese, he did also admit that his "sane mysticism" was founded on the view that questions arising from moral doubts about the character of the New Order as proclaimed by the myth-makers of the Axis were improperly formulated. But he seems to have realized this only because in this instance he shared the doubts. All that "the Spirit always acts well" can legitimately mean is that one should not set oneself up as someone else's conscience; but taken at its face value it appears to derive from this true premise the invalid conclusion that since I cannot be someone else's conscience I need not trouble my conscience about anything that he does. "Am I my brother's keeper?" appears this time in the sheeplike guise of "Judge not that ye be not judged."

The task of moral judgment for an actual idealist is twofold; or, more accurately, there are two duties that he must fulfill. First he must 'prove,' as far as possible, the concrete morality of the action, by entering into it and reliving it in the process of historical explanation; and then he must 'judge' it concretely, by saying, or rather by doing, what he feels called upon to do about it now or in the future; or if it touches his own life only indirectly, by saying what is to be learned from it for the guidance of his present and future action. The process is perfectly illustrated in the story of Jesus and the woman taken in adultery. He did not say that she had not sinned, or that "the Spirit always acts well." In fact he challenged her accusers to say just that in their own cases, and they saw that they could not, just as Gentile would have done if he had been thinking 'actually.' Jesus went much deeper, and by understanding the ground of the action, understood also its limitation; and on this basis he said, "Neither do I condemn thee; go, and *sin no more.*"

It might be objected that I am not myself employing the canon of 'actuality' that I have set up; for there are many witnesses, even among his most extreme opponents, to the ready sympathy and the personal goodness of Gentile himself. But I am not concerned with that here. I am concerned only about the public policies that he chose to support or oppose and with the reasons that he gave for so doing. Even in dealing with his public career it is now no longer part of my purpose to exhibit its 'concrete morality.' I have tried to do that already, with what success the reader himself must judge. History has already said to Gentile, "Go," and it is *we* who are left with the problem of 'sinning no more.' We must therefore understand not why the sin came about in the past, but *how it was possible,* granting Gentile's good faith, for the sin to come about at all, since it is only by solving that problem that we can profit from his example in the future. My solution can be summed up by saying that Gentile did not always act as he would have acted if he had fully understood the philosophy that he professed; and that his attempts to use his philosophy to justify his policies and attitudes on these occasions transformed it from an absolutely moral idealism into an absolutely amoral positivism.

Concerning the relation between Gentile's idealism and positivism, Holmes makes an interesting remark: "[The] situation in the realm of value typifies the entire difference between the two doctrines. It involves the meaning of 'I think. . . .' To the neopositivist this gives a hypothetical character to all assertions: to the actual idealist it gives a necessary and universal value to them." [12] Holmes of course is talking about the logical or truth value of assertions. But we can formulate a roughly corresponding statement about ethical values. On the one side, in deference to his logical theory, Gentile has to insist that "the Spirit always acts well"; while on the other side, an extreme positivist like A. J. Ayer in *Language,*

---

[12] Holmes, *op. cit.,* p. 217.

Truth and Logic is driven to assert that sentences of the form "X acted well" are not really statements at all. Thus in practical terms the contrast Holmes sets up amounts to this: whereas the positivist *refuses to put any meaning into ethical assertions,* Gentile's insistence that morality is a necessary and universal characteristic of all action *takes all meaning out of* such assertions. In a sense the opposites coincide in good Hegelian fashion; and this is because both parties agree, in effect, that ethical judgment is entirely subjective.

But the formal contrast to which Holmes directs our attention does make a practical difference. For Ayer the fact that ethical judgments were merely expressions of personal feeling was a conclusion from which nothing further could be deduced: an anarchy of feeling was simply all that there was. But for Gentile the recognition of the subjective character of ethical decision was simply a basic premise, a point of departure. Since your own feeling is 'absolute for you' in the sense that it is absolutely all that you have, your whole existence as an agent is dependent on your ability to make it effective. In the phrase that Bradley borrowed from Goethe one must either "be a whole or join a whole," and what follows from this was worked out in detail by Hobbes in *Leviathan.* Where there is no rational solution for a problem and yet we must solve it or die, reason itself requires the setting up of an arbitrary will to "stand for right reason"; and in this way a philosophy that starts from moral autonomy leads to the search for a hero and the acceptance of a dictatorship.

'Fascist' Idealism

Croce saw very early that a strictly 'logical' insistence on the actuality or positivity of experience was self-stultifying in practical matters. For if "the Spirit always acts well" then whatever *is* is right and that is the end of the matter. This recognition was the root of his continual insistence that the distinction between theory and practice is a fundamental one; and the acute moral discomfort that he evinced from the beginning about Gentile's solution of the problem of evil sprang from the same cause. Gentile countered his complaint that according to actual idealism every man is good in the immediacy of his own conscience by saying that *no* man exists in the immediacy of his own conscience, for if he did he would not be a person but a thing. This answer provides a way of escape from the Hobbesian consequences of absolute moral autonomy; but it is, *ipso facto*, at the same time a moral condemnation of dictatorship. The doctrine of the 'pure act' appears to lead to Hobbesian consequences as long as the transcendental Ego is regarded as a unique reality (or in Holmes's terminology as long as the act of thought is regarded as a unique impersonal process). As soon as we regard the unity of the Ego (or of the act) as an ideal, a duty to be performed, Croce's complaint becomes absurd, but so does the actual existence of 'Man,' *l'Uomo,* in the shape of Mussolini.

So far as I am aware, the first critic who emphasized the wholly 'ideal' character of actual idealism was Ugo Spirito. In his book *Italian Idealism and Its Critics* (1930) he wrote:

Idealism, in short, is not a philosophy that one can grasp as a theory, which, when once it has been grasped, gives us once and for all and without further ado the explanation of reality. When it is truly understood idealism makes us aware that it has not given us a knowledge of the world, but has set it before us as *what ought to be.* And to say that the world *is* what ought to be is in its turn an affirmation that is never a result, a conquest, but only an ideal.[13]

But Spirito when he wrote this passage was himself one of the most prominent Fascist idealists, and presumably, even if he did not share Gentile's paradoxical faith in the man Mussolini, he felt that the Gentilian distinction between the Party as a reality and the Regime as an ideal was adequate to the needs of his philosophical conscience.

This distinction must always be remembered if we wish to arrive at a balanced judgment of the political activity of Gentile and his followers. But at the same time it was the negation—or at least the *reductio ad absurdum*—of the claim that their idealism was a philosophy of actuality. Boas said that Gentile "does not see that Fascism is more than an idea—how could an idealist?—that it is an actual flesh and blood government. He does not see that it is a collection of men like other men with no deeper intimacy with God than their fellows. It is these men, after all, who enjoy the prerogatives of pure spirit." [14] This was not quite true, for Gentile learned by bitter experience, and did publicly acknowledge, that most Fascists—Mussolini always excepted—had no special intimacy with

---

[13] *L'idealismo italiano e i suoi critici,* Florence, Le Monnier, 1930, pp. 126–27.
[14] "Gentile and the Hegelian Invasion of Italy," p. 188.

God. But his acknowledgment merely reveals more clearly the devastating force of the criticism contained in Boas' ironical parenthesis: How can a Fascist idealist see that Fascism is more than an idea? For the sake of politeness, at least, if not of clarity, we must translate this into the idealist's own terms and ask: How can he admit that Fascism is or may be *less* than its idea? Once the admission is made it would seem that a gulf is admitted between the ideal and the actual, and hence the very possibility of a completely actual idealism is denied. This gulf, created by the admission of the empirical arbitrariness of actual existence, must somehow be bridged.

Now arbitrariness is, of course, a necessary condition of freedom. But a political system in which the distinction between the rulers and the ruled is in large measure arbitrary, and there is nothing to be done about it except wait and hope, can scarcely be regarded as an adequate expression of the 'method of absolute immanence.' Yet after all the idealism that sets before us the world as it *ought* to be is as old as Plato; what characterizes the whole Hegelian tradition is the further claim that there is some sort of necessary relation between the world as it ought to be and the world as it is. 'Actual' idealism is the 'logical' conclusion of this tradition inasmuch as it purports to be a final and irrefutable demonstration of this relation—that is what the 'method of immanence' amounts to. Arbitrariness is required by the method itself, for the immanence of the rational will is a conquest of this arbitrariness. But there cannot be anything arbitrary in the actual process of relating what is to what ought to be, for it is precisely here that the conquest is to occur, and the immanence is to be demonstrated. Waiting patiently for the passing of time to heal some evil is not a part of the method of immanence, but a confession that it has either failed or has not been properly applied.

Gentile would probably argue that waiting with quiet confidence is an appropriate policy in some particular historical situations, and go on from that premise to the conclusion that my whole line of criticism rests on an 'empirical' conception of actuality. The actual world, he would insist, is the world of actual thought; the world in which the reconciliation of existence with the ideal must take place is the world as you, the thinking personality, actually formulate it. But one cannot preserve the unity of the world in this way. This merely substitutes the subjective anarchy of Protagoras for the Platonic gulf between the Forms and the world of becoming. The breach between what is and what ought to be may thereby be healed, but only at the expense of giving every man a private world of his own, making him a windowless monad, who appears to his neighbors to be living in a dream. This was in fact how Gentile appeared, not merely to those non-Fascists or anti-Fascists who recognized his personal integrity, but even to Fascists who were not members of his 'school'—and even among his 'school' there cannot have been more than a handful who did not feel that he had lost contact with the actual world as *they* saw it by the time that he met his death. Gentile himself certainly felt that he was misunderstood, but he did not urge this in his own defense as his surviving followers have done; for he condemned the doctrine of the windowless monad on moral grounds, thereby implying that one has a moral responsibility to communicate successfully. His own failure in this respect arose precisely from his dismissal of 'empirical' considerations as irrelevant to speculative thought. The empirical world, the world of the Cave, must have its rights in any philosophy that claims to be 'actual,' for the aim of such a philosophy is not to escape from it but to transform it. Gentile admitted the existence of these rights in general, but he never stopped to work out what they were; and the Cave took a grim revenge on the philosopher who felt bound to remain in it, but could not come to terms with it.

The bitterest irony of all is that insistence on what I have called "the subjective anarchy of Protagoras" is the first step toward the solution of the problem. For the world of Protagoras is just the world that Plato has pictured in the Cave; and Gentile's idealism deserves to be called 'actual' because it begins by insisting that ordinary experience is not a prison but an experience of freedom, and that poetry and art are the demonstration or celebration of this freedom, rather than a shameful gilding of the Cave dwellers' fetters with trickery and deceit. The shadows on the Cave wall are the world that we create for our own experiencing; but to 'have' experience at all means to interpret it, at least to ourselves, so that even the free play of the imagination is an expression of our fundamental desire to communicate, to objectify, and hence to share our experience. To achieve a coherent community of experience is thus our whole aim and object, and it is no mere accident of coexistence that makes it necessary for us to agree with our companions in the

Cave about the shadows on the wall. This coherent community remains always an incomplete ideal, but it is an ideal to which every interpretation of every shadow must refer. The perfect system of the Forms can never be achieved in the Cave, because the Cave is, by definition, the realm of becoming. The Forms are thus, in a sense, 'outside' of the Cave; but to suppose that we can somehow get closer to them by going outside of the Cave ourselves was the error that created the unbridgeable gulf between existence and the ideal in the first place. It is only *from* the Cave that the Forms can be seen at all.

Actual idealism cannot therefore be a 'system,' for a 'system' is always an attempt to get out of the Cave, to escape the flux of ordinary experience by finding something more solid and abiding 'behind' it. But equally it cannot be a mere description of the predicament of the Cave dwellers. For then it would have no answer for the skeptics, who deny the existence of the Forms; no answer for those who believe that the ideal of a rational or freely accepted and voluntarily shared community is itself only a shadow on the wall, and that there can be no real community except by arbitrary convention. Actual idealism cannot be a science of the Forms; it cannot even be a way to the Forms, such as Plato provided in his educational theory; yet it must not be simply a shadow on the wall. The only thing that it can be, and the one thing that it must be if there is to be any answer to the skeptics at all, is a set of criteria for securing or measuring the immanence of the Forms in the shadows.

The problem of political action for an actual idealist, therefore, is contained not so much in the question of *what* ought to be done as in the question of *how* it ought to be done. About what ought to be done actual idealists, since they are human beings born in determinate historical contexts, are bound to disagree almost if not quite as much as other people. But if their philosophy means anything at all, it must lay upon them certain duties regarding the way in which they settle their disagreements. This is the point at which the duality of theory and practice must be attacked; the practical value of actual idealism lies in its uncompromising insistence upon the dialectical unity of method and result.

The *real* unity of *method* and the *ideal* unity of *aim* are the two roles of the Ego in the 'logic of the concrete' which so perplexed Roger Holmes. On the one hand the transcendental Ego appears as a reality from which the dialectic begins, on the other as an ideal toward which it moves. To make explicit the substantial unity of these two appearances—the morning and the evening star so to speak—is the highest purpose of conscious life. We have suggested above that actual idealism begins from a thoroughly Protagorean conception of 'nature,' or the world as 'given'—it is given yet not given, since absolutely nothing can really be 'taken as given,' and to bring order out of chaos depends entirely on us. Bringing order out of chaos means establishing a world of experience that is unambiguously shared; and so in terms which are appropriate to Protagoras as well as to Gentile we can say that the transcendental Ego is the ideal of a 'common logos.'

But a 'common logos,' a coherent community of experience, is not even a possible aim, unless we can have some assurance that we do in fact *share it as an aim* from the beginning. Agreement about the content of the aim, even supposing we could reach it, would never provide such assurance, since as long as the aim remains to be achieved we cannot discover whether the 'agreement' is more than a verbal ambiguity. Precisely at the point where we expect to enjoy the fruits of our labors we may discover that we have wasted our efforts.[15] But if we can agree upon a method for achieving our aims we are proof against this kind of disappointment, since the ambiguities will be resolved when and where they arise, and there is, moreover, an ever renewed hope that even explicit disagreements about the content of the aim may turn out to be only ambiguities after all, when we are finally obliged to choose between them. In the meantime the very fact that these disagreements are acknowledged and tolerated is the proof that the aim of our activity is a *genuine* reconciliation and not an artificial one. The real community of method is thus the immanent expression of the ideal community of aim.

On this view it is instantly apparent that no actual idealist should have aligned himself with the Fascists after the institution of the dictatorship in January 1925, since the dictatorship was a *practical* denial of the right of anti-Fascists to express their disagreements

---

[15] It is after experiences of this sort that moral skepticism arises, and egoism becomes for the first time a consciously held philosophy; the egoism may perhaps have existed previously, but only implicitly, for at the conscious level it is cloaked by the ambiguous 'common good.'

with the dominant party in any publicly effective way. The verbal or theoretical denial of this right, which was more or less coeval with the Fascist movement, was not in itself an insuperable barrier to cooperation. To demand explicit recognition of the community of method would be self-stultifying, for since this community is a presupposition of conscious cooperation it cannot be brought about *by* conscious cooperation, it must reveal itself to consciousness as already present; in most circumstances it is certainly *better* that it should remain unconscious, implicit, taken for granted. To attempt to make it explicit in order to procure agreement in a merely theoretical conflict would be to risk destroying it, and suffering the fate of the dog in the fable who dropped the bone he was carrying in order to snap at its reflection in the water. All that mattered was to see how far the Fascists were prepared to put their theoretical denials into practical effect. In this respect the record of the *squadristi* was a grim augury; and the best thing would certainly have been to meet their denial with an even stronger counterdenial the moment it assumed practical form. In other words the State should have taken vigorous police action against *squadrismo* as soon as it raised its ugly head. But if we assume, as Gentile and other conservatives did, that the State did not do this because it was moribund and had lost the power to assert itself, cooperation became legitimate as the best means of ensuring that the fundamental community would not again be set at nought. The establishment of the dictatorship in 1925 made complete nonsense of any such hope, and thus made further cooperation illegitimate.

Of course the Fascist theorists, notably Gentile, continued to insist on the ideal community of aim. All we have to do in order to comprehend even their weirdest assertions is to take them as statements of intention, and translate them from the present sense into a kind of 'future indefinite.' "Fascism is the highest form of democracy," says Gentile—but he knows quite well that this 'democracy' is something that can only exist for the perfect Fascist, rather as the service of God would indeed become perfect freedom if we were saints. Gentile's identification of Fascism as a new 'religious' spirit was in his meaning of the term exactly accurate; but it was also, by implication, a devastating critique of Fascism as a political movement. For religion is the objective moment of the spirit: to the religious man the ideal unity of the spirit is no longer an ideal that he must strive for but an achieved reality in face of which he and his strivings are reduced to nothing. His only hope is to become reconciled with this reality that has revealed itself to him. Thus the man who finds faith is transformed from a sinner on his knees to a prophet who speaks with God's voice. The whole problem of attaining the truth, which is vital to the philosopher, or of creating a community, which is our task as political animals, inhabitants of Plato's Cave, vanishes altogether. The only problem is how to spread the truth, the only task is to get it accepted; and this task which for the philosopher or the political man is only another way of formulating the more basic problem of attaining the truth, or creating the community, is no longer a speculative matter but merely an empirical question of expediency and maximum utility. The prophet has to make men see that their destiny is not in the Cave; that they must eventually pass beyond it and be judged worthy or unworthy of membership in the real community that exists 'outside' or 'beyond' in the Kingdom of God. If necessary he must go out into the highways and hedges and *compel* them to come in; but the community is already perfect and cannot be modified to accommodate new members—so the man without a wedding garment is cast into outer darkness.

The wedding garment cannot be put onto a man by force. This much the churches have always recognized; and because of this they have been able to accept as 'expedient' the requirements of toleration and freedom of conscience imposed on them by political authorities. Generally speaking they did not perceive the expediency until they were faced with the imposition; and it is important to see that they could not impose absolute respect for the individual conscience upon themselves, since that would be to make a principle out of something that is for them *only* expedient. For if, on the one hand, it is true that only a voluntary acceptance of the faith has value, it is equally true, on the other hand, that no will has value except the will that receives the faith. The unconverted will has a conditional value as long as there appears to be any chance of its conversion. But there is also the risk that, if he is too lightly ignored, the heretic or the unbeliever may corrupt the faith of others. Thus St. Thomas held that one must treat heretics as gently as possible and do all that one can do to reason or persuade them out of their errors; but he recognized also that there comes a point at which forgers of truth must be sent from our earthly community to be judged by God Himself, just as in his time the forgers of money were.[16]

Even a religious person, if he feels any concern for the things of this world at all, must regret the intrusion of the religious spirit—with its absolute and objective truth, and its correspondingly absolute judgments, which if they cannot be perfectly objective will certainly be reviewed objectively in the other world, where the pure light of objective truth shines—into earthly politics. Few, even among the most devout Catholics, would dispute the historical verdict that the old Papal State was one of the worst-governed principalities in western Europe. For an actual idealist, of all people, to have welcomed a political religion was little short of lunacy. 'Religious' faith by its very nature, by its concentration upon the objective content of the faith, tends to corrupt and destroy its own subjective foundations.[17] The religious wars that followed the Reformation, for example, were hardly an edifying chapter in the history of the Christian church. We may well hold that a world in which massacres of Catholics by Protestants, or of Protestants by Catholics, are quite inconceivable has achieved a higher conception of Christianity; but we must also admit that it is incapable of the intense religious fervor that produced the wars and thereby destroyed itself in an agony of spiritual weariness, economic misery, and political cynicism.

Fascism in general perhaps, and Gentile's Fascism in particular certainly, was a religion of the Nation. That is to say it took for its absolute object the community which all loyal Italians had been striving for, and some parts of the tradition which enshrined what they had achieved, and then treated this ideal as a reality of which the Fascists, especially Mussolini, were divinely appointed guardians. The Party card, or at least loyalty to Mussolini and the Regime, became a necessary 'wedding garment' which distinguished the elect from the damned. The only result was that 'patriotism' be-

---

[16] *S.T.* II[a] II[ae], 11, art. 3 (and art. 4 *ad* obj. 1).

[17] I must emphasize at this point that I am using the term 'religious' in the special sense that Gentile gives to it. I mean by it a belief in some object (person or world, etc.) whose real existence is quite independent of the believer, but which intimately affects the duties or destiny of the believer. I do not wish to imply that all the faiths that have been called or are called religious are of this character. Nor do I want to deny that even a religion that is of this basic character may contain other elements that provide checks and balances against corruption. (I have tried consistently to indicate peculiar usages of this sort by placing Gentile's terms in single quotation marks.)

came an ambiguous term. As Croce said in his notorious antimanifesto: "To describe as a religious struggle the hatred and rancor that blaze up in a party that denies to the members of the other parties the character of Italians and abuses them as aliens, and in that very act sets itself before their eyes as an alien oppressor . . . sounds like a very poor joke." [18]

But alas, even by the time Croce made his protest, the religious struggle had gone beyond a joke. The Fascists recognized no conception of the ideal community except their own. By this refusal they effectively reduced it from a genuine focus of spiritual loyalty to an artificial system of discipline, expressed in arbitrary conventional forms such as the taking of an oath or the possession of a party card. This discipline produced a material or external appearance of unity which was only a façade covering a deep spiritual disunity which decayed into apathy, as the ideal that had been denied gradually faded in men's minds. There were of course those for whom the Nation remained an ideal; but they were either helpless exiles or genuinely convinced but equally helpless Party members. They maintained contact with an ideal but they lost all control of the historical situation. For a moment, almost as it were by accident, Mussolini united the nation again during the Ethiopian crisis. But the pursuit of military glory and imperial expansion, to which that crisis was the prelude, led ultimately to the agony of the civil war in which the spiritual corruption produced by the religion of the Nation was made completely manifest. Where could one look for the Italian nation at the end of 1943? On the one side there was the Fascist puppet government of one foreign army, and on the other the royal puppet government of another; one was supported with bitter regret by Gentile, the other with grim disgust by Croce, but neither deserved the loyalty of a true patriot and neither survived the conflict. The Italy that the young men of the resistance fought for was as tenuously rooted in historical reality as the Young Italy of Mazzini; and the Italy of De Gasperi and Togliatti that arose from the ashes had scarcely more in common with the Italy of Cavour, Crispi, and Giolitti than it had with the Italy of Mussolini.

The consistent actual idealist cannot possibly adopt this religious attitude in any sphere of social relations, since it is not merely

---

[18] "Protesta contro il 'Manifesto degli intellettuali fascistici,'" *La critica*, XXIII, 1925, 318.

expedient but necessary for him to avoid coercion, unless as a last resort and then only negatively, in self-defense. In place of a *religious* faith, or a commitment to certain truths, he has what we may call a *philosophical* faith, a commitment to certain methods or methodological ideals. He must recognize the spiritual value of his opponents unconditionally, for he knows that without their willing assent and cooperation the Kingdom of Heaven—which the religious man thinks of as already existing somewhere else—can never come into existence at all. Gentile rightly argues that where coercion is employed the conscious situation of the agent differs absolutely from that of the patient.[19] But monadism or solipsism of this kind is exactly what the actual idealist has a moral duty to avoid. Hence he cannot leave out of account the ways in which his actions affect the conscious situation or attitude of his opponent; and for this reason Gentile's distinction of two diametrically opposite aspects of force, though it may have some value when we are seeking to understand the past conflicts of people who did not attain to the idealist point of view, provides no acceptable explanation for the actions of an actual idealist. The belief that it does was the worst of Gentile's many mistakes in the theory and practice of politics. The practical aspects of this error were clearly exposed in Croce's analysis of his notorious contention, in the speech of 1924, that all force, even the blackjack, is essentially moral force:

It is a philosophical proposition that human affairs are governed by force, and that every force is a spiritual force. What else would they be governed by? By lack of force? Or by material force, which not even the physicists succeed in finding, and which they posit at best as a convention or an expedient? For the philosophy of absolute spiritualism (and perhaps for every philosophy, if every philosophy, voluntarily or involuntarily, is always idealism) material forces cannot exist. And this, at least to me, is a transparent truth. But if at a certain spot on the planet called Earth, the citizens of a State in which it was previously the custom to debate their affairs through those "methods of force" which are called criticism and oratory and association and voting and other such things, have adopted a different custom of employing clubs and daggers, and there are among them some who regret the passing of the old custom and set to work to stop the new custom which they describe as savage; what part then does the philosopher play, who intervenes in the contest to pronounce his verdict that every force, and therefore even that of the club and the dagger, is a spiritual force? It would not be enough to say that he is only an inopportune theorist [*fa solo la parte dell'inop-*

---

[19] Cf. Chapter 4, p. 113, herein.

portuno e dell'astrattista]; because unfortunately he also takes on the less harmless role of one who encourages the use of clubs and daggers, and does it in a more than usually blasphemous fashion. For he does not offer political necessity as the motive for his encouragement, or passion, or the *voluntas* that stands *pro ratione*, but bases his stand on a philosophical proposition, which, uttered on such an occasion, amid people who are philosophically uneducated, loses its true and universal significance and is corrupted into a verbal sophistry; it degrades the office of philosophy and takes the sincerity even out of politics. The ignorant bullies will imagine that the new severe and heroic philosophy condemns civil methods as fatuous and recommends the savage ones as valid. . . .[20]

Unlike some of Croce's polemics against Fascism—for instance his criticisms of the Corporate State—this analysis was not based on distinctions peculiar to his own philosophy; it expresses the spirit of actual idealism far more adequately than any of Gentile's apologias for Fascism. And although Gentile might protest that he did not mean to imply that brute force was as good or better than rational persuasion, even a man as politically ingenuous as he was could hardly have been ignorant of the significance of his words in the minds of his audience. That is why, although I have the heartiest contempt for the moral theory preached, doubtless in their own defense, by the staff of the *Giornale d'Italia* to the effect that "acts of servile surrender . . . would perhaps have deserved pity as the result of a weak temperament," I am compelled to admit that their indictment of Gentile, to which I referred earlier, was in one sense justified: "He broke the front of culture, which ought to have been the front of liberty and human dignity . . . with acts of deliberate corruption and perversion of intellectual and moral values, which gave a false appearance of liberty to servitude, of national dignity to party faction, of high educational value to the brutal use of the blackjack." [21] False appearances is all that his ideals were in the eyes of the nation at large; and however much one may respect his sincerity in pursuing them—it was indeed *respect* that he deserved, and not *pity* which he would rightly have scorned—one cannot help feeling that had he been a better actual idealist he would have perceived that false appearances was all they could ever be as long as such methods were used to inculcate them.

---

[20] Postilla, "Fissazione filosofica," *La critica*, XXIII, 1925, 253–54. It is interesting that Croce ignores the theoretical ambiguity of the contention that "every force is a spiritual force"—an ambiguity which Gentile analyzed clearly in 1916—but fastens unerringly on the practical ambiguity that Gentile ignored.

[21] Quoted in *Vita e pensiero*, IV, 23; cf. p. 250, herein.

All of the equivocations on which Fascist idealism was built stem from the realistic or 'religious' interpretation of the *ideal* role of the transcendental Ego in the dialectic of the act of thinking. Thus if it is *really* the case that man is absolutely free and his freedom can never be taken from him, it follows that we may act as tyrannically as we please without endangering his freedom. And anyone who wishes to establish his authority may legitimately use any means to attain his end, which is always moral because it is universal. Of course his intended subjects may not perceive this universality, and for this reason they may resist; but the force he uses against them will only be 'real' insofar as it is spiritualized, or in other words insofar as they come to accept it voluntarily. Physical damage to their bodies is tacitly and perhaps almost unwittingly eliminated from consideration because pain is merely negative—the non-being of the spirit.

History itself has demonstrated graphically enough the inadequacy of this purely positive interpretation of human experience with its narrow concentration on the point of view of the agent. The very possibility of community presupposes that although the conscious situations of two or more persons who have to come to terms with each other may differ even to the point of absolute opposition, nevertheless what takes place between them is a unitary transaction; and hence the positive aspect of it, as an actualization of the spirit, does not express its whole meaning. Inevitably it will have also a negative, involuntary, coercive aspect for some or all of the parties concerned. Where the transaction is a simple case of the coercion of one party by another, they are not united in it but divided by it; it is simply the boundary line between two quite separate worlds. Now although it is clear that this duality must eventually be resolved, there is no necessity for its immediate resolution and no means of telling which of the opposed wills possesses moral authority, or which of the two worlds will eventually absorb the other. The necessity for a resolution is not immediate, because it is not yet moral. It is not moral because the compulsion is physical or 'natural,' and no one would say that a man's relations with Nature are moral, as long as Nature and not he is dominant. A situation of spiritual stalemate may persist almost indefinitely, with everyone retiring into the private world of his own selfish egoism because the unity of the public world has been shattered. Apathy and cynical indifference, which Gentile regarded as the supreme evils, were exactly what the Fascists with their religious spirit succeeded in producing. During the second decade of the Regime, Gentile continually protested that too much emphasis on discipline and religion would make both merely outward and formal. But he does not seem to have recognized that authoritarian methods could never be relied upon to produce anything except outward conformity.

Of course Fascism was not purely authoritarian. There was a certain measure of flexibility about it. But the career of Gentile himself, who as a friend of Mussolini and the most prominent Party intellectual certainly had more freedom than most of his compatriots, provides a graphic illustration of how narrowly human critical spontaneity was confined. In view of the sense of futility that grew up in *his* mind in the later years, the despair of any ordinary citizen who was sincerely concerned about the public good can scarcely even be imagined. That is why I said earlier that the 'good' Fascists were as helpless as the anti-Fascist exiles. The present was lost to them; they could only pin their hopes to an indefinite future.

The best that can be said for the 'actual,' effective, concrete philosophy of Fascism is that it was a very naive interpretation of the politico-historical theory of Hegel. The employment of authoritarian methods can only be justified by the assumption that the truth exists already, the assumption that forms the fundamental tenet of what Gentile called 'intellectualism.' In a dialectical theory of reality this presupposition emerges as the *logic* of the world-process, which is studied by the philosopher. Since freedom lies in the realization of this logic, the ordinary man only achieves freedom through obedience to an elite who understand its nature. The political history of the West since the Reformation is one long rejection of this abstract rationalism; and therefore its revival may fitly be described in the words which Gentile applied to Marxism: it was "one of the most calamitous deviations of Hegelian thought."

Actual Idealism and the Theory of Democracy

It was the more calamitous in that the source of the perversion lies at the point at which Gentile advanced farthest beyond the position that Hegel arrived at. The 'positive' interpretation of actual idealism has its roots in the strict definition of actuality given by Gentile. Hegel recognized a world of mere appearance which did not possess that inward substance of rationality which would make it real; whereas Gentile, because of his insistence on actual conscious experience, cannot allow any distinction between appearance and reality. It would seem, therefore, that the famous Hegelian dictum affirming the identity of the actual with the rational and of the rational with the actual must mean for Gentile just what ignorant and prejudiced critics have said that it means in Hegel's mouth—that the only criterion of historical rationality is success.

But for anyone who considers the matter from a strictly *actual* point of view, it is precisely here, at the deepest root of the trouble, that the fallacy of the realistic interpretation of actual idealism is most clearly apparent. For from this point of view reality is always *in fieri:* the act of consciousness is never completed. Gentile himself protested on occasions against the *punctual,* instantaneous interpretation of the pure act, and gave as an example of an experience which came somewhat nearer to the eternal, nontemporal character of *pensiero pensante* the reading and appreciation of the *Divine Comedy* as a whole. There is no fragment of experience that is not part of a wider experience which can be considered as nearer to the total complex content which would alone be an adequate object for the transcendental Ego. It is to these wider contexts that we must always appeal in order to understand the concrete significance of a punctual moment of present experience. It may be true, as Gentile insists, that every moment of experience is a complete and perfect act, involving the whole universe and containing all the riches of the spirit; but we cannot hope to understand in any moment, taken by itself, the way in which it expresses the whole. The total significance of an act is never explicit: our perspective is limited and determined by our own part in it, and much of it is hidden in the secret hearts of others. Even our own part we cannot completely understand, for some of our motives are hid from us, and amid the welter of hopes and fears that fill our minds we cannot tell which tendencies are mere velleities, passing shadows of feeling, and which have the solid substance of the moral will behind them. As Leibniz said, every instant is *gros de l'avenir;* and it is the nature of the future to be only partially definite. Only by first acquiring some concept of the whole can we begin to understand how that whole is mirrored in the instant of action; and even then the wholeness of the 'pure act' is only to be grasped as an ideal.

It is here that we part company with Croce. Croce argued that the "fixation" which was typical of Gentile's "philosophical cretin-ism" was due to a failure to add to a speculative theory the deter-minate practical content given by a particular situation. He con-ceived that this content of passion and emotion was something fundamentally different from pure thought and not reducible to it. In his view, therefore, no speculative theory could ever be turned to direct practical account, except by means of ambiguities of the sort that we have noted in Fascist idealism. Yet in practice no one —least of all Croce himself in his work as historian and critic—has ever been able to maintain the rigid distinction between theory and practice which his theory requires. If "the efficacy of logic is in the realm of logic, of doctrine in the realm of doctrine, of philosophy in philosophy," [22] it would seem that all theory is practically value-less, and that man is a rational intelligence grafted on to an irra-tional animal.

The truth is that Croce's criticism is as much an example of 'phil-osophical fixation' as the doctrine that he was criticizing. He took the analysis at least one step further than Gentile did, but he still stopped short before it was complete. He perceived clearly that the penumbra of passion and emotion, which surrounds any action at the moment of performance, makes the application of the canons of abstract historicism impossible—i.e., we cannot infer its 'ration-ality' from its 'reality.' Only when the act has receded into a his-torical context, in which the significance and implications of this penumbra have received determinate form, is an objective evalua-tion possible. But he did not see that out of a deepened understand-ing of these same canons a way might be found to determine the flux of emotion *subjectively* in the channels in which it *ought* to flow. Yet who more eloquently than he has argued that all con-crete practical experience is governed by the moral conscience? And what is this conscience but the concrete form of the universal (reason, philosophy) in practical life?

Because of the terrible difficulties that beset any attempt to divide reason from emotion as Croce does, we should not sacrifice Gentile's doctrine of the union of theory and practice, method and result, until we have made every effort to find an interpretation that will give a certain measure of concrete content to our a priori judgments. In these few concluding pages I shall try to show that the 'ideal'

---

[22] *La critica*, XXI, 1923, 127.

interpretation which I have offered will supply such a content, since through this interpretation the theorems of the intellect become imperatives of the will.

We have already laid it down that the problem of political theory on this interpretation is not the problem of what ought to be done but of *how* it may legitimately be done. The fundamental conclusion that I have to urge against Gentile, Croce, Hegel, and almost every other dialectical philosopher since Fichte (who perceived this truth quite clearly), is that the method whereby the spirit attains to actuality is not something empirical, accidental, and relatively unimportant. It is the very substance of the spirit, and is ultimately more vital than mere power or effectiveness, despite the fact that power is a prerequisite of actual existence. In practice, means are more important than ends because the ends can only become actual in the means.

Actual idealism purports to be a 'philosophy of *freedom*'; and freedom means the explicit realization of the spirit, in the fullness of all its aspects, as a harmonious whole. This may sound like a Pickwickian definition designed merely to procure a verbal triumph. But all that is meant is that a person can only be free if he knows what he wants, and a community of persons can only be free if the wants and needs of its members can be so understood as to preserve the possibility of community between them. The harmony of the whole does not involve the abolition, or even, necessarily, the reduction, of tensions; but it does involve the reduction to a minimum of sheer frustration or sheer waste. The most general form of the moral imperative, therefore, is that every act of conscious life should refer to or express a whole of this sort. This means that the spirit informing every action should be as philosophical, as self-critical as possible.

But the word 'self-critical' is ambiguous. We cannot criticize an action so long as we look at it only from the point of view of ourselves as agents, for this is by definition the point of view from which the act cannot appear to deserve criticism or we should not perform it. To perform an act self-critically means to try to see it, throughout the process of its execution, not merely with our own eyes but with those of others. Obviously the *best* way to do this is not to ask oneself "How would I feel about this if I were X" but to ask X how he does feel about it, making every effort to secure a frank answer. Nothing could be further from the truth than Gentile's contention that because the only effective criticism is self-criticism, the Fascist party did not really need an acknowledged opposition. The fact that they could not tolerate an opposition was rather the best possible proof that they were not capable of true self-criticism as here defined. If there is one thing above all that must be banished from the actual idealist's world it is the righteousness—the narrow concentration upon his own truth, his own sincerity, and his own vision—of the Pharisee in the parable. His prayer was quite heartfelt, and we should remember that he gave to God the credit for his success. But the spirit of actual idealism is contained in the prayer of the publican. Tolerance itself must be the first article of the idealist's *credo*.

Tolerance is important, not merely negatively because we are all sinners, but positively because it is the condition of the full and explicit realization of the spirit, which is the highest end. We only speak of 'tolerating' something if it appears somehow alien to us. But everything is initially alien to us, and the toleration of it pro tempore is the only way to find out what capacity for good is contained in it. It is the fundamental duty of every actual idealist to see that all other men are enabled and encouraged to live *like* actual idealists. This does not mean that he must strive for their conversion to actual idealism in a theoretical sense. Certainly he may and he will do this wherever he feels there is some hope of success. But since his main aim must be to secure the adoption of rational methods, he will not insist on the theory underlying this aim if by so doing he jeopardizes the aim itself. His aim is a community in which every member freely contributes all that is in him. That there should be at once freedom and community means that every member must have, and must strive to express, *his own* conception of the community; and he can only feel that it is his own if he is to some degree pulling *against* his fellows, or at least against some of them. The more of this sort of tension there is in a community, the healthier it is—as long as the tug of war remains just a tug and does not become a war to the knife.

A community to which every one contributes in this way is the ideal of democracy. The weakness of classical democratic theory is that in it every man is assumed to be capable of creating and sustaining the same degree of social tension—that is what is involved in "all men are created equal." But in practice, of course, people are capable of creative freedom in different degrees, or at least in different directions and respects; so that what is important is that every man should have maximum opportunity to try his strength, and no man should be tried beyond it. Authoritarian governments cannot destroy man's freedom, in the sense that they cannot destroy the moral strength a man has—though if they have been in power throughout the period of his education they can see to it that he does not have very much, or at least does not know that he has it. What they can do in any case is to render his strength virtually useless by trying him beyond it. The individual who can stand alone, relying entirely on an ideal 'transcendental' community, is even rarer than the religious martyr who has faith in a real but transcendent one. It is so much easier to conform. But since conformity means sacrificing one's social conscience, one's personal conception of the community, the only way to preserve some measure of self-respect is to retire from the public world altogether, and so not need a social conscience. At the theoretical level this retreat can be justified either by restricting the notion of community as in the case of Epicurus, or by extending it ad infinitum as in Stoicism or in most religious flights from the world. But since it is in the first instance a practical concern it can occur without the development of a theory; in fact it does occur to some extent in any society, no matter how it is organized, for even in the best democracy one can find a tyrant if one is looking for one as an alibi for evading the burdens of citizenship—the 'mob,' 'big business,' the 'machine,' etc. The thing is that in an authoritarian society one finds the tyrant without looking for him—and that makes the alibi genuine.

It is the object of the actual idealist to strengthen and consolidate the public world and the public conscience which sustains it. This is the real meaning of all the blather about the Ethical State being a 'strong' State. Militarism is the practical antithesis of this doctrine, inasmuch as it substitutes a policy of political discipline at home and imperialism abroad for the moral solidity that comes from spontaneous inward acceptance. By doing this, the Fascists, for example, steadily corroded the ethical bonds that bound Italians to one another and Italy to the rest of the world. No Ethical State can make an ideal of militarism; and no State that is not ethical can long remain strong if the 'humanistic conception of the world' is generally accepted. Gentile was right in his contention that war is a test of sincerity; and he was equally right in saying that there are many forms of it. What he never stopped to consider was that the different forms test sincerity in different ways and at different levels. Military war was not a very useful test, even in the old days of hand-to-hand conflict, because it rejected as inauthentic everything except physical courage and tended to destroy the courage and endurance that it revealed. Such absolute life-or-death heroism is of doubtful value in any case since it is usually accompanied by fanaticism, which is a form of moral blindness ('transcendental loneliness,' or absolute incapacity for self-criticism). War to the death produces as much hatred as it does heroism; and the hatred is conserved in institutions, while much of the heroism is wasted in death. What is needed is some less absolute form of conflict, something that is not normally thought of as war at all, for it is the 'religious' conception of a dialectic opposition as a 'war' that gives birth to slogans like "unconditional surrender" and all the other tragic shibboleths of the fanatic.

If in a physical conflict one's primary object is (as recruits are always told) to kill the enemy, then from the point of view of actual idealism such warfare is the most irrational of all activities. For one is striving to defeat the whole purpose of one's existence in the way that is most nearly irretrievable. The death of an opponent destroys the possibility of community with him. Thus the only circumstances in which an actual idealist could legitimately risk such an outcome would be in defense of his own life or that of his community, which after all is no less essential to the achievement of his purpose. He *may* even elect to make an absolute principle of nonviolence, on the grounds that his own death at the hands of an enemy would be a defeat for the enemy, but at least ideally a victory for him, in that he remained true to his principles. There would still be the possibility that even the survivor might come to recognize his defeat and his opponent's triumph, and thus salvage all that could be saved of the community wrecked by his own violence.

It should be noted, however, that even if we feel that by the 'method of immanence' we are absolutely committed to the principle of nonviolence, we must still admit that up to a point there is justification in Gentile's philosophy for his romantic idealization of war. Seen from the actual point of view of a patriotic combatant, war is a struggle in which he risks his own life for the sake of his total way of life. Whatever the sergeant-major instructors may say, a man in battle is probably more conscious of this personal risk than of his military 'duty' to destroy the enemy; and this sacrifice of the lesser for the greater self *is* what is demanded by the dialectic of the pure act. But even upon this more limited view of the situation it is clear, as we have said, that only self-defense can justify war; we can say *salus populi suprema lex* only because the 'safety of the people' is an indispensable minimum. When the community agrees that its existence is threatened, therefore, it can legitimately require that its members risk their lives as long as the risk is distributed in a manner that is generally recognized as equitable. This justifies the principle of conscription, and also the principle that service involving special risk must be performed only by volunteers. It also delimits the right of conscientious objection established in the preceding paragraph. The person committed to nonviolence has the right not to bear arms but he can have no right to escape the risks generally accepted by those who are in other respects his peers. He may be called on, for instance, as a front-line stretcher-bearer.[23]

What makes nonsense even of this very restricted justification of war as an instrument of defensive policy is the development of military techniques which, if they are actually employed, will completely annihilate whole communities and make the annihilation of the race itself a real possibility. The argument that if I must die at least I'll take the other fellow with me is the most outrageous absurdity possible in the context of the social theory here put forward; for by taking him with me I destroy the one possibility that my death may have some meaning and value. When the logic of war itself is pushed to a conclusion, as it has been in this century, the impossibility of regarding it as an educational device is made finally and completely manifest. The community has no moral right to sentence even one of its members to death, because by so doing it ceases to be his community; its members have no right to commit suicide either individually or collectively, because they belong to a community which includes the dead and the yet unborn.

This is the negative limitation immanent in rational political action. We must avoid the destruction both of ourselves *and* of

---

[23] In the short section on "Absolute Ethics" in *Speculum Mentis* (Oxford, Clarendon, 1924, pp. 304–5), R. G. Collingwood appears to have come very near to the interpretation of actual idealism offered in this chapter. But his contemptuous dismissal of the right of conscientious objection shows that he was as far as Gentile from grasping the logical implications of his view.

our enemies because death is the final dissolution of transcendental society. We must, as far as humanly possible, avoid or at least minimize coercion in social relations because it jeopardizes transcendental society at least temporarily; that is to say what appears as a social interaction between man and man tends to become for the coerced party merely a setback in his attempts to dominate his natural environment.

At the other extreme there is the positive ideal of all rational action. Every act should as far as possible be *the* act of the transcendental society. Hence it follows that everyone involved in the action should be encouraged to make public the whole significance that it has or seems to have for him. From the individual point of view this requirement yields what we may call the 'canon of politeness': that no one should make this publication difficult—or at the very least that he should not make it more difficult for others than it is for himself. From the point of view of the State, as the organization of the public world, this duty of individual citizens becomes the 'right of free speech,' and all the various 'freedoms' that go with it. Only through the free exchange of opinion can we discover whether a public act expresses a unitary spiritual situation for all of its participants; and this spiritual community is the very substance of the State. The whole of Mill's discussion of freedom of opinion falls directly into place here as a logical development of this principle.

But this is only a beginning. For in this free outflow of private conscience into the public world, a great deal of chaff issues along with the seed that is destined to bring forth fruit. A method of winnowing opinions must be devised that is recognized and accepted by all as a truly objective discipline which does not fall harder on some than on others. It would be wrong to see this discipline as something that has a purely negative significance, as a curb on irresponsible chatter and arbitrary or idle fancy. Rather it is a positive fulfillment of the right of free expression. No one can be expected to give his opinion honestly, or to devote serious attention to the disciplining of his own passions and particular interests, if he does not feel that his opinion, when given, will be attended to. In the respect that is paid to him by society he finds the objective realization of his own self-respect; without it he is unable to live in the public world. It is not a matter of responsibility being forced upon him; it is a matter of his being allowed to accept it.

I hope the reader will grant that through a detailed development of this argument I could arrive at a plausible semblance of a transcendental deduction of modern parliamentary democracy. To continue on this road would be a mistake, however, and the resulting plausible semblance, so far as it affected our approach to existing political problems, might well do more harm than good. What I am aiming at is a metaphysics of democratic *method;* and this is far from identical with a metaphysical theory of the ideal State. A method does not begin to exist until there is a problem to which it can be applied. Detailed development of the theory of parliamentary democracy is only valuable or even desirable as a moment in the critical or comparative analysis of actual political institutions with a view to their improvement. To set up a theoretical model as if it had a kind of universal applicability would be a most dangerous error, the folly of which ought by this time to be apparent to everybody. The reason for this limitation can be seen by considering the difficulty of applying even the very general principles that I have already stated. Even the existence of a 'right of free speech' presupposes that a measure of concrete agreement actually exists; there are always laws against 'sedition' that express this limitation. The universal acceptance of a method of making social decisions (through an elected body of representatives, for example) presupposes much more; for it requires either that there be no absolute or 'religious' conflicts of principle, or that these conflicts be so 'other-worldly,' so theoretical, that they can be treated as neutral—that is to say they never enter the domain of practical politics. Many of the most pressing political problems in the world involve communities where these requirements are not met. In India, for example, during the earlier years of this century, the British administration systematically destroyed the possibility of a unified democratic community by playing on religious differences, with the object of making its own continued presence essential for arbitration. India, as the event has shown, was large enough to divide, though not without tragedy and bitter hardship. But in many cases this simple recognition of the division as a fact is not practicable; and in such cases the existence of a neutral body as a court of appeal would seem to be the only way of preventing the complete corruption of the community by tyranny of one kind or another.

I have emphasized that in politics the means are more important than the ends. What I am now pointing out is that this statement must not be interpreted abstractly. What it asserts is precisely that it is no use considering ends-in-themselves apart from available means. But equally it is no use considering a means-in-itself. For the most part there is no point in uttering such an empty platitude, because no one supposes consciously that means exist 'in themselves.' But when great weight is laid on the moral importance of the means there is a danger that this may be forgotten, not because a means ever exists apart from some end, but because some means is in fact a means to *our* end, and this means can at the same time be made to appear abstractly legitimate. Thus majority groups are quick to emphasize how 'democratic' their position is; and the resulting sense of their own righteousness is apt to make them all the more tyrannical. We must remember that the transcendental Ego is always *both* an ideal *and* a reality. It cannot play either role unless it plays both. The guiding end which can never be neglected in political action is the preservation and development of the sense of community. The political problem is peculiarly a problem of *means* only because this *end* must in actual practice assume the form of an institutional *method* of resolving the conflicts which arise in the life of the community. Democratic institutions are 'ideal' for this purpose because wherever a solution arrived at by democratic process is acceptable the real unity of the community is explicitly demonstrated in the process. But the unity is not complete and perfect in any community, and unintelligent insistence on 'democratic process' may simply intensify existing disunities, when the tensions of the actual situation bring them to the surface. Concretely the problem is to find a method of making political decisions which invokes the unity against the disunities. If it is not straining the accepted use of the word too much to call *this* the proper definition of 'democracy,' then we must say that the ultimate essence of democracy is not that the majority should rule —which is simply a practical limitation, or what is called metaphorically a 'necessary evil'—but that the rights of the minority should be respected, i.e. that their conception of the ideal community should not be so far violated as to become incapable of realization.

The application of this criterion to a particular case is still far from easy partly because of the difficulty of acquiring adequate understanding of the empirical facts in a concrete situation, and partly because "man lives in the future," so that political decision always involves an element of adventure, of creative guesswork. Take for example the present situation in Cyprus. Here the community involved is too small to divide and perhaps even too small to be viable as an autonomous unit. Partition is therefore not feasible, and the path of independence, which is in prospect, will not be an easy one. The Greek Cypriot majority undoubtedly desired union with the mother country; but the Turkish minority has the best of historical reasons for fearing this since their very existence is proof of the sins of their fathers. There is no obvious solution to this problem in terms of 'democratic process.' The Turkish minority might have been handed over to the tender mercies of the Greek government; and perhaps in a generation or two they would have found that there was no foundation for their fear except a guilty conscience. The Greek government would no doubt have been willing to guarantee their rights. But the past record of national states in such situations is not good. The solution arrived at, whereby certain rights are reserved to the Turkish minority, including a kind of parliamentary veto power, and the British, Greek, and Turkish governments have the right of intervention as guarantors, does provide effective safeguards against communal tyranny. But in view of the continuing pressure for *Enosis,* the most hopeful expedient from the point of view of the philosophy of community here expounded would have been some sort of union with Greece *together* with constitutional safeguards and international supervision as proposed in the present plan.[24]

To end this lengthy investigation of Gentile's social philosophy with these desultory and amateurish remarks about 'plural communities' may seem strange. But there is a purpose to it, for if they make any sense at all these comments have important consequences

---

[24] When this discussion of the Cyprus situation was originally written, early in 1958, I assumed that the Greek majority would not compromise over their demand for *Enosis.* In 1959, before the manuscript went to the printer, my suggestions were overtaken by events and had to be rephrased as contrary-to-fact conditionals. But now as I read the proofs in June 1960, the path of independence is indeed far from easy. The emergence of the new republic which should have occurred no later than this February has been postponed temporarily thanks to disagreements about the implementation of the Zurich agreements. Only the acceptance of supervision and arbitration involved in the very making of those agreements now gives some grounds for hope that the spirit of compromise will not again be submerged in communal faction. If the deadlock long continues the suggestions here made may regain their practical relevance.

in several directions. To begin with they offer a way of dealing with one of the surds in Gentile's theory—the problem of an oppressed minority. He wrote from Trieste in 1919 a most graphic and enthusiastic account of the way in which Italian schools in Trieste had resisted the attempts of the Austrian authorities to turn them into organs of Austrian 'patriotism.' [25] But then a few years later he actively supported the policy of 'Italianizing' the predominantly Austrian-speaking Tyrol. Secondly, they give a hint of how to deal with the problem of securing self-determination without endless fragmentation, the problem which became acute when Wilson carried the democratic nationalism of the nineteenth century to its logical conclusion. These two problems are really one, for it was the atomism of the principle of 'national self-determination' that produced the national egoism of which Fascism was one of the most virulent symptoms.

Since the conception of 'transcendental society' avoids this atomism it contains an implicit solution of the gravest political problem of the present moment. In a world in which the autonomy of the sovereign nation seemed to be an obvious reality, the existence of minorities, groups too small to enjoy this autonomy, was an incidental problem, one of those casual evils from which life is never completely free. But in a world where all the nations have achieved their coveted sovereignty, and have uneasily begun to recognize that the autonomy was a myth, that they are really members one of another and must act in concert, the problem of minorities becomes the crucial and typical form of their dilemma. They can see that the conception of democratic self-determination needs to be revised in the direction of cooperation in an international order; but at the same time the cry of their own 'unredeemed' compatriots has a paramount urgency and priority. That is why plans for a world government or a unified system of international law remain mere utopian ideals, which in practice are more apt to hinder than to help the cause of peace because they presuppose the acceptance of conditions which *all* parties feel bound to reject. The international organization and system of law which the planners envisage must be created piecemeal by resolving the contradictions or conflicts of national sovereignty as they arise; the means for this resolution is to be found in the gradual extension of a system of interna-

---

[25] B.539.

tional guarantee and supervision of the rights of minorities, troubled frontiers, etc. In this way nothing valuable in the tradition and experience of 'national sovereignty' will be sacrificed, for the whole system of international supervision will be directed toward protecting this tradition and experience.

The problem of the 'one and the many' has generally been central in idealist metaphysics; in the political theory of the Hegelian tradition it arose in its most exacerbated form. But the 'method of absolute immanence' shows how it can be resolved. There is no need to imagine an ideal state or a universal kingdom of perpetual peace either here or elsewhere. We need merely a conception of international order applicable to immediate problems; this we already have and it has been gathering effective force for quite a long time. It began when nations first cooperated to bring criminals to justice, to eliminate piracy on the high seas, and so forth.

I realize that, in trying to apply the theory of transcendental society at the level of international politics in a world whose problems Gentile never foresaw, I have completely lost contact with anything that he himself wrote. My aim has been to discover how the initial community required for the transcendental dialogue can be established without recourse to violence. Once a community is well enough established to have put violence behind it, the direct application of the method of immanence will generate all of the 'universal human rights' in whatever form is most appropriate for that community. A citizen must have the right to express his opinion, to challenge received ideas and express new ones; he must have the right to form associations with others of like opinion in order to make his ideas count in the public world, etc. Of course these rights carry heavy moral responsibilities; but they are rights which the community must respect and guarantee because they are its own actual substance. To the extent to which they are abridged the community itself ceases to exist; this is the truth hidden in the dangerously ambiguous thesis that "maximum liberty coincides with maximum force of the State."

Neither of the major traditions of political thought in the West has succeeded hitherto in producing a theory of human society which is adequate to explain the actual experience of political democracy at its best. On the one hand the classical school of liberal individualism has tended to treat government as an evil. The moral implications of this speculative hypothesis, which is a denial of the possibility of any community between individuals except on the basis of the crudest material interest, seem to me to be so abhorrent that I am at a loss to understand how so many intelligent and public-spirited men could have accepted it. The salvation of this pluralistic approach has lain in its strong empirical bias. An instinctive respect for the actual facts of social experience kept the more influential representatives of this tradition from perceiving the logical consequences of some of their fundamental theories. But this does not alter the fact that their speculative formulations are full of disastrous ambiguities. Mill's attempt to distinguish 'private' and 'public' realms of activity, for example, is a failure, as anyone would discover who tried to apply it literally in the complex structure of modern society.

On the other hand the organic theory of society which stems from Rousseau's theory of the General Will has always been vitiated by a failure to understand the nature of individual freedom. According to this tradition, freedom, like truth, was to be found only in the whole. Thus, government was seen as the source of the good, and freedom was no more than the civil duty of obedience, which the citizen might, at need, be forced to perform. A freedom to which men can be compelled is not that moral freedom of the spirit to which men have always aspired. The salvation of this tradition —in the work of men like Royce, Bosanquet, and Hegel himself— has lain in the religious convictions out of which it arose. But here too the ambiguities always remain; and the history of Fascism and Communism clearly shows how dangerous they can be.

The difficulties of both traditions arise from the fact that one of the two terms 'individual' and 'society' has to be taken as a basic presupposition. The theory of individual personality as an internal society makes it unnecessary to presuppose either term, and thus gets rid of the egoistic pluralism which is the bane of one side, and the immoral exaltation of power which is the bane of the other. The fact that Gentile was misguided enough to associate himself and his philosophy with a political movement that inclined strongly to this second form of barbarism should not blind us to his speculative achievement. It would be not merely an injustice to him but a tragic loss for us if a man whose whole life was devoted to the ideal of education as voluntary self-formation were remembered only for an unfortunate remark about the educational use of the blackjack.

BIBLIOGRAPHICAL INDEX

to the Writings of Gentile Referred to in This Book

An edition of Gentile's *Complete Works* in fifty-five volumes has been planned by the *Fondazione Gentile*, and twenty-one volumes have now been published. But this index is based for the most part on V. A. Bellezza's *Bibliografia degli scritti di Giovanni Gentile (Giovanni Gentile: La vita e il pensiero*, Vol. III), Florence, Sansoni, 1950. Bellezza's numeration has been employed for references throughout the book. The few additions, corrections, and notes added by the present writer are indicated by the use of brackets. All relevant items have been listed, including a few to which no explicit reference has been made. I have indicated which among these I have failed to trace and examine.

1897

11. "Una critica del materialismo storico," *Studi storici*, VI, 1897; reprinted in 1157, pp. 149–96 [and now in *Complete Works*, XXVIII, 11–58] (see also 30).
    (pp. 45–48, 49, 51)

14. Review of B. CROCE: *Il concetto della storia nelle sue relazioni col concetto dell'arte, Studi storici*, VI, 1897; reprinted in 615, pp. 379–93.
    (pp. 45, 78)

1898

21. *Rosmini e Gioberti*, Pisa, Nistri, 1899, xii + 318 pp. [2nd ed. revised, Florence, Sansoni, 1955, xix + 327 pp.; this is now Vol. XXV of the *Complete Works*].
    (p. 7)

1899

30. *La filosofia di Marx*, Pisa, Spoerri, 1899, v + 161 pp.; reprinted in 1157, pp. 141–303 [3rd ed., Florence, Sansoni, 1955, 169 pp.; this is now Vol. XXVIII of the *Complete Works*].
    (pp. 45–46n, 47, 48–51, 56, 78)

31. "Il concetto della storia," *Studi storici,* VIII, 1899; reprinted in 615, pp. 1–60.
(pp. 45, 78)

1900

49. B. SPAVENTA: *Scritti filosofici . . . con un discorso sulla vita e sulle opere dell'autore da G. Gentile . . .* , Naples, Morano, 1900, clii + 408 pp. (see also 775).
(pp. 13–14, 40, 42)

1901

59. "Il concetto scientifico della pedagogia," *Rendiconti Accad. Lincei,* IX, 1901; reprinted in 1056, pp. 1–47.
(pp. 51–52)

1902

68. "Filosofia ed empirismo," *Rivista di filosofia, pedagogia e scienze affini,* Bologna, 1902; reprinted in 618, pp. 45–67.
(p. 40n)

70. "L'unità della scuola media e la libertà degli studi," *Rivista filosofica,* fascs. 2–3, 1902; reprinted in 813, pp. 9–54 [page reference misprinted in Bellezza].
(pp. 53–54, 56, 57, 61–62, 78n, 108, 242n)

74. Review of F. JAJA: *Per la giovane madre, Rivista di filosofia . . .* , Bologna, 1902, pp. 5–7.
(p. 52n)

1903

76. *La rinascita dell'idealismo,* Naples, Tip. della R. Università, 1903, 23 pp.; reprinted in 618, pp. 1–25.
(p. 40)

1904

98. B. SPAVENTA: *Principi di etica a cura di G. Gentile,* Naples, Pierro, 1904, xxiii + 186 pp.; Preface reprinted in 618, pp. 141–58 [page reference misprinted in Bellezza].
(pp. 40–44, 116, 118)

105. Review of J. BAILLIE: *The Origin and Significance of Hegel's Logic, La critica,* II, 1904; reprinted in 701 [and now in *Complete Works,* XXVII, 69–96].
(p. 43n)

115. Review of A. PIAZZI: *La scuola media e le classi dirigenti, La critica,* II, 1904; reprinted in 813, pp. 55–68.
(pp. 57, 58)

1905

121. "Nuove minacce alla libertà e alla filosofia nell'insegnamento liceale," *Rivista d'Italia,* April 1905; reprinted in 1056 [pp. 225–33].
(p. 56)

1906

143. "La riforma della scuola media," *Rivista d'Italia,* January 1906; reprinted in 813, pp. 71–115.
(pp. 54, 55, 60)

1907

154. *Per la scuola primaria di Stato,* Palermo, Sandron, 1907, 55 pp.; reprinted in 1056, pp. 169–201.
(pp. 53, 60n, 61, 62–63n, 64–65, 93)

158. "Il concetto dell'educazione e la possibilità di una distinzione scientifica tra pedagogia e filosofia dello spirito," *Cultura filosofica,* March 1907; reprinted with a postscript of 1908 in 1056 [pp. 49–63].
(pp. 52, 108–9)

159 and 160. "La preparazione degl'insegnanti medi I–II," *Nuovi doveri,* April and May 1907; reprinted in 813, pp. 194–231.
(p. 71)

161. "Istituti o cattedre," *Nuovi doveri,* June 1907; reprinted in 813, pp. 116–32.
(p. 61n)

163 (= 187). "Scuola laica," *Nuovi doveri,* September–October 1907; reprinted in 1056 [pp. 93–137] (see also 165, 183).
(pp. 58, 67–74)

165. "Discorso sul tema 'Scuola laica,'" *Nuovi doveri,* October–November 1907; reprinted in 1056 [pp. 137–53].
(pp. 71–72)

176. "Ancora del prof. De Sarlo e della sua scuola," *La critica,* V, 1907; reprinted in 618, pp. 238–41.
(p. 66n)

1908

183. *Scuola e filosofia,* Palermo, Sandron, 1908, x + 388 pp.; reprinted partly in 813 and partly in 1056.
(pp. 62, 74; for Gentile's Epilogue to "Scuola laica," first printed in 183, see pp. 74–76, 95)

187. See 163.

189. "Per la dignità dell'insegnamento superiore, l'on. Rava combattuto con le armi . . . dell'on. Rava," *Nuovi doveri,* January 1908, pp. 17–20.
(p. 97)

191. "La preparazione degli insegnanti medi: La Scuola Normale Universitaria di Pisa" in 183; reprinted in 813, pp. 232–96.
(p. 97n)

192. "Per l'insegnamento dell'italiano," *Nuovi doveri,* July–August 1908, pp. 227–28.
(p. 54n)

1909

216. "Questioni pedagogiche. Il sofisma del doppio fatto," *La voce,* 1909, n23; reprinted in 1056 [pp. 341–48].
(pp. 57n, 64)

217. "Dopo il Congresso. Esigenze ideali e tattica nella riforma scolastica," *La voce* and *Nuovi doveri,* October 1909; reprinted in 813, pp. 133–42.
(pp. 55, 156, 211n)

1911

252. B. SPAVENTA: *La politica dei Gesuiti nel sec. XVI e nel XIX, a cura di G. Gentile,* Milan-Rome, Albrighi e Segati, 1911, 314 pp.; Gentile's Introduction is reprinted in 898, pp. 173–96.
(p. 74)

270. Review of J. ROYCE: *La filosofia della fedeltà, La critica,* IX, 1911, 297–99.
(p. 63n)

1912

275. "Veritas filia temporis," in *Scritti in onore di R. Renier,* Turin, Bocca, 1912; reprinted in 1223, pp. 333–55 [page reference misprinted in Bellezza].
(p. 106n)

277. "L'atto del pensare come atto puro," *Annuario della Biblioteca filosofica di Palermo,* I, 1912; reprinted in 701 [and now in *Complete Works,* XXVII, 183–95].
(p. 39)

1913

290. *La riforma della dialettica hegeliana,* Messina, Principato, 1913, viii + 306 pp. See 701.

292. *Sommario di pedagogia come scienza filosofica,* Vol. I: *Pedagogia generale,* Bari, Laterza, 1913, xi + 272 pp. See 1251.

296. "Intorno all'idealismo attuale. Ricordi e confessioni," *La voce,* 1913, n50; reprinted in 898, pp. 11–35.
(pp. 7, 23, 52n, 63)

297. "Idealismo e misticismo," *Ann. d. Bibl. fil. di Palermo,* III, 1913; reprinted in 1279, pp. 243–65. English translation in 660, pp. 253–77.
(pp. 9, 19)

1914

305. *Sommario di pedagogia come scienza filosofica,* Vol. II: *Didattica,* Bari, Laterza, 1914, 246 pp. See 1252.

306. *La filosofia della guerra,* Palermo, Tip. Ergon, 1914, 31 pp.; reprinted in 497, pp. 1–24.
(pp. 103–4, 110, 129, 131–32, 148n, 233, 286)

308. A. ROSMINI: *Il principio della morale, a cura di G. Gentile,* Bari,

Laterza, 1914, vii + 258 pp.; Gentile's concluding remarks are reprinted in 1157, pp. 3–33.
(pp. 98–101)

1915

333. "Disciplina nazionale" (1 January 1915 in unidentified newspaper); reprinted in 497, pp. 25–31.
(p. 131)

334. "Proclama ai cittadini di Pisa" (26 March 1915 for the *Comitato Pisano di preparazione e mobilitazione civile*); reprinted in 497, pp. 32–34.
(p. 132)

341. Review of G. A. FICHTE: *Discorsi alla nazione tedesca, La critica*, XIII, 1915; reprinted in 497, pp. 156–61.
(p. 132n)

1916

350. *Teoria generale dello spirito come atto puro*, Pisa, Mariotti, 1916, 237 pp. See 1279. For the English translation see 660.

354. *I fondamenti della filosofia del diritto*, Pisa, Mariotti, 1916, 76 pp.; reprinted in 1157, pp. 3–139.
(pp. 63n, 98, 101–3, 105–7, 110, 111–22, 301)

361. Review of V. DELBOS: *L'esprit philosophique de l'Allemagne et la pensée francaise, La critica*, XIV, 1916; reprinted in 497, pp. 162–74.
(p. 132)

372. Review of M. DE WULF: *Guerre et philosophie, La critica*, XIV, 1916; reprinted in 497, pp. 174–75.

1917

375. *Sistema di logica come teoria del conoscere*, Vol. I, Pisa, Spoerri, 1917, 284 pp. See 1224.

381. "Cultura e letteratura nazionale," *Resto del Carlino* (Bologna), 22 February 1917; reprinted in 497, pp. 36–41.
(p. 134n)

382. "Critica di luoghi comuni. Nazione e nazionalismo," *Resto del Carlino*, 2 March 1917; reprinted in 497, pp. 48–52.
(pp. 127, 133)

384. "Esame di coscienza," *Resto del Carlino*, 13 December 1917; reprinted in 497, pp. 60–64.
(pp. 135, 148n, 248)

386. "Proclama ai cittadini di Pisa" (6 November 1917 for the *Comitato Pisano di preparazione e mobilitazione civile*); reprinted in 497, pp. 34–35.
(p. 135)

401. Review of E. VON TREITSCHKE: *La Francia dal primo impero al 1871, La critica*, XV, 1917; reprinted in 497, pp. 176–90.

1918

408. "Il significato della vittoria," *Rassegna italiana*, II, 15 November 1918; reprinted in 561, pp. 3–25.
(pp. 133, 144, 147)

409. "Politica e filosofia," *Politica*, I, December 1918; reprinted in 561, pp. 188–216.
(pp. 153n, 254, 288)

410. "Intendere per amare o amare per intendere? (Frammento di una gnoseologia dell'amore)," *Nuovo convito* (Rome), September 1918; reprinted in 1179, pp. 11–13 (but not in 660).

411. "La Società delle Nazioni," Agenzia Alessandro Volta, *anno* II, Bulletin 649, 5 February 1918 [2 pp.].
(pp. 140, 142)

413. "La riforma fondamentale della scuola," *Messaggero della domenica* (Rome), 20 and 27 August 1918; reprinted in 562, pp. 63–84.
(pp. 155, 156)

415. "Un prestito della vittoria per la scuola," *Messaggero della domenica*, 10 November 1918; reprinted in 561, pp. 31–36.

416. "L'unità della cultura," *Volontà* (Vicenza), I, September 1918; reprinted in 937, pp. 1–15.
(pp. 128–29)

Articles in *Resto del Carlino* (Bologna) during 1918

418. "La guerra del Papa," 3 January; reprinted in 497, pp. 124–28.
(pp. 138, 140)

419. "Il grande equivoco," 11 January; reprinted in 497, pp. 129–33.
(p. 138)

420. "Responsabilità" (unsigned), 19 January; reprinted in 497, pp. 69–73.
(p. 136)

421. "Il gran colpevole" (unsigned leader), 21 January; reprinted in 497, pp. 74–78.
(p. 136)

422. "La colpa comune," 25 January; reprinted in 497, pp. 79–83.
(p. 135)

423. "Chiarezza e lealtà," 30 January; reprinted in 497, pp. 134–37.
(p. 138)

424. "Il Sessantasei," 7 February; reprinted in 497, pp. 191–94.
(p. 135n)

426. "Il Papa e il patto di Londra" (unsigned leader), 21 February; reprinted in 497, pp. 142–45.
(p. 137)

427. "Il socialista nell'imbarazzo" (unsigned), 28 February; reprinted in 497, pp. 237–41.
(p. 138)

428. "Resistere," 10 March; reprinted in 497, pp. 95–99.
(p. 136)

429. "La crisi del marxismo" (unsigned leader), 14 March; reprinted in 497, pp. 242–46.
(p. 138)

430. "Le due Italie," 20 March; reprinted in 497, pp. 100–104.
(p. 137)

431. "Il nemico interno" (unsigned leader), 24 March; reprinted in 497, pp. 105–9.
(p. 137)

432. "La politica di Treitschke," 10 April; reprinted in 497, pp. 203–6.
(p. 133)

433. "Morale e politica," 19 April; reprinted in 497, pp. 207–12.
(p. 133)

434. "I pessimisti," 29 April; reprinted in 497, pp. 110–14.
(p. 137)

435. "Esiste una scuola italiana? Lettera aperta a S. E. Berenini," 4 May; reprinted in 562, pp. 7–21.
(p. 155)

437. "La sacra data," 24 May; reprinted in 497, pp. 115–19.
(pp. 134n, 148n)

439. "L'invincibile," 3 July; reprinted in 497, pp. 315–18.
(p. 139)

441. "La rivolta ideale," 17 July (also L'Idea nazionale, 18 July); reprinted in 497, pp. 309–14.
(p. 139n)

443. "L'equilibrio dei Cattolici," 25 August; reprinted in 497, pp. 146–49.
(p. 137n)

444. "Il problema adriatico da Tommaseo a Cavour" (book review), 27 August; reprinted in 497, pp. 323–29.
(p. 141n)

447. "XX settembre," 20 September; reprinted in 497, pp. 319–22.

448. "La giustizia in cammino" (unsigned), 21 September; reprinted in 497, pp. 342–45.
(p. 140)

449. "Fatalità" (unsigned), 27 September; reprinted in 497, pp. 346–50.
(p. 140)

450. "Equivoci e profezie," 2 October; reprinted (but misdated) in 497, pp. 330–35.
(p. 141)

451. "Prova suprema" (unsigned leader), 7 October; reprinted in 497, pp. 351–55.
(p. 140)

452. "Ricordi e ricorsi," 11 October; reprinted in 497, pp. 356–60.

454. "Disciplina" (unsigned), 16 October; reprinted in 497, pp. 361–65.
(p. 140)

455. "Forche caudine" (unsigned), 26 October; reprinted in 497, pp. 366–70.
(p. 144n)

456. "Epilogo," 11 November; reprinted in 561, pp. 26–30.
(p. 147)

457. "Lo spettro bolscevico," 19 November; reprinted in 561, pp. 37–42.
(p. 150n)

458. "Ordine," 1 December; reprinted in 561, pp. 42–48.
(p. 149)

459. "Ammonimenti" (unsigned leader), 2 December; reprinted in 561, pp. 49–53.

460. "La punizione del Kaiser," 11 December, p. 1.
(pp. 142, 143, 144, 145–46, 147n)

461. "Stato e categorie" (unsigned leader), 24 December; reprinted in 561, pp. 95–100.
(pp. 139, 179n, 180)

Articles in *Nuovo giornale* (Florence) during 1918

462. "Chiarimenti," 20 January; reprinted in 497, pp. 138–41.
(p. 137n)

463. "Vita e morale militare" (book review), 29 January; reprinted in 497, pp. 231–36.

464. "L'esame nazionale," 10 February; reprinted in 497, pp. 84–88.

465. "Per la futura scuola del popolo" (unsigned), 22 February; reprinted in 497, pp. 269–74.
(p. 155)

466. "I due Stati," 26 February; reprinted in 497, pp. 150–55.

467. "L'educazione nazionale," 3 March; reprinted in 497, pp. 263–68.
(p. 139)

468. "Le contraddizioni del Treitschke," 19 March; reprinted in 497, pp. 195–203.
(p. 133)

470. "Il progetto Berenini," 24 April; reprinted in 497, pp. 275–81.
(p. 155)

471. "Lo specialismo della cultura," 30 April; reprinted in 497, pp. 282–87.

472. "Antinomie socialiste" (unsigned), 16 May; reprinted in 497, pp. 247–52.
(p. 138)

474. "Tra Hegel e Lenin," 29 May; reprinted in 497, pp. 213–18.
(pp. 127, 133)

475. "La ripresa parlamentare. A lumi spenti" (unsigned), 13 June; reprinted in 497, pp. 120–23.
(p. 139)

476. "Patto nuovo" (unsigned), 28 June; reprinted in 497, pp. 258–62.
(p. 139n)

480. "I luoghi comuni della guerra. Idealismo e Kultur," 31 July; reprinted in 497, pp. 219–23.
(p. 133)

481. "Il regime della borghesia produttiva" (book review), 17 August; reprinted in 497, pp. 53–59.
(pp. 134, 168)

484. "Edificare la patria," 17 September; reprinted in 497, pp. 89–94.

485. "La democrazia e la scuola," 24 September; reprinted in 497, pp. 288–93.

487. "La Germania alla conquista della Russia" (book review), 29 October; reprinted in 497, pp. 336–41.

488. "L'alibi dei popoli," 17 December. [This item has eluded me.]

489. "Natale," 25 December; reprinted in 561, pp. 54–62.

1919

497. *Guerra e fede. Frammenti politici*, Naples, Ricciardi, 1919, xi + 381 pp. [This will become Vol. XLIII of the *Complete Works*.]
(pp. 103–4, 127, 129, 131–44, 148n, 155, 168, 233, 248, 249)

498. *Il problema scolastico del dopoguerra*, Naples, Ricciardi, 1919, viii + 121 pp. See 562.
(p. 155)

504. "L'idea monarchica," *Rassegna italiana*, II, March 1919; reprinted in 561, pp. 147–61.
(pp. 94n, 110n, 122–25)

505. "Mazzini," *Politica*, I, January 1919; reprinted in 1280, pp. 1–32.
(pp. 141, 170)

506. "Ciò che è vivo di Mazzini," *Politica*, I, March 1919; reprinted in 1280, pp. 33–63.
(pp. 141, 170)

508. "La crisi morale," *Politica*, III, November 1919; reprinted in 561, pp. 69–91.
(pp. 147–49)

512. "Scuola di stato e libertà d'insegnamento," *Messaggero della domenica*, 15 June 1919; reprinted in 562, pp. 100–108.
(p. 158)

515. "La Società delle Nazioni," *L'Idea nazionale*, 26 January 1919; reprinted in 497, pp. 371–77.
(pp. 142–43)

Articles in *Resto del Carlino* (Bologna) during 1919

516. "Fede e volontà," 6 January, p. 1.
(pp. 140, 143)

517. "Abuso di parole," 13 January; reprinted in 561, pp. 101–6.
(p. 141)

518. "Le due democrazie," 25 January; reprinted in 561, pp. 107–13.
(p. 123n)

519. "L'Italia dei combattenti," 7 February, p. 1.
(p. 152)

520. "Il buon sangue della Nazione," 11 February, p. 1.
(p. 152)

521. "Ognuno al suo posto," 6 March; reprinted in 561, pp. 175–79.
(p. 150)

522. "Confessioni di un liberale," 23 March; reprinted in 561, pp. 169–75.
[Bellezza passes over the first article in this polemic with M. Missiroli
in silence; see 561, pp. 162–69, where the date, 28 February 1913
(i.e. 1919), is given.]
(p. 150)

524. "Il pericolo," 6 April; reprinted in 561, pp. 180–87.
(p. 150)

525. "Wilson o Lenin," 16 April, p. 1.
(pp. 141, 144n, 147n)

526. "Scuola e insegnanti," 20 May; reprinted in 562, pp. 94–100.
(p. 160)

527. "XXIV maggio," 24 May, p. 1.
(pp. 147, 148, 148n)

528. "Lo Stato e gl'impiegati," 5 June, p. 1.
(p. 149)

529. "Lo sciopero dei maestri," 11 June, p. 1.
(pp. 152n, 156)

530. "I paradossi della giustizia," 23 June, p. 1.
(pp. 142n, 144n, 145–46)

531. "La politica dei combattenti," 28 June, p. 1.
(p. 152)

532. "Parole di fede," 13 July, p. 1.
(pp. 147, 150n, 152)

533. "Ricostruzione," 23 July, p. 1.
(pp. 148, 152n)

534. "La sensazione della realtà," 29 July, p. 3.
(pp. 147, 148n, 149)

535. "La questione romana," 23 August; reprinted in 561, pp. 134–40.
(p. 150)

536. "L'esempio del governo," 24 August; reprinted in 561, pp. 63–68.
(p. 150)

1921

615. *Frammenti di estetica e letteratura*, Lanciano, Carabba, 1921, 406 pp.
    (p. 45)

618. *Saggi critici, serie prima*, Naples, Ricciardi, 1921, viii + 257 pp.
    (pp. 40–44, 66n)

620 bis. *Lezioni di pedagogia, parte Iª: Psicologia dell'infanzia. Raccolte da* v. BATTISTELLI. *Anno accademico 1921–1922* [not 1920–21 as in Bellezza], Rome, Libreria della Sapienza di A. Sampaolesi, 229 pp. [This is not the 1st ed. of *Preliminari allo studio del fanciullo* as stated in Bellezza but a *continuation* of the lectures (see 655) on which that work was based.]

625. "Il problema della scuola," *La cultura*, I, 15 November 1921; reprinted in 813, pp. 391–401.
    (pp. 151n, 159)

629. "Esami di Stato," *La tribuna*, 8 February 1921; reprinted in 813, pp. 386–91.
    (p. 159n)

1922

655 and 704. "Per lo studio dell'infanzia. Appunti di scuola," *Levana*, I and II, 1922–23 [the lectures of 1920–21 to which 620 bis are sequel]. See 1225.

656. *Lezioni di pedagogia, parte IIª: La pedagogia di G. B. Vico. Anno accademico 1921–1922*, Rome, Libreria della Sapienza di A. Sampaolesi, 90 pp.
    (p. 7n)

658. *Lavoro e cultura* (lecture, 15 January), Rome, Tip. F. Centenari, 1922, 19 pp.; reprinted in 937, pp. 16–37.
    (pp. 129, 180, 275, 276)

659. *The Reform of Education*, tr. by D. BIGONGIARI, with an introduction by B. CROCE, New York, Harcourt, 1922 [and London, Ernest Benn, 1923], xi + 250 pp. (see also 1128).
    (pp. 21, 87n, 89n, 221)

660. *The Theory of Mind as Pure Act*, tr. from the 3rd ed. with an introduction by H. WILDON CARR, London, Macmillan, 1922, xxviii + 280 pp. See 1279.

664. "Educazione e libertà" (lecture, 11 May), *Levana*, I, 1922; reprinted in 1056, pp. 403–16.

668. "Discorso all'inaugurazione della sessione del Consiglio superiore della pubblica istruzione, il 27 nov. 1922," *L'Educazione nazionale*, IV, December 1922; reprinted in 1057, pp. 11–17.
    (pp. 76n, 218)

673. "Benedetto XV," *L'Epoca*, 23 January, and *Resto del Carlino*, 24 January, 1922 [very brief obituary comment].
    (p. 150)

736. "Lo spirito informatore della riforma" (address to the *Consilio superiore della pubblica istruzione,* 15 November 1923), *Levana,* II, 1923, 413–38, and elsewhere; reprinted in 1057, pp. 189–227.

755. "Dichiarazioni sul bilancio" (senate speech, 12 June 1923); reprinted in 1057, pp. 145–56.
(p. 160n)

768. "Appunti per la storia della cultura in Italia nella seconda metà del sec. XIX. V. La cultura piemontese: 5°. Un ritratto della cultura piemontese del decennio" [1850–60], *La critica,* XXI, 1922, 10–27 [Gentile's last contribution to *La critica*].
(p. 221)

1924

775. *Bertrando Spaventa,* Florence, Vallecchi, n.d., 215 pp. [New edition of the "Discorso" in 49 above. Bellezza quotes the following passage from the Preface: "I republish it newly revised [*con nuove cure*] and with some additions, but without changing a line of what I said or knew how to say formerly." Unfortunately this assurance cannot be relied upon. Comparison of p. cxi in 49 with p. 131 of this edition shows a substantial alteration in the judgment passed on A. Vera for example. This will become Vol. XXIX of the *Complete Works.*]
(p. 42)

776. *Il fascismo al governo della scuola,* Palermo, Sandron, 1924, 331 pp. See 1057.

778. *Il fascismo e la Sicilia* (speech at Palermo, 31 March 1924), Rome, De Alberti, 1924, 21 pp.; reprinted in 818, pp. 41–63.
(pp. 171, 174–76)

783. *Riforme costituzionali e fascismo,* Rome, Tip. de "L'Idea nazionale," 1924, 32 pp.; reprinted in 818, pp. 199–218.
(pp. 174, 179)

785. F. FIORENTINO: *Lo Stato moderno e le polemiche liberali, con pref. di G. Gentile,* Rome, De Alberti, 1924, 73 pp.; Preface reprinted in 818, pp. 125–35.
(pp. 169, 171, 174n)

789. "L'insegnamento religioso e i programmi della filosofia" (interview), *Corriere italiano,* 17 February 1924; reprinted in 1057, pp. 257–62.
(p. 167)

794. Reply to G. BOTTAI: "Saluto" *L'Idea nazionale,* 12 July 1924; reprinted in 1057, pp. 303–4.
(p. 178)

796. "Le attualità del fascismo" (letter), *La montagna* (Naples), December 1924; reprinted in 818, pp. 139–41.
(p. 172n)

837. "Il contenuto etico del fascismo" (lecture, 8 March 1925), *La Nazione della sera*, 9 March, and elsewhere; reprinted in 818, pp. 9–39.
(pp. 172, 173, 174, 178, 190n, 202, 233n)

838. "Il manifesto degli intellettuali italiani fascisti agli intellettuali di tutte le nazioni," *L'Educazione politica*, III, March 1925, 137–40.
(p. 183)

843. "A lavoro compiuto" (interview), *Il Popolo d'Italia*, 2 July 1925; reprinted in 818, pp. 225–29.
(p. 180)

844. *Relazioni e proposte della Commissione per lo studio delle riforme costituzionali*, Rome, Stabil. poligr. dello Stato, 1925; Gentile's "Relazione" is reprinted in 818, pp. 231–41.
(p. 179)

845. Preface (July 1925) to c. LICITRA: *Dal liberalismo al fascismo*, Rome, De Alberti, 1925; reprinted in 818, pp. 171–77.
(pp. 160n, 168n)

1926

873. "Il maestro della scuola riformata," *Nuova scuola italiana*, 23 May 1926; reprinted in 1057, pp. 377–97.

875. "*L'Enciclopedia italiana* e il fascismo," *L'Educazione politica*, IV, April 1926; reprinted in 937, pp. 110–15.
(p. 186)

877. "L'Accademia d'Italia (relazione e discorso)," (senate, 13 and 16 March 1926); reprinted in 937, pp. 122–40.
(pp. 121n, 184)

883. "Fascismo e idealismo," *L'Educazione politica*, IV, December 1926; reprinted in 937, pp. 67–69.

889. "Avvertimenti attualisti," *Giornale critico della filosofia italiana*, VII, 1926; reprinted in 1075, pp. 249–81 [2nd ed., pp. 226–55].
(p. 280n)

890. Postilla to V. ARANGIO-RUIZ: "L'individuo e lo Stato," *Giornale critico*, VII, 1926, 151–52.
(p. 254n)

1927

898. *Saggi critici, serie seconda*, Florence, Vallecchi, 1927, 218 pp.
(pp. 7, 23, 52n, 63, 74)

912. "La questione romana," *Corriere della sera*, 30 September 1927; reprinted in 937, pp. 182–88.
(p. 198)

912 bis. "Nuovi documenti sulla questione romana," *Corriere della sera*, 16 October 1927; reprinted in 937, pp. 189–95.
(p. 198)

919. "Continuando," *Educazione fascista* [= *L'Educazione politica*], V, January 1927; reprinted in 937, pp. 70–75.

921. "Il problema religioso in Italia" (lecture at the *Università fascista*), *Educazione fascista*, V, January 1927; reprinted in 937, pp. 146–81. (p. 190n)

922. "Stampa fascista e responsabilità di partito," *Educazione fascista*, V, February 1927; reprinted in 937, pp. 116–21. (p. 185)

924. "Il nostro programma," *Educazione fascista*, V, May 1927; reprinted in 937, pp. 82–91. (p. 219)

1928

937. *Fascismo e cultura*, Milan, Treves, 1928, 207 pp. (pp. 121n, 128–29, 180, 181, 183, 184, 185, 186, 198, 218, 219, 275, 276)

940. "I problemi presenti della cultura italiana," *Lo Stato* (Naples), 24–25 January 1928. (p. 184n)

941. "The Philosophic Basis of Fascism," *Foreign Affairs*, VI, January 1928, 290–304 [translation of a condensed version of 948]. (pp. 189, 191)

942. "Brunofobia, ipocrisia e altre cose," *Educazione fascista*, VI, January 1928; reprinted in 937, pp. 196–200. (p. 198n)

943. "La costituzionalizzazione del Gran Consiglio fascista," *Educazione fascista*, VI, February 1928; reprinted in 1104, pp. 72–73n. (p. 202)

944. "Il discorso di Napoli e la gazzara clericale," *Educazione fascista*, VI, February 1928; reprinted in 937, pp. 201–5. (p. 198)

945. "Filologia maligna e ipocrita," *Educazione fascista*, VI, August 1928, 491–94. (p. 222)

946. "La legge del Gran Consiglio," *Educazione fascista*, VI, September 1928; reprinted in 1104. (p. 202)

947. "The Philosophy of the Modern State," *The Spectator* (London), 3 November 1928 [centennial issue supplement], pp. 36–37; Italian text in 1104.

948. "L'essenza del fascismo," in G. POMBA (ed.): *La civiltà fascista*, Turin, U.T.E.T., 1928, pp. 97–118; reprinted in 1104 (see also 941). (pp. 189, 191, 192)

960. "Benedetto Croce," *Giornale critico della filosofia italiana*, IX, 1928, 79–80 [note on the *History of Italy*, 1871–1915].

964. "Filosofia come vita morale e vita morale come filosofia," *Giornale*

critico, IX, 1928, 233–34 [note on an article with the same title by Croce in *La critica*].

965. "Alleanze imprevedute," *Giornale critico*, IX, 1928, 319–20 [note on the article by Croce translated in *Politics and Morals*, London, Allen and Unwin, pp. 125–30].

1929

968. *Il concetto delle arti decorative* (lecture, 20 August 1928), Faenza, Stabil. grafico F. Lega, 1929, 35 pp.
(pp. 276, 280n)

970. "La Conciliazione," *Educazione fascista*, VII, February 1929; reprinted in 1104, pp. 93–97.
(pp. 73n, 199)

972. Inaugural address for the establishment of the Fascist Institute of Culture at Palermo, *L'Ora* (Palermo), 8–9 February 1929.
(p. 184n)

973. "La politica scolastica del Regime," *Corriere della sera*, 20–21 March (also *Educazione fascista*, VII, March) 1929; reprinted in 1057, pp. 439–51.
(p. 194n)

974. "Politica ed economia," *Politica sociale*, I, April–May 1929; reprinted in 1104, pp. 84–86.
(p. 203n)

975. "Fascismo e università," *Politica sociale*, I, July–August 1929, 333–36, and *Educazione fascista*, VII, September 1929, 613–15.
(pp. 184n, 195n, 196n, 197)

976. "Doppia anima," *Politica sociale*, I, December 1929; reprinted in 1104, pp. 86–89.
(pp. 202, 203)

976 bis. "La Scuola Normale Superiore," *Il campano* (*Riv. mensile del G.U.F. di Pisa*), April 1929, pp. 71–72.
(pp. 97n, 186)

977. "Una scuola celebre," *Corriere della sera*, 17 July 1929, pp. 1–2.
(p. 186)

980. "La filosofia e lo Stato," *Giornale critico della filosofia italiana*, X, 1929; reprinted in 1075, pp. 174–88 [2nd ed., pp. 157–70].
(pp. 189, 217n, 229, 241n)

982. "Benedetto Croce stizzito," *Giornale critico*, X, 1929, 79–80.
(p. 222)

1930

989. "Diritto e politica," *Archivio di studi corporativi*, I, 1930; reprinted in 1157, pp. 121–32.
(pp. 98n, 237, 238)

990. This is the Italian edition of 1031 (q.v.).

991. "I problemi attuali della politica scolastica" (senate speech), *Educazione fascista*, VIII, April 1930; reprinted in 1057, pp. 453–77.
(pp. 97n, 195n, 196, 200, 201)

993. "Il sistema corporativo dello Stato," *Politica sociale*, II, May 1930; reprinted in 1104, pp. 90–92.

994. "Questioni quasi personali," *Educazione fascista*, VIII, February 1930, 65–67.
(p. 200n)

995. "Il Partito e lo Stato," *Educazione fascista*, VIII, October 1930, and elsewhere; reprinted in 1104, pp. 79–83.
(p. 202)

997. "La formazione politica della coscienza nazionale," *Educazione fascista*, VIII, December 1930, 675–86.
(p. 197)

998. "Stato e cultura," *Resto del Carlino*, 10 March 1930 [an item that I have not seen; for its importance see A. PIGLIARU, "Fondazione morale della democrazia nel Gentile," *Studi Sassaresi*, 1953].

999. "Lo Stato e la libertà," *Il Popolo di Romagna* (Forli), 3 March 1930.
(p. 205)

1002. Preface to E. BURKE: *Riflessioni sulla rivoluzione francese*, Bologna, Cappelli, 1930 (also *Educazione fascista*, VIII, July 1930).

1931

1012. *La filosofia dell'arte*, Milan, Treves, 1931, viii + 377 pp.; reprinted, Florence, Sansoni, 1937 (1158) [2nd ed., Florence, Sansoni, 1950, viii + 325 pp.; this is now Vol. VIII of the *Complete Works*. Fragments of a complete but unpublished translation by E. CARRITT are given in his anthology *Philosophies of Beauty*, Oxford, Clarendon, 1931, pp. 320–30].
(pp. 108, 217, 223, 224, 276, 297–99, 301)

1013. *Der aktuale Idealismus. Zwei Vorträge*, Tübingen, Mohr, 1931, 40 pp.; Italian text reprinted in 1075, pp. 1–37.
(pp. 7, 10, 26–27, 30, 108)

1017. "Il concetto dello Stato in Hegel," *Nuovi studi di diritto, economia e politica* (Rome), IV, fasc. 6, 1931; reprinted in 1157, pp. 103–20.
(pp. 98n, 239, 240, 242, 243)

1019. "La R. Scuola Normale Superiore di Pisa e la preparazione dei professori per le scuole medie," *Annali dell'istruzione media* (Rome), VII, October–December 1931, 380–85.
(pp. 97n, 186)

1020. "Il carattere morale della previdenza," *Le assicurazioni sociali*, VII, January–February 1931.
(p. 279n)

1021. "Ideologie correnti e critiche facili," *Politica sociale* (Rome), III, March 1931, 167–70.
(pp. 205, 206)

1023. "Risorgimento e fascismo," *Politica sociale*, III, December 1931; reprinted in 1139, 115–20.
(p. 213)

1025. "Buffonate antifasciste," *Educazione fascista*, IX, January 1931, 44–49 [polemic against Croce].

1026. "Il fascismo e gl'intellettuali," *Educazione fascista*, IX, February 1931; reprinted in 1104, pp. 68–71.

1027. "Le dichiarioni del Direttorio e il Concordato," *Educazione fascista*, IX, July 1931; reprinted in 1104, pp. 98–103.
(pp. 199, 218)

1028. "Parole chiare," *Educazione fascista*, IX, October 1931, 963–64. [Strictly speaking the *parole chiare* belong to A. Marpicati—Gentile merely added a comment to his deputy's letter.]
(pp. 187–88n)

[1028 bis. Inaugural address and contributions to the discussions at the Second National Congress of the Fascist Institutes of Culture, November 21–23, *Educazione fascista*, IX, December 1931, 1069–1170 (stenographic record of the congress; the address was also printed separately, Rome, Tip. del Senato, 1932).]
(p. 204n)

1031. "The Italian Encyclopedia," in T. SILLANI (ed.): *What is Fascism and Why?* London, Ernest Benn, 1931, pp. 169–73.
(p. 186)

1032. "Tribolazioni di un enciclopedista. I. Come si distribuisce l'immortalità. II. Come si taglia e si cuce il libro per tutti," *Corriere della sera*, 4 and 11 February 1931, p. 3.
(p. 186n)

1033. "Lo Stato e l'educazione nazionale. La fine dell'A.N.I.F.," *Corriere della sera*, 15 February 1931, p. 1.
(pp. 183n, 202n)

1034. "Ancora delle tribolazioni di un enciclopedista. Critiche e difese dell'*Enciclopedia italiana*," *Corriere della sera*, 27 February 1931, p. 3.
(p. 186n)

1035. "L'Associazione fascista della scuola," *Corriere della sera*, 6 March 1931, p. 1.
(p. 202n)

1036. "Beati possidentes," *Corriere della sera*, 11 March 1931, pp. 1–2.
(p. 204n)

1037. "Coda a una polemica" (see 1034), *Corriere della sera*, 18 March 1931, p. 3.
(p. 186n)

1039. "L'*Enciclopedia italiana*, una lettera del sen. Gentile," *Regime fascista*, 22 March 1931, p. 5.
(p. 186n)

1042. Preface to M. GANDHI: *Autobiografia a cura di* C. F. ANDREWS, Milan, Treves, 1931.
(p. 216n)

1932

1056. *Scritti pedagogici I: Educazione e scuola laica, 4ª edizione riveduta ed accresciuta,* Milan, Treves, 1932, viii + 430 pp. [This will become Vol. XXXIX of the *Complete Works.*]
(pp. 51–53, 56, 57n, 58, 60n, 61, 62–63n, 64–65, 67–76, 93, 96, 108, 115)

1057. *Scritti pedagogici III: La riforma della scuola in Italia, 2ª edizione,* Milan, Treves, 1932, viii + 495 pp. [This will become Vol. XLI of the *Complete Works.*]
(pp. 76n, 81–84, 97n, 160n, 166n, 167, 171, 178, 194n, 196, 200, 201, 218, 276)

1063. Inaugural address for the *Istituto italiano di studi germanici, Educazione fascista,* X, April 1932, 295–98.
(p. 187)

1064. "Nel primo decennale," *Educazione fascista,* X, November 1932, 831–32.
(p. 206)

1067 or 1084. Inaugural address for the new buildings at the *Scuola Normale Superiore di Pisa, La Nazione* (Florence), 11–12 December 1932 (or in *Inaugurazione dei nuovi locali della R. Scuola Normale Superiore,* Pisa, Lischi, 1933, pp. 8–16).
(pp. 97n, 186)

1073. "Individuo e Stato," *Giornale critico della filosofia italiana,* XIII, 1932, 313–15 (or *Educazione fascista,* X, August 1932).
(p. 203n)

1933

1075. *Introduzione alla filosofia,* Milan-Rome, Treves, 1933, 289 pp. [2nd ed., Florence, Sansoni, 1952, viii + 285 pp.; this is now Vol. XXXVI of the *Complete Works*].
(pp. 7, 10, 26–27, 30, 108, 229, 241n, 280n)

1085. "La nuova università italiana e il problema dei giovani," in *Inaugurazione degli studi dell'anno accad. 1933–1934,* Pisa, Lischi, 1933; reprinted in 1139, pp. 341–61.
(pp. 206n, 207)

1087. "Tutti d'accordo no," *Leonardo* (Florence), IV, March 1933, 89–92.
(p. 208n)

1088. "L'Istituto per l'*Enciclopedia italiana*" (interview), *La stampa.* (Turin), 1 July 1933.
(p. 186)

1089 [= 1120]. Inaugural address for the *Istituto per il Medio ed Estremo Oriente, Il Tevere* (Rome), 22 December 1933; reprinted (1120)

as "Proemio" to F. DE FILIPPI: *I viaggiatori italiani in Asia,* Rome, Ist. per il Med. ed Est. Oriente, 1934, pp. 6–8.
(p. 187)

1090. "XXVIII ottobre," *Educazione fascista,* XI, October, 833–36 (and *Corriere della sera,* 27 October), 1933.
(pp. 206n, 213n)

1091, 1092, 1093. "Hegel, Orestano e fascismo," *Educazione fascista,* XI, June, 494–98 (and *Il Tevere,* 2 June); "Una lettera di G. Gentile sul caso Orestano," *Il Tevere,* 15 June; "La questione dello statino," *Il Tevere,* 20 June, 1933; [all reprinted in *Leonardo,* IV, July 1933].
(p. 188n)

1934

1100. *Discorsi di religione, 3ª edizione riveduta,* Florence, Sansoni, 1934, viii + 107 pp. [Now reprinted with additions as Vol. XXXVII of the *Complete Works,* xii + 173 pp.]
(p. 173)

1103. *La donna e il fanciullo. Due conferenze,* Florence, Sansoni, 1934, 57 pp.
(pp. 79n, 84n, 89n)

1104. *Origini e dottrina del fascismo, 3ª edizione* [of 948] *riveduta ed accresciuta,* Rome, I.N.F.C., 1934, 108 pp.
(pp. 73n, 189, 191, 192, 199, 200n, 202, 203, 217n, 218)

1107. "Economia ed etica," *Leonardo,* V, May 1934; reprinted in 1139, pp. 271–93.
(pp. 22, 42, 230, 231, 232, 234)

1115. "Parole preliminari," *Civiltà fascista* (= *Educazione fascista*), I, January 1934, 1–3.
(pp. 207n, 213n)

1117. "L'unità di Mussolini," *Corriere della sera,* 15 May 1934, p. 1.
(pp. 213n, 219)

1120. See 1089.

1935

1128. *La riforma dell'educazione. Discorsi ai maestri di Trieste, 4ª edizione riveduta,* Florence, Sansoni, 1935, viii + 187 pp. (see 557 and English translation 659). [This is now Vol. VII of the *Complete Works.*]
(pp. 2–4, 85–89, 92–94, 96, 108–9, 125–28, 153n, 164, 185)

1132. "Ricordi di Alessandro D'Ancona," *Pan,* III, May 1935; reprinted in 1139, pp. 183–203.
(pp. 97n, 186n)

1936

1139. *Memorie italiane e problemi della filosofia e della vita,* Florence, Sansoni, 1936, 387 pp.
(pp. 22, 42, 97n, 169, 186n, 206n, 207, 213, 230, 231, 232, 234, 245n)

1144. *L'ideale della cultura e l'Italia presente*, Rome, I.N.F.C., 1936, 20 pp.; reprinted in 1139, pp. 363–83.
(pp. 207, 213, 245n)

1145. "Dopo la fondazione dell'impero," *Civiltà fascista*, III, June 1936, 321–34 (also in *L'Italia nel mondo moderno*, Rome, I.N.F.C., 1936, pp. 7–20).
(p. 214)

1149. "L'Istituto Nazionale di Cultura Fascista," *Civiltà fascista*, III, December 1936, 769–74.
(pp. 183n, 216n, 220n)

1152. "La prolusione del sen. Gentile all'inaugurazione dell'anno accademico dell'Istit. Fasc. di cult. di Cremona," *Regime fascista*, 22 December 1936, p. 5.
(p. 215n)

1937

1157. *I fondamenti della filosofia del diritto* (*3ª edizione riveduta ed accresciuta*) *con aggiunti due studi sulla "Filosofia di Marx,"* Florence, Sansoni, 1937, vii + 310 pp. [The *Filosofia del diritto* will become Vol. IV of the *Complete Works*.]
(pp. 45–51, 98–103, 105–7, 111–22, 173n, 195n, 237, 238, 239, 240, 242, 243)

1166. *Dal Comitato nazionale per la storia del Risorgimento al R. Istituto storico italiano per l'età moderna e contemporanea*, Sancasciano Val di Pesa, Tip. Stianti, 1937, 28 pp.
(p. 186)

1167. "L'Italia e l'Oriente," *Nuova antologia*, May 1937, pp. 146–57 (also published separately).
(pp. 187, 216n)

1168. *Dottrina politica del fascismo*, Padua, Cedam, 1937, 22 pp. [I have also seen a fifteen-page offprint bearing no indication of origin.]
(pp. 190n, 216)

1173. "L'Impero nel quadro dei suoi scambi con i paesi dell'Oriente Medio ed Estremo e del continente africano," in T. SILLANI (ed.): *L'Impero A.O.I.*, Rome, Rassegna italiana, 1937, pp. 131–46.
(pp. 213n, 231n)

1175. "La calunnia antiaccademica," *Leonardo*, VIII, January 1937, 31 (signed A. Z.).
(p. 208)

1176. "Vox clamantis," *Leonardo*, VIII, February 1937, 68 (signed A. Z.).
(p. 209)

1177. "L'antica minaccia della scuola unica," *Leonardo*, VIII, March–April 1937, 119–20 (signed A. Z.).
(p. 209)

1178. "Programmi, programmi . . . e il signor de La Palisse," *Leonardo*, VIII, May 1937, 170–71 (signed A. Z.).
(p. 209n)

1179. "La scuola unica e i corrucci del Signor de La Palisse," *Leonardo*, VIII, June 1937, 207 (signed A. Z.).
(p. 210)

1180. "Protesta del signor di La Palisse (lettera al direttore)," *Leonardo*, VIII, October–November 1937, 363 (signed Giacomo di Chabannes, signor di La Palisse).
(p. 210)

1938

1190. "Dichiarazione . . . Lapalissiana," *Leonardo*, IX, January 1938, 26.
(p. 210)

1939

1207. "Il Centro nazionale di studi manzoniani," *Annali Manzoniani*, I, 1939, 5–21.
(p. 187)

1213. "La Carta della Scuola," *Corriere della sera*, 22 March 1939, p. 5.
(p. 210)

1940

1223. *Il pensiero italiano del Rinascimento, 3ª edizione accresciuta e riordinata*, Florence, Sansoni, 1940, xii + 432 pp.
(p. 106n)

1224. *Sistema di logica come teoria del conoscere*, Vol. I, 3rd ed. revised, Florence, Sansoni, 1940, viii + 287 pp. (see 375). [A 4th ed. prepared by Gentile in 1943 has now been issued as Vol. V of the *Complete Works*, viii + 281 pp.]
(pp. 5, 9n, 10n, 11, 24–25, 63, 222, 293–302)

1225. *Preliminari allo studio del fanciullo, settima edizione riveduta*, Florence, Sansoni, 1940, viii + 96 pp. [This will become Vol. XLII of the *Complete Works*.]
(pp. 79–82, 108–10, 118n, 263, 301)

1232. "Discussione sul disegno di legge: Istituzione della scuola media" (senate, 15 June 1940); [reprinted in G. BOTTAI: *La nuova scuola media*, Florence, Sansoni, 1941, pp. 88–90].
(pp. 212, 245)

1941

1241. *La filosofia italiana contemporanea. Due scritti*, Florence, Sansoni, 1941, 50 pp.
(pp. 246, 252)

1243. "Filosofia italiana e tedesca," in J. DE BLASI (ed.): *Romanità e Germanesimo*, Florence, Sansoni, 1941, pp. 375–90.
(p. 187n)

1246. "La filosofia del fascismo," *Il libro italiano nel mondo*, May–June 1941, pp. 21–33.
(pp. 190n, 246)

1249. "La distinzione crociana di pensiero ed azione," *Giornale critico della filosofia italiana*, XXII, 1941, 274–78; [now reprinted in the 2nd ed. of 1075, pp. 271–77].

1942

1250. *Sistema di logica come teoria del conoscere*, 3ª edizione riveduta, Vol. II, Florence, Sansoni, 1942, 388 pp. (see 699). [This is now Vol. VI of the *Complete Works*.]
(pp. 9n, 24–25, 63, 107, 108, 109n, 110–11, 221, 222, 255, 278, 293–302, 311)

1251. *Sommario di pedagogia come scienza filosofica*, Vol. I: *Pedagogia generale*, 5ª edizione riveduta, Florence, Sansoni, 1942, xii + 270 pp. (see 292). [This is now Vol. I of the *Complete Works*.]
(pp. 7, 28–38, 52n, 78, 86, 93–94, 96, 108, 113n, 297, 302)

1252. *Sommario di pedagogia come scienza filosofica*, Vol. II: *Didattica*, 5ª edizione riveduta, Florence, Sansoni, 1942, 224 pp. [not 254 pp.] (see 305). [This is now Vol. II of the *Complete Works*.]
(pp. 38n, 52n, 78, 87–92, 94, 96–97)

1261. "Giappone guerriero," *Civiltà* (*Riv. trim. dell'Esposizione Universale di Roma*), III, January 1942, pp. 5–12.
(pp. 187n, 216n, 247)

1262. Inaugural address to the *Amici dell'India* (29 April 1942), in *Italia e India*, Rome, Società "Amici dell'India," 1942, pp. 5–6.
(p. 187n)

1263. "A Benedetto Croce," *Giornale critico della filosofia italiana*, XXIII, 1942, 120.

1943

1264. *La mia religione* (lecture, 9 February 1943), Florence, Sansoni, 1943, 36 pp.; [now reprinted in *Complete Works*, XXXVII, 121–43].
(pp. 73n, 253)

1265. *Discorso agli Italiani* (24 June 1943), Sancasciano Val di Pesa, Tip. Stianti, 1943, 39 pp.; [now reprinted in B. GENTILE: *Dal Discorso agli Italiani alla morte* (*Giovanni Gentile: La vita e il pensiero*, Vol. IV), Florence, Sansoni, 1951, pp. 65–81].
(p. 248)

1267. "L'immanenza dell'azione," in *Il problema dell'azione e le sue diverse concezioni*, Milan, Bocca, pp. 65–76; reprinted in 1288, pp. 173–88.

1268. "L'esistenzialismo in Italia," *Primato* (Rome), 15 March 1943, p. 102.
(p. 252)

1269. "Parole di G. Gentile," in *Commemorazione di Michele Barbi,* Florence, Sansoni, 1943, pp. 5–7. [This item has eluded me. I rely on the passage quoted by Bellezza in his note.]
(p. 245n)

1272. Speeches at the *Primo Convegno nazionale di studi filosofici,* (Rome, 13–14 December 1941), in Vol. II, *Discussioni,* Rome, R. Istit. di studi filosofici, 1943, pp. 8–10, 27, 67–77, 84.
(p. 246)

1274. "Ricostruire," *Corriere della sera,* 28 December 1943; [now reprinted in B. GENTILE, *op. cit.,* at 1265, pp. 83–87].
(p. 285)

1277. "Postilla a 'La mia religione,'" *Giornale critico della filosofia italiana,* XXIV, 1943, 210–11; [now reprinted in *Complete Works,* XXXVII, 143–44 (cf. 1264)].
(p. 253)

1944

1279. *Teoria generale dello spirito come atto puro, 6ᵃ edizione riveduta,* Florence, Sansoni, 1944, viii + 272 pp. (see 350 and English tran' ʾ- tion 660). [This is now Vol. III of the *Complete Works.*]
(pp. 6, 9, 12, 16, 19, 44n, 63, 109n, 217n, 221)

1280. *I profeti del Risorgimento italiano, 3ᵃ edizione accresciuta,* Florence, Sansoni, 1944, viii + 220 pp. [This is now Vol. XXVI of the *Complete Works.*]
(pp. 141, 143, 170)

1282. "Ripresa," *Nuova antologia,* LXXIX (Florence), January 1944; [now reprinted in B. GENTILE, *op. cit.,* at 1265, pp. 89–93].
(p. 286)

1283. "Giambattista Vico nel secondo centenario della morte," *Nuova antologia,* LXXIX, April 1944; [now reprinted in B. GENTILE, *op. cit.,* at 1265, pp. 105–19 (cf. 1283 bis)].
(p. 287n)

[1283 bis. "L'Accademia d'Italia e l'Italia di Mussolini" (speech introducing the Vico commemoration (1283), Florence, 19 March); now first printed in B. GENTILE, *op. cit.,* at 1265, pp. 99–103.]
(pp. 286–87)

1284. "Il sofisma dei prudenti," *Civiltà fascista,* X (Bologna), fascs. 1–4, April 1944, 35–37 [issued a few days before his death; now reprinted in B. GENTILE, *op. cit.,* at 1265, pp. 121–26].
(p. 288)

1285. "Questione morale," *Italia e civiltà* (Florence), I, January 1944; [now reprinted in B. GENTILE, *op. cit.,* at 1265, pp. 95–98].
(p. 286)

1286. Letter dated 11 January, *Corriere della sera,* 16 January 1943 (concerning 1274 above); [now reprinted in B. GENTILE, *op. cit.,* at 1265, pp. 87–88].
(p. 287)

1946

1288. *Genesi e struttura della società. Saggio di filosofia pratica,* Florence, Sansoni, 1946, 192 pp. [This is now Vol. IX of the *Complete Works.* English translation, *Genesis and Structure of Society,* with Introduction, notes, and a bibliography of Gentile studies in English, by H. S. HARRIS, Urbana, University of Illinois Press, 1960.]
(pp. vii, 51, 108, 111, 118n, 224n, 244, 251–84, 288, 292n, 300, 301)

ANALYTICAL INDEX

Abbagnano, N., 252

Absolute formalism: Gentile's, 19

Absolute triad (Art, Religion, Philosophy): in Hegel, 40, 44, 47–48; immanent interpretation of, 77–79; in educational theory, 276

Abstraction: as freedom from past, 118

Abstract logos: as object of intellect, 4; as past, 18; economics as, 22n; sensation as, 33

Abstract theorizing: in G.'s theory of pain, 304

Academic snobbery: in G., 158

Accademia d'Italia (Italian Academy), 188n, 195n, 284–85, 289

Actual humanism: and logical idealism, distinguished in G., 25–26, 39; reconciliation through concept of feeling, 242–43, 297

Actual idealism: character of, 63, 311; two schools of criticism, 292, 293, 304

Address to the Italians: by G., 247–49

Adriatic question, 141, 149

Alfieri, V., 190n

Alphabet: as 'baptism of reason,' 53

Amici dell'India, 187n

Analysis and synthesis: relation in G.'s early thought, 53

Angst: G.'s account of, 255n; produced by error and sin, 264; root of pessimism, 280–81

A.N.I.F. (*Associazione Nazionale di Insegnanti Fascistici,* National Association of Fascist Teachers), 183, 202n

Antigone: justified, 237–38

Antonio and Shylock: as a case of subjective right, 122n

Apathy: results from external discipline, 319–20

a priori method: conflict with method of immanence, 44–45, 50, 78

a priori synthesis. *See* Synthesis a priori

Arcadian ideal: of Benedict XV, 137–38; implicit in Society of Nations concept, 143

Ariosto, L., 280n

Aristotle: theory of individual, 16, 52n, 55n; on justice, 87; natural slavery, 89; will and intellect distinction, 101; on unanimity, 106n; conception of the State, 142; friendship with self, 257; mentioned, 238n, 291

Armistice 1943: 124n, 284, 285

Art: and dream, 80; G.'s philosophy of, 224n; pure act reformulated in G.'s philosophy of, 224n, 242–43, 297, 301; personification in,

of, 92; corporal, 92n; must be internal, 136. *See also* Discipline

Pupil: and teacher, duality, 52; liberty of, denied, 57–58, 86; liberty of, reconciled with teacher's authority, 59; teacher relation and G.'s social theory, 78; school and, 84–94; liberty of, asserted, 85–86; school as internal to, 85; responsibility of, 86–88; punishment as 'right' and as *dissidio*, 90–91, 93, 116; liberty of, incoercible, 92; liberty of, none in *Riforma*, 164

Pure act. *See pensiero pensante*

Pythagorean *ipse dixit*, 112, 173n

Racialism: Fascism and, 244–45, 246

Rationalism: tradition of, 6; in ethics, G.'s denial, 63; of elite theory, rejected, 319

Realism: of common sense, 1–4, 8, 29, 64; and idealism, 1–4, 153–54; in culture, 85, 128, 164–65, 185; speculative ground of, 164–65. *See also* Intellectualism

Reality: value concept not logical category in G., 18, 295

Reason: sense and, in Hegel, 48; concrete historical, 61, 62, 322; force and, 115–17; vital to culture, 207; and actuality, 320–21; inseparable from emotion, 322

Red bogy: G. anticipates, 138; unimpressed by, 150n

Reformation: wars of, 315; elite theory rejected in and after, 320

Reform of Hegelian dialectic. *See* Dialectic

Regulative ideals: in education, 87, 96

Religion: mythical transcendent character, 5; primitive animism, 26; in education, 56n, 68–73, 75–76; religious authority in the State, 66–68, 74–75; and

philosophy in education, 68, 73–74; three senses of, in G., 72n; Hegel and G. on, 72n, 95; transcends State, 75; as childhood of spirit, 76; religious aspect of domestic education, 82–83; problem of instruction by lay teacher, 94–95; internal other as religious moment of consciousness, 110; religious spirit in G.'s mature works, 110; Fascism as religious spirit, 121n, 171–73, 182–83, 247–48, 313–15, 316, 319–20; in *Riforma*, 162–63, 198, 199–200; Fascist religious spirit in schools, 206–7; terminology of, in G.'s account of State, 267n; and politics, 269–70, 313–15, 326; contrast with economics, 270; transcendental society in, 271–72; and eudaemonism, 278–80; of Nation, 315–16

Renaissance: humanism of, 6, 55; neo-Platonism of, 7n; individualism in, 144n; unity of art and work in, 276

Repentance: force and, 116; original sin and, 264–65

Representative government. *See* Government; Parliamentary government

Responsibility: ideal of freedom and, 3, 281; of teacher and pupil, 58–59, 86–88; authority and, 69; institutions as relief from, 164–65; of spectator, 288; and pain, 303–4; for communication, 310–11

Resto del Carlino (Bologna newspaper): G.'s association with, 134

Revisionism: G.'s attitude to, 148n

Revolution, continual: in Marx, 49; Fascism as, 51, 94, 195; State as, 228–29, 267

Ricasoli, B., 169

Riforma Gentile: 'lay' school and, 73, 162, 218; economic poverty

ℹ️ Illini Books

IB-1	Grierson's Raid: A Cavalry Adventure of the Civil War	D. Alexander Brown	$1.75
IB-2	The Mars Project	Wernher von Braun	$ .95
IB-3	The New Exploration: A Philosophy of Regional Planning	Benton MacKaye, with an introduction by Lewis Mumford	$1.75
IB-4	Tragicomedy: Its Origin and Development in Italy, France, and England	Marvin T. Herrick	$1.95
IB-5	Themes in Greek and Latin Epitaphs	Richmond Lattimore	$1.95
IB-6	The Doctrine of Responsible Party Government: Its Origins and Present State	Austin Ranney	$1.25
IB-7	An Alternative to War or Surrender	Charles E. Osgood	$1.45
IB-8	Reference Books in the Mass Media	Eleanor Blum	$1.50
IB-9	Life in a Mexican Village: Tepoztlán Restudied	Oscar Lewis	$2.95
IB-10	*Three Presidents and Their Books: The Reading of Jefferson, Lincoln, and Franklin D. Roosevelt	Arthur E. Bestor, David C. Mearns, and Jonathan Daniels	$ .95
IB-11	Cultural Sciences: Their Origin and Development	Florian Znaniecki	$2.25
IB-12	The Legend of Noah: Renaissance Rationalism in Art, Science, and Letters	Don Cameron Allen	$1.45
IB-13	*The Mathematical Theory of Communication	Claude E. Shannon and Warren Weaver	$ .95
IB-14	*Philosophy and Ordinary Language	Charles E. Caton, ed.	$1.95
IB-15	Four Theories of the Press	Fred S. Siebert, Theodore Peterson, and Wilbur Schramm	$1.25
IB-16	Constitutional Problems Under Lincoln	James G. Randall	$2.95
IB-17	Viva Mexico!	Charles Macomb Flandrau, edited and with an introduction by C. Harvey Gardiner	$1.95
IB-18	Comic Theory in the Sixteenth Century	Marvin T. Herrick	$1.75

*Also available in clothbound editions.

IB-19	Black Hawk: An Autobiography	Donald Jackson, ed.	$1.7
IB-20	*Mexican Government in Transition	Robert E. Scott	$2.2
IB-21	John Locke and the Doctrine of Majority-Rule	Willmoore Kendall	$1.2
IB-22	The Framing of the Fourteenth Amendment	Joseph B. James	$1.4
IB-23	*The Mind and Spirit of John Peter Altgeld: Selected Writings and Addresses	Henry M. Christman, ed.	$1.2
IB-24	A History of the United States Weather Bureau	Donald R. Whitnah	$1.7
IB-25	*Freedom of the Press in England, 1476-1776: The Rise and Decline of Government Controls	Fredrick Seaton Siebert	$2.2
IB-26	*Freedom and Communications	Dan Lacy	$ .9
IB-27	The Early Development of Henry James	Cornelia Pulsifer Kelley, with an introduction by Lyon N. Richardson	$1.9
IB-28	*Law in the Soviet Society	Wayne R. LaFave, ed.	$1.9
IB-29	*Beyond the Mountains of the Moon: The Lives of Four Africans	Edward H. Winter	$1.7
IB-30	*The History of Doctor Johann Faustus	H. G. Haile	$1.4
IB-31	One World	Wendell L. Willkie, with an introduction by Donald Bruce Johnson	$1.7
IB-32	*William Makepeace Thackeray: Contributions to the *Morning Chronicle*	Gordon N. Ray, ed.	$1.4
IB-33	Italian Comedy in the Renaissance	Marvin T. Herrick	$1.7
IB-34	Death in the Literature of Unamuno	Mario J. Valdés	$1.2
IB-35	*Port of New York: Essays on Fourteen American Moderns	Paul Rosenfeld, with an introductory essay by Sherman Paul	$2.2
IB-36	*How to Do Library Research	Robert B. Downs	$1.4

Also available in clothbound editions.

B-37	Henry James: Representative Selections, with Introduction, Bibliography, and Notes	Lyon N. Richardson	$3.50
B-38	*Symbolic Crusade: Status Politics and the American Temperance Movement	Joseph R. Gusfield	$1.75
B-39	*Genesis and Structure of Society	Giovanni Gentile, translated by H. S. Harris	$1.95
B-40	*The Social Philosophy of Giovanni Gentile	H. S. Harris	$2.45

*Also available in clothbound editions.

University of Illinois Press   Urbana and London